The Five Great Elements

A Comprehensive Guide
to the Expression of Life
in Earth, Water, Fire, Air and Space

A Completely Revised Third Edition

by

Swami Nityamuktananda

British Library Cataloguing In Publication Data
A Record of this Publication is available
from the British Library

ISBN 978-1-84685-565-8

Published 2007 by

Exposure Publishing, an imprint of Diggory Press,
Three Rivers, Minions, Liskeard, Cornwall, PL14 5LE, UK
WWW.DIGGORYPRESS.COM

Offered to
The One that unfolds as the Many

**'Come forth into the light of things,
Let nature be your teacher'**
(William Wordsworth)

If only we could understand the songs of birds, if only we could interpret the pattern of clouds, if only we could tune into the whispers of stones, we would not need books. But as we can't, we need help to understand life and ourselves. To truly understand, we need guidance and grace. I would like to offer this book, with immense gratitude, at the feet of my Gurus, teachers from whom I receive both.

In the Jnana Sindha it says: 'the five Elements are the very body of the Guru!' In the Bhagawat Purana (ancient Indian scriptures), Lord Dattatreya lists 24 Gurus, people, nature and the elements - who taught him well; ultimately he exclaims: "Learn above all, from the rhythms of your own body." I would like to join him.

The emphasis in this book is neither on any specific concept of East nor of West, its purpose is to find wisdom in both; to see beyond separating individual concepts, to the common source which binds us together. For the path and the purpose are the same: just following the path will change our relationship within the ultimate 'Play' that is life.

CONTENTS

Endorsement:

I am very happy to see this book entitled THE FIVE ELEMENTS. The conception of life and the universe, which she uses in her book relates to Hindu, Buddhist, Christian and Taoist beliefs. I was personally very interested to see she has added her own experiences of the five elements as well as making relevant references to modern science. This kind of synthesis of Eastern and Western, ancient and modern knowledge is exactly what is required right now. By following one system, religion or viewpoint we receive only a partial view of any given situation because our views are coloured by cultural and historical factors.

Taking the best of the good news and positive information from all the traditions, we find many new and innovative solutions to our personal, mental and physical health difficulties, as well as finding solutions to the complex social and environmental problems now besetting the global village at the beginning of the third millennium.

Through the balancing of our five inner elements and the healing of the five outer elements we can create inner peace and thus contribute towards the development of world peace. I hope that the readers of this book will use it as a resource on their personal paths to healing and peace.

T.Y.S. Lama Gangchen Rinpoche; Tulku; Via Milan, Italy

And:

I am more than pleased to have the honour of forwarding a book like this, which offers a fresh approach within our complex social world that has become a labyrinth of moral and ethical confusion. We need to look for new paradigms. The author skilfully uses the ancient theory of the 'Five Elements' to lift the reader out of conventional approaches, and widens the awareness through contemplation. Yet the simplicity of these barely hides the profound knowledge of Eastern and Western Philosophy, Psychology and Medicine quite obviously behind such an approach.

Rather than boring the reader with complex foreign systems of the past, the author transcends these concepts, making them relevant to modern thinking. She entertains the reader with stories and examples and even, I must add, with a lovely poetical touch.

The reading of this book consequently results in a joyful experience that also provides a deep contribution to philosophy and a much-needed 'value' education.

As we say in my mother language, this useful book is 'Deja poso,' that is: it makes a mark, and given the inherent poetry of the language used, it will surely be permanent. As somebody said in her mother tongue: "Was bleibt aber, stiften die Dichter."

Prof. Dr. J.M.Ramirez, Departmento de Psicobiologia,
Universidad Complutense, Madrid, Spain

ACKNOWLEDGEMENT

This book contains work from many great writers and visionary thinkers; it is to these that I owe my greatest debt, whether they be dead or alive. I bow to these teachers; sincere gratitude for their original creativity fills my heart.

I would like to thank the SYDA Foundation, who allowed me to use some of their materials. Direct quotations are, as is customary, marked with footnotes, thoughts might be 'quoted' from memory and in this form, they have become my own.

But there are many others that helped to give birth to this book. Special thanks must go to Sonia Moriceau, my Shiatsu teacher, whose guidance was essential to finding the door to understanding my own body; furthermore she sowed the seed for this book many years ago. Since then, teachings of numerous wise men and women have been added.

Note: In order to distinguish some nouns, which have become specialised terms in this context, I have taken the liberty of using capital letters (example: the Earth; Air Element; Metal Energy; Water person; Bladder-organ-network). The usual spelling is retained where the word is used in its common meaning.

INTRODUCTION

IT FEELS odd to write about something so natural and part of our life that we are almost unaware of it. The world is unthinkable without the Five Elements, namely Earth, Water, Fire, Air and Space. Yet talking about these makes us aware that behind the apparent, there are universal concepts, reaching back to antiquity. In recent years they have become widely known due to several revivals:

- Yoga and its philosophy (Vedanta/Samkhya) have spread through the West like wild fire! Patanjali, the 'Father of Yoga,' describes in his Yoga Sutras the importance of focused contemplation on the Five Elements and its consequence.

- Holistic approaches to life (from Feng Shui, American Indian wisdom and simple eco-philosophy) further point to the necessity of studying these energies in depth.

- Complementary medicine in all its different forms, however, plays probably the most prominent role in the 'rediscovery' of the Five Elements (Traditional Chinese Medicine, Acupuncture, Ayurveda etc. etc).

- Contemporary science of energy fields and their vibrations might be another surprising contender for the wisdom of the Five Elements.

Throughout time, man perceived himself and his surroundings through these elements and as his perception and ability to cogitate and relate information grew, so his knowledge of the Elements grew. Ample global evidence, from the earliest civilisations to the modern day, show that the Elements have been observed and seen as a link between the gross manifest world and its subtler dimensions, in the end opening to the highest powers. What form this path of manifestation took and to what extend it was used, depends of course on the climatic and cultural context.

One cradle of civilisation is the region of Asia that descends into the Indian subcontinent. Scholars maintain that the worship of earth, fire, wind, water and the heavens existed there from the earliest times... 'Philological investigation reveals distinct traces of such worship... they were worshipped for their mysterious power, the divine, manifested in them. The formation of gods is a later development...' [1]

It is easy to picture.

Ancient people might have sat at the foothills of the Himalayas, in the Mediterranean sunshine, or the plateaux of South America – and become aware of the conditions of their environment. They absorbed the warmth of the sun, walked by any river and watched its flow adapt to the riverbed. They felt pushed from behind by a strong wind, experiencing its power of movement. The ancient ones felt the support of the earth under their feet and got lost in space by staring into the beauty of a night sky.

In comparison to these forces, man felt and feels insignificant, powerless and delivered to their action and it is only 'human' to ask: "'what are these energies that I experience?" Furthermore, when suffering from their impact as devastating fires, floods, storms, earthquakes - even meteorites - or when plagued by fevers, depression, lung-diseases, decay or disorientation, man wanted to appease these powers. He tried to understand and manipulate them; knowledge was gathered and used in everyday life and in worship.

Observing the characteristics of these Elements led into more and more subtle realms, leading the 'investigators' into transcending the Elements and finding their common source. This process of discovery and learning was obviously influenced by cultural traditions. In China, strong emphasis on concrete help for physical disease led to the blossoming of medical knowledge; in South America, the knowledge of interaction between the Elements found its peak and for the wise men of India, the concepts were part of their vast spiritual tradition.

In this book we will explore four levels of this vast knowledge: the universality of the concept (philosophical), how it helps us know our body, in ease and disease (physical/medical), and how, via a typology, it can help us understand ourselves and our relationships (psychological). Lastly we will explore some aspects of how knowledge about the Elements can help in our spiritual evolution (Yoga).

There is at times confusion: do we recognise four or five Elements? What are they called? In time these issues will be explored further. It suffices here, to say that most such issues revolve around the fifth Element; this, the most subtle, is rejected by the Greek tradition with great consequences for the Western culture.

The Chinese in accordance with a structured temperament call it Wood, (and the fourth 'Metal' or even 'Iron and Nature') even though their associations and characteristics tally with their equivalent in the rest of the world's traditions.

Although the fifth Element is known around the globe by many names, in essence it remains the same. It mirrors the global awareness that matter alone does not explain the world we live in. There must be an intangible element that holds all together and goes beyond matter. The word 'Space' best expresses that realm where transcendence and immanence touch; others speak of 'Ether,' 'Faith' or in the tradition and language of the Europe of the Middle Ages, the fifth Element is expressed as the 'Cosmic Christ.'

It is obvious that the 'fifth Element,' connecting heaven and earth/ matter and spirit, leads ultimately to contemplation of the unlimited, the Absolute. Some call this Ultimate force 'God' and name it according to their tradition, yet essentially 'That/He' is indescribable. Only once 'IT' expresses in energy we can perceive, furthermore energy is never static, it interacts on all levels; it is this interaction we call the 'Movement of Life.' This is 'the Stuff' that constitutes our world.

Chinese sages, Indian saints, European mystics, quantum physicists and modern biologists agree that everything is made of the same 'stuff.' But due to the fact that we can only experience things via our five senses, our nervous system and the accumulated conditioning of our mind (i.e.

traditions and culture), we perceive things only via our 'points of view.' We see the objects out there in the world - we see the tree, the car, the cat, the other person, quite distinctly as solid, individual shapes. But what we see, is not what is. If we would look at the same objects through the reference point of an electron or any other subatomic unit, all these are nothing but dancing, scintillating energy.

We see the piece of wood, can imagine its cells are made of carbon – but for most of us that is as far as our mind can go. Any deeper - most of us are lost. An image from ancient Indian scriptures can help us understand:

When we look at the sea, we notice the many waves, each with its different shape and notion of rising and falling. We overlook the fact that the wave is no different from the ocean – and that both are nothing but water.

Looking at the differences, or looking at the sameness – produces two different views of the universe.

Modern science and ancient wise ones tried to perceive both; thus coming closer to Truth, or Reality. So Einstein said: "Life and death flow into one, and there is neither evolution nor destiny, only Being." David Bohm described the world as a web where 'consciousness and matter is married in one intricate order with n-th dimensions.' H. Skolimowski talks of a subjective, participatory universe. Quantum physicists and even biologists such as Rupert Sheldrake talk of the 'unified field' which is held in the general background field - there is no separation between one object and another. These interacting fields of energy have inherent intelligence, which come together as a 'unified field,' as a field of supreme consciousness. Are the five energy fields, that the ancients globally recognised as the Five Elements, these very fields? Sheldrake's 'morphogenetic fields' are an open and closed system. Open to constant change and interaction, closed within a certain character/frame (wave constantly interacts with ocean). It 'transacts.' [2]

The ancient 'seers' or *rishis* of India also testify to this unified field in which all existed *para* (beyond) our normal perception. They called this unified field *Prakriti (or Shakti)*. The wise of many cultures investigated the nature of this shared ground which expresses in five categories, or base types of energies. They contemplated the nature of these FIVE ELEMENTS in great detail. We can step into their 'shoes' and, looking beyond the superficial perception of our senses, contemplate the wisdom behind these five types of energies.

You might say, "'I know what the Elements are - what is all the fuss about, after all, water is what comes out of the tap and is used to wash, drink and brush my teeth." Yes, but have you ever really mulled over what water is? The deeper we contemplate each Element, the deeper our understanding of how one Element relates to another, the more we understand about ourselves, our relationships and our place in this universe. From the moment we are born, we relate to others. However much we are made to believe that each one of us is a separate individual that can be put into a box, named, classified and codified for a computer – we are in essence one universal energy.

And yes, this energy has different characteristics - due to its expressions in five different types. We can know them, can even ask: what makes the fire burn, what makes the water flow, what makes the air move, and what is it that gives the earth its solidity? Even, what is behind the breath of life? And like the sages all over the globe, we will return to the only answer there is: some great creative force, that like a womb gives birth to everything; it is the place in which all is contained and from where all comes forth. This creative energy is linked (in most parts of the world) and frequently worshipped as the 'Great Mother' – who herself rests in the One Unknowable (Shiva/God father/the Luminous Ground etc), who is more elusive even than Space, with no form, no end and no beginning.

The Honourable Lama T.Y.S. Gangchen Tulku Rinpoche, a world-renowned Tibetan teacher, encourages us to use the Five Elemental Energies to re-educate ourselves. Using his ancient tradition, he teaches that these Five are likened to Five Supreme Mothers. The Great Goddess, who is creative energy per se, appears as Five Supreme Mothers which we experience at the gross level 'in the elements around us in the form of mountains, sea, air, space, fire...' [3] and we can call on them on the subtle level to give us their blessing:

> Please, Great Earth Mother Mamaki, All knowing One,
> reveal your wisdom to us.
> Please, Great Water Mother Lochana, All knowing One,
> reveal your wisdom to us.
> Please, Great Fire Mother Pandaravasini, All knowing One,
> reveal your wisdom to us.
> Please, Great Wind Mother Samaya Tara,All Knowing One,
> reveal your wisdom to us.
> Please, Great Space Mother Vrajavahari, All knowing One,
> reveal your wisdom to us.

PART I
INSPIRATIONS FROM AROUND THE WORLD

Chapter 1: From the One to the Many:
One Energy, Three Qualities, Five Elements

BOLDLY speaking, man has inherently a need to understand himself and his relationship with the world. The whole 'living experience' is about finding out who we actually are, what the world is, and how the two fit into each other.

Historically the first two questions: who we are and what the world is, has been answered by the various religions; lately it has been explored in the West by focus on quantitative analysis of matter. From this latter angle, we are so much water, so much Carbon and so many molecules of trace elements etc. The same basic 109 chemical ingredients make up the entire universe. What makes me different from the dog - you different from the tree, is how these chemicals are put together.

Hence the first point: essentially we, and everything that exists, have the same building blocks!

Take for example a cell from your body, a tree or a cat - chemically analysed each consists of the same 'stuff,' left to itself, it is merely a pile of dust. Yet somehow the ingredients are put together in a way that make a living, procreating cell with different functions, my liver cell works different from a bone-marrow cell. Obviously the chemicals aren't randomly heaped together, but ordered intelligently for a specific purpose.

Think of a house: there are bricks, cement, stones, sand, wood etc. All of these are nothing but a pile of materials until an architect puts them together in an intelligent way and a builder (energy) executes the plan. So one could say the house is made out of the idea, the practical energy and material.

Transferring this to the universe as a whole, we can say there exists some energy, which by acting with knowledge and/or intelligence, moves ingredients together in the infinite possibilities we perceive as Creation.

'Creation' is not static - whatever we look at (or experience) has been there previously as something else. The tree was a seed, the bookshelf was a tree; brick was clay, the clay was rock, and so on. This also applies to my existence. The adult I am now, was a child, was my parents' sperm and egg, was genes within my grandparents and so on, ad infinitum... What exists now is only ever temporary form.

Imagine you take a photo of a flower, and two months later go back and take another one of the fruit – they appear to be radically different, but are they? They are both Cucumber. We look at anything in the world with our senses, sort of taking one frame of a film, one picture, one moment in time - and think this is how it is. But even seconds later one form shifts into another. Nothing in Creation is ever an end product! To think that it is, is nothing but a trick of the mind. The 'camera' of the mind freezes one moment as finite. In reality, the picture of the energy that was a flower shifts in the next to be a worm. This ever-changing aspect is described beautifully in a Buddhist text, Visuddhi-Maggai VIII:

'The being of a past moment of thought has lived, but does not live; nor will it live. The being of a future moment of thought will live, but has not lived, nor does live. The being of the present moment of thought does live, but has not lived, nor will it live.' [1]

Second point: every thing that exists, is constantly changing form.

What is it that changes? If what we perceive are constantly changing forms, there must be something that changes. Formless energy is the action in every shape-shifting, just as electricity is the unchanging energy behind millions of lamps, heaters and fans. That energy behind all phenomena has many names: some call it Reality, some Creative Power, Primordial Energy, Cosmic energy, n-th dimension, morpho-genetic field, Chi, Shakti or Reiki, The Great Mother, etc. etc. All cultures and religions have their own name for it.

Furthermore, how do we perceive that change occurs? Simple logic tells us that change can only be perceived against the backdrop of something static, something that remains the same. What can we say about this 'One Constant' ...which has been called the indescribable 'Mystery?' All we know, is that there are two aspects: on the one hand there is energy that constantly changes...on the other there is some still base/ground about which we can't say much.

We live in interesting times, because what the saints and sages of many religions have said all along, is now confirmed by quantum physics. Both recognise these two concepts, which must merge somewhere, and yet struggle for a language to describe it. We can sense the oneness of the two aspects by contemplating a river: the Water in the river is water, remaining the same throughout. But the micro-climate, the ground, the speed in which it flows, what lives and grows in it, etc., continually alter the river with every pebble that falls into it, with every rock that is in its way. Yet despite all changes, the river keeps its identity throughout.

Approximately 6000 years ago in India, the Vedic tradition began describing what lies beyond our ordinary perception - they clad their findings in poetry and stories, here is such a story. When Svetaketu, at his father's bidding, had brought a ripe fruit home from a banyan tree, his father said to him:

"Split the fruit in two, dear son."

"Here you are father, I have split it in two."

"What do you find there?"

"Innumerable tiny seeds."

"Then take one of the seeds and split it."

"I have split the seed."

"And what do you find there?"

"Why, nothing, nothing at all Sir."

> Ah, dear son, the subtlest essence of this fruit appears as nothing to you. Even if you cannot see it with your eyes, it is present nonetheless; the Being, that is the essence, which pervades everywhere and is all things, the supreme reality! That is the SELF, which lies at the root of all existence. That art thou, Svetaketu." (*Chandogya Upanishad*) [2]

Relying on our senses, we accept what we see as reality, we study, analyse, dissect and proudly insist that inside the 'fruit' are nothing but 'tiny seeds.' The father's answer reveals this method as blind, unable to see the 'hidden' essence – with quantum physics we can say that we can see the underlying unified field – whatever name we want to put on it.

We feel our body, we see the world around us, we experience our emotions – we know, because 'my mind, my inner computer' tells me: I exist as Me! I belong to me. I am different from others, plants, the tree, my cat and my neighbour. My existence is separate from anyone else (Latin: *existere* means 'to stand out'). So the world and myself exist as so many separate, different objects... or? Yet Svetaketu's father has an entirely different view. Instead of looking at the separate object that one can taste, touch, see, put in a box and stick a label on saying, 'Banyan tree seed,' he, like sages throughout cultures and times, looked at the split seed with different 'eyes.' They did not perceive things with the five senses; they thought that this limits us. How can our five senses be limiting us?

Our eyes can see even the stars and with a telescope, even galaxies undreamed of. Oh yes, our senses are excellent tools that relay information to our mind - and there, so brain research states, it gets registered as new memory, after comparing it to old memory, i.e. previously registered knowledge. What we can't link, have no 'hooks' for, we can't understand, moreover we don't even see it – because our minds might have no previous blue-print, no record, no language to name it, understand it, describe it. It is a bit like a computer using one language and being unable to read a 'floppy disc' that is programmed in a different one. Let me illustrate this with another story:

> One day a frog from the sea paid a visit to another frog.
> "Where do you come from?" asked the frog of the well.
> "From the ocean", he replied.
> "How big is the ocean?"
> "It is gigantic."
> "You mean about a quarter of the size of my well here?"
> "Bigger."
> "Bigger, you mean half as big?"
> "No, even bigger!"
> "Is it... as big as this well?"
> "There is no comparison."

"That is impossible! I have got to see this for myself."

They set off together. When the frog from the well saw the ocean, it was such a shock that his head just exploded into pieces. 3

It is near impossible to imagine such a completely other dimension as described in Svetaketu's story as 'no-thing.' Our everyday mind can only process what it perceives through the instruments of our senses i.e. sight, taste, touch, hearing or smelling. If something has no form to see, no taste, no texture, no sound, no smell, our limited minds cannot grasp it.

And yet the wise ones of old seem to have another way of reaching knowledge, understanding which comes from a different level, something beyond our normal ways of perceiving (which we share with animals). This 'other level of perception' is beyond ordinary human being, this 'beyond human' is the dictionary definition of 'divine.' The wise, sages and saints can thus somehow tap another means of knowing reality by tapping into the 'divine.'

From there they describe the world in a much deeper way, e.g. in the 'Guru Gita' (an Indian scripture) the cosmos is compared to a 'wise Being:'

by whose reality the world is real,
by whose light it is illuminated...
by whose existence the world exists...
by whose knowledge this world will
no longer be perceived to be divided by differences...
All this universe appears in various forms
but there is no difference from anything...4

Most of these notions a quantum physicist could go along with; in ancient times people reached this insight by shutting out the five outer senses and directing their focus inside themselves. *In that inner isolation they developed a faculty of expanded knowing. This process we call meditation.* They understood that with ordinary 'vision' through our senses, we only see the gross manifestation of the world – but beneath it lies a deeper level from where we recognise that we are part of what we perceive. Ordinary perception is like trying to see your own face with your own eyes - it's useless, the eyes cannot see themselves! Once we learn to step back from our individual perception, we 'see' the web of moving energy that includes us, we understand the essence of life as holistic.

W. K. Heisenberg, physicist from the beginning of the 20th century, declared 'the researcher can not stay objective, but participates in what is happening.' We are part of the same happening - who we are and how we see the world, is one and the same. We are a field of pulsing energy, held in a unified field of pulsing energy. Once we shift our perspective from onlookers to participants, from 'outer-scientists' to 'inner-scientists,' we have a vantage point from where to 'know' the essence of life, that mysterious power that is said to be beyond normal human perception. Having cast off the inherent human limitations of experiencing only through our senses, we perceive 'the divine,' which is what Svetaketu's father referred to: 'That are Thou,' or better *Tat Twam Asi,* a state experienced as one essence, many forms. Henry Skolimowski, a modern philosopher, talks of the *participatory mind,* that mind which goes beyond superficial perceptions of phenomena outside and participates perpetually in creation. According to him, such a shift is available to all, but we don't use it. [5] And we don't, because we can't, due to the limited, conditioned mind-space that he calls mind-cone. What condition us are all the patterns and things we have learned during our lifetime; when we cast them aside, we find a 'different reality,' one where all energies are connected in a unified-field. Christian Mystics speak of the cosmic body of Christ, Indian Mystics speak of 'Guru' or *'Purusha.'* We simply have to give that mysterious essence some name, so we can talk about it.

The formless has to become form; the nameless has to be given names. The Indian Poet-saint Jnaneshwar Maharaj offers a simple, powerful description:

> That One who exists, when nothing else is,
> That One who is seen, when nothing else is,
> That One who is enjoyed, when nothing else is,
> That One Alone is. [6]

Third point : Beyond the plurality of what exists is One Reality

This 'One' is a puzzle to our mind; man has simply named it 'the Unnameable.' Each culture and each religion speaks of it embedded in its own words. Seeing only those words, we see differences; if we see the essence, we see similarities. Some cultures, being aware of this, have two ways of describing ultimate Reality.

For example: In India they know of Brahma Nirguna, Brahma without form, and Brahma Satguna (with form/matter), and Purusha and Prakriti (Shiva/ Shakti).

The American Indians differentiate between 'the Great Mystery' and the Great Spirit, wherein the Spirit refers to the energy that moves within creation to 'direct all things for the good of his children' (from an Iroquois prayer).

The Australian Aboriginals have Wanjina – the original source and Nangina - the earthly form.

In Christian terms there is the Holy Spirit, as the energy that moves, and its manifestation in Jesus Christ and the rest of Creation.

In Ancient South America, we have Quetzalcoatl, which is feather (Spirit) and serpent (Matter)

In this way, we could go through most cultures and acknowledge the point where the 'One' as **creative energy per se** in subtle aspect, is talked of as Spirit and in its most dense aspect as matter. Spirit by itself is most difficult for us to understand; our senses are not equipped to compute it. Like Electricity or sound waves, which potentially are all around, we can perceive them only once they express in light bulbs, heaters, radios etc. The analogy can be taken further. Electricity becomes heat through various transformers; how does 'the indescribable energy,' which is like 'nothing we can perceive,' become 'something?' Or simpler: 'how does pure Spirit become Matter?'

In this way – the fourth point has been made : The One becomes Two

Most people today are familiar with the Chinese concept of Yin and Yang. Together these two symbols express the 'indescribable,' the Tao. These two states are recognised and so is their constant inter-action. Actually there are three states: 1) light 2) action 3) dark. These three states or attributes of energy are also called Gunas (in Indian thought).

The notion of three co-operative forces, or stages, can even be seen in Quantum Physics. Yes, in the final stage we have something that is both wave and particle, energy and matter, yet in between those stages 'it' disappears... it is there, yet not there... In this third stage 'where the quantum object is transcendent... the wave-packet is collapsed...' it has no locality, it is in indescribable transition, in movement (termed 'non-locality'). 7 We could simply say: it is one thing, it is another, and sometimes it is neither.

Abhinavagupta (11th Century AD) developed the 'doctrine of vibration.' 8 Its tenet being that the entire universe is nothing but vibrating, intelligent energy expressed in different forms...

> In the night of Brahman...Shiva...rises from his rapture, and dancing,
> sends through inert matter pulsing waves of awakening sound,
> and lo! matter dances, appearing as a glory round about him.
> Dancing, he sustains its manifold phenomena. 9

Tibetan Buddhist Sogyal Rinpoche describes three states of energy as the ground (base), the rising (activity) and the created object (manifestation) – *Dharmakaya, Sambhogakaya, Nimanakaya.*

The three flavours of the original creative power are thought of as a thread (Sanskrit: *guna*) that is 'spun' out of the Absolute, akin to how a spider creates his web with a thread spun from its own body. This image is also found in Celtic myth where the woven Web of the world is the Wicca.

This three-fold thread is plaited out of three subtle energies. Although subtle, they can be perceived, even though more in the psychic realm – their wisdom constitutes something like an ancient Psychology.

The fifth point is: the two forces express through three types of energy.

It is accepted that at birth, we start this incarnation with a distinct combination of these three qualities, giving us a unique constitution and personality. The mixture is usually dominated by one or the other, providing distinct forms of existence or types of people. Satya Sai Baba, a modern day

Saint, gives a clue to the types and their dominant characteristics. 'The dull and the inert will hesitate to be active, for fear of exhaustion or failure of loss. The emotional, passionate individuals will plunge headlong and crave for quick results and will be disappointed if they do not come in. The balanced persons will be active, because it is their duty; they will not be agitated by anything - failure or success.'

These three energies are of course constantly moving, influencing each other, creating ever new combinations! Their interaction creates 'The Movement of Life,' they are the key to life being alive!

Through their interaction all phenomena become manifest, so that they can be seen, heard, touched, smelt and tasted. Once our senses can perceive them, we register them as Earth, Water, Fire, Air and Space.

Thus **three types of energies, by their interaction, create Five manifest Elements.**

It is easy to see how Earth is basically inert (*tamasic*); Water when stagnant (or frozen) is *tamasic* - yet its life cycle is characterised by fluidity thus it is also *rajasic*; thus it is a mixture of these two.

Fire is always 'on the go' (*rajasic*), constantly transforming, pure kinetic energy. Air is at times dominated by *rajasic* movement such as in storm, but is equally distributed, quiet, *light and sattvic*; Air like Water is 'a step in between.' Space then again is purely *sattvic*, all pervading, light with no form. From energy in total abstraction, via its main three qualities, we have arrived at five manifest forms of energy that we can actually perceive with our senses. In fact, we have five senses, because there are five gross elements to perceive. All around the globe, knowledge has been gathered about these Five Elements.

Chapter 2: The Universal Wisdom of the Five Elements

2.1: The Elements in Asia

Vedantic India provides rich pickings right from antiquity. Maybe as much as ten thousand years ago, people in the foothills of the Himalayas and the River valleys recognised, contemplated and worshipped the Elements. And most certainly during the early Vedic period they worshipped these, turning them eventually into 'humanised gods' which then fed 'the muddy pool of religious differences.' [10]

Man's experience with the elemental forces revealed an inherent hierarchy within them; Water is less solid than Earth, Fire less tangible than Water etc. In this way, Space is recognised as the most subtle, begging the question of whether it is still of this world? And furthermore, is it an element or is it the root of all the others? Thus Space becomes linked with the idea of the original cause of existence. And since man also is part of this caused universe, he too must be made up of the Five. The Bhagavad Gita (Chapter XVII/15) points out: 'whatever action man performs by his body, speech and mind - whether right, or the reverse - these five are its causes...' [11]

Man experienced himself and his world as a manifestation of the Five Elements, yet he knew them as the material cause. Space holds all the Elements yet there must be a 'root-cause' where Space itself must be included, as it itself had existence. How can something come out of nothing? Or as an ancient proverb expresses it, if something can come out of nothing, the son of a sterile woman can become father of many children.

In this way observation and reasoning led men beyond themselves to their cause - the 'indescribable Brahman Nirguna' (without form) – also named '*Sadasiva* who shines as the self-resplendent light bringing forth the five great elements...' So writes Swami Sivananda. Shiva is present in all elements, as there is nothing on earth that is not his sign. This Absolute manifests through creative energy or power called *Maya, Prakriti* or *Shakti* – as air, fire, water and earth. 'The five elements are... ever changing; they... have combined among themselves and created apparently materiality in the world.' [13]

Pure energy constantly changes from one form into another, this we recognise as movement; we saw previously how this action takes place in three forms, three threads (Gunas) *tamas, rajas and sattva*. These are mostly described in detail in 'Yoga-speak;' what is behind these words?

Tamas: most frequently translated with 'inert,' could be linked to the extreme Yin energy. *Tamas* is heavy and dark in an almost value free sense, not as 'bad' but the darkness of no differentiation, say as a dark cave – which is both, harbouring all potential – like a womb yet filled with the unknown. As the 'not known' and 'unknowing' it is referred to also as ignorance and in its extreme form, as thoughtless, mechanical action. This leads to repetitive mental patterns, dullness, clouded reasoning, heavy feelings, the refusal to think, small minded-ness etc.; it brings an impotent will, lack of faith and self-confidence.

Sri Aurobindo says that *tamas* left to its own, speaks of 'the shut soul... the callous heart; ... soon spent affection and languor of feelings; ... it's what makes a man coarse, heavy and vulgar in spirit...' [14]

But luckily one strand never exists by itself. For example: the form, the most solid aspect of our body is its flesh and bones; the lightest and most knowing is our awareness/consciousness, the action aspect is the energy that drives us. Thus there is *tamas* in every person and each phenomena, yet in inter**action** with others.

This action is the quality of **_Rajas_**.

Rajas simply translated, is: kinetics, motion, and passion. It is the power that transforms, that drives to do, to grow; expanding, seeking, and aspiring to... In people *rajas* is their vitality, is the power to strive. Desire is the strongest human and animal initiator, producing motivation and movement (mental and physical). We could say it is like Freud's libido, or Darwin's instinct of survival, the power behind evolution. *Rajas* works very hard to overcome inertia (the stagnant, mechanical or unconscious); it's effort is constantly fighting to overcome negativity, disappointment and suffering; it is the power of survival and evolution.

Again *rajas* by itself is again neither good or bad, it is simply the drive to act; yet action for actions sake brings prejudice, attachment to opinion and self-willed desires. As unchecked 'action-power,' it leads to the fanatic and sectarian mind, pride, arrogance, selfishness, lust, greed, cruelty, hatred etc.

On the other hand, when in co-operation with *sattvic* energy, it is the power that drives us to be compassionate, caring, brings love and self-awareness; it inspires to seek knowledge, drives to higher goals.

The third strand of energy is **_Sattva_** - or what you might know as pure Yang energy. *Sattva* is the energy of light and harmony; it brings equilibrium, purity and peace. *Sattva* is gentleness, adaptability. It is a vital tempering ingredient; within people it is the quality of the mind, mind not in the sense of the lower animalistic mind that strives for basic survival, but the mind that constantly thirsts to balance and assimilate knowledge. Not just to collect factual knowledge, but understanding; the more clarity, the wider the view of life and the more tolerance. *Sattva* brings a quality of ethical spirit, of self-discipline, love, and empathy. It brings an intense, satisfying sense of ease, poise, a happiness of mastery and security. Light and happiness are its ultimate characteristic.

The Bhagavad Gita describes the pure *sattvic* state as one where one can stand back, watch the energies that cause pain and suffering and remain impartial.

As the three gunas, the energy is subtle, not perceivable by our sense organs. Through interaction, they combine into ever more gross states. It is a bit like making a cake. First flour combines with water. It is already a mixture - yet no cake yet! This mixture then gets combined with sugar and it is a bit more cake like; then that mixture combines with Raisin and so on through many stages. Eventually we recognise it as cake mix, yet it still contains all the original steps. In this way each final Element, say 'Water' has aspects of each Element. One ancient text, the Vivekachudamani, describes this in verse 74:

'Having united with parts of one another, they become gross, and become the cause for the formation of the gross body... The theory that explains how these five subtle elements from their nascent condition have grossified is called *Panchikarana*...'[15] Through self-duplication and mutual combination, each gross element ends up consisting ½ of its own character (say Air), one eighth borrowed from ether (space), 1/8th of Fire, 1/8th of Water and 1/8th of Earth. Thus each of the five Gross Elements is a combination including all other elements. [17] Meaning: Air is 50% determined by its own energy, but in addition has some Element of Space (occupies space), some part of Fire (moves), has some characteristic of Water (is transparent) and Earth (consists of solid molecules, has weight). Because each Element contains all others, it can never stay still; always interacting, it changes into the variety of phenomena we perceive as the ever-changing world.

In Indian thought, it is furthermore thought that these different energies or elements come into being through <u>intent.</u> The intelligence or consciousness behind the universe is portrayed as a cosmic Persona, with supreme intelligence and will. Quantum theory agrees, stating that on ultimate energy, knowledge rides like a jockey on the back of a racehorse. This intelligence creates the conditions, which result in the obedience of the 'horse' - it acts with intent. 'If *IT* intends to experience sound, it creates space in which sound can travel; if *IT* intends to experience touch, air is created, unseen and subtle. Wishing to see, this cosmic person brings fire into being, and this fire expands into the numerous sources of light. Intending to experience taste, as well as coolness to counteract fire, water comes into being. And lastly, by its mere wish to smell, earth with its faculty of smell comes into being.'[16] This means the world is willed i.e. ideation or thought precedes word on the journey into existence.

This is noteworthy, because it goes one step deeper than in most cultures, where the world comes into existence through the spoken word. Here the idea precedes and, is the seed that grows into the word by the power of *Matrikashakti,* prime expression of creative energy. Sacred words in India are called mantra. One of the most ancient mantras is: *Ohm namah Shivaya*; these syllables stand for: *na* - earth, *ma* - water, *shi* - fire, *va* - air, *ya* - space. The mantra embodies the Five Elements.

Another expression of creative energy is certain marks, or symbols. The Sanskrit word here is *Linga*. In Southern India 'there are five famous *Shiva Lingas,* which represent the Five Elements.

> 1) In Kanjivaram (Tamilnadu) there is Prithvi *(earth)* Lingam. 2. In Tiruvanali Koil (Tamilnadu) there is Appu *(water)* Lingam. The lingam is always in water... 3) In Kalahasti (Andra Pradesh) there is Vayu *(wind/air)* Lingam. 4) In Tiruvannamalai (Tamilnadu) there is Tejo *(fire/light)* lingam (Arunchalesvaram). 5. In Chidambaram (Tamilnadu) there is Akasa *(space)* Lingam.'

Swami Sivananda explains. 'These five places (respected temples) represent the apex of five angles of a five triangled figure which represents the five *Bhutas* (Elements) of which the entire world is made up.' [117]

Of course man also consists of these Five Elements which dissolve in death: 'the physical body (flesh etc.) is earthy, so it returns to the earth. Blood etc. are liquid and they return to the water-element. The fire (heat) and the light in the body belong to the fire-element, they return to it. The air is offered to the cosmic air. Space merges into space... Furthermore earth dissolves in water, water in fire, fire in air and air in space. Space should be merged with cosmic space, which is the cause for all.' [18]

The thing though is, that man experiences the five Elements via his senses, which by themselves are mere instruments producing nothing, they do so only in collaboration with the mind. The labelling of the perception, the working with the observation, is a function of the mind, which in turn is made up of the *sattva guna* (calm energy) of all the five elements and processed by the brain.

(It is interesting to note here that modern brain science acknowledges various locations of energy transformation connected to the senses, and the Elements, as well as various functions of the brain to the elemental energies. Space is especially experienced through the temporal and parietal lobes of the brain; spatial memory is here. Air is especially experienced through the parietal lobe and the frontal cortex and connected to technical and factual memory. Fire and light are especially experienced through the temporal and occipital lobe and are connected to long and short term memory, as well as vision. Water is experienced through the frontal lobe and the Lymbic System, i.e. Amygdalla/Midbrain and connected to traumatic memory, fears and trauma. Earth is experienced mainly through the upper frontal lobe (smell) and the cerebellum, seat of ancient security, planning, genetic memory etc).

It is the non-physical mind though, that houses our identity, our personality and ego. It is the 'sense of I' which is the glue that binds knowledge together with the body. Self-awareness is a key issue, with which to gain knowledge. According to Indian tradition we have five different layers *(koshas)* which make up our body: some even think of it as different energy bodies. With self- awareness we can know and experience these. They are the anatomical (earth), physiological (water), psychological (fire), intellectual (air) and spiritual (ether). [19] These bodies are characterised by the five elemental powers and they determine even such aspects as the character of a person's knowledge and his happiness, as will be shown when contemplating each Element individually.

A modern day Indian Saint, Sri Nisargadatta Maharaj, said, "You are the manifest, dynamic principle, not the body... You have identified with the body, but you are not the body... you put on various uniforms in order to give it (that principal) identity... It has no form – the forms are given because of the elemental play. Now that principle gets completely lost in the uniform (the five elements) and is recognised by the uniform only...'[20]

Finally, ending this glimpse of Indian thoughts to the Five *Mahabhutas*, (Great Elements) let me share a myth. Legends often speak far more eloquently than ideas, because they arise from the subconscious of people. Here a story told about Sankaracharya, probably the most well known philosopher of India, nicely sums up Indian philosophy: It is said that when he was a young man, he went in search of his teacher. He had travelled a long distance, arriving at the hermitage in the evening. Tired, he walked three times around the hermitage and was directed to the cave where Govindapada lived; he prostrated at his door and began to chant a hymn in praise of the sage, than continued. "Praying to Thee for instruction in the truth of Brahman, I salute Thee, the repository of all great virtues!"

Praised thus, the sage came out of his super-consciousness state, and asked, "who are you?" In reply Sankara said the following, indicative of his great spiritual enlightenment:

"Revered Sir, I am neither the earth, nor water, nor fire, nor air, nor sky, nor any of their properties. I am not the senses and the mind even. I am Shiva, the division-less essence of Consciousness."

Hearing these words, pregnant with the spirit of non-dualistic consciousness, the sage was delighted... [21]

The above kind of thinking affected daily life in the Indian Culture, especially in **Medicine/ Psychology.** Around 3,500 BC the sages of the ancient Indus culture gathered in the quiet of the Himalayan foothills and contemplated how to alleviate sickness and suffering. The Caraka Samhita, an ancient text, describes the knowledge we call Ayurveda (Sanskrit: *vid,* which means knowledge and *ayus,* which means daily living or life cycle). So Ayurveda is the knowledge of daily living, also referred to as 'the science of life.'

According to Ayurveda, the material world is composed of combinations of the five elements, and these are not understood in a purely literal fashion but are rather meant to 'communicate the essential universal principle inherent in a particular element. Thus air is transparent, a rarefied, kinetic force which sets the created in motion. By fire is meant the force in nature that produces heat and radiates light. By water we understand the cohesive aspect of reality which holds things together, perfectly and simply witnessed in the ubiquitous H_2O molecule. Both earth and space are understood in the same prototypical sense.' [22]

The five physical elements are expressions of the life energy called *Prana,* which flows through the body like electricity. Ether (Space) is the first physical element, which interfaces directly with *Prana.* These two are like a positive and a negative force working together: (*Prana* (+) and Ether (*Akasha*) (-). The 'Movement of life' flows as the current of Five Elements through us; when there is imbalance in this process, it effects our life-force, pronounced imbalance produces 'dis-ease.' Three states influence biological decay - they are called *doshas* (meaning 'that which darkens'). Each *dosha* receives its characteristics from particular elements. Thus the *dosha* called *Vata* reflects disharmony in Space and Air; *Pitta* reflects disturbances in Fire, (some say Fire and Water); *Kapha* reflects on Water and Earth.

The particular combination of energies (mixture of Elements) present when we enter this world at birth, is known as our 'innate constitution' or *prakruti*. The Elements stay with us all our lives, yet the *doshas* refer only to biological disturbances. These are the concern of Ayurveda, which consists of a complex medical system around these; here is not the place to go into details. Less well known is that Ayurveda also includes a special brand of **Martial arts and Music**. (Martial arts and specific physical movement (*asana*) is used to cure disease even today. See research in the SVYSA, Swami Vivekananda Yoga Anusandhana Samsthana, AIIMS (All-India - Institute of Medical Science etc).

Music too is used since ancient times to cure illness. The chanting of *slokas* and mantras is said to cure ailments: 'the musical notes have tremendous power and help to exercise the elemental energies on all levels, physical, mental and spiritual' (Dr. M. H. Paranjape, 1998).

A vast body of nutritional science pays tribute to the importance of 'right food' in India households. For a time in history, this knowledge went underground and became 'family history' and 'secret knowledge,' but in today's India and increasingly world wide, **Ayurvedic food** is almost equally as well known as its medicine. Ayurvedic food is vegetarian, and each ingredient has an elemental character and as such has an effect on the entire system i.e. Almonds are said to increase Kapha (Water and Earth), control Vata (Space and Air) and increase Pitta (Fire/Water). Cabbage is said to increase Vata (Space/Air); Capsicums increase Pitta and decrease Vata; Cucumber increases Kapha; Grapes reduce Pitta; lentils increase Pitta; potatoes increase Vata and so on.

There are countless more subjects that are affected by the Five Elements, as life itself is the Five Elements. We saw its effects in the Temple **Architecture** above (including a science of sacred space called Vastu); and there is a vast body of knowledge around **Astrology** (Jyotish), considered a path of self-knowledge leaning strongly on the *Gunas* and Five Elements. Last not least there is **Yoga**, a practical path spread all over India and the West, that effects probably millions of people – using the knowledge of the Five Elements. We will hear much more about this further on.

The Five Elements in Buddhist thought reflect their roots in Hindu India. The historical Buddha, Prince Siddharta Gautama, born 563 BC, taught (in a time where Hindu thought had calcified, against a background of mindless, empty worship) a doctrine of mindfulness as the way back to a state where we can return to our true pure states of being.

Buddhism spread from Northern India into China and Tibet, and south into Thailand, Burma and other South East Asian countries. The Northern School became the Mahayana, the Southern, Theravada. Within the Mahayana school, in the period between 3-7 AD, a third form developed – Tantra. It is concerned with transforming the gross body, speech and mind into those of a Buddha (Awakened One) through working consciously on subtle processes.

On this 'journey' through various countries Buddhism inevitably took some already existing concepts on board and thus enlarged its knowledge on the Elements.

For example the Vietnamese monk, the Venerable Thich Nhat Hahn, lets Buddha himself explain the teachings of the Five Elements:

'The Buddha understood that Rahula was ripe to receive certain teachings. He said: "Rahula, learn from the earth. Whether people spread pure and fragrant flowers, perfume, or fresh milk on it, or discard filthy foul-smelling faeces, urine, blood, mucus and spit on it, the earth receives it all equally without clinging or aversion. When pleasant or unpleasant thoughts arise, don't let them entangle or enslave you... Learn from the water, Rahula. When people wash dirty things in it, the water is not sad or disdainful. Learn from Fire. Fire burns all things without discrimination. It is not ashamed to burn impure substances. Learn from the air. The air carries all fragrances whether sweet or foul. Rahula practice loving-kindness to overcome anger... Practice compassion to overcome cruelty... Practice non-attachment to overcome prejudice. Non-attachment is the way of looking at all things openly and equally. This is because that is. That is because this is. Myself and others are not separate. Do not reject one thing only to chase after another." ' [23] The all-encompassing detachment of Space is unmistakably represented.

Buddhism grew under Ashoka, a powerful Hindu warrior king who (centuries before Christ) was converted to Buddhism, renouncing all violence. Somehow it had the effect of revitalising Vedic teachings and Ayurveda during that time. As Buddhism spread, with it spread this system of medicine. Especially in the remote regions of Tibet, there was a melting pot of knowledge from India and China. The Elements were a distinct part of this knowledge; they were understood as states of being (*skandas* or aggregates); these aggregates of <u>matter</u> were 'analysed in terms of four elements (solidity, fluidity, heat and motion and their derivatives)' [24]

Sogyal Rinpoche writes 'the potential and quality of these five elements also exists within our mind. Mind's ability to serve as the ground of all experience is the quality of earth; its continuity and adaptability is water; its clarity and capacity to perceive is fire; its continuous movement is air; and its unlimited emptiness is space.' [25]

An ancient Tibetan medical expresses it more graphically: 'Flesh, bones, organ of smelling and odours are formed from the earth element. The blood, organ of taste and liquids in the body arise from the water element. The warmth, clear coloration, the organ of sight and form are formed from the fire element. The breath, organs of touch and physical sensations, are formed from the Wind element. The cavities in the body, organ of hearing and sounds are formed from the space element.' [26]

W. Y. Evans-Wentz, scholar on Tibetan matters, describes how the elements reach into cosmology in the *Bardo Thödol*: 'In the First Round of our Planet, one element alone - Fire was evolved. In the fire-mist... cosmos assumed a rotary motion and became a blazing globular body of undifferentiated primeval forces, all other elements lay in embryo... In the second Round, as the Element Fire assumed definite form, the Element Air separated from it and enwrapped the embryonic Planet as a shell covers an egg... In the Third Round, as the Planet, bathed in the Element Air and fanned by it, abated its fiery nature, the Element Water came forth from the vaporous air... In the Fourth Round, in which the Planet still is, air and water neutralised the activities of their Parent Fire; and the Fire, bringing forth the Element Earth, became encrusted with it.'

A similar thought is conveyed by the old Hindu myth of the churning of the Sea of Milk, which was the Fire-Mist, whence came like butter, the solid earth... on which the Divine Progenitors incarnated becoming the human race.

This inherent divinity of man expresses itself through a system of Channels and Nadis, through which the divine life energy flows; each Element has its special channel through which it constantly creates and dissolves the manifestations of the body. Through these, the interaction between the Elements outside and inside the human body take place. This theory of meridians plays a major role in Tibetan, Chinese and Ayurvedic Medicine.

Tibetan Buddhism gathered a unique wealth of knowledge about the interaction of these energies in the outer environment and its interaction with the inner human 'environment,' devising countless rituals and healing practices for purifying both. Dis-ease has its root-cause in ignorance. Ngakpa Chogyam Ogyen Tongden writes that this *ignorance* takes on five recognisable patterns of distortions 'which take their character from the Elements (Earth, Water, Fire, Air and Space) as they manifest in terms of our emotional/psychological energies' (be it positive or negative). In this way he links arrogance/obduracy as well as equanimity to the Earth element and anger/aggression as well as clarity/insight to the Water element. The indiscriminate and obsessive consuming nature is related to Fire, as well as discriminating awareness/compassion. Paranoia is linked to Air as well as confidence/ability and self-accomplishment. Torpor and depression is linked to Space as well as ubiquitous intelligence and pervasive awareness.[28]

To redress dis-ease and lead us back to the natural state of oneness, help is sought from five Meditation symbols, the *Dhyani Buddhas*. These Buddhas are not to be regarded as personal deities, but as personifications of primordial and universal forces; (they are accompanied by their female counterparts, which we met at the beginning of this work). For example at the end of the Tibetan Book of the Dead, prayers for Guidance upon death are written. The 10th prayer says:

'May the ethereal (Space) elements not rise up as enemies;
May it come that we shall see the Realm of the Blue Buddha,
(Vairochana).
May the watery elements not rise up as enemies;
May it come that we shall see the Realm of the White Buddha,
(Akshobya).
May the earthy elements not rise up as enemies;
May it come that we shall see the Yellow Buddha, (Ratnasambhava).
May the fiery elements not rise up as enemies;
May it come that we shall see the Realm of the Red Buddha,
(Amitabha).
May the airy elements not rise up as enemies;
May it come that we shall see the Realm of the Green Buddha,
(Amoghasiddhi).' [29]

The most crucial Element to understand is Space. Lama Gangchen talks about it as the backdrop for all others: 'the four elements of wind, fire, water and earth are all moving or dancing together in the element of space. It is the space element that gives the capacity for the other four elements to manifest, in both subtle and gross forms.' [30] Women possess a very special intuitive wisdom quality... On the absolute level, this female energy is space quality, the wisdom of emptiness and dependent arising. It is from the space of emptiness that all phenomena of the outer and inner world arise, (much like a womb), and this we sensed when we called our planet Mother Earth.

Elements in Buddhist life.
Buddhism has its own form of **Yoga**, Yogācāra; it combines discipline and good conduct. Its main tenet is that external objects are unreal, but the mind itself is not - if it were, all reasoning and arguments would be false. According to this school, mind follows the rule of dependent origination and change – but these are mere effects on the mind, the mind itself is pure. The task of Yoga is to return to this purity. Which is no different from Patanjali's ('Father of Yoga') goal for Yoga as: Yoga-cittavritti-nirodha (Prevention of Modifications of the Mind). [31] If we look at a more unique use of the Elements in Buddhist life, a typology (Psychology) stands out. The five Elements are said to be 'five families' - they relate to psycho-sociological states, behaviour patterns that have evolved in the struggle between the ego and 'others.' We belong to these families just like we consider ourselves to belong to our biological families. Naturally not everyone fits neatly into a category and many people are mixtures of several families. Chogyam Trungpa describes the five families: *Vajra* (diamond), *Buddha*, *Ratna* (Jewel), *Padma* (lotus) and *Karma* (action).

The *Vajra* family person reflects the environment with sharp accuracy, there is fear; surprises result in anger. But then this angry, controlling intellect can be transformed into 'Mirror-like Wisdom,' which is associated with the **element water**, the Buddha *Akshobya* and the *dakini* (mother) *Dhatisvari*.

The *Buddha* **family** person is associated with the **element of space** or ether. In its neurotic state, such people seem dull and thick; 'spaced out,' 'they don't bother to wash the dishes or take care of themselves,' everything is too much effort; yet when in a positive state, they are clear, calm and with a spacious mind like sky. The name of the *Buddha* of this family is *Vairochana* and the *dakini Locana*.

The *Ratna* **family** is associated with the **element earth;** in its un-evolved state this energy must fill up every corner because it never has enough; these people are said to be greedy and domineering, accumulating food and possessions. But in the same way they attract positive wealth, riches and 'All Enriching Wisdom.' The Buddha of this family is *Ratnasambhava* and the *dakini Mamaki*.

The *Padma* **family** person is seductive (**Fire**); he/she is interested in relationships and wants to accumulate desirable feelings; scattering the energy she starts projects, then drops them when the superficial glamour wears off. Pleasure is very important. When purified and the energy freed from the ego's hold, it becomes 'Discriminating Awareness Wisdom.' The family is related to Buddha *Amitaba* and the *dakini Pandaravasini*.

The *Karma* **family** person is very active, always working; too busy to look at you straight on. This need to always be doing comes from **the air element** and can be very aggressive and compulsive. These people like to organise and control everyone. After transformation the energy turns into 'All-Accomplishing Wisdom,' benefiting many beings. They are associated with the Buddha *Amoghasiddi* and the *dakini Samayatara*. [32]

As for **Medicine**? The Tibetans have a vast and ancient medical system based on types of constitution. Their 'humours' are similar to the Indian *doshas* (not to confuse with the Indian 'humour, 'which are more positive influences).

'Wind' gathers the energies of Space and Air, and describes a type of people that is dry skinned, bent from the shoulders, talkative, they are nervous and agitated, have a rapid heartbeat; they are easily aggressive, are especially affectionate to family, suffer from attachment and avarice etc. etc.

'Bile' describes mainly the effects of the Fire element, and people that are thirsty, sweat excessively – or not at all and have a high metabolic rate; they like the cool; have too much ego, and an active (monkey) mind. They are sharp and learn quickly, they can be cruel, full of envy, anger and hatred.

'Phlegm' describes types of people dominated by water and earth qualities. They are said to be nice looking, fair, slow and patient, they are tolerant, resist difficulties, they are secretive, don't show emotions much, are more stable and have a longer life; they are calmer and have a more controlled life energy . They suffer from ignorance and selfishness; they have a deluded mind.

These characteristics (just as in Ayurveda) effect the science of **Food,** i.e. a person characterised as 'Wind' should avoid fat food, junk food, tomatoes, coffee etc. and instead eat plenty of oily food, pasta, butter, wheat, rice, eggs, cheese etc.

A person characterised by 'Bile' should avoid hot spicy food, alcohol, eggs, onions, bitter and salty foods and should eat plenty of cold food, rice and barley, radishes and lentils, fresh food, watery vegetables etc.

A person characterised by ' Phlegm,' should eat cooked and heavy food, plenty of beans, and avoid dairy products, ice cream, animal fats, raw vegetable, raw fruit, salads, sweet food etc. So there is really very little difference between the two systems.

Tibetan Buddhism details these three types even further. The physical realm i.e. vitality (Tibetan: *Srog)* is influenced by one element, the elemental nature of the body, by another (Tibetan: *LU)*. *Wangtang* the power and quality of our energy, is influenced by a third, the energy which plays upon us as personal luck (Tibetan *Lungta*), by a fourth, and the general overall energy as manifest in the Aura, by yet another. Thus the person as a whole has a constitution made up of the <u>influence of five different aspects</u>; they might show a dominance of one, or can be influenced by different elements. This must be the most complex constitutional model that can be decoded by Astrology.

Furthermore, there is a science about **the Aura** based on two aspects, the strength and health of the elements in us, and the cosmic energies around. Astrology helps to calculate which elemental energy within our Aura needs strengthening. This is a complicated process linking the character of the year and its animal symbol - related to the Five Elements with the person i.e. someone born in the year 1945 is under the influence of the Wood/Space element and the symbolic animal of a bird. This means that the life force of him/her has the character of Earth (solid and strong) and the body is under the influence of Water (dissolving things). Its power and strength of will comes from Wood/Space (the intellect and spirit); its luck from Water (being flexible and supportive to others), and Earth (strength) will be noticeable in the Aura.

In **Buddhist Astrology**, using the Five Elements is not regarded as superstition, but rather as a practical tool 'to understand and heal our body and mind on the gross, subtle and very subtle levels.' [33] The influence of the Elements is through the planets, each linked to an Element as well as every single day in our lives: i.e. Space/Wood is linked to Thursday, Air/Metal with Friday, Saturday is linked to Earth, Sunday is linked to Fire; Water is linked to Monday, Tuesday is also linked to Fire, Water is linked to Wednesday.

And further recognition of Elements is found in Buddhist **Art and Architecture**. Buddhist (and Hindus) are fond of and famous for *mandalas*, meditative ornamental symbols, painted, made of the finest sand or found in architecture.

In Indonesia, in Central Java, is the largest surviving tantric, Buddhist Mandala in the world and it has as its subject, the five Elements.

T.Y.S. Lama Gangchen Tulku Rinpoche says: "Encoded into the *stupa mandala*, is a very detailed map of human consciousness, from its grossest and most impulsive state, up through successive higher levels of purity, until it finally reaches the pinnacle of human development - full enlightenment and the awakening of the Buddha mind." 34

Furthermore, **Music** (sound or chants) or chants and purification mantras are connected to the Elements. Each Element has a sound mantra with which to purify the respected Element in our own body, as well as in the environment. Such chants are for example:

Eh Ho Shudde Shudde Soha (for the Space Element)
Yam Ho Shudde Shudde Soha (for the Wind/Air Element)
Ram Ho Shudde Shudde Soha (for the Fire Element)
Bam Ho Shudde Shudde Soha (for the Water Element)
Lam Ho Shudde Shudde Soha (for the Earth Element) 35

Finally, in the Asian context we look at **the Five Elements in Chinese Tradition.**

Although the roots are vague, we know Taoism as the base of Chinese thinking. Before 600 BC Chinese philosophy was incredibly varied and its explanations difficult for the ordinary mind - traditional thoughts were constantly swamped by new influences. Then there was a great surge of knowledge when Lao-tzu formulated Taoist knowledge and Confucius soon after contributed his ideas (some think the two were nearly contemporaries). A few centuries later Buddhism joined. The indigenous practise of ancestor-worship paved the way for 'Buddha' joining the position of first-ancestor, then of God - 'from a clod to divinity.'

So what we know as Chinese Tradition is an amalgamate of Taoism, Confucianism and Buddhism and indeed we find many temples which share worship between the Three; frequently depicted as 'The three Pure Ones' (or symbolically: Heaven, Earth and Water; or wealth, health and longevity).

For a basic understanding of Chinese philosophy though '...it is sufficient to concentrate on three features which originated long before the development of any formal cult... 1) Tao, 2) Yin and Yang and 3) the theory of the elements... ' 36

The prime concept of the Tao holds that: "Everything is what it is... is all One... The Tao," so said Lao-tzu. Who was he? When Confucius asked this question, he was told: "*The men* about whom you talk are dead, and their bones are moulded to dust; only their words are left." Is Lao-tzu an amalgamate for 'old men', wise ones?

What is the Tao or 'the Way?' Man's 'co-operation with the course or trend of the natural world, whose principles we discover in the flow patterns of water, gas and fire.' 37 Confucius, so legend has it, was obsessed with order. He systematised every aspect of existence; making the heavens into an ordered state that included a Ministry of Thunder and Storms, a Ministry of Water etc. He was not satisfied with three Elements (Heaven, Earth, Water) he 'ordered' it to be Five!

In the 'people's knowledge' nature always was observed, people delighted in it, believing nature is all there is - whatever is thought, felt and experienced is brought about by nature. Tao is the name for what ever happens naturally, and man is part of it. The quintessence is captured thus:

> The Sage falls asleep not
> Because he ought to
> Nor even because he wants to
> But because he is sleepy! [38]

The Tao happens of itself because everything is affecting everything else, not because a ruler, creator or anything external decrees it (i.e. Confucius). Tao is the ultimate energy of the universe, the Ground-of-Being. Anything else that is said about IT limits it; nothing can be outside it, no-thing can be said about it. 'The Tao that can be told of is not the Absolute Tao.'

'The Tao does nothing, and yet nothing gets left undone.' [39] Chung-tzu explained: 'The fluidity of water is never the result of the effort of water; and so water became the main symbol for TAO, whose natural property is fluidity.'

Fluidity taking form becomes movement, this energy that moves is *Chi/Ki*. To this, both environment and man owe their existence; to know and to live within this movement is The Way, *The Tao*.

Movement is always from - to, i.e. it happens between two 'poles.' So at the very roots of Chinese thinking and feeling lies a second principle, that of polarity. Never though are the 'poles' seen as fixed; they have not the character of opposites, but are harmony in dynamic; without this dynamic state, there would be no change, no life. Light and dark are mutually completing, they are not in opposition; Taoists hold with harmony of opposites.

In Chinese thought, these two poles of cosmic energy are Yin and Yang. This, the original split into dual power, is instigator of all change which then unfolds and is 'broken down into tangible components... the five elements' [40]

These are called *wu-hsing* and are first mentioned in connection to a map, describing: 'Water in the north has sprung from the one of heaven... Fire in the south... Wood in the east... Metal in the west... Earth in the middle... ' [41]

In the above described ancient diagram (or map), there are also five heavenly numbers and five earthly numbers mentioned; these are distributed among five places, each with its complement. This organisation of the 'Five' shows the Confucian influence of 'right order.' It put a grid over the world by which to understand the physical world via Five Elements, and yet they maintain the polarity of Yin and Yang energies and have their origin in the Indescribable, the Tao.

This grid finds **applications in everyday life**, most prominently in **Medicine.**

Chinese medicine (just like its Indian sister) is said to originate in the dawn of time. It certainly goes back to the 'Nei Ching' – (the Yellow Emperor's Classic of Internal Medicine) which is entirely based on the Five Elements. The contents of the book is said to date back to 2500 BC even if the present book is probably composed as late as the third century BC.

According to the above, Yin and Yang extend into fire, earth, metal, water and wood, each with innumerable associations. Its detailed anatomy, organised according to the Five Elements, will be considered later in more detail. Suffice it to say, it includes the organs and their functions, as well as emotional, mental and subtle states of being. Thus a state of well being (health) is not only seen as a balance between Yin and Yang but also as a harmonious mixture of the elements.

The creation of this balance is aided by considering a host of correspondences to each Element, such as: seasons, time of day when an Element is most active or passive, the season, a direction on the compass, climate, the tissues or parts of the body, colour, smell, taste, and foods, emotions and their expressions, reactions in times of crisis, the movement of *Ki/Chi* etc. etc. Chinese medicine is no doubt the most well known use of the Five Elements and its influence spilled over to Japan, modern American and European awareness.

As within Indian and Tibetan tradition, the Five Elements also found their way into Chinese **Astrology.** Like the Western Zodiac, it works with 12 signs. However, unlike the western Zodiac, the Chinese Horoscope is based on a 12-year rather than a 12-month cycle. Furthermore Chinese Horoscopes take into account 28 divisions of the sky (marked on the 'lo pan' compass (pa kua) in order to position Sun, Moon and Stars etc. Furthermore, they linked the Elements to certain heroes (sage or ancestor-spirits), days of the weeks, planets etc. **Feng Shui** uses this knowledge in the art of determining and changing auspicious energy of places, homes, relationship etc. etc.

Like Tibetan Astrology, the years undergo a 60 year cycle. Each year corresponds to an Element; for example the year 2000 was influenced in all actions and ways by the character traits of the Air/Metal Element.

In Chinese medicine, a host of herbs and foods are governed by their elemental qualities, either for healing or preventing illness. Again many different rules apply, such as using the right food at the right time, for example: The Earth time, summer, is a good time to strengthen spleen and stomach, thus it is advised to earth foods, such as maize, sweet rice, carrots, fennel, pumpkin etc. On the other hand, in winter for example, pulses should be eaten just as fish and other seafood, because they strengthen the kidneys and the bladder. [42]

The Elements also influenced **Art**. The special character of Chinese art is the result of the influence of the contemplative branch of Hsien whose prime adept was Chung-tzu. Through contemplation of the Elements 'Chung-tzu shows how the sage through intuitional enlightenment, finally comes to know the spiritual unity of all things as a personal experience.' [43] The emphasis on personal spiritual experience combined with Buddhist teachings to form Ch'an (Zen) and its unique Art. Here emphasis is not on the resulting painting, but on the state of the painter. The painter as a person would go through spiritual training and discipline in order to balance first his life and character according to the Great Elements. Once he was in a state of harmony himself, in a state of what we call deep meditation, then and only then, would he take up 'his brush and create, moving intuitively.' The painting was then a result, not of the painter, but his inner state i.e. the harmonised energy of the Five Elements. The inner state mirrored the hidden spiritual power of *ch'i yun* and always displayed reverence to earth, the characteristic flow of its waters, the unusual light of its misty sun, whispering mystery (air) of green bamboo groves. Most of all it tried to intuit the mystery of the Tao, as the indescribable emptiness of Space beyond.

The focus on knowledge that goes beyond the material world yet is in harmony with nature is the foundation of Ch'an and Zen, the latter was not embraced without conflict by Japan, yet eventually captured the entire nation and life. It brought forth most beautiful arts which, completely infused by the theory of the Five Elements, are mirrored in all aspects of Japanese life and culture, from archery to gardening, from the tea ceremony to architecture, from flower arrangement to Noh-theatre, and from brush painting and calligraphy to haiku, ceramics and cooking. The secret is that Zen Art is always a servant to spiritual ideas, and with this it is less concerned about depicting nature as it appears, and more with the natural flow of energy that is beyond ordinary perception. Keep in mind that 'perfect' depiction only leads to critical analysis, thus only involves the left side of our brain, but 'imperfect' art is alive, and challenges our intuition to get involved.

Thus the emphasis in this art is on the dynamics that happen between the Elements; they hint at the point where activity seizes (the pause between the breath). This space within is especially honoured in both **architecture and painting**. Space is always of major importance as it holds earth, water, air and fire - or shall we say: mountains, rivers, clouds/mist and light.

2.2: The Five Elements amongst the Aboriginals in Australia

The above abundant theories of the Five Elements are especially accessible to the western mind because they are organised into systems. Yet there exist other, more contemplative forms, which are equally rich and help man to understand himself within his environment, which he knows himself to be part of. If one lives in such an integrated, holistic world, an awareness of essential participation in nature presupposes a different state of perception than our ordinary waking state.

Such an expanded state of awareness is what we find in the ancient culture of Aboriginal Australia; their people seem to live continuously in the awareness of being one with nature. They refer to this state of being as 'Dreaming.' Creating Dream-time is a manner of life which is 'an ongoing metaphysical, rather than historical event... Dreaming is a state of mind;' [44] it is acted out through ritual and ceremony.

As nomads, the Aboriginals of Australia have a different relationship to Space. They are not bound to one place where one feels safe and belongs, sheltering from an alien world. As they occupy the world in which they are, every moment in its totality, there is no past, no future. Meaning, that man is present in every moment; he is always in tune with his environment, with his ancestors and the Father of Fathers, *Bai-a-mi*. 'He carries his whole world within him. He does not need to rely on outward exigencies to define his personality.' [45] Thus man doesn't 'exist' separately (*existere* - standing out) on the contrary he and his entire world are permeated by the numinous. Totems and *churingas* are the sacred tools for ritual and ceremony, a gate for communication in this divine world – in its entirety. This is a primarily metaphysical culture.

This makes clear that there can be no body of philosophy separate from its effects on daily life. Daily life is totally permeated by spirit. For Aborigines, the numen is embodied in all things manifest. Myth, legends, 'science,' daily life, spirit world - you name it - they are one. Life is truly holistic - only intrusions from outside, i.e. European culture, led to a division of subject and object, of observer and observed.

For us to understand this deeper knowledge we have to overcome the idea that there is only one way of talking about the Elements (categorising language). For true knowledge, we must open our limiting minds to look for wisdom beyond concise theories; we must suspend our judgement and enter into the space of 'dreaming,' must expand our awareness to include answers lying in myth, in legends and Dream-time-stories. 'We pay for the exactitude of factual language with the price of being able to speak from only one point of view at a time. But the image is many sided, many dimensional and yet at the same time imprecise; here again, it is like nature itself.' [46]

The Aboriginal is embedded in his community, not only his tribal community, but the community of birds, animals, the earth, the rain, rocks, water-holes, all are filled with life-essence, *kurunba*. 'Aborigines had no conception of themselves as the 'crown' of God's creation in the way that world religions often deify man. Life per se was a web of interactive particles, of which mankind and nature were co-equal partners.' [47]

In this way the experience of the Five Elements are within and without man, an integral sacred part of all. Lore about these is clad in myth, which must be distinguished from religion, science or even philosophy; it does not give factual knowledge but tries to catch something that is wider, deeper - goes beyond, capturing complex metaphysical ideas.

Their culture is as varied as any; many different tribes with different traditions have innumerable stories to tell, revealing great treasures. Let's listen:

> There is the cold West wind she 'is called *Gheeger Gheeger*.
> She is guarded by *Wahn* the Crow, who keeps her confined in a
> hollow log. He has to do this because she has such a turbulent

nature. Some times she escapes, and *Wahn* is kept busy trying to catch her and bring her back. The log is slowly decaying. When it finally falls to pieces, *Wahn* will be unable to control the west wind, which will run wild and devastate the whole earth.

The South wind, *Gooroon-doodilbaydilbay*, is accompanied by *Mullian* the Eagle Hawk, who can be seen in the sky riding on her back in the form of towering cumulus clouds.

The South East wind, *Yar-rageh*, has three wives, the *Budtha, Bibil and Bumble trees*. When he makes love to them, they begin to grow and put forth flowers and fruit as a sign that *Yarrageh*, the spirit of spring, has arrived.

The North wind, *Douran Douran*, is also a great lover. From his kiss come the floral dresses of the *Coolah Noongah* and *Kurrajong* trees. The East wind is *Gunyahmoo*.

Twice a year there is a *corroboree*, which is attended by all winds, including *Gheeger Gheeger*, who is released for this special occasion by *Wahn*. The female winds are unpredictable and wild. They rage through the trees, breaking branches and moaning because their lovers have been stolen from them...' [48]

The first thing to note is that the winds blow from different directions. Secondly J. Cowan tells us that in the north the seasons are irregular which is mirrored in journeys the tribe takes. Such Dream-journey follows special directions, associated with an animal and its character is linked to a certain wind. So crow, a scavenger, guards the West; his hiding place is a hollow log that decays. The wind can be so turbulent that his movement is unexpected, there is even danger of it being uncontrollable and causing death and devastation etc.

Without wanting to fall into the trap of pressing this into a known mould, it is surprising how many parallels we can find here to descriptions of the Air Element elsewhere. The Air Element is globally associated with 'West,' signalling an end-phase, the state of decay, rotting, sinking into the Earth etc.

Similarly the South, in the above watched over by an Eagle, a high flyer, he explores the periphery of the sky and has to turn 'her' back from the outer edges 'of cumulus clouds.' Again parallels can be found to the universal associations to Fire (spreading, ascending, high performance, high achievement, light, eagles, sight, having to be controlled). The South East (or East) brings new beginnings, brings spring, and starts the growth of flowers and fruit. These attributes are generally associated with Space/Wood ('bringing forth' and 'greening power').

In the above, little is said about the North except: 'he is a great lover.' To talk about love is talking about emotions, about feelings, about aspects that are otherwise connected with the Water Element.

Here is another story, this time about the **origin of fire**. There are many variations of this, but this particular one stems from people who lived on the North Western coast of Australia:

Two brothers named *Kanbi* and *Jitabidi* lived in the heavens. Their camp was near the Southern Cross, and their fires were the Pointers, Alpha and Beta Centaurus. At that time there was no other fire in the universe.

Food was getting scarce in the sky-world, so *Kanbi* and *Jitabidi* came to earth, bringing their fire-sticks with them. They established their camp, and laid their fire-sticks on the ground while they went to hunt *opossums*.

The two hunters were away so long that the fire-sticks, becoming bored, began to chase each other in the grass. This game started a bush-fire, burning out much of the countryside. Seeing the smoke and the flames, the brothers returned at once, recaptured the playful fire-sticks and restored them to their place in the sky.

It happened that a group of hunters saw the fire and felt its warmth. Realising the value of this strange element, they took a blazing log back to their own camp, from which many fires were lit. Now all aborigines have the fire that once belonged only to the men of the Southern Cross.' [49]

Note: fire needs entertainment, is joyous and playful, when it does not get entertained it gets bored – even depressed and seeks 'further afield.' Fire is linked to a great deal of activity and speed i.e. friction! It 'feeds on others' and it leaves nothing! It has to be recaptured, harnessed, and 'put in its proper place.' These Fire-characteristics describe equally well real fire, a personality trait or a physical body.

Here is a third example the story of ' *Tiddalik* the Flood-Maker.'

Tiddalik, an enormous frog, woke up one morning with an unquenchable thirst. He started to drink, and he drank until there was no fresh water left in the world. All creatures everywhere were soon dying and the trees were shedding their leaves. It seemed that very soon *Tiddalik* the frog would be the only one alive.

The animals could not think of a way out of their terrible plight, until a wise old wombat suggested that if *Tiddalik* could be made to laugh, all the imprisoned water would flow out of his mouth.

So everyone gathered by the frog's resting-place. For a long time they tried to make him laugh, but in vain. The kookaburra told his funniest stories, so good that he himself had to laugh... but the frog's face remained blank and indifferent. Then, the eel, driven from his favourite creek by the drought, began to dance. He started with slow graceful movements, but as the dance became faster, he wriggled and twisted himself into the most grotesque and comical shapes, until suddenly *Tiddalik*'s eyes lit up and he burst out laughing. And as he laughed, the water gushed from his mouth and flowed away to replenish the lakes, swamps and the rivers. [50]

Here several points are made about the Water element. Firstly - it is necessary for all life forms; when withheld it damages life; 'withholding' is a dark, unbalancing facet of water. Water, when frozen is withholding, withdrawing, and becomes useless as a life-support. In a person this expresses as stoicism, lack of interest. Its opposite pole is fire; its quality of joy, humour and play 'defrost' Water and thus keeps it functioning.

The frog is amphibian, living in both Elements of Earth and Water! It is Water's task/nature to nourish others, when holding back it is selfish, egoistic even and that has terrible consequences, i.e. drought. 'With-holding' he cuts his own life force; immovable, he himself becomes life-less.

The Aboriginals of Australia believe in reincarnation; what reincarnates is the mythical being *muramura*, this is the essential Dream-time-hero, the ancestral spirit. Initiations and life-experience fulfil the path of the inner spiritual hero. *The Diyari* 'religion' said that 'without the power released by the *muramura*, it was believed humans could not survive.' [51] The Dream-time-hero or ancestral spirit is man's animating power. *Ankotarinja* is such an ancestral spiritual hero, who reincarnates in ordinary man. He lies in the depth of the earth until spoken about; the speaker then is his incarnation. Stone symbols and songs are used to tell **his story**:

Ankotarinja was lying asleep in the depths of the earth (much of Australia's Earth is red), his bones bare (the following verses describe this state).

"Red is the down, which is covering me;
Red am I as if I were burning fire.
Red too is the hollow in which I am lying..."

In this state he thinks, 'it might be nice to rise up.' Having done thus, he looks around himself... and staggers to a nearby swamp and sits down, gazing at himself in the water. He becomes aware that from the crown of his head, rises a pole, a great *tnatanja*.

Looking at this ceremonial pole he realises that it 'touches the sky.'

Like a whirlwind, it is towering into the sky
Like a pillar of red sand, it is towering into the sky.
The *tnatantja* is towering into the sky...

He then starts to breathe heavy and 'like a dingo he sniffs the four winds... when he turns to the west he feels a warm breeze on his face, he cries out "The breeze that warms my heart comes from the west!" As he speaks the great *tnatanja* towering above his head topples to the ground. Disturbed by the wind, he decides to travel underground.

'An underground pathway lies open before me,
Leading directly to the west, it lies open before me...'

He comes against tracks of other human beings, and eventually women; (they fall mysteriously ill i.e. lovesick) '...like a dog he follows the trail by scent...'

He watches the women, then attacks them, biting into their waists (seat of liver, life); he comes to another camp and finds men sleeping.

' Irresistible and foaming with rage
Like a whirlwind he rakes them together...'

He devours them, and full and tired falls asleep under a *tnatantja* (sacred pole).

A traveller also to the West, comes across the scene, wonders what has been gone on, and horrified, he hurls a sacred (*churinga*) stone at the monster, hitting him in the nape of the neck. *Ankotarinja's* head rolls away, making it possible for the men he swallowed to escape; 'they flow forth from his trunk like water... to celebrate their rebirth... *Ankotarinja's* head reflects, 'My home isn't so far away, really. Let me go back there for my last rest.'

'Out there, not far from me lies *Ankota*;
The underground hole is gaping open before me...
A cavernous pathway is gaping before me...'

Then his head rolls back towards *Ankota* underneath the ground, to emerge finally in the creek-bed where he was born.'

The story ends like it started: ' Red am I, like the heart of a flame of fire, Red too, is the hollow in which I am resting.' [52]

He has gone full circle; his head enters the womb again. It's an ancient and universal story. The hero is born, becomes aware of himself, goes underground (into the worldly activities of matter), fights with man, consumes women, falls asleep, is attacked by 'others,' is killed and returns whence he came.

Let us just look at those points that relate to the knowledge of the Five Elements.

The power of imagery mingles fire, earth, air and water. At the beginning *Ankotarinja* exists in fire, in spirit alone (bare bones, pure thought), the fire decides to come out of its spirit nature into real fire into the 'light of nature.' This mercurial act happens in the bowls of the Earth; Spirit has to become total manifestation, total Earth, total matter. *Ankotarinja* himself decides to move out, to become matter, his persona looks into the mirror of water. The contemplative nature of water gives the insight that tells him: I am part of the spirit world, I carry the *tnatanjas*, the ceremonial pole, the fifth dimension, the axis mundi in me/with me as that I reach the sky. The *tnatantja* points beyond earthly existence. But as the hero orientates himself in the world, he positions himself in the four directions, this earthly focus makes him lose his spiritual dimension, the *tnatantja* falls off. He becomes man, physical animal. He sniffs the four winds.

The element air gives him the motivation to move. (Air and Movement are classic associations). 'He smells out the warm winds in preference to 'cold' winds from the other quarters. He has addressed the four cardinal points... 'and chooses the west; he has to go forward to walk full cycle, through the underworld, through all suffering, to completion, to walk to sapient knowledge.'

His underground travels lead him to explore man and woman, physical life; and then he falls asleep, full with his experience, complete. He is found by a 'wise' man of the West (associated universally with wisdom) who is the light in the centre of this 'monster'; his soul 'glows red.' The soul needs liberating; for that, all the unconscious images and bad karma (result of bad deeds) need to 'flow forth like water.' The men trapped inside the 'Earth man' now are free and they drink water - water brings greening power, it leads to rejuvenation, joy and celebration.

Decapitation here is not death but simply finishes a cycle. The cycle of the Elements is completed, we met Fire and Earth, Wind and Water and Space - the *tnatanjata* that holds all upright as the spiritual principle that reaches the sky.

The deep knowledge of the Australian Aboriginals about the Five Elements is beyond doubt, as they find expressions in their myths, songs and art. Although 'Art for art's sake' is a concept foreign to their culture and their languages have no words which corresponds exactly with 'art' and 'artist,' [53] their ceremonial objects, poles and stones, as well as tools and their own bodies, were richly decorated. Often the paint used was either red earth hardened with human blood, or white clay (earth). This combination of red and white symbolised Earth and Water (blood), both intrinsically sacred.

2.3: The Five Elements in Africa

Africa has an enormous mixture of cultures and such a varied past that we have to define which Africa we talk about. The influences of ancient Europe, Islam, Christianity and Judaism were present in Africa almost from their beginnings. Unfortunately as a result part of the original African myth, culture and language is lost. For example the creation myth has been so strongly influenced by the story of 'Adam and Eve' that 'the *Swahili* word for human being is *mwanaadamu* - child of Adam.' [54]

One of the strongest and most ancient influences show in the myth of the Queen of Sheba, which goes back to 900 BC. Her union with Solomon resulted in a son, who became Menelik I, founder of a dynasty of which Haile Selassie was the last.

This might suffice to illustrate the difficulty of separating out what is Semitic, Islamic and Christian Africa, and what is indigenous. The former brought with them the monotheistic-anthropomorphic deities and with it a division between God and nature. Furthermore some of the indigenous Africa has been destroyed by adaptation to modern secularism, which includes most of Southern Africa.

Amongst the indigenous Africans, hunters, gatherers, herds men (the Massai, the Fulani of West Africa, the Khoisan, Bushmen, the BaMbhuti etc.) people lived in harmony with nature and animals, often having no rulers as such but living in a civilisation of simplicity. Amongst these the awareness of interconnectedness with nature and its Elements was well alive. The Elements are understood as the multifaceted expression of One spirit force, a divine energy that lives in trees, animals, people, mountains and rivers alike. The power manifesting the whole of nature is frequently referred to as *Jok*.

J.H. Driberg defines this concept among the Langi of Uganda:
> '*Jok* like the wind or air is omniscient and although its presence may be heard and appreciated, *Jok* has never been seen by anyone... His dwelling is everywhere; in trees, it may be or in rocks and hills, in some springs and pools... or vaguely in the air.'

The distinguished Kenyan Nilote, Bethwell A. Ogot confirms this: 'the spiritual part of Man, the only part which survives death is *JOK*; and it is the same power which is responsible for conception as well as for fortunes and misfortunes. Hence to the Nilote, *Jok* is not an impartial universal power, it is the essence of every being, the force which makes everything what it is and God himself, the greatest *Jok* is life-force in itself.' [55]

This sounds like a holistic, non-dual world-view. *Jok*, the divine and all pervasive, is 'primarily the process of being, the essence of universal power, which inherent in life as a force, is... the universe and the force of life in all manifestations... All the different elements in nature can be expressions of 'God'... God is everything in everything. Each tree, each blade of grass and each stone that you will see out there and each one of the things that live... the hairs on your head, and each flea in your hair... Him who was and yet was not, and him who will be and yet shall never be... because there never was a time when God was not and there never is a time when God can never be...' [56]

Malidoma Patrice Somé, shaman and scholar, takes this one step further, when he describes the cosmology of his people, the Dagara of Burkina Faso: 'In the beginning there was no earth as we know it. In its place was a burning planet, a ball of fire... Therefore Fire is the first element of the Dagara wheel. Fire is present in everything... Water became the second element in the cosmological wheel. The shock from the collision of fire and water... chased the fire into the underworld, leaving the surface as a hot steamy place, fertile for breeding of all kinds of life forms. This surface, hospitable to life, is what is known as earth, which constitutes the third elemental principal of the Dagara. A steam of great density formed the atmosphere around earth (Air)... which made it conducive to the birth of life and thus the fifth element, vegetative nature, came into being.' [57]

In fact the first four elements exists within Nature, within the fifth element.

As with the Aboriginals of Australia we find rich understanding in lived traditions, ritual, myth and accounts of 'secret,' or Shamanic knowledge, handed down through generations, in villages. Vusamazulu Credo Mutwa, Hereditory High Witchdoctor to the Zulu nation tells a creation myth told by the Bushmen and amongst the Zulu and Bantu (*Ba-ntu* means walking upright, human):

Nothing existed but nothingness...
Nothingness had been floating, for no one knows how long,
Upon the invisible waters of Time....
Then one day, the River Time desired Nothingness...
And as a result of this strange mating of Time and Nothingness
A most tiny nigh invisible spark of living Fire was born.
This tiny spark of Fire could think and grew conscious of its lonely state...
'I exists, I am what I am'
Was the living thought that pulsed through the 'mind' of the tiny spark...
'I must grow or end my life...' There was nothing for the spark to feed upon...
It fed upon itself... grew in size... and grew until... it devoured its mother, Nothingness
But River time was very cross with what the Spark had done and sent the Spirit of Cold... their mighty battle... still rages unabated...

Because of their unceasing conflict, all Life depends. (Fire and Water)

From the still warm ashes... arose the Great Mother Ma... (Earth)

(But she felt lonely and cried; her tears became rivers and lakes and floods that damaged the earth, and the Great Spirit ordered her to create)... a perfect Universe from Chaos. (Considering it a pointless task) she thought:
'How long will I work here, creating all this? This utterly senseless rubbish!'
... "Thy duty is to create... to do and not to doubt... I command thee to do...
The purpose behind creation of all the Universe, is known to me alone..." (thundered the voice of the Great Spirit).
"Oh, imperfect being, you wish for a partner? You are what ... will be known as a female and your opposite shall be your companion - a Male.
... He shall bring contentment to you and both you and he will bring forth Life upon earth." (The next morning, she heard a voice and it called her).

"Come, oh my mate, I await thee here."
And the shimmering silvery Goddess arose with a cry of immeasurable joy...

held her arms outstretched... "My mate! My Mate!"

(What embraced her) were not arms like her own, but great creeping vines...'

"I am the Tree of Life, thy mate and I desire thee!"
(The tree is of matter, crystals, sharp granite stones, rock hard roots, its branches of jagged pieces of granite, diamonds and iron ore. A thousand years later, the Goddess experienced birth-

pains)... and the first mighty nation of flesh and blood was born...
and the strangest change came over the Tree of Life.
Green buds burst from its writhing limbs, clouds of seeds emerged
and fell upon the rocky plains... soon all manner of plants grew
forth - a creeping carpet of lush living green. Soon mighty forests
covered the earth... and the 'Tree of Life' bore living snarling,
howling animal fruit... and so on and on... to different generations
of stories. [58]

The story is beautifully told; its content has many of the Elements we
came across in the Dagara cosmology. In the beginning there was vast
Nothingness, e.g. the void, emptiness, potential, Space; there was time, or
rather motion described as a river. Out of these two components, life unfolds
under the directive of Spirit; earth and 'tree' unite to create 'the tree of life' -
yet Spirit, the fifth Element, is the instigator.

In man he takes the form of a personal Spirit called *Ena.' Ena* rides on
the Soul, like a man in a canoe.' The Bantu (like most indigenous Africans)
believe in reincarnation, and the *Ena* and Soul reincarnate in phases in the
grass, trees, beasts, human, reptile, birds and stars. Vusamazulu Credo
Mutwa describes life of an indigenous African (similar to the Australian
Aboriginal), as totality inseparable from recognition and reverence for the
Five Elements, and the One who 'inspires' them. Everyday life, places and
rituals for the hunter and farmer are bound to the Five Elements.

The eloquent Shaman Malidoma Patrice Somé, shares with us that
people and cultures also carry the characteristics of the Five Elements. In
this way there are cultures that are dominated by the Fire-Element, 'its
people's perception of the world is red. As they rush ceaselessly forward with
a consumer's mentality, they pollute everything in their way, conquering and
destroying anything that interferes.' (Who does not recognise both aspects in
our Western culture)!

By contrast Water cleanses and reconciles, nurtures and 'does not want
the natural environmental harmony to be perturbed. It is a slow culture... It
prefers to see the potential good in anything...'

An Earth culture is a culture of homeless people, maybe of refugees;
'without grounding people... (are) missing the nourishment that earth offers.
Yet after they have gained all the material things they need, they will still feel
uncertain...'

A culture impregnated with the Air/Metal Element, is 'frenetically
involved in communication at every level. In such a culture, language is an
impressive instrument of power (the great orators who persuaded millions
by sheer power of communication and propaganda speak eloquent of
this).' [60]

He also reports that his people understand individuals to have
characteristics of the 'Wheel of the Five'; each person has dominant
characteristics of one. Moreover people are grouped in clans, each
representing an Element: we have a group of water people, a group of fire

people etc. (much like the Tibetan Buddha family). At birth, elders decide according to which element the child should be named and educated, to make sure there is a balance in the clan.

Overall, the Dagara associate with **Fire**: the South, red, ancestral knowledge, the spirit and psyche that knows, ability to intuit, running out of control, violence, completion etc. Fire 'makes us do, feel, see, love and hate. Fire has power. We act and react because the rising power is in us... Inside of us, the fire pulls the spiritual forces beyond us, towards us... From the realm where the ancestors dwell, this fire can be seen... fire in us is never dead, therefore it never needs to be reborn...' [61]

They associate with **Water**: cooling, generating life, reconciling, serenity, the North, blue, black, cleansing, balancing, focus etc., represents the coolness of water. IT provides peace of the body and soul...

Earth is associated with support, comfort, inclusion, belonging, healing, caring, yellow, the Centre, nurturing, contentment etc.

Air/Metal is associated with the West, white, receiving messages, communication, memory, listening, knowledge stored, etc.

The generative aspect of **Space** becomes associated with its product, **Nature** and as such, is associated with the principle of change, green, the East, consciousness and spirit, magic, rhythm etc.

Malidoma writes about his initiation 'the coach was dividing us into five uneven groups, the earth people, the fire people, the nature people, the water people and the iron people...' [62]

Note: three of the Gross Elements are as per usual, two have unusual names: The fourth Element (Air) group here is referred to as 'iron people' (just as in some Tibetan Texts; he also talks of Mineral/Metal just as the Chinese).

The fifth Element here is 'Nature,' easily linked to what is called 'Wood' in the Chinese tradition as symbol for the life-force; he even points to the tree as essence of consciousness for the indigenous people.

In the tradition described by Malidoma Patrice Somé, the Elements also play a role in the **Judiciary** system. Elders representing each Element clan, meet at the Earth temple of the village, which is in the centre. Justice is based on the fact that estrangement from the tribe, custom and right behaviour results from losing one's centre; losing one's connection to the essential nature!

It is easy to see that the Five Elements are not only found in myth, but that they are an integral part of the community, social structure and law in parts of Africa.

2.4: The Elements in the Americas

The Five Elements in Meso/South America

South America, as we call it in a sweeping statement, has two distinct parts, Meso-America and the Southern part of the continent. Their cultures ancient and modern share one focus, the Sun whose symbol is the royal eagle.

From earliest times nomadic tribes lived in these regions, according to their legends seven tribes emerged from seven caves. Many ancient civilisations and their descendants, such as today's Kagaba Indians and their forefathers the *Tairona* feel that they stem from these. Even though some of the tribes and great civilisations we know of belong to different linguistic groups, they still consider themselves connected to these seven tribes and share many base beliefs. One of these is the conviction that the number Five holds special significance i.e. the world evolves through Five Sun-ages. The Chimu further described how five eggs develop into five falcons, which turn into men; two of these turn into gods, *Pariacaca*, the God of Rain, who chases *Caruincho* the God of Fire.

These two representatives are thought of as the primal duality, which again we find in many cultures; here they are later joined by *Viracocha*, the creator God, or as modern day Yanomani call him, *Omainé*.

Unfortunately much detailed knowledge is lost, as the skill of reading the early methods of 'aid memoir' has died out with the Spanish Conquest. People used to record history by certain knots on strings. So in most cases we have to rely on archaeological remains and living myth.

One of the most known cultures was the kingdom of the *Incas,* the kingdom of 'the Four-Corners'; the four Quarters of the World were thought to meet in the capital Cuzco. Their state was built on the principle of co-operation and harmony. In fact co-operation with each other and God was the reason for existence; this was written in the constellation of the sun and the stars. In fact each tribe and their homeland was linked to a star, each had special talents and gifts to contribute.

'*Mayan'* is often used as an umbrella term and some argue [63] that they were simply 'one people' in different periods of high profile. They flourished in the same region as the Olmecs, Toltecs and of course the Aztecs. (The Aztecs were a barbaric, nomadic hunter tribe from the North-west who flooded over the Toltec civilisation at the end of the first millennium)

All of these left many clues in the ruins of the southern continent; we find rich pickings in **archaeological** ruins about their knowledge of the Five Elements. The Artwork, together with surviving myth and legends, shows a language of symbolism, which has been called *Nahuatl*. In *Nahuatl*, certain symbols appear to dominate such as the jaguar, the condor or eagle, the snake, the fish, and the frog. The first three refer to the sun in various parts of its journey and thus are physical representations of **Fire.**

The snake represents dense matter, and is always associated with terrestrial gods; the god of **Earth** itself is at times represented as a frog.

The fish, waves, starfish, pearls, tears and shells are symbols of **Water**, and relate to the Rain God.

Flowers, the symbol of impermanence and delicacy, are symbols associated with **Air**; the Wind God represents the breath, spirit.

The Fifth Element is represented by the '**Fifth Sun**' - its symbol is the human face, and the cross (holding together the four directions).

According to the *Nahuatl* tradition, the present age is the Fifth Solar Age. These Ages, governed each by one of the Elements themselves are to be followed by the Age of Consciousness. This sixth age, according to Computer prediction and the Mayan Calendar, is supposed to start in 2011.

Each age was destroyed by the extremes of its nature. The present, the Fifth Solar Age is preceded by **the age of Water**, which was destroyed by floods and man turned to fish; yet one couple survived to repopulate the world.

The **age of Air** was destroyed by Sun-winds, man turned into monkeys; again one couple was saved to repopulate the world. (Sun-winds? This symbol is an exact design of the whirling winds emanating from the surface of the sun, as per modern astronomy). 'As the sun rotates, the particles which solar wind is composed of, fan out rather like droplets of water from a garden sprinkler' [64]   The **age of Fire** was destroyed by fire. It is said that the nature of fire is to turn organic matter into its primal constituents, releasing heat and light, thus earth and the heavens were created with one couple surviving.

The **age of Earth** was destroyed by lava raining from the sky and man having to turn into birds. The destructive power of earth finds its symbol in the tiger - here linked to dark, destructive animalistic power.

The wisdom revealed here, is that the four Elements left to themselves are destructive; 'As long as these four principles remain isolated, they perish... the only means of survival ... (is to) act upon another dynamically.'[65]

Therefore the **Fifth Sun**, holds all Elements, just like Space, and has as its guiding principle **Movement.** Through movement (co-operation, interaction) balance among the elements can be achieved. Its symbol is *Naollin,* a human face, the face of the divine incarnate. It is embodied in the original hero Quetzalcoatl.

Furthermore, the four ages are portrayed in four directions - the fifth 'direction' is the centre; which incorporates what is above and what is below; its symbol is the cross. Why the cross? It has the ascending line of fire and water, the movement line from left to right, or spirit to matter, Air and Earth meet in the centre, which is 'the fifth dimension.' Many symbols for the Five are found such as five dots, five circles, five corners of a mandala etc.

Our age is deemed the Fifth Sun-Age, it has a great chance of survival through freeing creation from duality (matter and spirit, serpent and feather/ flower). It has the task of showing man his way back to divinity and it does that through the movement of balancing energies. In *Nahuatl* a feathered serpent depicts the harmonious union of matter and spirit, the conscious man who sings of inner freedom.

The wisdom of these Five Ages, the search for harmony amongst the Elements is personalised in the ancient figure of *Quetzalcoatl*.

Just as the present Western era is linked to the birth of Jesus Christ, South American culture roots in Quetzalcoatl (who probably appeared around the same time in history). Quetzalcoatl is not only a god but could be a composite man (ancestral hero) or even a mental structure. His symbol the plumed serpent, has in its cultural context the same importance as the 'empty Crucifix' for Christianity (the risen Christ).

Quetzalcoatl is at the core of '*Nahuatl tradition*'; probably originating with the Toltecs, the image was 'fine-tuned' by the Mayans and led to the extreme by the Aztecs. Quetzalcoatl played a social and religious role. He is said to have given people maize, the knowledge of precious stones, the arts of weaving and making mosaics. 'He taught man science, showing him the way to measure time and study the revolution of the stars; he showed him the calendar and invented ceremonies and fixed the days for prayer and sacrifice.' [66] Here is his story:

> The story shows a man as basically good and of heavenly origin, yet he has to become matter (Earth) to experience life. This happens by looking in a mirror (brought by a plodding priest): "What is this thing that is my body?"
> The priest says: "Son of mine, Priest *Ce Acatl Quetzalcoatl*, I greet thee and come, oh Lord, to show thee thy body."
> Quetzalcoatl answers: "I know and welcome thee, grandfather. What is this concerning my body? Let us see." On this he is given a mirror.
> "Look and know thyself my son...." Quetzalcoatl, looking at himself, got frightened; demons then offer him drinks to appease his fear; he gets drunk and sleeps with a woman. Ashamed of his deed, he retreats for four days into a coffin, and decides to burn himself.
> He goes to the seashore (the divine waters) and lights a funeral-pyre onto which he throws himself. Thus having purified his heart, his soul rises into the heavens and becomes Venus.
> The planet Venus rises and falls with the Sun. It appears first in the Western sky and then goes 'underground' to rise again in the east united with the rising Sun.
> The pilgrimage of the human Soul is like this journey of Venus, having to go underground, becoming matter; then the fire of the spirit frees it for the journey home to reunite with the eternal Divine, the Sun. 'The Sun is called the 'King of those who return.' The aim of Nahuatl religion is this unity. [68]

While Quetzalcoatl is in the underworld, he takes the form of a dog; *as dog he is matter, as Venus he is total spirit*. As dog, or serpent that slithers over the ground he is total **Earth**, as Venus, as star or as feather he is total **Fire**, the fire of spirit. Other times he is portrayed as Wind-God, then he is 'the giver of breath.' **Wind/Air** is the energy that sets in motion the movement of life, the universe, thus providing the necessary dynamics to move from matter to spirit. This harmony of opposites is a continuous theme; the Quetzalcoatl symbol of union is the One, the same rising in the East and setting in the West.

To illustrate this union of opposites he is portrayed in a ship on water encircled by flames. He wears a breastplate with an image of '**Burning Water' opposing elements, in union.** Creation does not rise out of heat or water alone, but out of the dynamic interaction of the two.

It is this dual aspect which is represented also in the character of *Tlaloc*, the 'Water-God, who nurtures and sustains physical life.' As Water-God, Quetzalcoatl is portrait with the characteristics of the Fire God (such as yellow hair, butterflies, rhomboid eyes, special marks etc).

In this tradition, emphasis is on the interaction of the Elements, which have a mutually balancing effect. Why else is, for example *the ancient Fire God depicted in a pool of Water surrounded by flowering stones?*

Just as water and fire are on one axis of opposites of the elements, so are stones and flowers (inert matter - flowers, Air and Earth). The message is strong: seek harmony amongst opposing Elemental forces.

The Great Temple of Tenochtitlan was dedicated to this idea of uniting. The gods of rain and celestial fire were placed side by side at the top of the pyramid, with blue and red water flowing freely, showing 'that the gods ruling over it, symbolised the mystic formula of 'burning water.' [69]

The battle between these opposing forces happens within man, within the world, within the universe. When one element dominates, imbalance or destruction follows (illness or hell). Such illness though, serves as a warning to wake up, to restore balance. A New Age is born 'out of a man covered in sores.' The myth of creation of the Fifth Sun tells us that this age is created through the sacrifice of a man whose body is covered by sores and scabs. Physical matter has broken open revealing the need for inner purification. Through it rebirth comes, it calls for movement and balance of the Five Elements. Some cultures have developed an intricate system to work with numbers to calculate such harmony.

One such theory is the **'Twenty Count'**; it combines knowledge of the Elements, tracking their movement and using it for balancing opposing energies. This esoteric teaching is found in South and North American tradition. The Twenty Count, frequently depicted as circles within circles, evolved out of a way of praying to the four directions with constant return to the centre (and its cross directions). It is indeed a multidimensional meditation much like the Mandala of the East. One familiar use is the **Mayan calendar**, which has meticulously recorded the wisdom of the flow of natural relationships; computed to fit the 365 days of the year, putting together philosophy, science, mystics and art.

The Twenty Count defines a path of life in which the physical being prepares and aspires to higher levels of being. The first seven numbers refer to the body, the latter thirteen to the evolution of higher mental activities.

They are counted by fours, being classed according to the directions, in the order of East, North, West and South, making five groups. Each of these also belongs to one of the directions, like a family with certain attributes. These attributes often tally with the attributes given to the Elements in other contexts.

The actual numbers thus relate to concepts, forming archetypal patterns:

1) relates to East, to Sun, to primal Source, to unity, to original perception , the serpent/dragon.

2) relates to Air/Wind, respiration , cosmic energy , movement, polarity, duality, reflections, mysteries.

3) relates to Earth , to rhythm of day and night, places of mystery, the heart, the child and projection.

4) relates to Water, geminating seeds, generative Principle, balance and measure, animals and the elk.

5) relates to the Centre, integration and attainment and the wolf.

6) relates to North, organic balance, to understanding of mortality, death of the physical body, ancestor spirits.

7) relates to West, to mystic powers, knowledge and power, the sacred dream of life and order.

8) relates to South, stars intuitive realisation of patterns of higher life, harmonic resonance, cycles of laws and laws cycle, relationships and will.

9) relates to East, to the awakening consciousness, communication and expansion, to cyclic movements of the moon, choices and the 'Red Thunder Cloud.'

10) relates to the Centre and finally, to becoming physically manifest, thus its symbol is the dog (see Quetzalcoatl); also emotional life, loyalty and faithfulness etc. etc. [70]

It seems that in the South American Indian Culture, the Five Elements have in the main been explored and used to explain the evolution of man, universe and even the cosmos in a spiritual manner. They created a system, almost an anatomy of spiritual energies, focusing on the interrelationship of the Five Elements. These found their expressions in Astronomy, Art and Metaphysics; one may ask, is anything of this **still alive today?**

Let me tell you a story from my own experience:

Some years ago, after an international conference, I visited the home of one of the participants. Her husband was a Peruvian artist. I was welcomed into the living room. By the comfortably looking settee, stood a beautiful round table; it was made from leather and had intricate designs embossed on it by the man of the house, and to protect it a big glass pane was laid over it. We sat down and intrigued by the table, I asked for its story.

The tabletop was designed to show the interaction of the Five Elements, and the Five Sun Ages, in so many symbols and images.

What appeared a very 'cool, modern' table-top, was in fact based on ancient South American wisdom; in the mind of the artist, the ancient culture was alive

The Elements in North America

The focus in South American traditions was/is especially on the interrelationship between the Five Elements; this concern is also alive in present North American Indian Culture.

" ...to be Indian is an attitude, a mental state of being; to be Indian is a state of being that has its place in the heart. To allow the heart to be a source of energy, to allow your heart to give energy to the planet, to allow your feelings to spread your energy, to draw that energy from the earth up and from the sky down into the heart, the centre of our Being, and then to share it - that is our task!

Some philosophies talk about five different worlds and say that the creator has given all these worlds a simple law: to live in harmony and balance with all things, including the sun. And again and again men have destroyed this harmony and we too have destroyed this harmony. And again we have done so, without any necessity to do so.

If we don't restore this balance, this will be our last chance." So says Brooke Medicine Eagle of the Nez Percé and Sioux.[71]

In the same spirit, Chokecherry Gall Eagle writes: 'From all the adventures and mysterious happenings, nothing strikes me as important as balance, harmony, centring, generating Light' [72] He continues that this is achieved with the help of '*Skan (sh-kan) or Taku Skan Skan. Skan* means something like divine substance in movement. 'It is something moving, always moving but only through itself and yet touching all of creation.'

The fundamental quality of 'Movement' around and within all the Elements, is probably the most widely known Native American tradition, shared by many different tribes, from the Navajo, Hopi, Ojibwa, Tewa, Nootka to the Mazcteka, Chippewa and Lakota - as **the 'Medicine Wheel.'** The actual 'wheel' originated in ceremony; they were also called fasting circles or healing circles.

The base idea behind the Medicine Wheel, is the recognition that everything in the universe depends on everything else, including man. Life is thus not seen as linear, starting at a point and proceeding to an unknown point in the future, but is better expressed in circles. Linear thinking isolates man from the happenings around him, he forgets his home, his roots and interconnectedness. 'We have forgotten that we are connected to all of our relations on the earth, not just the human family... We have imprisoned ourselves in tight little worlds of man-made creations. We have forgotten how to hear the stories and songs that the wind can bring to us. We have forgotten to listen to the wisdom of the rocks that have been here since the beginning of time.' [73]

We have lost the ability to perceive the light and joy that dancing fire shows us; we have lost the ability to let our dreams float on the water to nourish our souls. The Medicine Wheel is a living symbol reminding us of all aspects of the world. Spirit moves constantly through this circle.

The Medicine Wheel, also called the Sacred Hoop, is used like a 'book of life.' It is used when people built their houses, when they purify their bodies, when they come together in council. It governs tribal activity in war and peace, and the life of the individual in health and sickness, shows each person the lessons they have to learn through their journey of life. Amongst others, the wheel represents also the year, a calendar, and thus astrology.

Man enters the 'Medicine Wheel' at birth, at one point. This point gives a certain constitutional character, gifts and talents that relate to the element of that day, and represents the family clan and the totem that protects that day.

The Medicine Wheel, although usually a circle made out of specially selected stones, encapsulates the idea of constant Movement; it is a physical representation of energy in all its different hues, moving without beginning or end. The elemental energies find expression in different sacred spaces within the Medicine Wheel and have been honoured for centuries as 'cycles of planting, gestation, birth, growth, change, death and rebirth; (they) are the life lessons of the Sacred Hoop.' [72]

Chokecherry teaches that 'everything vibrates at its own speed. Everything is one vast whole... merely different manifestations of the same thing... What differentiates one form of matter from another form are the vibrations, rates and speed...' [73]

Each sacred space differs in vibration, despite the fact that we are of the same spirit, connected by movement. This is the most important understanding about the Medicine wheel: in essence it is 'movement of life.'

The wholeness of the circle remains undisturbed as the movement of life courses through the four sections, representing Earth, Water, Air and Fire and their associated directions and seasons. (Occasionally these are subdivided into North-west, South-west, South-east, North-east). Each facet depicts a stage on the journey of life, a particular personality trait, a talent, gift or lack of such etc. There are numbers attached to them (just like in the Twenty Count); each has totem animals (representing certain gifts or talents); each has a Clan Chief, myth and special symbols attached. Together, they include all human interactions, all possible states of being, and all manifest and un-manifest creation.

Two points ought to be mentioned here, so as not to 'paint over differences.' In some traditions, such as the Chinese/Australian, the Centre stands for the Element of Earth – in the American Traditions (North and South as well as here, in South America and as we will see in Christian Europe, the Centre stands for the Fifth Element, Space etc.

Secondly, the East in some traditions (i.e. Chinese/Indian) is associated with Wood/Space for its generating quality, the new beginning, and Air (such as above) with the West. Here is not the place to argue why.

The East in the Medicine Wheel 'is the home of the Golden Door, the entry point to all other levels of awareness and consciousness...' [74]

It is the place of illumination and the home of the eagle. Here live the 'Clan family' of the Wind or Air, it is the air on which the spirit travels, life-force itself, and so the East brings spring and renewal. It also has a special relationship to the Self - it speaks of mystic revelations, the dawning of Light in the heart.

The North is the place of the Water Clan. It relates to Winter, the White Buffalo, and the wisdom of elders; it stands for clear-mindedness.

The West is the place of the Earth Clan, the home of the Bear who lives in the cave, the womb of introspection and female energy. It is the place of quickening, which awaits 'the rising of spiritual illumination which helps us to see further and live in warmth and light;' [75] it relates to spirit, or psyche.

The South is the home of the Fire Clan and Coyote, or the Butterfly, it is where innocence and play live, where there is faith and trust, joy and child energy. It is the place of full body experience and relates to passion and sensations.

When we have balanced these four parts of the self in body, mind, heart/spirit, we have reached our centre, an inner balance. We realise that all is One, we have reached the hub of the wheel where the Higher Self lives and from there we have access to the collective consciousness, the Great Mystery.

The Centre, just as in the South American Tradition, is the dimension of Spirit, the Fifth Phase, the Fifth Sun, and the Fifth Element. We fulfil our task 'by returning to ceremony, ritual and using the wisdom of the Ancestors to heal any old wounds and bitterness.' [76] Ceremony, whether in the formal Medicine Wheel or 'in life' is celebrated by the Pipe.

The pipe is another symbol shared by all 'brothers and sisters of Native America.' It too represents the Five Elements, (there are variations in how this is expressed) yet the following is common: the bowl is made of stone (or clay) representing the mineral kingdom of the Earth, its form is a symbol of the female energy. Its stem is of wood, representing the plant kingdom; its shape is a symbol of male energy. It is decorated with fur and feathers, representing the animal kingdom and is used by a member of the human kingdom. All these symbols of life forms gather in the smoke, as a representation of life spirit and Air. 'With the smoke, an ethereal substance capable of penetrating between realms of the physical and spiritual worlds, go our prayers.' [77] The sacred tobacco in the pot is lit and burnt, representing Fire. This transforming agent is saluted, and a puff of smoke is offered to all directions, the Elements, Mother Earth, Father Sun and the Great Spirit.

The message is strong - we live in connection with everything else, and we change and learn and grow with everything else. Constant change is brought about by the **interaction of the Elements.** Their relationship is at the heart of matter, in us, and the teachings of the Medicine Wheel challenge us to seek harmony with the rest of Creation.

The teachings of the Medicine Wheel echo in many ways, what we have heard from the South American Indians. With some variations the following story is told amongst different tribes:

The Great Spirit created Earth according to his vision, but when he saw what had become of it in time, he grew sad. The minerals, the plants the animals and even the humans, they all had forgotten the law of unity by which they were to live. They were fighting with each other constantly over the smallest thing. They were unwilling to share their talents, possessions and wisdom. They were full of greed and hatred, only caring for themselves.

The Great Spirit thought that the earth could not continue this way, so he send messengers to all creatures, yet few listened and humans acted deaf. So he called the spirits of water and they descended upon the earth. Rains came until the water covered the earth and few survived. Still the Great Spirit felt sad, for an earth without humans was not what he had envisaged.

Up in the clouds there lived the spirit of a woman, and she was lonely for a companion. Plants and animals were lonely too and remembered the days when there was harmony. They knew about the woman in the sky, but thought she would need earth to live on. The plants and animals sat in council to ponder this, when a giant turtle arrived.

'Friends," the turtle said, "I have a strong back, the sky woman could come and live on it." The animals thought it was a great solution, they could ask the woman to come down and her children could grow up to learn how to live in harmony. So they called upon the sky woman. She accepted and came down; she walked around the turtles back and thought it was a fine new home. She thanked the turtle for offering her back as a home for herself and, "all of the humans that will come from me. But if we stay on your back as our home, you will not be able to do what turtles do. So let me help you."

She called all the water-animals together and asked them to join in helping turtle, by diving deep into the water and bringing up some earth.

They did, but none could get deep enough to bring up earth, except the Muskrat. She took the earth from the Muskrat, who had tried hard and was exhausted. She gave him healing medicine, and then took the fist-full of earth and dried it in the sun light; then she rubbed it into dust and sprinkled it in the waters all around the turtle; then she blew life over it, and the earth was born again. "'Now, you may return to your own life," she told turtle, "we will always remember you, even though you are a creature of the water, you will also be thought of as the creature of this land." In this way a water creature became the totem of the Earth Clan. [78]

The Water Element has, in the tradition of the Chippewa, the Frog as a totem, which is described as living near Water, but also on trees and the Earth.

The butterfly is totem in Chippewa for Air and describes how the 'crawling one' went to his grave (Earth) and its spirit soared into the Air afterwards.

The Totem of Fire used to be an arrogant Hawk, a bird of the Air that became greedy - the qualities involved here are of Air and Earth - until he became a fiery shape created by lightning, called the Thunderbird.

Each Totem undergoes change, growth. It seems that the totems are carefully chosen for their interaction with other Elements, change and movement again lead to harmony and unity.

To illustrate the deep awareness of North American Indians of the Elements and associated directions, I refer to a myth told by Black Elk, a Sioux of the last century. [79]

Long ago two Sioux were out hunting when they saw an apparition of a beautiful woman. One of them became lustful and she reduced him to dust.

She told the other one to go home and built a ceremonial tent. The tent was to be erected around twenty-eight poles, "of which the central pole, the main support, is compared to the Great Spirit... (amongst other symbols are) one for the fire, one for the water, one for the rock, and finally one for the two legged people."

The tent was built and the beautiful woman appeared in ceremony. She appeared in the East and proceeded anti-sun-wise south, west, north and again east, walking around the circle of the tent. The woman gave the chief a sacred parcel. "No impure man should ever be allowed to see it; for within this bundle there is a very holy pipe... with this sacred pipe you will walk upon the Earth, for the Earth is your Grandmother and she is sacred. ...The bowl of this pipe is of red stone; it is the Earth. Carved in the stone and facing the centre, is a buffalo calf that represents all the quadrupeds that live upon your Mother. The stem of the pipe is wood, and this represents all that grows upon the Earth. These twelve feathers that hang there... are feathers of the spotted eagle. They represent all the winged things of the air. When you smoke this pipe all these things join you, everything in the universe; all send their voices to *Wakan Tanka*, the Great Spirit, your Grandfather and Father. When you pray with this pipe you pray for and with all things."

The Ceremony continues and finally the pipe is lit, the first smoke flows through it for *Wakan Tanka*, then smoke is blown in the different directions.

After more teaching and ceremony, the woman leaves and turns into a buffalo calf and in turn into a white buffalo and a black buffalo; she, in the centre, was herself the *wakan* woman, the feminine aspect of the cosmic energy, the Divine.

2.5: The Elements in the European Tradition

Until the sixth century BC in Europe, science, philosophy and religion were not separate. The Sages of the Milesian school of Iona had the same aim as their brothers on the rest of the globe, namely to discover the essential nature of things called *physis*. The Milesians saw no difference between spirit and matter, animate and inanimate; all forms of existence were supported by cosmic breath, *pneuma*.

Heraclitus (544-483 BC) talked of the universal principle, 'the sublime concept' as a dynamic and cyclic interplay of opposites.

Yet slowly the divine principle was seen as that which was <u>above</u> the world, and thus the first step was taken in separating matter and spirit - yet both notions co-existed. Pythagoras and his followers felt that the highest level of spiritual experience came from contemplating the essence of reality in total. Even Plato still felt that matter could not be so easily separated from spirit. Amongst the Neo-platonists, Plotinus markedly distinguishes between the One, the Intellect and the Soul, which exist within each other. He states that 'man is not the centre of the universe, it is rather the universe, including the transcendental One, which is the centre of man.' He accepts a substratum that pervades all existence and yet allows each thing to have "'its own voice.' It is here that we find the place of the Elements. He described them as 'earth (ornate with all its growth...) the very sea... the great air... the ether and the far spread heavens,' with the sun from which fire derives. All these compounds - earth, fire, water and air - are permeated by the great soul, the supreme pure Intelligence, whose consciousness streams throughout existence, as though 'from all sides pouring in its light.' [80]

Each element has its own voice, so the Earth, for example has 'the indwelling earth-principle. The growing and shaping of stones, the internal moulding of mountains as they rise, reveal the working of an en-souled Reason Principle fashioning them from within and bringing them to that shape; this we must take it, is the creative earth-principle... '

Fire too has its own inherent principle: 'fire certainly does not originate in the friction to which it may be traced; the friction certainly brings out a fire already existent in the scheme and contained in the materials rubbed together. Matter does not in its own character possess this fire-power; the true cause is something informing the Matter... to bring fire into being... It is with this in mind that Plato says there is a soul in everything of this sphere. That soul is the cause of the fire of the sense-world... and the same principle applies to the other elements water and air.' [81] What underlies the material world is the fifth dimension or Element; it is consciousness or the very spirit that Aristotle (384-322 BC) denied. He fully and finally pronounced world as pure matter, paving the way for our typical Western science and philosophy. Without the spiritual dimension, the holistic world-view is lost; science and philosophy are split and 'Spirit and Soul' were fully pushed into the arms of Religion alone.

With this development, the Fifth Element disappeared from mainstream European thought; four Elements alone were recognised, the 'Quinta-Essentia,' the Fifth Element with its metaphysical connotations, was cut out. 'Thus for the greater part of the last 2000 years, the prevailing view was that of Aristotle. He proposed that everything in the universe is formed from just four basic constituents: earth, air, fire and water. It appears very naïve now, but in fact it is easy to appreciate the natural appeal of such theory against the backdrop of a mythic cosmology.' [82]

This fundamental split of Spirit and Matter could never silence all voices; again and again some rose to point out the gap. We find them mainly amongst Christian Mystics. Hildegard von Bingen is probably the prime example. For this remarkable woman, the cosmos is a living organism – portrayed as the Cosmic Christ. She was a German Abbess from the Rhine Valley, theological scholar, medical doctor who wrote Music and a famous Artist; her 'Illuminations' [83] as the drawings of her visions are called, frequently show the Cosmic Christ containing the universe within him, propelled by Wind energy: the breath of God! There are many of these *mandalas*, and all of these have five inner circles, woven out of the Five Elements.

More astonishing is that she not only recognised the Five Elements in the cosmos at large, but also within the human body; much of her medical work is based on balancing these Five Elements. She was adamant that to create peace and health, the Five Elements within the body have to be balanced. Inner peace is the cause, outer peace is the result, because the Cosmic Christ, or Christ-consciousness finds its incarnation in us and our life's work.

For her, the Five Elements are Fire, Earth, Water, Air (Wind) and Ether (Spirit, the Divine). These work together: 'Each relates to the whole. Everything comes out of God and goes back into God; akin in all creation as Fire, Air, Water, Earth... ' [84] The Great Elements, held in the Cosmic Christ, are responsible for people's characters, illnesses etc. 'God created the Elements of the world. All Elements are in the human being, and with them Man lives. These are called: Fire, Air, Water and Earth. These basic elements are within themselves so interconnected, that none can be separated from the other, and they hold so tightly together, that one calls them the essential structure of the universe... Four winds are the might of God... The East (Wind) embraces the air and mild dew sinks on everything that is dry... this wind penetrates everything with humidity and lets the seeds sprout.

The West (Wind) mixes with the driving clouds so they hold their contained water, so as not to burst forward... this wind dries up everything that starts to green.

The South (Wind) hinders the Fire, containing its power and stops everything from being singed... this wind ripens everything, brings all to fruition, the leaves in the woods, the grass, all seeds, fruits and wine and all the harvests of the earth. The North (Wind) finally holds the darkness in check, so that it does not grow out of balance... this wind brings the cold with him, presses everything together with icy cold and lets it freeze. So that it cannot flow.' [85]

In her medical book: 'Causae et Curae,' she gives a detailed description of what she understands by each Element and how each is part of the other. For example: Fire is the highest power under the heavens... it has five powers... just like man has five senses. Fire burns, yes, but the coolness stands against him so that the heat does not get out of balance. Water serves with its dampness to produce steam, so it can rise. Air is needed to ignite fire and movement is part of the flame, enabling it to shine.

Air has four powers: she sends dew, and lets greening-power sprout... it spreads warmth, which lets everything ripen. Air spreads itself to the four corners of the earth...

Water has... dampness, rising, speed, movement; it provides the sap for trees to grow, for flavouring the fruit, for greening-power of herbs; it nourishes all things with its wetness, supports the birds, feeds the fish, enlivens animals, keeps the worms in slime...

The Earth... is cooling in the summer and warming in the winter; she carries within herself the greening-power (*veriditas*) and the drying power (*ariditas*); she lets things grow out of herself; she carries animals and supports all creatures. [86]

In the human being, the Elements are connected to certain psychological tendencies and organs, as well as their illnesses. In this way Hildegard von

Bingen writes: 'the elements in the human... work in him and in all his actions they circle like a wheel turning.'

Fire... sits in the brain and the bone marrow... from here the blood derives its red colour... the powers manifest as heat in the vision...

The Air comes... into its own in breathing and in consciousness. She serves the divine life-breath of the soul, who carries man... with each breath....

Water... itself is fluid in the blood... gives man its humidity so that the greening-power can keep him living... manifests as juice in the process of fertility... the freezing coldness of water lends its quality to the bones. Earth... is in the flesh and the cells of bones, manifests in the warmth and coolness of the flesh, in the greening-power (growing); in its ability to reproduce... it holds sensitivity and sympathy... This might suffice to show the incredible depth and breadth of the use of the Great Elements.

Consider that Hildegard von Bingen lived in 12th century Europe, three hundred years before the first book on 'the working of the body' (Andreas Vesalius) i.e. anatomy, was known. The work and knowledge of the Woman can only be admired. Within our study, it is a rich example of how even in medieval Europe, the Great Elements played a considerable role.

It is clear that the Elements belong to a holistic way of perceiving the universe. And so it is here, but we have to look further for it in European thought.

Although mediaeval society was governed by 'reason' it included God; he had a powerful place outside of man, in the heavens. God ruled from above, through his church, with an iron, patriarchal hand. Man had to 'submit to the preordained plan of God... Man thought of himself as pre-eminently a rational being... with everybody knowing his place and serving his purpose.'[87]

This thinking within a hierarchical structure, with God at the top, the church and the bishops underneath ruling with rigidity and dogmatism and the peasant at the bottom, was accepted and provided safety. If you questioned it, you might be burned at the stake.

The same hierarchy can be found in theological thinking; it became more and more scholastic and academic; thus the schism between secular, analytical thinking on one hand, and belief in what the church held as sacred, grew bigger.

In this climate, the Renaissance brought a new perspective. Renaissance thinkers looked at nature and, seeing it anew, filled it with their own sensual metaphors. 'They impregnated nature with their dreams and visions, they brought sanctity to nature... they infused (it) with spiritual energy.' [88] This found new expression amongst painters, poets and ordinary people. Renaissance man rediscovered his love of the four Elements, which resulted in introducing 'four *humours*' for describing people: i.e. the melancholic (earthy), the phlegmatic (watery), the sanguine (airy) and the choleric (fiery).

But this love of nature did not result in returning to *Five* Elements, nor did it bring much in terms of a new paradigm for society; still, it maintained a counter point to the ever increasing mechanistic and technical thought that grabbed hold of the Western World; it could serve as a foundation, as fertile ground on which holistic thinking could eventually re-grow... and that in the most unexpected corners...

Recently I visited the monastery of St. John of the Cross, in Segovia, Central Spain. He was a Carmelite monk, famous Mystic, poet and contemporary of Hildegard von Bingen. The church of this monastery had recently (1982) been renovated in honour of a visit of Pope Juan Pablo II. A fellow Carmelite monk (Rev. P. Gerardo Lopez Bonilla) was asked to create an altar-piece according to the mystical poetry of St. John of the Cross.

When I arrived at the church, I could not believe my eyes - there were five panels depicting the Five Elements in strong colours of abstract paintings. In short, the lowest panel (horizontal) consists of a painting of Water, in strong blues of concentric circles. Above left, a panel shows the folds of Earth in a dark brown rock face; the centre panel is light blue Air, with white clouds on which the Virgin Mother ascends, her child reaching with his hand to the devotee kneeling at her feet. To the right is a panel of a single, vibrant red flame; across the top is the fifth panel, in yellows dissolving into brilliant white light... the Space of Christ consciousness. As one of the monks described it, it is 'synthesising the spiritual teachings of this mystical Doctor (referring to St. John).

Space is associated with Mount Carmel, symbolising the divine union with God, the goal and perfection of life.

Earth relates to the 'dark night of the soul'; where we are stuck in solid matter, in desperation and insecurity; it is a gestation period for spiritual ascent.

The panel of Water refers to the fountain of divine water that nurtures us - symbolising the Eucharist. The central panel, Air, relates to the Holy Spirit, the divine elevating power; the theme is repeated on the front of the altar, where the hands of God protect a dove, that enable it to fly. The flame symbolises the fire of love, purifying fire burning with mystical love and devotion.'

The Five Elements - in today's world - depicted in a catholic monastery by a South American padre; indeed a global, timeless, living symbol!

But all over Europe, **Astrology** reminds us of the Four Great Elements, used to classify the Zodiac signs. In this way Taurus, Capricorn and Virgo belong to the Earth; Leo, Aries and Sagittarius belong to Fire; Gemini, Libra, Aquarius are Air signs and Cancer, Scorpio and Pisces are Water-signs. The elemental character was used to reveal different attitudes of personalities and other forces that act upon our behaviour.

Astrological interpretations today use **Carl Jung**'s classification of the four functions of consciousness, which he classifies in his book of Psychological Types according to the Elements. In this way he links thinking to Air, feeling to Water, sensations to Earth and Intuition to Fire. Within these, 'intuition and thinking are considered active, self-expressive, extrovert, yang and masculine; and water and earth are considered passive, receptive, introvert... fire and air are associated with levity, tending to spread out and rise, while earth and water are associated with gravity, being affected by it and tending to concentrate and collect at the lowest level.' [89]

In this way a person born in the Zodiac Sign of Pices, will be under the influence of the Water Element, as a predominant Character shaping influence. As Water is associated with the Jungian category of 'Feeling,' this means the person will be sensitive to others, able to feel what others feel, have compassion and empathy etc. The Four Elements as used in Astrology and Jungian Typology, is probably the most well known use of the Great Elements in the Europe of the past century.

At the Beginning of the new Millennium, we are aware that our universe is larger in dimension, and more complex than man ever thought. It provides us with a sense of mystery, and a newly intensified wish to search for meaning. This expresses itself in the surge of spirituality that is not necessarily part of the established religions, but strives for 'truth, purpose, validity, obligation and meaning' to use a phrase from T. S. Eliot. The tendency of many thinkers is to rise towards wholeness and inter-connected-ness. Fritjof Capra writes: 'Each event is influenced by the whole universe... it is the whole that determines the behaviour of the parts... The world-view of modern physics is a systems view.' [90]

This new focus on wholeness brings about a new awareness of nature and it is, as we live in the global village, fertilised by knowledge from many cultures. Probably the most influential has been the rebirth of complementary medicine, influenced by Chinese and Indian Medicine, but also very much creating new brands. They all use and base their knowledge on the Five Elements; they include various forms of psychotherapies, Kiniesiology, Shiatsu, Acupressure, Touch for Health, etc). The new trend of 'Energy Medicine' has been linked by Donna Eden to five rhythms, rhythms that have the characters of the Elements. [91]

'We each vibrate at a core rhythm that reflects the current season of our soul... You are born into a particular rhythm or combination of rhythms... Your body, your movements and your disposition, were formed within the energy of one of the seasons of nature, and they are imbued with a rhythm that blends that season's rhythm with the rhythm of the season preceding and following it... Beyond the rhythm that is embedded in your character, you move through all five rhythms many times... during your lifetime.'

Modern Architecture borrows more and more from Feng Shui; sacred Architecture has always existed, but it has become common knowledge with this Chinese art form. A Western equivalent emerges as 'Space Clearing' and 'creating sacred space' even in the most normal office building. It holds a concoction of assimilated wisdom from many cultures. It is recognisable in the following: 'One method I use for Space clearing is based on the Sacred Circle of Life... it is the sacred circle that infuses all of life... It is a mandala of the greater Medicine Wheel of the universe in which everything created has its proper place. It is our bodies and our mind, our spirit and our heart. It is the zodiac, the Wheel of Life, the serpent swallowing its tail, Ezekial's vision, the calendars of the Aztecs, Navajo sand-paintings showing the creation of the world, the Four Winds, the Four Elements and the Four Directions... The elements of Air, Water, Fire and Earth, as well as various colours, plants and animals are assigned to the cardinal points... How each of the various elements are assigned to each of the Four directions varies... The important thing is to understand that each direction has its own power... use your intuition.' [92]

Europe has woken up to the universal wisdom; yet still falls short where the fifth Element is concerned.

Chapter 3: 'Anatomy' of Energy Concepts

IN ORDER to understand how deeply we are connected with the five Elements, we need to look into the many aspects of our bodies. Western understanding of our body was and largely still is, based on the Cartesian view of the world, rooted in the Newtonian model of reality. Just like the world, the body was looked upon as an intricate mechanism, a type of grand machine or clock that is controlled by the brain and the peripheral nervous system, the ultimate biological computer. Along with this perspective, 'a dichotomy of mind and body has been imposed on human beings. The body is divided, in order to comprehend the phenomena of life such as anatomical structures, cells, tissues etc. Health has come to be viewed in terms of the state of our physical components.' [93] This view, prevalent in traditional allopathic medical understanding, is only slowly changing with the insights of new physics and biology. According to the 'new' science, we have to wake up to the fact that we are 'unified networks of events' (Valerie Hunt) – no mere clockwork.

Since Einstein's understanding of Reality as a unified field and Quantum physics, we have to accept that all matter (including our bodies) is organised energy. If my body and the world around me are nothing but energy, how do I distinguish between the two? How do we notice differences? Our sense organs take in information our brain processes this. We have an organ of smell inside us- with which we smell what is outside us. But we ourselves give off odour; it means we smell anything from the outside through, or mixed with, our own personal smells. This illustrates the problem that whatever energy we perceive as 'out there,' we can only perceive through - and because of - the same energy 'in here.' The macrocosm, the world around us and the microcosm of our bodies, are so intricately linked that they are nearly indistinguishable. We only perceive the outer on the backdrop of the inner. Some cultures are more aware of this than we. So in India, the word *prana* has two distinct meanings: it describes the general life-giving energy as well my breath; Swami Rama states: 'From the centre of consciousness arises the wave of the life-force. This life-force turns into breath.' [94] In Japanese tradition the word *Rei-Ki* separates the two forces even more clearly; '*Rei*' being universal energy, and '*Ki*' the personal Life-force (two parts, one word). For the Chinese, *Chi* or *Qi* is an energetic substance that flows from the environment into the body - one current, one flow!

Whether the energy is called prana, Chi or Ki, this energy is always moving purposefully, indicating that it has intelligence. Without intelligence, energy or matter would be undirected, formless and chaotic. Intelligence makes the difference between the house designed by an architect and a pile of bricks. Consequently our own body must be credited with an immense fund of such 'know-how.' Every cell is not only programmed by DNA, but also empowered by knowledge to do a specific job. Each cell knows what to do; just as each river knows how to flow, each lettuce knows how to grow. This inherent knowledge in every part of creation is called consciousness. Thus life-force is said to be intelligent and conscious. Quantum physics speaks of knowledge riding on matter.

Once the conscious, intelligent life-force leaves the body, the physical matter returns into a disorganised collection of chemicals. The 'personal' energy is simply reabsorbed back into universal energy. This process is no different from a wave that falls back into the ocean; its individual demise has no effect on the existence of the ocean. In this sense, death is just a change of form by the **one energy** which is itself immortal; neither born nor unborn, nor yet to be born.

Energy, by its very nature, has vibrations; different forms of energies can be recognised by different vibrations. The energy form that is me thus differs from the energy form that is you. We have different vibrations. Many factors contribute to me having a certain vibration. The happy me - today - has different vibrations, than the unhappy me yesterday. The energy that is my heart differs from the energy-form of the Bladder. Thoughts, feelings, everything has its own vibration and adds to the whole. The overall main frequency-band, characteristic for a particular body, accounts for the trends and dominant tendencies that we call personality.

The frequencies of our personal 'vibrating field' are affected by all other vibrations that bring about constant minor, or major changes. This has been used quite directly in ancient and modern times, when illness has been treated by vibrating energy fields that we call music i.e. Indian, Tibetan medicine and even modern therapies (i.e. Dr Guy Manners, Bradford Hall Clinic, England). Most dramatic results were recently achieved by A. Tomatis, who studied the human ear for over fifty years and treated people successfully with sound, curing deafness and even such complex illness as schizophrenia, paralysis and illiteracy. But in general, relative little research has been done into how our bodies react to vibrations. More studies are needed even on influences of mundane vibrations such as caused by cell-phones, microwave ovens, radio, television etc.? We know next to nothing about how emotional vibrations given off by violent videotapes, 'heavy metal rock' etc. affect us. We think we know our bodies, but do we? When our bodies manifested an illness, do we even consider finding out what energetic disturbances are involved? And why - as vibrating energies, our bodies have consciousness and intelligence, so science and mystics tell us. But will we listen to it, when will we learn from our own bodies?

In the Bhagavad Gita, Lord Krishna compares the body to a field. He says to Arjuna: This body is called 'the field,' the wise, who understand such things call the One who knows this, the knower of the field. I, the knower of this field and every field, hold it that you must understand this (BG 13/1). [95]

Why does Krishna use the image of a field? The base of a field is Earth, supporting growth of ever-new forms, brought to life by pure Water that essentially nurtures and nourishes. It is warmed by the Fire of the Sun; covered by Air providing oxygen etc. for all that grows: grains, flowers, fruits, trees and all the 'grazing animals ' that feed on these. The field occupies Space; in fact the inherent purpose of a field is to be space in which things can happen. So the field, like the body, is made up of the five primal aspects of one, all-pervasive, divine and intelligent energy.

The five different aspects, states or fields we call **ELEMENTS**. The unified field that is our body consists of **five fields of different energies;** observing these opens understanding of ourselves and the subtle energies of the physical world that includes us.

First we need to consider our bodies and its different levels, then we will consider the five energy fields that effect it.

Contemplating the analogy of the field for our body, one becomes aware that in both cases, the physical body and the field, there is 'someone' who owns and uses this field. The owner can do what he wants, turn the field into an apple orchard or a flower garden. One can split it into little plots and build a house for people to live in or make it into a cemetery to receive the dead. One can also do nothing and let thistles and thorny bushes grow on it. Just as the field, the body is ours to do with what we want. We can train to be a boxer, become a potter, a wise man or a fool, a good man or a bad man. We can do with this body what we want - and men have done anything to it, from reaching enlightenment to crippling it, selling it and humiliating it.

An interesting question arises: who then, is the one that owns and works through the body? To find out you need to understand your body, listen to it, observe it and know it. But who does this listening; who does this knowing? Previously, it was said, the material body itself is inactive matter - yet in every cell there is constant awareness of what needs to be done. If you see somebody else's beauty and get jealous, there is no sense in cutting your eyes out, the eyes are mere material instruments; it is our conditioned minds (ego) that tells us to be envious, jealous. If it is the conditioned mind that suffers, we have to purify it to get to 'Know the Knower' behind the scenes, our true Self, our true nature; then it is a pleasure to be in the body.

There is a story told about a saint who, when his death approached, thanked everybody, bowed to the five elements and his Guru, then with folded hands thanked his body: 'My dearest body, with your help and grace I saw God. I thank you. I may have often neglected your needs and frightened you. I have made you suffer but you have always helped me. I am in your debt. You gave me a quick and perceptive mind. Sometimes I unknowingly wronged you, even though, you always helped me, did everything you could for me! Whatever I did, you returned only friendship and support. Without you I could not have followed my spiritual path, would not have realised God.' With these words he left his body behind.

What is this entity we call 'our body'?

3.1: Body-Mind-Soul and the Aura

Frequently we talk about 'my body ' as a composite: body, mind and soul. Note that we call it 'my body', confirming the above, that there is somebody or something different from body 'who' owns it. Secondly, the three different aspects are in modern vibrational medicine considered as 'subtle energy fields, condensing and influencing electromagnetic energy fields, which in turn condense into matter i.e. chemicals. Then Chemistry creates structure, structure functions in a way that reinforces structures. It works like a feedback-loop where chemistry influences electromagnetic fields, which then reflects on the subtle energy field. Thus body is soul, and soul is body.' [96] This revolutionary sounding idea is in accordance with what philosophy and religion has said all along, that matter is intelligent, self-aware energy which acts in coherent fields. So if one of these three is consciousness, they all are. The highest of these three we call soul/Self; second is the mind through which we experience; that experience is then recorded in the brain, the most physical, gross vibrating manifestation of this intelligent self-aware field.

If we apply the above to the Five Element theory, then the subtlest energy field, with highest vibrations - soul - is an expression of indefinable, all pervading consciousness (Space); the second energy field is intelligence, mind generating thoughts (Air); next is mind generating passion/enthusiasm, driving us into action (Fire). Actions result in emotions, physical feelings, which are manifestations we associated with Water; finally the whole process shapes our physical body down to the flesh (Earth)! Because these energies are not static, but in constant interaction - as long as there is life, the physical body constantly changes.

The physical body you see today in the mirror was not there yesterday! 'Ninety eight percent of the atoms in your body were not there a year ago. The skeleton that seems so solid was not there three months ago. The configuration of the bone cells remains somewhat constant, but atoms of all kinds pass freely back and forth through the cell walls, and that means you acquire a new skeleton every three months. The skin is new every month. You have a new stomach lining every four days.' [97] So what actually appeared a solid body is more akin to a river (or interactive fields of energy).

As for the mind? In classical science, until recently, the mind was assumed to be in the 'closed jar' that is our skull and solely identified with the brain. Today we know, brain cells are only one kind of cells with the task of digesting (converting) and storing experience (as knowledge/memory). In fact, each cell has an intelligent centre in its nucleus, which reproduces itself and receives and gives messages. Thus the whole body has intelligence. Mind is not an object, not limited to the brain, but an intelligent field... or as other traditions have it - a 'subtle body' of 'knowing energy' that reaches even beyond our physical body, providing interaction between various 'fields,' throughout mind, body and soul. Anything that happens in one leaves tracks in the other; their vibrations are different aspects of one conscious, unified field. They act as and are One.

People of all times and cultures have said that one can 'see ' the radiance of this field as an 'aura.' A simple way of understanding is this: Look at a candle flame; there is in its centre a wick, a physical thing – vibrating in a way that we call burning. We know that 'burning' is energy at work. The process of burning produces various layers of light, we see in the centre a blue flame and around that many different layers of less intense heat and light (or 'ever subtler' layers of energy). In the same manner, the human body is a physical entity that constantly 'burns,' transforms energy. In *Yogic* language, it is burning by the power of its 'digestive fire' (Agni) which is fuelled by the breath, turning food into energy. This burning - this transforming - we call life! The energy, the radiance resulting from this process, is perceptible as the glow of the human Aura.

'The human energy field is the manifestation of universal energy that is ultimately involved with human life. It can be described as a luminous body that surrounds and interpenetrates the physical body... Based on their observations, researchers have created theoretical models that divide the aura into several layers. These layers are called bodies, (sheath or fields); they interpenetrate and surround each other in successive layers. Each succeeding body is composed of finer substances and higher 'vibrations' than the body that it surrounds and interpenetrates.' [98] The layers defined by locations, colour, brightness, form, fluidity and function, are grouped into different systems. Suffice it to say, traditions talk of five, (seven, or even twelve) such layers. To give you a taste, just dim the light in your room, and put your outstretched fingers in front of a white wall, soft focus your eyes, and most likely you can see some kind of luminous outside rim of your hand. If there is a 'New Age' or 'Health Fair' near you, you could probably get an electromagnetic photograph taken of it. The different layers vibrate at different frequencies and interacting via 'energy transformers' called *chakra*. The first four chakra, (East and West seem to agree), relate mainly to the physical, more animalistic functions. The physical/etheric body (associated with the Element Earth), the emotional (associated with Water), the mental (associated with Fire) and the astral (associated with Air). The latter three are much subtler and are all considered to be in the realm of Space, the etheric template, the celestial and the ketheric or casual body. They are of a spiritual nature and of such high frequency that, Barbara Brennan postulates, when we bring our consciousness to the seventh level of the aura, we know that we are one with the Creator.

If indeed we consist of fields of high and low frequency energy in constant flux, when something blocks this flux it would cause dis-ease or behavioural problems. Conversely people with higher frequency vibrations might be specially gifted people. Furthermore could there be people with altogether higher frequencies? People who have 'purified' their lower energy fields and raised their energies to such an extraordinary level that they do not have the same lower energy bodies, but are pure (subtle) spiritual energy? Then they would have no body! That could explain the trans-cultural phenomena of angels and celestial beings. One step below that, would be people who have a body of almost pure energy, pure consciousness? In old times these beings were recognised as 'living Gods' or Saints, which appear to be like us and yet qualitatively different from us by the high purity of their energy. Meditating on the higher energy frequency within, the Kashmir Shaivist Saint Lalleshvari said, while gazing up at the glaciers crowning the mountains of Kashmir, "Water freezes into ice and ice, grazed by the suns rays, melts into water. Just so, all pervading consciousness congeals into the ephemeral material universe. But when matter is grazed by the compassionate glance of God, it releases itself once more into all pervasive being." [99]

If the energy frequencies are vastly different, like in that of a 'divine' person, the energy field of any person in their presence will be drastically elevated. This is why ordinary people flock to sit in the energy field of such 'perfected Beings.'

How far does our energy field extend? When do you make contact? When do you start to interfere in somebody else's space? How about our intimate relationships, where does our space start in the matrimonial bed, where does intimacy start, where invasion? How about people who are forever tired, are they spending endless energy, constantly converting their or other people's low frequencies into higher ones? Are they working hard although doing 'nothing,' just because they are surrounded by people with the 'wrong' frequencies? Instead of taking pills, people who feel unwell, tired and without energy, ought to look at their way of living, maybe even the place they are living and the earth's vibrations in that place. How much our everyday life needs to change if we take notice of these concepts is anybody's guess. Is the purpose of human existence eventually to convert lower energy fields to higher energy to return to the light we came from? This process is called doing *Sadhana*, spiritual practices. Allama Prabhu compared *Sadhana* to looking after a garden:

> My mind is the spade
> With it I dug up the illusions like weeds
> I broke the clods of worldliness
> I raked the earth and sowed the seed of the spirit
> My well is the thousand-fold lotus
> My waterwheel is my breath, the nadis channel the water
> I set up a fence of patience and poise
> To stop, the oxen of my senses to trample my crops...

3.2: Chakras and Nadis

The different levels of energy communicate by transformers, which as above mentioned, are called chakra. These have been observed by people who spent long periods of times meditating, some call them 'inner scientists.' These rishis experienced these Chakras, but like any subjective experience, to communicate, their experiences have to be clad in words. What words are used to describe these phenomena, varies slightly according to tradition and cultures. Furthermore as mentioned earlier, the body and its energies are in constant flux. Thus for example, in the Tibetan Healing practices it is acknowledged that *chakra* have one colour when there is a healthy activity – another when it is being healed.

Acknowledging the differences, there is however, common ground. Most traditions agree that layers of energy interact amongst themselves and with the universal, divine energy through these chakra and energy is then distributed through a warren of channels, called *nadis*/meridians.

The majority of oriental cultures hold either with five or seven main *chakra*.

However it is said that there are 360 to 600 *chakra*. They are lined up with the central channel called *sushumna* (*nadi*). The Shiva Samhita mentions 350 thousand of these *nadis* (with 14 main ones). The 'channels,' like blood-vessels, cross each other in the body; where they cross they look like 'spokes of a wheel' or numerous lotus leaves – which gives the phenomena its Sanskrit name: *chakra* - (wheel). There are those that are major, those that are still important as they supply energy to joints (minor ones), and those that are really of little importance.

Each *chakra* is associated with a nerve plexus and a major endocrine gland, a psychic perceptual function and many other associations; according to the energy they metabolise (frequency), they <u>are associated with one of the Five Elements</u>. In this way the base *chakra* is related to Earth, the second *chakra* to Water, the third to Fire, the fourth to Air, the Fifth with Space and the upper two with pure divine energy. Dis-functioning at the level of the *chakras* and *nadis* is associated with pathological changes in the nervous system, endocrine glands and abnormal changes in the cells of the entire body. This will be considered in more detail in the context of the Elements.

Each *chakra* metabolises different frequencies of energy. Energy of the highest frequencies (heavenly) enters in the Crown *Chakra* and descends (on the way being transformed to usable energy); the denser frequencies of earth electromagnetic energy are absorbed by the root-chakra (the lowest) and refined and transformed upwards. This two way traffic happens 'in' the spinal cord (*sushumna*) and is, i.e. in the Tibetan System, described as white Boddhichitta (male) descending and Red Boddhichita (female) ascending. Similarly in the Indian concept Shiva's energy (white) filters down, Shakti's energy (red) ascends (as *Kundalini*). The two energies merge (marry) in the Crown *Chakra*. In addition each *chakra* also can metabolise energy horizontally.

Similarly the *nadis* (symbolic of the fine roots of the lotus) distribute the life-force into the physical body, by affecting foremost the nature and quality of nerve transmission within the extensive network of the brain, spinal cord and peripheral nerves. There are three special *nadis: ida, pingala* and *sushumna*. They are envisaged as 'incomparably subtle hollow tubes' that criss-cross each other in the centre of the spine, like the caduceus symbol of medicine.

Which brings us to the point where something has to be said about the *Kundalini.*

If **the One unfolds as the many**, then there is basically one creative vital energy, which unfolds in all of Creation. This vital energy unfolds as us, in us. There is however a storehouse, of this energy in its pure state, and this is called in India *Shakti,* or in some contexts *Kundalini*; it lies dormant at the base of the spine. The spine with the cerebral-spinal fluid, is the first physical manifestation of our existence; from here the human being unfolds in its physical state, but also in its highest spiritual states. To awaken to the latter is the purpose of this potent, slumbering energy reserve. When it awakens, it ascends through the *sushumna,* (central channel, in the spinal column), eventually right up to the *Sahasrara,* the Crown *Chakra.* The image of a slumbering energy that unfurls and rises up straight, has been likened to the movement of an awakening snake. The experience of this rising energy is universal, and many cultures share the symbol, from the Hopi Indians in North America to the Kung people of the Kalahari Desert in Africa. We find it in carvings of spirals and snakes on Celtic stones, in Ireland and Scandinavia, and as a symbolic snake in Egypt, and the serpent deities of the Aztecs and Australian Aboriginals.

It is said that the energy 'pierces' different levels, different Chakra. Yet the Sanskrit word used in this context, is *bheda,* meaning learning the lesson! Potentially all beings are capable of waking this source of spiritual energy and learning the lessons that each step of man's evolution has to teach. When we learn, change happens. In this case it is sometimes accompanied by physical cleansing - yet always leads to notable transformation in consciousness. (Again we will hear more about this in connection with each Element).

Ayurvedic and Tibetan medicine have used the above knowledge to heal by balancing energies through work with the *chakra* and nadis, for thousands of years. Imagine someone has thyroid problems, the thyroid itself can be taken out, and that is just what conventional medicine might do. (The patient then substitutes hormones originally produced there, by pills). It certainly seems to fix the problem! But does this change the energy pattern that caused the illness? The thyroid is linked to the fifth *chakra* and the fifth auric field, thus to the energy of Space. Both feed energy to certain organs and mental functions associated with Space. If the 'feeding process' is blocked, the energy can not properly fulfil its job. Here this is associated with the vocal apparatus (on the physical level) and a sense of self-worth, one's place in society and a sense of belonging (on the psychological level). So even if the malfunctioning thyroid is taken out, disturbance in the energy flow is not 'fixed.' The person has to ask, what am I not expressing? Why can't I vocalise my wishes? Where do I want to belong? Am I willing to accept the answer? If the person then changes these aspects, clears the blocked energy flow, the thyroid problem will change – and might never need an operation. Disturbances in the flux of energy cause problems; if not changed they will manifest illness whether operated on or not. In the above case, it could mean if the thyroid glands are taken out, where will the next illness manifest, in the ears, mouth, teeth?

3.3: Meridians

Much of what has been said about nadis applies to the meridian system, which has come to us via Traditional Chinese Medicine. It is based on observing different energies flowing through our body - you might like to try it yourself.

Lie on the floor, flat on your back. Allow your attention to come gently to your feet. Tell yourself to let go of any tension in your feet; then take your awareness to your ankles and consciously let go of any tightness you feel there. Take your mind to your calves; be aware of any tension there and let it go... and so on. Work up through your whole body (you might be familiar with this). Once you have relaxed your body, relax the tension in your head; let it go! With it, let go of your mind. You are completely relaxed, yet fully alert; be the witness of what is going on in your body.

When I lay there in the stillness of my body, I became aware of a flowing sensation in me, a floating, and then a feeling as though honey or molten gold flew through me. First I became aware of it along the spine and then in the sacrum, a warm flowing, glowing feeling. Then the inside of my arms seemed to have light streaming through them! The back of my legs started to 'sparkle.' The back of my head felt like a 'Spaghetti Junction,' then suddenly there was physical activity there, even though I lay perfectly still. The 'Spaghetti Junction' smoothed out as though someone said 'Ah-h-h-h' and something flowed over the crown of my head. It was/is as though an unknown universe moves inside me, it flows, streams, glides! While in that total relaxed state of awareness, I witness energy flowing **like water, in a sort of line from the back of my legs to the crown of my head.** These lines of energy flow are called meridians.

Since time immemorial some people have been able to see or feel these energy lines in themselves and others, we can also become aware of disturbances in these, and several healing arts have evolved to redress these. Acupuncture being the oldest one, it is mentioned in the Vedas, and the Buddhist University (Takshshila) also taught such techniques from earliest times. The science of Acupuncture was probably spread by travelling monks and flourished most in China.

Consequently the Chinese have for thousands of years studied these energy flows and amassed an enormous amount of knowledge about these 'rivers of energy' through which *Chi*, the divine energy flows. They use fourteen such channels but twelve are considered together. The traditional acupuncture system envisages them as absorbing energy into the human body via portals of energy on the skin (minor chakra/ Tsubos/ Points). Others see them as more a flexible,   loosely processing energy. (All pay attention on the points of entry and exit).

Loosely one can say that one group of meridians enters at the fingertips, journeying through the body and gathering the heavenly energy of *Yang*. Other such lines start at the toes journeying upwards, gathering the energy of the earth, the *Yin* energy. Some like S. Masunaga propose that the energy can be contacted anywhere along the line, others pay more attention to accessing it at fixed points. (Iyzak Bentov and Dr. Valerie Hunt, scientists that have measured the epidermis on points along the meridians, find that their electrical resistance is lower than that of the surrounding skin by a factor of ten to one). They also found the electrical quality being influenced by different states of consciousness, i.e. waking, sleeping and meditation or a state of 'dis-ease.' Dr. Hiroshi Motoyama has not only measured the electrical characteristics of various meridians but has, with a device called AMI (machine diagnosed imbalances), taken some sort of photos akin to Kirlian's electrography. Kirlian photography is a technique whereby living objects in the presence of high frequency, high voltage, low current electrical fields are photographed (re: Aura). The danger of a 'fixed' approach lies in compartmentalisation, thus completely missing the point that the energy is flowing in different levels (bodies) or energy fields and constantly interacting in nth-dimensions. This has been revived by W. Ohashi and S. Masunaga, who also insist that meridians are channelling energy in interaction with energy fields that can not be separated from the context of the Elements. [100]

Although Meridians channel subtle energy, energy of higher frequencies than what we normally term physical and visible, we can feel their vibration. The energy channel can be experienced as 'full or empty,' as present or lacking; as contracted or flowing or as *kyo* or *jitsu* (Japanese). As each Meridian channels the energy of a certain vibration, linked to the vibration of one of the Five Elements, their balancing balances the elemental energies! Living is a process of interfering in the flux of energies, we can uses the 'interference' for a positive result; this is indeed what complementary medicines does (Acupuncture, Shiatsu and Touch for Health, healing through intention or laying on of hands etc).

Let us look a bit closer at the meridians: The first pair appears literally straight after conception, and is called the Conception Vessel (CV) and the Governing Vessel (GV). On the grown body, they run central to the front and back respectively. They form the core of our energy system and act as regulators to the overall body (much like we have heard about the ida and pingala, the two central nadis, that weave around the central channel). They affect energy at a deep, constitutional level.

The other 12 channels are, in Indian and Chinese tradition, grouped together in a brother or sister relationship, based on the Taoist Chinese principle of *Yin* and *Yang*. Each pair is connected to a hollow or solid organ, thus I refer to it as the Organ-network.

Each Organ-network shares the energy of one of the Five Elements.

The *Yin* meridian and the *Yin* Organ are called 'core-organs' or respectively 'core-meridians' because they lie deeper in the body and deal with deeper more refined energy processes. The pure essences of these Organs are difficult to replace. The *Yang* organs together with the *Yang* Meridians protect and support the *Yin* Organs and meridians, therefore they lie closer to the surface, creating a conductive internal environment in which the latter can operate.

One more point: If we drew a stick man with his arms raised and legs spread wide, it would appear quite naturally that the body forms two triangles; the lower is formed by the distance between the parted legs, both legs and the lower abdomen. Above the waist is another inverted triangle, resting, seemingly on the tip of the first one (arms raised above the head form the sides of the second triangle; the base is the distance between the hands). The area where both triangles meet, according to such diverse people as Michelangelo and C.G. Jung, is the point of balance, 'the centre of man.' This centre is what is in the Indian tradition is called 'the heart of Shiva,' or what the Japanese call the *hara*. Here in the *Hara* converge all Organ-networks and their meridians; thus each of the Five Elements has its core here. A strong, healthy representation of these energies here, make for strength, energy and focus. The significance of this area is recognised in many cultures. Do you remember seeing pictures of Chinese, Japanese or even medieval Christian sculptures and paintings with gods, monks and saints which have huge exaggerated bellies? They are symbols for 'a strong centre-of-man' where all energies are represented as full and healthy.

From the centre, from the belly, the meridians rise to activity and stretch out, filling the body with energy, and then flow out even further beyond the physical body, reaching into the energy field around us characterised by five elements. In turn, energy fields of the environment reach inside us, affecting the nature of the meridians. In this way, these five elements give their qualities to the meridians. It is a living, breathing interchange from outside the body at large, to inside, down to the smallest component, and back again. To gain understanding of the meridians as they go about their work of being and becoming, we have to focus on the 'Five Elements.' Before we focus on the Elements themselves, let us be aware of the limitations of our understanding - however much we 'push' at the boundaries of knowledge.

"Cottleston, Cottleston, Cottleston Pie,

A fly can't bird, but a bird can fly."
Ask me a riddle and I reply
"Cottleston, Cottleston, Cottleston Pie.
Cottleston, Cottleston, Cottelston Pie,
A fish can't whistle and neither can I."
Ask me a riddle and I reply,
"Cottleston, Cottleston, Cottleston Pie.
Cottleston, Cottleston, Cottleston Pie,
Why does a chicken, I don't know why?"
Ask me a riddle and I reply,
"Cottleston, Cottleston, Cottleston Pie."

... A fly can't bird, but a bird can fly, very simple, it's obvious isn't it? And yet, you'd be surprised how many people violate this simple principle every day of their lives, and ignore the clear reality that things are as they are...

"Tell them about Cottleston Pie - what it means," whispered Pooh...

"Pooh wants to know that the words 'Cottleston Pie' are a way of saying 'Inner Nature'..."

Ask me a riddle and I reply,
"Inner Nature."
"Hmm."
"Cottleston Pie sounds better," said Pooh.
"Well how about this, Pooh?"
Ask me a riddle and I reply...
"Things are as they are."
"Better... but it still doesn't rhyme"
"All right, how is this?"
Ask me a riddle and I reply...
"Cottleston, Cottleston, Cottleston Pie."
"Just right," said Pooh. [101]

PART II
THE FIVE ELEMENTS

SWAMI RAMA (founder of the Himalayan Institute of Yoga) said:
"Everything in this manifest universe is connected to everything else, and
experiencing the fullness of our own beauty and bliss depends on having a
direct experience of this connection. This law applies at every level of our
existence. Nature is the manifest form of the Divine Mother, the
transcendental ocean of beauty and bliss. To enjoy her protection, love and
care, we must live in her lap... Exploiting nature is like abusing our own
mother. Out of ignorance we fail to see that we are constantly receiving
nurturance from the sun, moon, stars - air, fire and water. We are made of
these forces; they are integral to us... gravity... holds us fast to the bosom of
the Earth. Punching holes in the ozone layer is like drilling holes in our skull.
(Only)... once we are in harmony with nature we begin to experience divine
love... as this happens, the curtain of duality is lifted and we no longer
experience ourselves as entities separate from her."

This divine creative energy is in and around us; it changes from in-breath
to out-breath, from one physical state to the next, from day to night and
night to day, season to season, from health to illness. It changes from
fortune to misfortune, from love to hate, from anger to joy, from aggression
to peace, from growth to decay, from manifestation to dissolution and so on,
ad infinitum. One way to describe the flow of energy is *the Five Elements*, or
five fundamental powers. But despite classifying life into these five forces
one has to be aware that in each phase, each element is also made up of the
same Five again. For example: there is the 'earth of Fire,' which is the Flame;
there is the 'Water of Fire' which is the fluidity, its movement and 'rippling'
effect. There is the 'Fire in Fire,' which is its heat; there is the 'Air in Fire,'
which is the movement itself; and there is the 'Space of Fire' in which Fire
happens, which spreads its radiance and light. Like a hologram, each part
contains the whole picture. In the same way, whether we look at the rotation
of the planets, or the growth of your fingernail, the explosion of a volcano or
the working of an ant colony, the digestive process of our stomachs, the
growth of a tree, or the emotional make up of my daughter, all reflect each
and every part of the whole of nature. They serve as a map 'that charts the
course of process, a guide for comprehending our unfolding.' [2]

For instance, as the year goes through the seasons of spring, summer,
late summer, autumn and winter, so the human being goes through cycles in
their life. Each phase has the character of an Element. We begin with birth,
followed by adolescence; in these years we take form (are in a phase of the
Earth Element). As we proceed, we spend years of establishing a family/job
(Water). Then there come years where we are collecting the fruits of our

labours, where we enjoy and celebrate them (Fire), followed by a phase that is movement in transition - the phase of retirement (Air); finally we enter the last phase of the cycle - dissolving back into Space. To understand the elements helps us to understand the nature of all things, including ourselves, be it in health or illness.

Here we look at the cycle from the manifest to the subtle; we can equally look at it from the opposite way, as a cycle of Creation. Space (which supports all) represents the phase of expansion, the outward movement, which then culminates in the phase of Fire, which spreads the energy on the surface. At its furthest point we encounter Air (Metal), the phase of contraction, an inward breath feeding the core. It culminates in the co-operation of Water and Earth. The former through its inherent quality of nurturing and strength, becomes the site of germination, the latter being the one in the centre that stabilises, the ground on which balance and activity takes place. Earth is the axis, or churning stick in the Indian creation myth. It is the centre of manifestation, of abundance.

All these states/phases are represented in the body, mind and soul; discord manifests itself in the physical form in organs as illness, in the mind as fixations, blocks, character traits, and in the soul as distress and anguish (*karma*) - or bliss (*ananda*).

Before we look at the elements individually, a word of caution. We must honour the holographic concept; each aspect contains all creating constant movement. We must not consider an element as a box in which to put a person or event; i.e. a person can be, for example, an apprentice learning a new trade – expansion in the Space-phase of his life. His most apparent character trait might be his humour; all his life he managed to look at things with a pinch of laughter, thus he probably has a dominant Fire Element. Yet as he is at present going through a patch of fear and anxiety with the approach of his final exam, he is filled with fear: will he pass or not? Thus temporarily his Water Element is strong and overriding the others. He has a strong bond to his hometown and likes to be with his large family; e.g. he has a well-developed Earth Element. Unfortunately at present he suffers from constipation. His Metal Element has become blocked by sitting for so many hours of studying, being hunched over his books, not moving, not breathing properly and overriding all elimination processes (effectively blocking them) with acquisition of knowledge.

Chapter Four: Invocation of the Earth

I am Woman
    I and the Goddess are one
    I am the mother of all that exists
    I walk in tune with the universe.

My head- is Saraswati, delivering all from ignorance.

My mouth - is the mouth of Kali, drinking the blood of those who dishonour me.

My eyes - are the jewels you find in the diamond mines of South Africa.

My nose - is disgusted by stench of human sacrifice, be it on slabs of an altar, the computer of a tycoon or the sweat shops of the Third World.

My cheeks - are those of a young girl meeting her first lover amongst cherry blossoms in Nara.

My ears - tire of hearing your cries of "more, more," are you deaf to 'enough;' has your drum lost the memory of the rhythm of gratitude?

My hair - is the cornfields, swaying in vast grain-belts of America and Russia

My throat - gets irritated by the acid rain, do you want me to treat you with the same disdain?

My chest - heaving with sympathy and compassion brings forth healing plants

My lungs - are the forests of the world, be aware how you treat them, unless you want to suffocate.

My heart - is a molten core immensely powerful, linked to Grandfather Sun, who gives light, life or death. Yours is the choice.

My veins - are the rivers, through them pulses the water of life.

My liver - and kidneys are the beds of sandstone and lime that filter the water, So I can sustain you with clear, clean blood.

My stomach - is wherever death occurs, for I digest and transform manure into the sweetest smelling rose and the most succulent peach.

My guts - are the sewers of every civilisation, from Mohenjo Daro to the favelas of Rio de Janeiro.

My faeces - are the opals, golden nuggets and other treasures, you grovel for in the dirt.

My spine - is the Himalayas, my bones, the mountains of continents and oceans; they support me and in turn are your strength.

My breasts- are the breasts of every female, nurturing without judgement, providing for the weakest cub, the most crooked tree, generously I provide – yet you have lost the ability to share, how dare you treat each other with such shameless disdain?

My pelvis - is the valley of the Tansa River, where lingam meets yoni, where Shiva meets Shakti, where earth meets sky.

My womb- is vaster than the surface of this planet, every inch brings forth life, is sacred space to be honoured in my name. Even what seems dead to you, swamps and deserts support microbic life.

My vulva - is the rift valley in central Africa, from where man originated, on the banks of Lake Turkana.

My skin - did you not realise that my skin covers all of this planet? Then why do you stab out a burning cigarette on your mother's skin, or cover more and more of it with tarmac, is nothing sacred to you?

My arms - reach out to each starving child, to offer rest in my heart.

My hands - shower grace and blessings on everyone, they caress each creature with equal love and tenderness; even those that are too blind to see.

My thighs - are the thighs of each grandmother that rocks a child on her lap, secure and immovable like a mountain.

My calves - are the vital support and strength of Durga, upholding dharma

My feet - are tapping out the rhythm of life, the animation of all creatures, decorated with bells creating the original sound.

The soles - of my feet are decorated with the cave paintings of the first people, whose symbols are dear to me, they knew the earth was sacred!

My toes - are islands in the sea, decorated with jewels, shells and flowers.

My joy - is in the first smile of a baby.

My wrath - is in the rumble of an earthquake.

My smile - is like the dawn.

My tears - are like the ocean.

My pain - is your pain.

My memory - is long, many thousands of years. Be aware of the hurt you inflict on me, what waste you bury in me, what suffering you cause in my name, for in...

My revenge - I am Woman
    I and the Goddess are one
    I am the mother of all that exists
    I walk in tune with the universe.

4.1: Contemplation of 'Earth'

Every civilisation generated their own myths and stories about this stable, seemingly immovable ground, that with the 'kiss of rain' turns into a fertile field, abundantly supporting life. Several years ago I spent some time with the Igorots of the Philippines, a mountain tribe that still lived as though in the Stone Age (doubtless that has changed since then). Apparently everything they needed was provided by 'mother' earth and her daughters. The behaviour of the different daughters was responsible for changes in seasons, in day and night, human fortune or mishap, yet 'mother' was the stabilising, balancing centre.

The earth is the ground on which we stand; it locates us in space. Odd how we have no difficulty in accepting that plants and trees need to be firmly rooted in the ground or the wind will kill them; yet we forget that we too need to acknowledge our need for grounding. Of course we have a choice (in more ways than one) where and how. There is an abundance of places that could nourish our life. From the Himalayas to the Andes, from the African plains to the fjords of Norway, from the Siberian tundra to the tropical island, we can choose to grow in crevices, shallows or on mountain slopes. We can live on plains, flatlands and open spaces. And each venue has many different features and textures. In places earth has a loose surface of gravel and sand from where a weed is easily pulled up; in some others she has the most waterlogged swamps where only specially adapted life can exist. In some, she has heavy clay soil, rich in minerals that holds things firmly in their place and some have wonderful, rich fertile soil where much can grow.

Nearly everywhere we find people, tribes and nations that have their roots firmly planted in the fields, paddies or forest, and not only people but also all manner of plants and animals. Earth provides for all, there is no other source other than her. And once we have lived, earth takes us back! All - good and bad, beautiful and ugly, she does not judge; **Earth holds all**.

As I hold a bit of earth in my hand and muse over its magnificence, I suddenly realise that not I am holding the earth, but that the earth is actually holding me. The spot where my feet touch the ground is holding me - just I hold earth in the palm of my hand. Gravity, the core of earth, is holding both, so that we don't 'fly off' or dissolve. It holds me, as I hold it. I could not hold it without being held by it. It gives total stability, unshakeable security to me and all else. She holds the trees, the houses, the water, the cars, the factories, the good people, the bad people, the crops and the weeds, the tiger and the mosquito. She holds all creatures whether we deem them useful or not, whether we deem them dangerous and harmful or not. She just holds!

What she holds goes through a cycle of change; seeds become plants, become trees, become rotten wood, become compost; becoming flowers, becoming seeds, to becoming plants; a baby lives, becomes an adult, grows old, dies - but at no time does the earth let go! There is no escaping; her job of holding is never done. She is the playing field where the other elements, Water, Fire and Air sport; whatever they do, they are still held by her gravity. Throughout she remains stable, true to her task, holding without **judging anything unworthy**.

Not so long ago I sat in a Cornish Fogou to meditate. A Fogou is a prehistoric earth tunnel with one or two chambers, built into and fortified by granite boulders. It was reputedly used for ceremonies, healing or simply as a shelter in times of tribal fighting. To sit in the bowels of the earth reveals her potentiality. Apparently there is nothing but stillness, yet one feels the potency, a fullness that can only be experienced, not described. As womb she is also grave; beginning and end, life and death, death and rebirth – **life is contained in her**.

Hold a handful of Earth, smell it, see it, pinch it between your fingers; what is it that you actually hold? A melange of many things! Contemplating this handful of 'something,' on a physical level we could answer: it is fibres, water, grains of sand, minerals, even crystals; a conglomerate also found on other planets!

Then there is the chemical answer that talks about feldspars, lime, H_2O, alkaline and acid balance, but also about pollutants, poisons, pesticides and radioactive waste.

Then there is a biological answer; it talks about millions of microbes, living organisms, cells, plasma, plant fibre and more; compost really – embodying decay and fertility, the Circle of Life.

Is it possible to hold pure earth? Even desert sand might have microbes and seeds in it. It became abundantly clear to me when one day travelling through the centre of Australia, I witnessed a 'miracle.' It rained, and within a few hours the 'barren' desert-earth changed into fields of flowers as far as the eye could reach. What is it then that we mean when we talk of earth?

It is a mixture, a synergetic mixture, where the whole has become stronger than all its parts. This mixture takes on a new character.

My handful of earth used to be a granite boulder eroded during thousands of years, yet as much as it contains ancient particles, it contains last year's leaves and living organisms born today. 'Now!' Earth is **timeless matter,** it speaks of the past constituents and shapes which it transforms into a present melange, which will be the womb of tomorrow's daffodils. Earth speaks of a stability that adapts - is not static; for earth a thousand years are no different then yesterday or tomorrow; despite the change it **maintains its integrity!**

Looking again at the handful of earth, I am reminded of my grandmother; on her sideboard she had a white china pot filled with earth. We used to lift the lid as children and look at its dark, almost black, crumbly consistency, and wondered how one could have 'dirt' as an ornament. But of course for her it was not an ornament, neither was it dirt, but a reminder of her homeland. She was a refuge from Silisia, and this handful of earth was her link to her past, and moreover it was her emotional support now. It was a link to her mother, and her mother's mother.

As we saw in the onset, many cultures consider 'earth' as mother. In Sanskrit (root of many of our familiar languages), the word for mother, for earth and for clay is the same: MATA. In Egypt, the syllable MA not only stood for mother but also meant to see, and the hieroglyph was that of an eye, its meaning was truth. **Earth, mother and truth** - powerful shared roots. The 'womb of all life' makes a strong image, and it is not surprising that most cultures around the globe (at one time or other), revered the Earth as a goddess. The Earth is Gaia and as the archetypal goddess she is a living organism, symbolising truth and sacredness.

One night in a certain place in India, I went to bed, just as usual. As soon as I relaxed, my feet felt like they were on fire. The burning sensation turned to intense heat *inside* the soles of my feet; then I saw actual flames around my feet. It was so real, I was perplexed and disorientated, yet the fire crept up my legs, encircling my calves and stayed there with painful, consuming heat. Gradually the fire moved up to my hips and into my pelvis; there it stayed, for what seemed a long time - then moved up to my chest. My feet were engulfed in flames; the rest of me seemed burnt by that heat. I saw the flames, yet was not scared, more mesmerised as my thoughts repeated:

'I walked on sacred Earth; all day I walked barefoot on sacred Earth; walked on sacred Earth; stood on sacred ground.'

This awareness of earth as sacred was lost in our Western civilisation due to the influence of later Greek philosophy. It focused on 'soul-less-matter,' which had a devastating effect – as such matter could be dissected, exploited, misused and destroyed at will, which is exactly where the focus on the material world took us, and there was no 'reason' to do otherwise.

Only with the new physics, the awareness returned that matter is intelligent light and it reacts; it communicates with the observer (and so earth becomes Earth again). Earth is not as our senses perceive - dense dead matter - but moving, conscious energy, even light. The Celts were aware of this, and thus saw the world as both worldly and 'otherworldly;' the latter we experience as a divine (beyond human), feeling it belongs to what is ' beyond' us.

Travelling through the Rift Valley in Africa, this quality frequently drew me to walk barefoot on the earth, sit, lie on it, meditate and gaze at it. I got absorbed in her – lost to powerful feelings of a timelessness sense of mother qualities, of the origin of creation; I felt I was in the centre of sacredness itself.

Earth wisdom is knowing that we exist only within her. She holds us, she provides - yet once we die, we give ourselves back to her.

Earth itself teaches us to look deep into the centre of things, deep into the essence of ourselves. 3 It teaches us to look beyond the appearance and discover our original nature as sacred beings. What looks like a handful of dust, or dirt, smells of compost (a musty, wet rotting material), tastes slightly sour and feels a mixture of rough particles and smooth slimy clay - is actually a form of divine consciousness, a form of light, a form of God.

Holding my handful of Earth – it fills me with awe!

Matter shares consciousness; consciousness is awareness: as such earth is a living, intelligent organism that knows. There is only One; there is only conscious energy, at the same time source and manifestation. Sacred is profane and profane is sacred.

The Australia Aboriginals of the Northwest, especially in the Kimberleys, have a beautiful way to express this in the story of Nangina. He is the first man. Originally sleeping in the ground, he wakes up and discovers nature and all that is around him. He feels the power of the spirit in himself and he recognises it as the source of all life. Although it is overpowering and he sees its frightening omnipotence, he bends it to his own will, using the energy of fire to transform his food, himself and his environment. Laying fire around his abode, he keeps his mountain of origin sacred, Ngalenga. In the act of naming things, he identifies himself with all things and their destiny, grass, birds and animals that have emerged from the earth. His own inner spirit gives them life by giving them names. As a 'spirit-being' he is a Wandjina; as an 'earth-being' he is Nangina, who takes a wife, gives her home and shelter, gives order and law and dreams a spirit-child into his wife's womb. Other tribesmen infringe on him and he imparts his wisdom to them, assuring continuity. Then he allows himself to be killed, to become a dream-painting on the walls of his place of origin; in this way his spirit merges back into the earth and becomes Wandjina, the sacred dream-time painting drawn with earth, on earth (rock). Nangina Wandjina the first man shows us: he is the earth forever. The Wandjinas, the rock-paintings, are the centre of the earth wisdom to remind all generations of the need to embrace the idea of unity of earth and spirit. There is only One, yet Wandjina the original source is Nangina in it's earthly form and Wandjina as 'timeless earth-spirit' - all three aspects are One. [4]

Contrary to most traditions in the Australian lore, earth is male; he is strong and in charge – and holding, looking after and protecting all of his creation. Interestingly that care goes beyond death, hence the ritual painting on the wall. Earth is a teacher who knows his pupils well; he knows their needs and fears, hence he teaches immortality! He teaches 'for all to see,' without judgement, giving unconditional attention. Earth instructs us to accept this world as it is! Be content.

Can we learn to be without judgement? It is hard, for we fall prey to this misbehaviour all the time. We judge people for wearing different clothes, having different hair or lifestyles or even for eating different food. We judge people because they laugh differently... talk differently... smile differently... play different games in the playground... buy different brands of consumer goods etc. Our judgement means we do not respect that person; at worst we deny them their job, their fun and even their lives, and persecute them: 'I do not like you because you have a bigger house, because you have more spiritual experiences, more wisdom, health... etc.

We are in desperate need of re-educating our minds!

Not just for other people's sake, but for our own; we pass the most terrible judgements against ourselves: I am not good enough... capable enough... clever enough... slim enough; I am too big... too small... too timid... too loud... too ugly... too... These self-judgements are constantly reinforced by families, schools and society. Which parent has not fallen into the trap of calling their child too slow, too thin, stupid, fat etc.? Or less obvious: we call our children... very clever... very beautiful... very talented etc. These judgements, positive or negative are harmful, and yet they are ingrained in our society; we take them as 'natural.'

The only way out is... to stay in our Centre. To be like the Earth, firm in our acceptance of life as it is – **without judgement yet with compassion!** The scriptures advocate a way out: awareness and discrimination.

We need to open our ears, listen, understand and decide: that is not worth listening to! I have heard it before – but need not judge.

We need to open our eyes, see, understand and decide: that is not worth seeing; and stop reading or looking, no need to judge.

Usually, we are closed off, stuck in routines, and thus repeat the same old patterns of behaviour, of mistakes, of pains and disease. It is our lack of awareness and our profusion of judgements, which keeps us in quicksand, rather than fertile Earth.

Our judgements take ridiculous forms; we judge it as more profitable to live in an urban environment than feel isolated from nature, separate from life and lonely.

We judge that eating a Hamburger is more important than the rain forest! (Cutting down forests to create grazing land for cattle).

We judge that mining uranium for atomic power is more important than the sacred sites of the Australian Aboriginals; and commit genocide to an ancient culture.

By implication, I judge that burning petrol to drive my car is more important than the acid rains caused by exhaust fumes that destroy the forests. We judge that the street children of Brazil have less right to live than us, or we would not allow their poverty to drive them into the sewers. The list is endless. Our attitudes, built on *hidden judgements*, penetrate every niche and corner of our existence. Let us wake up, and **learn from the Earth to hold creation safe, and be responsible without judgement, to hold and respect each other so we all can flourish.**

Let us return from our musing thoughts to focus on the 'real earth.' Have a look out of your window, or imagine being in a park. Look closely at the earth. On it lies a stone, it just lies there... see the tree, follow its root - they just root there, held by earth... See the person walking, the feet touch the ground, they just touch, held for just the right time by the earth.

Earth holds the tree adequate to the tree's need, so that it will not get 'blown over.' Look at the house. It stands there; the earth provides it with a base. People walk, sit, run, even lie on the earth; it just holds them in whatever position <u>they choose.</u>

To appreciate earth, we would need to change our 'glasses.' Normally we look at a stone and think 'it is too grey,' it 'is useless,' etc. We look at the tree thinking, 'it needs pruning;' ' it is big; too big?' or we might even think: ' it is beautiful;' yet all this - positive or negative - is built on judgements.

We never see the earth reject something because it is ugly, or hold something too tight because it is beautiful; can you see how holder and held co-operate? We look at the house and say: "How cosily it nestles in the valley," or "how dangerous it is so close to the road." We look at the people and think: 'He is careless walking on the grass.' We look and our mind judges; we see the world around us through a veil of conditioned judgement; the sad thing is that we miss appreciating what we really see. If we really look, without our judgmental projections, we see earth's **self-less generosity.**

We too can give such self-less service to our children, our parents, our community, our employers, our friends and our enemies. In our Western societies, a list like this will immediately raise opposition. We consider service and especially a service that brings no rewards, as having no value; even worse, we feel worthless if we render such service! Yet look at the Earth, it needs nothing back, nothing can be added nor subtracted from it. It all belongs to it already; a beautiful Indian verse declares:

Om pûrnamadah pûrnamidam

Pûrnat pûrnamudacyate

Pûrnasya pûrnamãdãya

Pûrnamevã vasisyate.

(Ohm, That is fullness. This is fullness. From fullness, springs fullness. If fullness is taken from fullness, fullness remains.)

We are all of this Earth; all is perfect as it is; she holds all reward already within herself. There is plenty, so give from a full heart; leave no emptiness, no obligations. It does not mean giving until we are empty; it does not mean constantly doing things for others, forgetting our own needs. To give selflessly and generously does not mean we have to be taken advantage of.

Think of a mother and her young baby. During pregnancy, the mother's womb is 'available,' holding the baby in all its needs, in its totality; they are one body. Even for a while after the baby has been born, there is such mutual bond. Mother fulfils the needs of the baby without regard for her own profit or loss, she just cares for the baby. Only because the mother (the earth) holds the baby (all life forms) safe and secure, the baby can grow into its own. The mother provides this selfless service, without knowing whether her love will ever be returned by baby, child or adult. She holds and loves without expectation of reward!

Yet if the mother does not take care of herself with adequate rest, food, enjoyment and so on, she will not be able to provide for the baby. Self-less does mean 'without ego' – not 'without caring for oneself!'

In the Mahabharata, one of India's most revered texts, is a section that tells about the famous battle between two families, the Kauravas and the Pandavas. At the heart of this epic is the Bhagavad Gita, a profound dialogue between Arjuna, the warrior and his charioteer, Lord Krishna. In this conversation, Krishna explains the duty of a warrior is to fight 'with detachment from the fruit of his labours.' This is selfless- service; to do what is necessary, yet not worry about the outcome.

Such detachment from 'the fruits of our labours' is most foreign to us. We can not imagine to - 'just give,' 'just do' - without thinking of the result, because we want to achieve something, get somewhere. We want the fruits, and to eat them. And we forget that as soon as we have eaten them, hunger and desire raises again the desire to yet get another fruit to eat. The 'desire' to have, never seems to sleep.

How can self-less, generous action be performed? An Indian poet saint, Jnaneshwar Maharaj, explains: "Oh, Arjuna, a person who performs his proper duties in this way, reaches the gateway to liberation. He is not tempted to turn towards any action prompted by desire, just as he couldn't willingly place his legs in the stocks, even if they were made of sandalwood."5

We need to re-educate the mind, cultivate a different attitude: something in our mind-make-up has to shift.

To give quality time to our children, rather than dash off doing our thing, is not easy.

To do a job well (even cleaning the toilet) without expecting to be praised or paid, is not so easy.

To give a friend, partner, husband or wife love, acceptance and support, without waiting for them to return it is not so easy. We feel 'I love him/her so, why doesn't he do 'anything' for me.'

To give to the poor, sick and old of our time, care and love without thinking: I hope one day in heaven (or in my own old age) this good deed will be rewarded - is very difficult for us. We are brought up in a culture where the thought prevails: if we simply **give generously, without wanting something in return** 'we would never get anywhere!' To give freely is difficult, because we judge the giver, judge the gift, and judge the act. "Aunt Sue was 'unfair' to give me some socks for Christmas! She should have thought more 'what I want'; I don't like the socks." This is not the way of the Earth - she is **infinitely patient with us**.

This morning, driving my daughter to school, I waited at some road works and I was reminded of the patience of the earth. She does not rebel when we pour hot tarmac all over her; when we bore holes into her, spray her with pesticides and even bury toxic chemicals or radioactive waste in her. She holds it all, processing it with infinite patience, transforming it to the good of all, even if it needs thousands of years (as in the case of nuclear waste). Such patience is timeless.

I m p o s s i b l e, you say! No business can survive on that, we need to innovate, change, grow, act, push, press! There is no growth without push. Not even learning can be without the desire to acquire knowledge! If we are content and sit on our backside, nothing progresses - no science, health or educational program can be carried out if we are content with the status quo. W r o n g! **Contentment** doesn't mean doing nothing- it means doing the appropriate thing! How can we recognise right, appropriate action? By forgetting what we want the outcome to be, putting our wishes on a shelf, forgetting them and doing what is necessary.

There is, no doubt, a lot more to contemplate about the Earth; I leave you to proceed on you own journey of contemplating the richness of the earth's teachings. But before that let us summarise:

Earth holds the potential for physical evolution; it is rich and plentiful. It shares its riches generously; it nurtures and supports indiscriminately; it is non-judgemental, giving. It synthesises opposites (life and death); it stabilises, balances. Earth is the quiet centre around which activity revolves; it is tireless in serving others; it preserves (family, society), it is compassionate and sympathetic to all in need, it re-cycles; it is strong, it holds and protects.

4.2: Associations to the Earth Element

Every Element has many, often universally agreed, associations. They are influenced by the kind of energy expressing in that field. In this way the Element Earth is the field that vibrates at the lowest, most dense frequencies. It expresses on three interactive levels: body, mind and spirit. Starting with the body, let us explore those associations that directly affect the body and most commonly are used in all manner of...

4.2: a) Complementary Medicine

The physical organs associated with Earth, are the stomach and spleen. Looking at these through the eyes of traditional Western anatomy reveals their intrinsic truth.

1) <u>The Stomach</u> is a part of the alimentary tract, which is a long tube through which food passes; it commences with the mouth and ends with the anus. The stomach has the shape of a 'J' and is a widened part of the digestive track. It starts as a continuation of the oesophagus and it ends in the duodenum (part of the small intestines). The stomach has a valve at either end. It is lined with four layers of tissue and is protected by the fatty skin of the peritoneum. When we have eaten something, the food accumulates in the stomach and is mixed with gastric juices that are secreted by special glands, (mineral salts, water, hydrochloric acid, 'intrinsic factor' and enzymes). The muscles contract in a constant churning movement, liquidating food as well as killing microbes; furthermore Pepsin begins the digestion of proteins here and Intrinsic factor helps absorbing Vitamin B12. Mucus prevents the acid from destroying the stomach. After being broken down, food or 'chyme' is moved on.

The stomach has a slightly different task from what is commonly believed. It only digests food in a very limited sense. Its main functions are to act as a temporary reservoir for food; it allows the food to be prepared and only begins the chemical process of dissolving it into nutrients.

2) <u>The Spleen</u>, also lying in the abdominal cavity, below the diaphragm, is part of the lymphatic system, formed (in part) by lymphatic tissue. It is slightly oval shaped and is enclosed in an elastic capsule which consists of pulp containing lymphocytes and macrophages. Blood flows through the spleen. After their life span of approximately 120 days, red blood cells, formed in the bone marrow, get broken down here as well as in bone marrow and liver. The broken down products of the spleen are passed to the liver. Other cellular material and microbes are ingested and killed in the spleen (phagocytosis). The spleen also provides many lymphocytes (B- and T-lymphocytes) needed for immune reactions.

The spleen cleanses and protects blood, thus ensures its function and healthy distribution. The spleen's role is one of support, transformation and protection. The Nei Ching, the ancient Classic on Medicine by the Yellow Emperor, talks about the spleen as 'the solitary organ, (that) can irrigate the four others that are nearby,' (meaning the liver, heart, lungs and kidneys). The spleen is mainly a supporting agent for the major body organs; it prepares, is in 'communication with (the major organs, they) influence one another.'[6]

This interaction gives the spleen a central role; if it is well and healthy it helps others, if it is ill it will affect the related organs.

It is interesting to note that the diagnostic area location for the spleen occupies the central position of the *Hara* (belly), [7] marking the fact that stomach and spleen play an equally central role to Earth.

Food is not just gathered and redistributed in the stomach, but the workings of this 'food-silo,' as well as its contents, determine how well the food supports the entire system. Food can be held in the stomach from 20 minutes to eight or twelve hours (in extreme conditions). In the latter case it creates nausea and tension. This mode of 'holding on' is an energy that prevents moving on and absorption, be it of food, or emotions. It might reveal a person's tendency to hold on to something, preventing inevitable moves, not wanting to change, learn, grow up... etc.

From this description of the organs and their function, it is easy to abstract some characteristics that we find similar to what was described about Earth. Both receive, accumulate and hold. Both are preparing or holding potential until it is ready to move on. Both are constantly active bringing forth, passing on, nurturing, and giving. Both, but especially the spleen, are of service to others, and even 'kill unwanted' stuff, for protection. It is obvious why these organs and Element Earth are connected in the same energy field or Organ-network.

This Network includes two energy lines (*Meridians)*. Both organs and meridians are referred to as sisters; the Stomach meridian is considered as *Yang* and the Spleen meridian as carrying *Yin energy*. As we know, meridians and their Organ-network include physiological as well as psychological energies.

Location of the Stomach Meridian (ST): It starts (mid-socket) underneath the eyes, runs central each side of the face, along the front of the body; parallel to the mid-line of the body, to the outside edge of the front of the legs and ends in the second toe.

ST meridian, just as the organ in general, relates to the intake of food, and integrating it, to the production of body heat, and to reproduction. It takes the energy from the food for the spleen to distribute. It is related to the entire upper digestive tract, from the lips through the oral cavity, oesophagus, stomach, and duodenum to the jejunum. ST controls appetite, lactation and to some extent the ovaries and the menstrual cycle [8].

Location of The Spleen Meridian (SP) begins on the big toe and runs up – through the middle of the inside ankle, along the inside legs, the front of the body. At shoulder height, one branch runs down the inside of the arm to the inside of the index finger, another runs off across the clavicle into the head ending above the temple. **SP** 'relates to the breaking down of food... It relates also to reproductive glands (breasts and ovaries). Since the spleen distributes the energy obtained from food through the body, the other organs depend on it for life.' [9]

At this point it is interesting to add that for the 12th century medic and mystic Hildegard von Bingen, just as in the Chinese and Ayurvedic systems, illness was based on distortions of the elements. She described illness and cures in great detail; she too links the stomach, the flesh, sexual organs and fertility, the mouth and all forms of ingestion and other similar concepts to earth. [10] Furthermore, Buddhist traditions such as Tibetan medicine also agree on the link between earth, stomach and spleen. In the latter especially, emphasis is also placed on the psychological and mental aspects: lack of stability resulting in fear, jealousy, frigidity etc. on one hand and sacred actions and secret offerings on the other hand. [11]

Further Associations with the Organ-network for the Earth Element:

The Cycle: The Chinese point out that we have something like a 'body-clock' or body rhythm. Each Element and their meridians have a designated time of optimal and minimal work. Stomach and spleen are working at their best between seven and eleven a.m. It means that this is the optimal time for digestion and assimilation. On the other hand twelve hours later between seven and eleven p.m. is the time of slackest digestion.

If a person does not like to eat during the peak time, even feels nausea at the thought of eating 'so early in the morning' they might have an imbalance in Earth energy. If a person habitually does not eat breakfast, he/she constantly injures the Earth Element.

On the other hand a person with a strong balanced Earth Element might feel especially fit, willing to eat and do things in the early morning. They might also feel that a late evening meal is making them feel sluggish, heavy and even give them indigestion. Even though this is true to some extent for all of us, it is especially significant for a person dominated by the influences of Earth.

This realisation can have far reaching consequences. Some diets, like the 'Hay Diet' or 'Fit-for-Life-diet' advocate no breakfast, or to eat just fruit. According to the Element theory this does not make sense. Ayurveda suggests a cooked meal of cereals as best; it will quickly be absorbed and give energy for the day! Porridge?! Furthermore, in some countries, especially the Mediterranean countries, the main meal is in the evening when the family is re-united after a day's work. So far so good, but, according to the 'body-clock-theory' this is inappropriate. The old English custom of a hearty breakfast and a small meal at supper-time (five o'clock) seems to fit well, if not for <u>what</u> is eaten, surely for <u>when</u> it is eaten. It is interesting to recall that farmers (people close to the earth) seem to adhere to this internal body clock quite naturally.

Disregard for these eating times can result in lack of energy and stamina because the stomach is unable to digest and prepare the food adequately to free the energy for use. Although one might have eaten a good meal, or even a big meal - the food just lies in the stomach, heavy and unused. Unprocessed food does not only deteriorate and gives no energy, but it rots, making the body toxic.

TCM and Ayurveda also both respect these times for administering medicine, or hold that acupuncture points are at these times treated with greater success.

The Season linked to the Earth Element is late summer, the three months of 'summer proper.' It is the time in the middle of the year when abundant green colour lingers, yet a hint of autumn already beckons. It is the central focus of all the seasons. The late summer is the time where all things seem to culminate; there is frantic activity in the insect world, changes happen fast. The berries suddenly change colour and are ripe to eat. We start harvesting the first fruit and vegetables (i.e. potatoes/*Pomme-de-terre*/the apple of the earth).

We also meet this time of abundant growth and ripening in people. The early summer of life is that of marriage and founding a family, yet late summer sees the children grow into adults, sees the fruit of one's professional life mature. In the East, people are conscious of the association between a stage of life and the seasons. In the summer of life family life blooms; duties towards society are being fulfilled; it is the stage of the *grastha*, the householder! The height of summer is the time to enjoy the richness of life and a stage of vigorous activity that almost unnoticed glides into the autumn, with the dawn of the mid-life crisis. Now our connection to the earth becomes especially important so that change does not toss us into chaos and a whirlpool of emotions.

The menopause and all the associated symptoms in women, often is heralded by imbalances in the Earth Element, just like illnesses to do with female hormones, infertility, the womb, ovaries or testicles. People who are drifting through mid-life like a rudderless ship, people who start many different things, never getting to see the fruition of any of their labour, people who dance through life like busy bees, doing 'this and that' never really settling down - might well have an Earth imbalance.

The Direction associated with Earth is the centre. It is a still point, yet holds all potential including that very first inclination to move out; from this point, that first stirring happens, which is called the heartbeat of the Earth.

Every tradition has its own way of expressing this initial movement, which is more a potential really. It is a messenger heralding abundance, a sense in the heart of freely giving positive energy, love! Indeed the contact point (alarm point) for the Earth energy is in the diagnostic area of the Heart, in the centre. This centre (*Hara*) holds two power points (used in Martial Arts and complementary medicine), the *tan tien* and the 'Core Star.' [12] Both are believed to carry the 'Core of our Essence' and both lie in the diagnostic area of the Spleen. Thus injury in the belly, the centre, results in serious damage to life and even death. This is familiar from the famous word *hara-kiri*, meaning splitting of the belly (stomach and area below the navel); this fatal incision is made because the belly is considered the seat of Life.

Man has a place in society; if he neglects that place, if he neglects what is central to his life, be it health, family, friends, job, values or any of his basic needs, it will affect his life negatively. If the centre is his divine core and he neglects to acknowledge or to live according to it, it will affect his life too. He will feel cut loose, uprooted, at odds, restless, frustrated, a strange unearthly loneliness, a lacking, a craving, but for what? He will be searching, always searching to fill his void centre with substitutes, e.g. overwork, thinking too much and worrying too much, or he will feed the void with snacks, sweets, sex and even turn to addictions such as alcohol and drugs. If we look at social problems in western society, we might find it indicative of a neglected Earth; our sense of belonging has been disturbed. We have lost our own 'intrinsic Earth.'

It is not without reason that the Bible describes man 'as made of Earth.' To recognise our place on Earth, in society, is the sacred duty of each person and a responsibility among the society of 'Earthlings.' We take into our Centre much more than the food we ingest. We take in air and 'digest it' and even rest (sleeping patterns); we take in movement (bodily co-ordination). We take in thoughts and ideas (brain activity); we take in sensory impressions (emotions); we take in seeds (female reproductive cycle); indeed it seems that the *taking in* is central to just about all human activity. Consequently, ailments that derive from malfunctioning of this *process of 'taking–in'* range from obesity, stomach ulcers, colds and nasal congestion, to too much thinking and worrying over details, forgetfulness and restlessness. They include being easily tired and yawning a lot, as well as a malfunctioning of the female organs and reproductive glands. It includes the inability to assimilate new ideas as much as the hardening of the arteries due to stress (the stomach has a direct link with the hypothalamus/endocrine glands).

The Climate related to Earth is humidity/dampness. Dampness stems from accumulation of moisture, it arises from a build up of fluids. It makes the person feel full and heavy, it causes stagnation and thus affects the circulation. Dampness at the roots gives a sense of contented-ness, with it comes stillness and peace. But too much damp is detrimental - when it is too damp the atmosphere becomes heavy. Within the body it leads to accumulation of phlegm, abundant mucus, water retention especially in the abdomen, joints and extremities, (oily skin and/or sticky perspiring hands and skin). The result is a heavy head, a dull feeling and general lethargy. Usually the dampness is accompanied by either heat, cold or wind.

If it appears together with cold, there is restricted circulation, stiffness and soreness of muscles, and fatigue. When it is accompanied by heat, it expresses as herpes, shingles, jaundice, bronchitis, cystitis and any amount of red, raised pus filled sores, such as abscesses, ulcers, or mouth ulcers. When it appears in conjunction with wind, it produces swellings that migrate, such as hives, swollen lymph nodes, wind in the stomach, sores and ulcers. In extreme cases, it creates obstructions that can cause seizures, strokes, vertigo, fuzziness and psychosomatic states like clumsiness, lack of co-ordination and such like.

The reverse of dampness of course is dryness. Too much dryness causes just as much hazard. If cells lack moisture they literally dry up and shrivel and illness result. States such as anorexia develop where mind and body waste away.

Tissues or Parts of the body associated with Earth are the flesh, e.g. muscles, lips, collagen and fat. Flesh signifies and describes body mass, relevant here is the condition of that mass. Its elasticity and temperature tell whether the owner feels tense, tight, overburdened or is simply 'bouncing' with health. Illnesses such as muscular dystrophy and other wasting diseases are linked to an imbalance in the Earth Element. The person lacks nourishment (on gross or subtle level) to the cells as and might well lack that vital relationship with the centre of being. Muscles are said to correspond to the mental energy. Knotted shoulders manifest such energy. Tight muscles in the upper back point to 'rage that was initially aimed at ourselves but then gets projected outwards towards others. This can be seen in what is known as the 'dowager's hump.' This is 'a formation of soft tissue that builds in the upper back, most often in older women, a collection of angry and resentful thoughts... connected with frustration and irritation in not doing what we really want to do, with thwarted ambition or achievement.' 13

Another quite common manifestation connected to gathering and hardening of mental patterns is fibroids, or fibrosis. Suppressed feelings of femininity, sexuality, motherhood or unexpressed guilt, confusion in what we want to do and how to live... all manifested in the flesh. Tight muscles in the legs and thighs might be related to not liking 'where we are going,' dissatisfaction or disorientation about the direction in life we are taking at that moment in time.

The Sense organ connected to the Earth is the mouth and the sense of taste. The mouth is like a gate, where we take in and reject physical and emotional energy, where we receive food, drink and even air. These are life sustaining raw energies (*prana*) needed for any organism. Furthermore the mouth is used - especially in young children - to recognise, feel and experience the world. The first such experience is the breast of the mother, yet for a long time after, toys and any other tangible objects are put into the mouth, either in order to recognise shape and texture or for emotional satisfaction. The first experiences of 'earth providing' are so powerful, that we crave to go back to it, which has lead to countless ideas about 'oral gratification,' including smoking and chewing gum.

The mouth is vital to communication. With the mouth we express our thoughts and feelings; just the way the lip is moved (or dropped) by my daughter, lets me read a whole array of states of emotions!

The mouth is also used to get rid of things and feelings, as in spitting, vomiting etc. Many illnesses affect the mouth with ulcers, swollen gums, throat diseases, roughness, blistering etc. Difficulties with, or illnesses of, the mouth can be related to not wanting to taste, swallow or digest the reality we live in, the feelings and thoughts with which we are presented. The same can be said for likes and dislikes of textures and flavours, be they concrete or abstract.

The Orifice related to the Element Earth is also the mouth.

The Fluid associated with the Earth energy is that of saliva. Saliva is part of the digestive process. Food is cut up and mixed with moisture in the mouth for easy swallowing. We say even emotional issues are 'hard to swallow,' or mere 'dry facts.' They are 'unpalatable'; our body, mind, soul entity refuses to moisten them with 'saliva' in preparation for taking them into the body. If a person suffers from too much or too little production of saliva, or complains about other difficulties in swallowing, it is obviously prudent to look at the Earth Element for imbalances. I remember my daughter complaining about meat being too dry, her mouth did not produce the same amount of saliva say, for roast beef, as for dry bread or crisps etc. and that was even when the meat was accompanied by gravy!

The External Physical Manifestation of Earth is the flesh, thus see under 'tissues,' parts of the body.

The Colour in Chinese medicine associated with Earth is yellow; for thousands of years they have taken the facial colour as an important tool for diagnosing and healing. It does not of course, relate to the genetic colour of the skin, but refers to subtle nuance, recognisably different from that person's normal colouring. In this case, an imbalance of the Earth Element will produce a yellowish hue. The Nei Ching even says, 'When their colour is yellow like oranges, they are without life.' [14] But colour gives clues in other ways: a person choosing to dress predominantly in yellow (or conversely dislikes yellow) shows characteristics of the Earth Element. One might well ask why? Colours vibrate at certain frequencies (see *chakras*).

A person who either desires or dislikes a colour, expresses attraction (need) or dislike (overproduction) of that frequency. So why does the Earth related Organ-network attract yellow? Yellow could to be connected to the Spleen, the colour of bilirubin, an iron by product of the spleen's breakdown of cells and blood. Furthermore iron is one of the most common minerals in the earth, it appears naturally in three different colours, yellow, red and black. We are familiar with the rusty red of many soils e.g. the soil of the County of Devon in England, the centre of Australia and many parts of Africa, but we may not be so familiar with yellow except when we go to China. Taking a boat trip in the South China Sea or along the 'Yellow River' gave me a clear demonstration; here the yellow mud from 'up-country' spills into the sea. Earth in large parts of China is yellow due to the presence of yellow iron oxide. The same goes for parts of the Himalayas, the mountains of Tibet are even 'lemon yellow!' [15]

The Smell connected to Earth is a sweet fragrance. The Nei Ching says: 'Humidity is created by the centre. Humidity nourishes the earth and the earth produces sweet flowers. The sweet flavour nourishes the stomach; the stomach strengthens the flesh.' [16]

A sweet smell or odour is not just what is liked or disliked; rather because of the condition of their organ network, a person actually 'takes on' these odours. Their skin smells in a certain way and thus the smell becomes a diagnostic tool. A strong, fragrant emanating smell from a person, or even a sickly sweet smell that reminds one of well-rotted manure, indicates an imbalance in the Earth Element.

The smell of a fragrant tree carries far; similarly actions of an Earth person can carry far. One of the main characteristics of an Earth person is giving abundantly, giving with compassion. The 'smell' of such a person can carry far; their 'charitable deeds' can involve world-wide actions. Unfortunately we do not always act so true to our character or with such conviction to our Earth-nature. We misuse our senses in a literal and metaphorical sense. To satisfy our senses we become their slaves and risk honesty, honour, commitment, dignity, wisdom, even our lives.

The Taste related to Earth is also sweet. The Nei Ching says: 'If people pay attention to the five flavours and mix them well, their bones will remain straight, their muscles will remain tender and young, their pores will be fine in texture, and consequently, their breath and bones will be filled with the essence of life.' [17]

Each taste is linked to one of the Elements and helps to balance them, excessive consumption of one, on the other hand, damages the related organ network. Thus a longing or even a craving for sweets, cakes, sugary dishes, points towards the Spleen. Spleen and pancreas are in Western medicine linked to illnesses as diabetes, hyperglycemia etc, for their part in the sugar metabolism. In the Nei Ching, the stomach is thought of as the seat of all the five tastes.

The Grain associated with the Earth is millet. **The Fruit** is the apricot. **The Meat** is beef. **The Vegetable** is the shallot. These foods are a guide to a balanced diet. Each individual has different needs, related to foods enhanced by that Element. Sometimes they simply support general harmony; at other times, to eat more or less of any of these is showing signs of an imbalance. It begs the question, why these foods are specially linked to the Earth? Fruit and vegetable might be chosen as much for their mineral content as for their colour or growth habit; their round shape could also be significant; even Millet, a complex carbohydrate, easy to digest and nourishing is understandable - but beef? Some texts translate the Chinese symbol as being the 'Ox' or 'Bull.' In Chinese the animal symbol for the bull or ox is described as a strong, hard working, down to earth animal, it is described as a family type, complacent until challenged; helpful and of service to man. [18] Strangely enough, these characteristics can all be attributed to Earth.

I venture to say there might be an older reason; behind the Chinese tradition stands ancient Indian wisdom. In India, the cow plays a *central* role in any village, as it provides the basics. It gives food (milk), tools (bones), fuel (dung), cloth and shelter (hides) and strength (working animal).

The Expression associated with the Earth is singing. And here is not just meant the ability to perform a song. It rather relates to the tone of voice during ordinary communication. We might hear an underlying, monotonous or melodic ring to a voice, a soft whining sound or even a continuing singsong. As with the colour, this refers to changes to the normal voice of that person. Sound rising high from the throat, quavering or quirking, or even trembling of a voice, point to an imbalance in the Earth energy.

The Sound attributed to Earth is belching. Belching is directly linked to the digestive process or rather the ability of the stomach to pass things on. If food lies in the stomach beyond a reasonable time, it starts to rot, releasing gas, which needs to escape. Just as belching indicates that food has been kept too long, sometimes ideas, patterns of behaviour, attitudes and arguments are held too long. We can't let go. The fruit of a tree needs to be harvested, otherwise it rots, the corn needs to be harvested or it will 'blacken.' Belching is an imbalance in the dharma of 'passing on.'

The Attitude associated with the Earth Element, is 'catching food in hand.' 'Attitude' here is a word employed to describe a behaviour that is not approved of. In that sense, 'catching food in hand' stands for an attitude where 'eating' is devalued; the person just snatches a bite on the run, as the time spent sitting down and having a meal is considered wasted time. Instead, the person would rather organise another village fete, a charity event; or their own body needs are ignored, but they like eating and of course need food – so they end up in this habit of constantly nibbling. The need for constant replenishing comes from a feeling of emptiness. Quite inappropriately one tries to fill it with food rather than care.

The Movement of the Energy is one of holding and embracing. Holding and embracing is an expression of being the centrifugal power. Some people are desperate to hold things, they need to embrace others for the lack of being embraced themselves; they fear, if they don't get what they need, that they will fall apart. They end up giving out too much, which then depletes the person, leading to imbalances.

The Quality ascribed to Earth is what we normally deem 'intellectual,' or rather what we associate with intellectualism (factual knowledge, stored but undigested). Intellect refers to more than just the accumulation of facts; it includes transformed (digested) knowledge. When heart and soul are partaking in this process, facts and experience are transformed into wisdom. Intellectualism i.e. accumulation of undigested ideas, indicate an imbalance in the Earth Element. On the other hand, when experiences are digested, also felt and understood intuitively with the heart, we speak of knowledge as in 'common sense.' If experiences and facts are only linked to the spiritual or soul-level, then understanding becomes unreal, up in the clouds, ungrounded, and can easily be considered or classified as insane. All true masters and teachers therefore place great emphasis on studying the scriptures as a grounding activity. To be balanced in the Earth Element and hold supreme knowledge, we need all three - body, mind and soul - or brain, heart and spirit.

I was brought up by a refugee family, with the belief that you have to study hard, what is in your head 'no-one' can take away. It took me decades to see that this is the view of uprooted, unearthed people, making an understandable virtue of a hard-learned lesson. I am grateful and feel fortunate to have the opportunity to begin to see otherwise.

The Activity associated with Earth is absorbing. The earth absorbs rain in order to gather humidity needed for growth, but she also absorbs matter, effluent, poison etc., decomposes it, and assimilates it as harmless substances so that life can go on. In this way Earth is the greatest recycling plant! The stomach too has a similar function, when it absorbs minerals, vitamins and nutrients. The mind absorbs knowledge; the soul absorbs pure energy. Absorption is the ability to make something part of itself. An inability to absorb, be it knowledge, nutrients or experiences, and make them one's own, points to an imbalance in Earth.

The Condition is one of poise. The image arises of Planet Earth poised in the universe, full, majestic, being without challenge, without purpose; it just is. It seems held by invisible strings of luminous energy. Just like the planet Earth, a person has poise, can stand on their own, stable in their centre; straight, almost proud, yet neither stiff, nor aloof. A person who is secure and balanced at their centre of gravity will, like a child, easily return to their centre when knocked off balance. That person acts like an island around which others move. By contrast, a person who has lost their centre, their connection to the Earth, has no poise, has no stance, no weight and is easily pushed over. Poise needs trust and knowing that all is well, needs a link of equal support to inside (belly) and outside (environment). It reminds me of a stalk of grain dancing in the wind, wafting elegantly like a prima ballerina - or indeed a whole field of grain, a field of plenty, poised in late summer, ready to be harvested to fulfil its duty, its *dharma*.

'Field of Plenty,
Abundance for all
No hunger
No more pain
Great mystery holds
Earth's children dear
And feeds them with
Eternal flame.
Children of Earth, trust again!
Be grateful and give praise!
The field of plenty will remain
To sustain us all our days.' [19]

At this point I would like to add a category not from Traditional Chinese Medicine, but from modern, **psycho-biological research.** Each person shows **differences in brain activity,** which can be linked to influences of energies. Taking this into account, the relative strength of certain influences produce dominance of certain traits.

Where Earth energy (low frequencies) is more prominent, the brain is more (or less) active in the frontal lobe with a direct link to the limbic brain - here smell is received; memory is especially active in the area where genetically encoded memory is stored, i.e. the caudate nucleus. On the dopamine trail, this stimulates action and planning memory, collecting base information. The limbic brain needs to express its state thus the person acts extrovert - yet is unaware of the roots of 'feelings.'

Increasingly research is being done into these influences on the brain. Our societies are getting increasingly aggressive, thus it is worth looking at this in connection to forms of Aggression; it seems **there are five types of Aggression** that increasingly plague humanity.

If Earth, solid, stable, immovable earth, 'holds' on too tight to its own state of being, tension results; earth breaks its crust! Earthquakes result. It shifts and changes and settles into a new position. Similarly with a person where predominant Earth-energies reach 'breaking point,' they might 'loose their grip,' be unable to cope, have a nervous breakdown, a change of heart, an explosion of feelings - but soon settle back into a new position. Thus Aggression in the earth energy – expresses as a powerful eruption of short duration that results in a 're-definition of position.'

The Relationship of Earth to the other Elements (in Classical TCM) is described in several models. One called the cosmological cycle, has the Fire Element at the top of an axis (cross-like), the Water Element at its opposite end. At the central cross point is the Earth, with Wood (Space) and Metal (Air) to either side.

The most frequently used model is that of the *Shen-Ko* Cycle. The Elements here are arranged according to their continuing support in a circle. Thus Fire supports Earth > Metal (Air) > Water > Wood (Space) > Fire etc. There is no beginning or end to this cyclic relationship.

There is another way to portray interaction according to their controlling effect on each other; it is depicted as a star (Ko). Each line portrays an arrow shot to control the flow of energy, thus it is revealed that each Element is controlling as well as being controlled. In this way Fire controls Metal, Earth controls Water, Metal controls Wood, Water controls Fire, Wood controls Earth.

Usually the aforementioned circle and the star are shown as a 'double' symbol to demonstrate how the Elements balance each other through mutual enhancement and control - just like parents balance the children by support and restraint.

This parental image is taken quite far; accordingly Earth <u>gives birth to Air</u>, and with it, she gives birth to the child of her own substance; eventually she lets go and the child takes on a separate existence. This is symbolically describing that each Element contains the previous, yet to a lesser extent. The mother nourishes *her* child; Earth transmutes her energy to Metal/Air. Earth and Metal (Air) are characterised by beneficial co-existence. Yet, Earth <u>controls Water</u> (re: rivers or canals are kept in their beds by banks of earth). Water is kept within its boundaries, restricted, prevented from flowing over and swamping everything by walls of Earth. The Earth needs to control Water to protect itself from becoming a deadly swamp; yet, in order to fulfil its *dharma* of bringing forth abundant life, it needs Water. Together they are fertility per se. Their relationship is co-operation at its best. Earth <u>is controlled by Wood/Space</u>. The roots of plants keep the soil in place, stop it from being eroded by either water or dryness (fire). They are limiting each other almost to exclusion. Finally Fire is the agent of rebirth; Fire burns matter into ashes, those very minerals that, mixed with water and aged in time, become Earth. Thus <u>Fire gives birth to Earth</u>; Earth is the child of Fire.

Fire nourishes the Earth, replenishes its contents, purifies it and dries it when it is too wet and warms it when too cold. The relationship of Earth to Fire is one of being nurtured, protected and enriched. And then the Circle starts again.

Ayurveda too describes the relationship between the Elements in models, it uses wheels, i.e. there is a 'Wheel of Creation,' one of destruction, one of control and finally, one of support. 'The Wheel of Support' is the same as in the *Che-Ko* Cycle. The Wheel of Destruction (*Vinasha chakra*) sets the Elements in the same order, but the spokes or arrows of the five-sided star are point in the opposite direction from the *Chen-Ko* Cycle; thus Earth destroys Wood (Ether) which in turn destroys (Air/Wind)/Metal. The latter destroys Fire (Wind fans, but it also blows the Fire out). Fire in turn, dries up Water and the latter washes away Earth.

These different symbols focus on a specific aspect, why: because they are used in different contexts. The Chen Ko cycle is especially useful in alternative medicine, where Imbalances are addressed. The Cycle of Creation shows the most accurate observation of how subtle energy fields become ever denser Matter. An indescribable source (outside the circle; i.e. *Prana*) becomes Ether (Space, Wood) and creates out of itself Wind (Air) Movement. Movement produces friction, culminating in Fire. Where there is Air and Fire, chemically speaking, Water molecules are made. Their interaction produces a 'liquid' state; the latter solidifies to Earth. From here a direct link feeds back to Space/Ether and closes the link. [20]

I will, as much as appropriate, stick to the latter cycle. Of course this is justifiable only as a working hypothesis. Indeed the interaction is more akin to a complex web of interacting fields of elemental energy on many different levels (be it body, mind, soul or - seven, even twelve or more up to n-th etheric bodies). They pull and churn and feed off each other with the Earth - on any of these interacting levels, as some central, stabilising axis, or three, or twelve or n-th axes. It generates the image of a super nova. Remember a clear, deep summer night sky with many levels of stars, forever more distant.

There is always one component, which is central; one that is more solid, more manifested, more practical; there is always one 'Earth.' Our belly is like the earth, the earth is like the galaxy, the galaxy, like the universe... as above, so below.

Hildegard von Bingen describes **the interaction of the Elements:** 'would the earth not fulfil its task of providing 'growing,' there would be no air. If the water would not be softening and taming the earth... and the earth not taming the water, and lead it into the right pathways, the water could not have its mirror-like quality that points to the depths... The dew is a symbol for right mixture of fire and air, bringing the right condition for abundant ripening of fruit, fulfilled in the fire of the sun. The hardness of one element supports the softness of another, and the softness of one, soothes the hardness of the other, in such mutual benefit the elements can exist in harmony and balance... ' [21]

4.2: b) Association with Personality and Relationships

All phenomena are manifestations of the Elements, including people. Their individual aspects come from a dominant presence of one of the Five. I would like to draw an exaggerated picture of *a person* who has Earth as their dominant, influencing Element. She may be a housewife and mother, but not necessarily so. She may be a teacher, a diplomat or in any serving job. If not, she will certainly be involved in helping others in some way, even if on a voluntary basis and in some kind of charity... or two... or three! She might be somebody spending a lot of time organising jumble sales, baking cakes for school fairs etc. She holds her family together with a practical, down to earth intelligence, circling around their needs and the needs of others, to the extent that she might forget her own needs, having difficulty in saying 'no' to the demands of others.

She might be fleshy and strongly built yet her feet and hands seem small. She has solid hips and thighs; her feet are firmly on the ground. In an unbalanced state however, she might have difficulties putting her feet on the ground. Her heaviness does not stop her from being quick and efficient, accomplishing her tasks with gusto. She is a patient listener who makes people comfortable, but is not somebody who hides her own feelings either. Her home is very important to her, as is family and where she lives; her surroundings are warm and cosy.

She is protective not only towards her family, but also to an extended network of friends. She feels good when needed by others. She might even get completely absorbed in them, which leaves herself at times feeling empty and unfulfilled. She mistakes this emptiness for hunger, cravings for food and eating become a 'must.' Eating despite being 'full' slows her metabolism down; food remains undigested, inflating her abdomen with stagnant energy, fluid and gas. As the body can't make use of the food, she feels 'low' and her remedy is to eat more. This leads to extra physical, as well as emotional weight, stemming from taking on other people's problems. Taking on this extra weight results in sluggishness and tiredness. The person feels 'stuck.'

She might have benevolent lumps of one sort and another in her tissue, since 'disease is located within the flesh.' [22] And since the Earth Element covers feeding others, her mammary glands might especially be affected. She is also prone to fibroids, especially in the womb.

If the environment is generous and without too much change, with lots of social tasks to fulfil, she will be happy and have a stabilising effect on the world around her, keeping her tendency to overcompensate well at bay. Her life is like a play: she supports the players, providing physical and mental nourishment, thus ensuring that the play of the world can continue and that every other player can do their part.

The Emotion that characterises her best is empathy - sympathy, which includes compassion and non-judgemental love. Sympathy and compassion arise from understanding that if I am a child of this earth, then you must be too. If my physical and emotional being roots in the earth, then yours must also. If I am a child of the divine (Earth), then so must you be. Out of the understanding of myself, comes the recognition that you are my brother, my sister, that you are indeed no different from me, that there is only one brotherhood of man. With this I can recognise the physical, material and psychological suffering that is yours. I can put myself inside your skin; I can 'step into your shoes' and feel your suffering. This goes far beyond shallow observation of a poor person who has ill fortune and reacting with 'compassion,' a 'suffering with.' Recognising the suffering, the earth person knows how to help. This centrally orientated empathy rises from the stillness of the belly; it is by nature not dependent on the other person being loveable; it is by nature non-judgemental. The Earth person understands that by helping others, she helps 'herself.'

But surely such empathy 'should' extend to compassion and love of oneself. If someone hurts the earth person, and she can re-connect with her centre, she realises that the person (or the circumstances), which hurt us are merely 'other fruits of the earth; of ourselves;' with this comes detachment; bitterness will vanish and make place for reconciliation. The same road leads to self-acceptance, self-love and sympathy towards oneself. Out of the reconciliation with the self, abundant growth of talents, ideas and feelings will blossom. A person who has lost the ability to empathise or feel compassion towards him/herself is uprooted and segregated from his original nature and shows an imbalance in the Earth Element.

There are people who simply can't see other people suffer, they can not 'stomach' being in the presence of the poor, hungry, dirty or sick; such people have lost the awareness of all beings, as children of one earth. We hear people say, 'to see these people makes me sick'; and they might quiet literally become nauseous.

Equally people who are constantly 'fussing over' others over the slightest mishap, i.e. a mother keeping her child so 'tight to her heart' that he cannot flourish, show imbalances in the Earth Element. They are over-indulging, completely identifying with the other, forgetting that 'although we are the same essence, we are all unique in our patterns,' that we are all children of the earth but not 'identical twins.' Such people 'worry themselves sick,' they are holding 'things' too long, too tight in their arms - just as they hold food too long in their 'stomach' with out passing it on to the next stage. The result: be it food or relationships - they rot.

The Manner in which such a person reacts in times of excitement is with stubbornness. Earth people hold on to what they've got, hold to ideas and opinions with unrivalled stubbornness. Stubbornness is a sign of holding on beyond reasonable time or circumstances. On the other hand, if a person has the habit of changing their mind quickly and cannot hold on to an idea, argument or feeling, then their Earth Element is equally out of balance. Why? They are not able to harvest their 'investment'! Nothing will bear fruit because they switch too quickly from one idea to the next, like dust in the dry deserts where nothing can take root.

A Person does not live alone. We might think ourselves as separate from others, even as alone and isolated, yet in truth, we never are. Not even on a mundane level. It is a game our mind plays with us, we need to free ourselves from this depressing illusion of aloneness; we are deeply connected to everything around us.

Observe yourself as you drink a cup of tea, sitting in your chair feeling depressed and lonely. Now, contemplate your cup of tea! Somebody, on the other side of the world, picked the leaves of the tea bush for you to drink. In order for the woman to go and pick the leaves of the tea bush, grandmother had to look after her children; her entire family is connected to you via the tealeaves. Furthermore, so are all the people who processed, transported, packed the tea and put it on the shelves in the supermarket. Via a cup of tea you are connected to just about the whole world - and further, to all of creation via the rain and sun which helped to grow it.

The secret lies in the focus; we normally keep our focus so narrow, that the wise of old just consider us as 'blind'; being blinkered or blind, is looking at one frame of a whole movie picture and saying: I don't understand the story! If we look with a wider angle or at the whole film, we realise that we are part of a vast, interactive community.

Let's look at how **a person with dominant Earth energy interacts** and reacts to people characterised by other Elements. To understand, let us simply look at nature: **Earth and Water!**

Earth's stability and solidity is contrasted by water's fluidity. Where earth is dense, opaque and stable, water is transparent, taking up any shape and colour of its environment. Water and earth intermingle closely. If there is more water than earth, earth gets swamped and loses its ability to hold freely and adequately. With the right quantity of water earth's ability to hold is enhanced. Many myths in all cultures see this fertile relationship between earth and water: earth, receptive female goddess is fertilised by water in the form of the rain–god. This fertile relationship is archetypal. Out of earth and water, the first life microbes and amoebas arose.

The deep connection between these two shows in the landscape. Earth banks channel the river's water to its destiny, the ocean. The ocean bottom, however deep, is still earth! Earth and ocean share mutual boundaries (coastline) and by and large they respect those boundaries (only slowly they erode; floods, earthquakes etc. are obvious drastic imbalances). Islands scattered in the oceans, show how much the earth can penetrate into the Waters, just as Water can penetrate into earth.

A relationship, even marriage between people characterised by Earth and Water is peaceful and fertile as long as they respect each other's boundaries; the stability of the one can be balanced by the flexibility of the other. They can be creative and inspired, supporting each other's duties, jobs and ambitions. As we saw above, danger comes if either one dominates; then a Water person will make the Earth person ineffective, slow, lethargic and 'drown' her/him. Conversely a dominating Earth person stifles the creativity of the Water person, making her/him stagnant and stale.

In a relationship between these two elemental characters, the key word is discipline. If Water disciplines its drive to 'go all over the place,' and accepts the guiding river banks of the Earth person, and the Earth person resists the temptation to 'close ranks' and become a stubborn, inflexible rock, then a balanced and unusual fertile relationship can grow. For example:

Imagine the headmaster of a large school, an occupation well befitting an Earth person. His school soon has its 25th anniversary and he has asked the music-teacher to prepare a musical event. The music teacher is a Water person, creative and flowing, imaginative. The music teacher goes ahead and chooses some music for the recorder group and practices it with a few people. Somebody suggests including a saxophone player; the teacher is off to find some older pupil that can play. Shouldn't the school choir be involved? She abandons the recent practices and sits down to write a beautiful piece of choir music; during the rehearsals with the choir, it becomes clear that all would benefit from a piano accompaniment and may be some drums. Of she goes to borrow some from the neighbouring school.

At the next rehearsal, the headmaster comes to listen; there are only three days to the big event. Panic sets as all instruments play 'a different tune.' The recorder players even stay in a corner of the room waiting for instructions. It is chaos! The teacher, in her long flowing skirt, swoops from one group to the other, not getting anywhere.

The headmaster is distraught; he looks at the situation, and realises it is partly his own fault; yes, he was leaving the music-teacher a generous amount of time, financing extra sheet music – but he paid no attention to the fact that the music-teacher was a 'water person.' His brief to her was too loose. (Water seeps here and there, flows, if unguided all over the place). The headmaster's patience and generosity had only supported her trend. Realising this, without judgement and attaching blame, he now constructs a framework for rehearsals to channel her energy (adding his ability to support and give boundaries to her abundant creativity). A wonderful performance is presented on the day.

Next, let's look at the relationship between **Earth and Fire.**

Imagine a bonfire; watch what goes on between the earth on which the fire sits and the fire itself, it is obvious that earth herself does not get consumed by fire. All else may be burned, but not the ground. If we go back to the site of the fire on the next day, we find a heap of ashes (minerals) on the earth. If we return after the next rainfall, the ashes have been washed into the earth: they have become more earth. The Chinese talk of the Earth Element as the daughter of the Fire Element. Cosmologicaly, this is certainly true: for millions of years ago, a fiery glowing star became – our earth. The same process still goes on as the core of the earth still cools. Occasionally we witness fire breaking out from within the earth and producing lava, which in turn, cooled and eroded, is again earth. For me, the close link became abundantly clear in Kagoshima, a small south Japanese island where recently thrown out lava stones, still warm, were found side by side with smaller eroded grains in which already, radishes and small oranges were cultivated.

Fire also affects earth from the outside. The sun warms the earth; as the sun goes down, the temperature changes (as it does for winter). Extreme heat, as well as its absence, splits granite rocks and turns them into earth. So looking from the point of the earth, fire is its creator, its generous giver; it doesn't destroy earth yet it might transform its shape.

We can observe the interaction of fire and earth in many circumstances. Think of a foundry. Ore/earth gets heated up so intensely that it turns liquid, yet as soon as it is cooled, it returns to being earth. By and large, Earth returns to what it originally was, it is true to its nature, its 'centre.'

What does this mean in terms of **relationships, even marriage** between an Earth person and a person with a dominant trait of Fire energy?

We look at it here from the perspective of the 'Earth person.' Earth gets warmed, comforted and supported by the Fire person so she can go about her duties. Earth's life becomes inspired by the relationship with a Fire person to such extend that ultimately the Earth person might be melted by a passion that changes her own being to light, to Fire. Enthusiasm and joy are infused in the otherwise heavy and dense Earth person, so that her innate glow of love and concern for others can 'brighten up the world.' If she finds the fire of devotion and love, her work might expand to great humanitarian work. But if for one reason or the other the Fire is removed (which is quite possible as a Fire person's character goes), the Earth person, left to herself, cannot maintain the warm lightness for long, and returns to her more heavy and dense states. To be nourished, she needs Fire.

It would be beneficial for an Earth person to discover her own source of Fire; the solution might not be in dependency on a partner, but in an inspiring job, charitable or humanitarian causes. It could be in finding a spiritual teacher or the discovery of divine love. Without the warming fire of inspiration from one source or other the Earth person finds it difficult to grow.

How then can a conflict arise between an Earth person and a Fire person? Back to our headmaster!

There is a very attractive, flamboyant but volatile girl in his senior class. She is very artistic and a good performer and manipulator. Other students like her, for she sets inspiring trends in the school. Her seemingly untamed temperament can bring disruption to the school routine. The headmaster finds it difficult to control her.

She and some friends want to have a school magazine, yet the headmaster thinks it will detract from work, especially from the exam. The boys and girls try to lobby through the teachers but eventually the senior-girl is send to the headmaster to talk for them. When she enters, the room seemed to 'light-up;' she burst in with much charm and sweet politeness. The headmaster listened patiently to her enthusiastic, sparkling pleas. Gradually he started to see her points and becomes infected by her enthusiasm; he has to admit that some benefit for the pupils could be gained. Eventually the headmaster melts and gives in. He promises his generous support, if- the schoolwork does not suffer. Soon the project gets under way. Even the headmaster adds some suggestions of his own; the senior girl has not only won, but has also inspired the headmaster.

After a few months, the paper is going well; the senior girl moves away, and with it the motivation of the other students, drops.

What to do? The headmaster ponders the situation and comes up with an idea; he contacts the local newspaper, and the professionals take up the cause and write an article about the school newspaper. The interest is rekindled, and now even includes the community at large and the headmaster gains a lot of prestige.

With her charm and inspiring ideas, the Fire person melted the solidity of the Earth person. He could not resist such warmth and used his own generosity, tolerance and patience to foster the scheme. Having been 'warmed,' the headmaster got into contact with his own centre of Fire; from the centre, the earth renews itself. When the 'Fire went out,' the Earth person used his residual warmth to rekindle it.

Earth and Air seem so different! Earth appears as solid matter, the most manifest form of energy - and Air is so light, so insubstantial; they seem opposite. Air is rarely still; it is so light it drifts here and there over the surface of the earth. Rarely is there any interference between the two, except may be in violent storms. Each keeps in their realm. Other agents like microbes and fungus are needed to bring air to penetrate into the earth. Earth is surrounded by Air, it almost 'suffocates' it; this band of air is subtle but never the less substantial, it is some 400km deep (atmosphere) gradually thinning. However strong the centre of earth (whose gravity holds 'all'), it can not hold the gases of the air eternally.

Without enriching organisms, the elemental relationship of Air, Earth is 'life-less,' at best peaceful, an uneventful coexistence – at worst stale.

There would be - in a **relationship, marriage or partnership** - little conflicting action, but a respectful coexistence. Lively storms and upsetting events are more likely to come from the outside than from within the nature of the two. The Earth person being by nature supportive and able to hold and serve with dignity, respects the Air person and holds them as close as possible, with understanding and respect. Yet the Air person can't help 'thinning-out' and eventually becomes something else. This self-removal of the Air person does not have to be linked to distance, or even be intentional, but can simply be a business-project the Air person gets involved in, or even a tendency to shut others out ('gone fishing!'). The Air person easily can remove herself mentally from the partner; it is like retreating 'into the garden shed.'

True interaction between them - from the point of the Earth - can only be through a catalyst.

Let us return to our headmaster; his secretary is an efficient Air person; they make an effective team, each knowing what their tasks are, and keeping to them. The secretary is a clear and precise worker, well liked by the staff for her punctual work and high standards. The headmaster recently agreed that the secretary could use the school's computer to pursue a project of her interest. It didn't take long before some teachers complained that this and that is not done.

Realising that the secretary is getting more and more involved in her project, the headmaster has to face the problem. From the 'Earth point' of view, he is aware that his tendency to be overly generous and patient is partly responsible for the problem. He knows that this can cause problems. He did not consider his secretary's tendency to get so involved in *her own* projects; she tends to 'fly off,' forgetting the responsibilities of her job.

On reflection, the headmaster realises the tendencies of the Air person and sets about to rectify the situation. With respect and generosity he establishes boundaries; i.e. when the secretary could use the computer; forbidding it altogether would deny the Air person her own nature!

Let us now contemplate the relationship between **Earth and the fifth Element;** it is kind of difficult to draw an accurate picture, because different traditions name it differently. First we shall look at the Chinese version: The name 'Wood' relates to the symbol of a tree; a tree roots firmly in the earth and grows skyward; branches stretch into all directions (all dimensions from the most dense to the most subtle).

Earth provides the base for the tree, it is where the tree is anchored. Without the earth's holding, the tree would not be fit to grow upwards. On the other hand, the roots of the tree hold the earth - without them the earth is vulnerable to be blown (or washed) away. Paradoxical as it sounds, the Earth needs the hold of the roots, just as the tree needs the hold of the earth. This mutual holding symbolises the relationship between an Earth person and a Space person; two polarities that can not exist without the other, they give each other meaning.

They also share meaning in the relative existence; earth's life cycle (and thus her span of thinking and action) is so vast, it is almost timeless. The tree stems from a seed of a predecessor (past generation) and makes seeds (future), thus it too has a 'timeless' quality.

Other cultures refer to the Fifth Element as Spirit (American Indians, Celts and Australian Aboriginals). In some Indian philosophy it is called Ether or Faith. All these point to strong 'spiritual overtones.' For other Indian, Tibetan and Buddhist traditions, this Element is named Space, and refers to that which 'contains' everything - even time and movement. It is the most universal image; thus I will use it.

Earth is the densest in the hierarchy of the elements, Space the least 'substantial;' it has no 'real' perceivable substance, is more spirit, life-force, *prana,* than anything else.

This subtlety shows in a person dominated by the Element of Space; she might seem detached from the humdrum of life, almost without substance; who knows whether she is confused, or simply disinterested? Her mind is filled with a plethora of ideas with great potential but she has difficulties in making them 'real.'

When looking at the **relationship between an Earth person and Space person,** it appears as though they have even less in common that

Earth and Air, but not so. Space is in every particle of Earth, down to the subatomic level. And... earth after all hangs totally within Space. Again we have this mutual integration, as was shown above between earth and tree/wood.

Earth knows that it is totally held and interpenetrated by space, if Earth is not assertive this could turn into a stranglehold. A weak earth can even be 'sucked into a black hole' by space. On the other hand if the Earth person has enough strength (gravity) from her centre, it 'hangs' rather autonomously in Space; the Earth person can lead a fulfilling, autonomous life within the Space person's orbit.

Being opposites, they are mutually completing, giving each other meaning of life; this is an avenue a couple could explore. Earth's centre is her own strength (gravity); Space lives in an altogether different dimension (consciousness, God?). For the Earth person, a quantum leap is required to get into touch with That. If Earth focuses within, Space focuses beyond. Such relationship needs a lot of awareness.

How would our headmaster cope in a conflict with such a person? He has a caretaker in his school that is a 'Space person.' The caretaker knows every little space, any corner and hideout in the school building, but also is familiar with anything that goes on in school. He prides himself in keeping inside and outside running smoothly. It sometimes seems as though he *is* the school.

The headmaster usually simply jovially smiles at the caretaker. Then one day the school needs some alterations. The caretaker objects straight out: What, change his Space? No way! But then he starts dreaming - his church has a boys football team - and his school could provide some practice ground; he could coach them, maybe they would get into the football league. All they need would be a new football pitch. Now if the alterations could include that... His dream gets over-ruled by the school governors and the headmaster.

Once the decision is made, the caretaker takes off and comes up with a new suggestion each day. Maybe his intention is to block the whole plan, maybe he is just dreaming... today he wants a new coat of paint for the WC, tomorrow a new carpet for the staff room! Finally, as he feels he does not get what he wants, he speaks of handing in his resignation.

The headmaster is at first surprised and when he finds the caretaker lobbying against him, he knows its time to act. Hmm, the caretaker is a 'Space person' and has a tendency to fly off in different directions, it should not be judged; he does a good job – so it is no good sacking him! So the headmaster tries to be patient - if he does nothing, by the time the school is finished, the caretaker will probably love 'his new school.' So he invites the caretaker for a chat, they sit together and the headmaster listens while the caretaker diffuses his energy. Listening to the complaints and suggestions, patiently the headmaster's confidence grows that this man is the right person for the job. Eventually the caretaker runs out of arguments and admits that he looks forward to see the building finished.

While being true to his own nature, yet respecting the nature of others, the headmaster in the school of life, has avoided and solved many conflicts just by being himself and by looking for help in the Five Elements; following the laws of interaction, he has lived his dharma.

4.3: Associations for Spiritual Evolution (Yoga)

The tendencies one has, that come from the kind of energy that influences us most, naturally also have an impact on the way one works with the relationship between God, the world and oneself. Depending on the dominant energetic influence we find our **spiritual or religious inclinations.**

Although Earth energy is bound to the physical world, it does not mean it finds no spiritual expression. Earth energies, providing strong focus on the physical world, can and have led to materialism and dogmatism no matter what background. On the other hand, Earth mysteries have, from the earliest times, played a vital part in any human culture, and frequently these metaphysics go through a revival. At their best they turn to the numinous forces behind nature (such as we have seen in the context of Africa and Australia). Shamanism works with the concept of 'soul retrieval' having found its very own way to answer Earth's question of 'who am I.' Other such positive spiritual paths under the auspices of earth energy, are the way of the American Indians, the Celtic teachings of the Druids and many more. At the core of these Earth Mysteries is always the wish to heal and understand the link between earth and man.

Qualities/Steps in Sadhana. In my understanding the spiritual aspect of the body-mind-soul entity undergoes an evolution; the development is called walking the spiritual path or *Sadhana* in Sanskrit. For much of this way, this too is influenced by the Five Elements, albeit in ever subtler ways, and there comes a point when such a subtle level is reached, that it is beyond the influence of the elements. Meanwhile I propose that for most of the path, the Earth adds distinct character.

Earth refers to the manifestation of spirit in matter and mind. The first step in understanding this, is characterised by becoming conscious of who we are. Naturally at first we identify with the body. On the 'Earth-level' we stay in the realm of this basic awareness – even though evolution happens here too: gradually through experience, we become aware that body is life-force in the most solid of states. (This insight is hoped for - through the *asanas*, practised in *Yoga)*. The body is **life incarnate**; it is en-livened by spirit, this is the end (or the beginning of the line). The bug stops here, all is worked out on this level. The path for doing that is Yoga (although other traditions use other words).

The path of Yoga takes different forms; traditionally it is no way limited to *asana* practise, but in fact describes a path of spiritual evolution offering different practices for differently inclined people. Those who fall under the dominant influence of Earth are best suited for Karma Yoga. As we have seen above, Earth people tend to enjoy selflessly working for others. This is Karma Yoga. It is not just 'doing good,' but doing it without self-interest. In what field depends on the other influences in the person, as we are always composites of elemental energies.

Indian philosophy recognises four **different stages of consciousness.** We traverse these as we develop as human beings into our fullest potential. They are the waking consciousness, the dream consciousness, the deep sleep consciousness and the *turya* state (the state beyond). The influence of the Earth Element belongs to the **waking consciousness.** When we are awake, what we perceive of the world is what we deem real. This perception is limited to what our senses can perceive; thus the focus is on sensual impressions of the physical reality. This is reflected in the role Earth energy plays in **energetic anatomy.**

We have referred frequently to **energy fields/energy bodies;** these formed around the cerebrospinal fluid, or rather the central subtle channels (be they called *sushumna/Ida/Pingala* or Governing and Conception Vessel). As the embryo evolves with it, five sheaths (*koshas* as they are called in Sanskrit) [23] are formed; the first sheath (associated with Earth energy) is called **Annamaya Kosha.** 'Anna' means food. This is our 'food-body,' the physical environment, where food is changed through the bodily processes into physical energy. Meanwhile in the central subtle channel, pure energy (Kundalini) works and travels, evolving our existence from raw matter to divine consciousness. Wherever this energy is at work a related 'state of being' unfolds within the person.

When work is done on the most manifest level, the energy works through the *Muladhara*, the lowest Chakra. The work here is influenced by the qualities of Earth- energies (raw life energy); work consists of transforming this energy to a higher frequency. In other words: when work is done by the Kundalini in this *chakra*, the person mainly identifies with the gross physical body, and primal physical energy which looks after the primal needs for self and others, such as food and shelter. By and large a child between the ages of one and seven acts out of this *chakra*. The infant grounds itself in mother and father, and gains a relationship to earthly existence. The young child will be self-centred and highly concerned with his or her own physical survival. Such actions are appropriate at this stage of life.

The energy of the **Muladhara**, the base *chakra,* is associated with a frequency of 460 Htz; meaning that it spins (metabolises energy) at that relatively low frequency. The Energy of **Earth** influences this Chakra (giving it the majority of its characteristics). In most traditions it is associated with the colour yellow and the base symbol for solidity: a solid yellow square with orange petals. [24] In Indian mythology the presiding deity over this Chakra is Brahma; his four heads look into four directions, representing the four aspects of human consciousness (the physical Self, the rational Self, the emotional Self and the intuitive Self). They also are said to represent the four forms of sound etc). The female divine aspect here is the Dakini/Shakti or Kundalini. She is the gatekeeper and should be worshipped as the Shakti of Brahma. The symbolic animal of the Chakra is the Elephant. As elephant–headed god, Ganesha bestows protection (supporting Earth's need for security) and removes all obstacles to further evolution. Each Chakra is also associated with organs, which work with their energy. In this way 'the physical organs associated' with this Chakra are all those that give physical support to the body, like the vertebrates (bone structure), but especially the coccyx, the sacro-coccygeal plexus, legs, feet, rectum and the immune system.

The more psychological, emotional and mental factor associated with it are: the importance of safety and security (physically and mentally) these aspects are needed for life to flourish and include issues of law and order. It was already mentioned that work done here relates to body identification, which of course includes the will to live, and to stand up for oneself! A material worldview derives from such orientation – yet evolving from here is including the desire to learn.

The metabolised energy in this Chakra shapes the perception and nature of information that can be processed. Environment is perceived primarily through touch and explored through kinetic movement, resulting in a sense of balance, a sense of physical pleasure – or pain.

The Need this energy generates is a need for physical comfort, pleasure and health and material wealth.

In the Tibetan system, which is kind of a bridging point between India and China, this Chakra is also associated with healing energy released by meditation on the symbol of Buddha Amoghasiddi, who grants the freedom from fear. It vibrates with the seed syllables vam, lam to sam. (Also, in the Tibetan system this and the next *chakra* have been combined under the name *Sang-Na)*.

Physical ailments that are associated with the dis-function of this *chakra* are: chronic lower back pain; sciatica; varicose veins; rectal tumours/cancer; depression; immune related disease.

As you know, the energy exchange between the various fields are not limited to *chakra,* but also function through channels (nadis/meridians). All of these are stimulated, stretched and balanced and purified through the postures (*Asanas*) in Yogic language. In fact it is said, that the practice of yoga asana in its plurality, comes from the need to detoxify the body organs.

Whenever one practices these asanas, the five Elements are involved. Patanjali writes in his Yoga Sutras (II/46), 'Asana is a steady, comfortable posture.' The most steady 'thing' is the unilateral triangle, hence we sit in a steady, comfortable posture in such a triangle, where the distance between the knees is equal to the distance between knee and shoulder. i.e. the classical meditation posture (padmasana, siddhasana). It means that this classic posture is 'earthing,' grounding us, connecting us to the material base, from which we can then rise, like a tree that is firmly rooted.

This strong grounding, the connection to the Earth, is mirrored in the practise of each asana, when reminded of a firm steady foundation, with focus on the placement of the feet, the steadiness of the legs and the alignment of knees and hips. But of course there are times where the thighs and hipbones become this grounding base or even the head and neck (shoulder stand). It makes it clear that 'foundation,' 'earthing,' has little to do with specific limbs of the body, more with a quality of movement, and a quality of being. And that not only physically.

Furthermore, different parts of the Yoga practice, under the influence of these energies, thus the posture itself, represent Earth; movement or fluidity (viniyasa) from one posture into another represents the Water Element. The 'victorious breath,' ujjayi breath (inhalation with closed mouth through both nostrils), heats the body, stokes its fire and thus is connected to the Element Fire. Air is in the lightness and ease with which an asana is practised, is in the upward movement and lift.

Stretching creates inner space especially in the body's core. Done with the right awareness this leads to stillness and silence within the spiritual heart, the hrdya. Reaching this space we are closest to our original nature, to what Yoga is about.

Furthermore, certain asanas work especially on energies related to the Earth Element and their associated organs (and related meridians) etc. After all the root of asana practice is thought to be a way of detoxifying the organs of the body 'by squeezing and stretching,' so that life could be long and healthy in order to be able to fulfil the purpose of life. Specific asanas relating to the Earth Element in this sense, are 'all techniques that are held in stillness,' [25] improving steadiness, for example: *Tadasana* (mountain pose), *Ardhalasana* (half plough), *Halasana* (plough), *Dandasana* (staff pose), *Ardapindasana* (embryo pose), and those that work on the Earth-meridians (Stomach and Spleen) i.e. *Urdhava Dhanurasana* (strong backbend), and some versions of *Virasana*. Of course many poses work on several Elements, and we must not forget that indeed, as one flows into the other, they all affect all aspects.

Indeed all is connected in this interconnected web we call cosmos. In it, like within one body, everything has its place and 'way of being'; this inherent way... is cosmic truth; living accordingly is 'walking our talk.' This inherent wisdom is called *Dharma*.

The **Dharma of Earth** could be said is to hold in respect and non-judgement. She fulfils her *dharma* by 'living from the centre' (gravity); from her core she holds us. Being held is a powerful experience that provides essential feelings, from birth to death. How can we learn this 'earthly virtue?' The Earth is the teacher, from her example we learn that we need to 'hold' each being; one way to do that is to listen, truly listen; listen and learn.

One of the most revered ancient Indian Sages was Patanjali, [26] he is referred to as a '*svayambhu*,' this means a soul who specially came to the world to help humanity to understand life and live in a righteous manner. This 'Father of Yoga' collected what was known about Yoga in short and direct phrases in a scripture known as '*the Yoga Sutras*.' They are timeless guidelines for spiritual evolution. In the second Chapter he gives ethical principles for the seeker called Yamas and Niyamas (things we shouldn't do and things we should do). Having contemplated the Elements, we can recognise their energies in the teachings. Often *Yamas and Niyamas* are like two aspects of one topic, such as **non- stealing, (asteya) and contentment**. Non-stealing doesn't simply mean: don't be a thief, but goes much deeper. In non-stealing, it means not taking things that are not ours. What is? Behind this, we recognise the qualities of earth energy: giving and supporting all without wanting anything in return, meaning, being content with what one has got. These earth qualities, we gain, so Patanjali suggests, by controlling our mind and senses. We start with being aware of our motives; let me give you an example:

We get a letter from 'Oxfam' through the door and face the question whether to 'support the needy child?' Reluctantly we put a 'fiver' in the envelope. What are our motives for doing so? Do we do it because we want to support the child, or because we hope to get some merit from it, even if it is that we can tell ourselves (or the neighbours) how generous we were?

Do we ever do things without self-interest? How far does this go? Are we able to look at the neighbour's new car without, in our deepest heart, desiring to have it? Equally, we need to learn to farm our lands in such a way as not to want more and more crops out of the ground. Learn how to be content with what you have. Understand that on the bottom of 'wanting,' is judgement; something is 'more valuable, than what I have,' ' he has a better deal than me,' 'she is more beautiful than my wife, more entertaining, more sexy...' From judgement comes want, from want comes 'stealing!'

The energies also influence our **mental concepts** (such as security, happiness, and knowledge). We already mentioned that people dominated by Earth energy or its lack, have security issues. We can look at it deeper: under the influence of the earth energy, the person experiences the security issue in the context of shelter and a job. Yet for someone influenced by Water, it is concerned with personal beauty and youth. The need for security expressed in the realm of Fire energy, concerns authority and status; a person under the influence of Air energy searches and finds security in the realm of faith, and finally for the Space person, security is looked for in knowledge! [27]

And **knowledge** itself has different states on the path of our evolution into our true human potential. The Bhagavad Gita gives insight into two mental patterns: knowledge and happiness and how they are shaped by the Five Elements.

Accordingly, knowledge 'which clings to one single effect, as if it were the whole, without reason, without foundation in truth and narrow, that is declared to be *Tamasic* (Dull). Single fixed ideas, dull - as in failing to see things as they are, self-important, crystallised, isolation, narrow vision and limited,' is knowledge that belongs to the base energy of Earth. [28]

Happiness is also experienced differently according to its conditioning through the elements. 'That happiness, which arises in our bosom when the appropriate world-of-objects comes in contact with our sense organs, is indeed a thrill that is nectarine at the beginning; but unfortunately it vanishes as quickly as it comes, dumping the enjoyer into a pit of exhaustion... This contact cannot be permanently established, for the objects are always variable... and changing... No man can fully enjoy even the passing glitter of joy that the sense organs give him... (because) it gets unfortunately tainted by an anxiety that it may leave him.' This sense-orientated happiness is thus always 'ere long a tomb of sorrow.' (Holy Gita XVIII/38)

Happiness characterised by the down side of Earth, is here described as happiness where the intellect becomes encrusted with negative values that ruin the personality. Holding and support has turned to stubbornness, is crystallised and frozen in the past. This 'happiness' satisfies mere sense-cravings, which arise, according to the Gita, from sleep (a dull-witted state of 'non-apprehension of Reality'). It stems from indolence (an inertia of the intellect, making the experiencer insensitive to life and people in the presence) and heedlessness, (carelessly avoiding the voices of the higher consciousness), sinking lower and lower into animal nature.[29]

The stages of evolution on the spiritual path are frequently described as '*Kundalini* piercing the *chakra*'; yet the Sanskrit word used is *bheda* which is more like: learning the lesson! The Earth–Element (and its associated chakras and energy bodies) invites us to 'learn a lesson!' The topic of the **Earth's lesson is 'Who am I?'** Am I simply this physical body? Of course as long as we 'know the answer' there is no point in answering the question. But start questioning the conditioned assumption: 'Earth' starts asking: Who are you? What is your dharma?

To find who we really are, to find our centre is the question that has occupied wise people throughout. Teachers from Buddha to Christ, from Mohammed to the Dalai Lamas, from Shamans to therapists and psychologists, rishis and yogis all unite in asking **us this central question of our existence. Who are you?** What is your centre? [30] Many paths of varying shades, countries and traditions have been suggested to solve this question. There are probably as many, paths as there are people. We can choose to follow a path that others have walked or try to find our own, yet answer we must! Indeed many would agree that this is the reason why we exist at all, the ultimate justification for human life: to find our core. Only from there, can we be truly be empowered. The Earth just poses the question, with tolerance, patiently and silently she provides the invitation to simply follow witness her example. Still like a mountain she is just there, stable and contained, resting, withdrawing from all distractions. 'To become like the Earth,' 'to be like a mountain' are metaphors often used in Zen Practices to describe the practice of meditation. 'To just sit,' with no distractions, no doing, just holding awareness of one's Self is in many traditions East and West considered 'the way' to the centre. Because in that silence, another voice can be heard, the voice of the Self, the original me.

The Oracle in Delphi had over its entrance the words 'know thy self.' Plotinius, the prominent Greek philosopher (3rd century) used a very graphic example to describe the job of self-inquiry; we are to look into ourselves and if we don't like what we see, we can be a sculpture; cutting away here, smoothing out there, polishing something here. In this way we can make all that is crooked, straight. He asked us to never stop until 'the godlike splendour of virtue shall shine from you.'

The African Shaman Malidoma Patrica Some writes: 'The centre is both within and without. It is everywhere. But we must realise it exists, find it, and be with it, for without the centre we cannot tell who we are, where we come from and where we are going.' [31]

The American Indians tell us we need to find our own drumbeat inside ourselves, the rhythm of Life that is specific to ourselves, yet fits totally into the drumbeat of mother Earth.

The Ismailii community (Moslem) has a manual (written in Pahlavi; from the 4th century), that contains questions and answers for young people. Everybody over fifteen is supposed to know the answer to these questions: 'Who am I and to whom do I belong?' 'Whence have I come from and whither am I returning?' ' What is my proper calling in earthly existence?' [32]

The Indian Saint Sri Ramana Maharshi, recommended a simple technique of self-inquiry for people regardless of status, gender, religion, or achievement: Just ask yourself. 'Who am I?'

Meditation

Meditation starts with the right posture, having a stable base puts us right in the 'lap and security' of the Earth. From this physical, material stability we can rise to subtler levels. Earth thus by its 'being ' is part of meditation. Once stable and rooted here (in life as well as in posture), the focus changes from the apparent physical, to a higher nature. Gradually one evolves from the more animalistic lifestyle to a more evolved being; this higher nature, this 'Higher Self' is universally recognised as the source for true moral behaviour. Our modern western society seems to have lost this simple truth. We know full well that when people have a sense of self, a point of belonging, of security in themselves, they behave differently. It is hard to imagine somebody lashing out at society, take drugs, hitting an old lady or starting a war if they feel secure, accepted, held and loved within themselves.

We recognise it in ourselves and others, but can we change it? To change others we first have to change ourselves, we have to drink our own medicine; it does not work by proxy.

Listening to the drum of our mother's heartbeat, it is her song that we are.

Chapter Five: Invocation of Water

I am Varuna, the Vedic Lord of the waters who rules the mysterious seas
- whose eye of conscious awareness is in every drop of water
- whose intuition is natural guidance

I am divinity within the waters of the Ganges of every country
I am Tialoc, the water snake of the Mayas,
I am Tiddalic and Gekko the water-beings of the Aboriginals,
I am Dagda of the Celts
I am the TAO, ground of being and non-being

I am the blood of the earth nurturing all living creatures;
- plants and trees gain their progression from me
- fruits and flowers obtain their measure from me
- bodies of bird and beast gain potential through me
- their stripes and markings are made through me

I am these, yet none of the various things is the result of any effort
on my part, my suchness is transparent, I am ten thousand things.

I AM WATER

I am fluid - taking any form - yet still and stagnant;
- changing effortlessly from tiny vaporised particles to the
most grand glacier
- moving gracefully as a ballerina and powerfully as a Sumo wrestler
- following a law unto myself, respecting no political borders
- adapting to water-pipes and sewers alike, unattached
- reflecting the image of the moon even from brackish marshes
- carrying the lotus flower in the muddy Balinese temple lake
- suffocating all life in the swamps of the Everglades
- breeding flies in a stinking puddle in the African village.

I am refreshing, cooling and freezing, deadly
- refreshing rainfall after a scorching summers day
- the ice-crystals that delicately hug the holly leaf
- moisture in the softest moss beside the river's bed
- the cool drink on parched lips of a fevered child
- a pregnant cloud that bursts asunder
- the blizzard that kills, the flood-wave crushing villages
- the ice-cap of the frozen north, endless reservoir of energy
- winter cold paralysing bones and joints with arthritic pain
I am gentle and strong
- the sacred water that washes the lingam

- the nectar the hummingbird drinks in the hibiscus flower
- the vibrations in your ear, the sound of Handel's music
- the slow drip from the ladle in the Zen garden
- the majestic wave that carries the ballast of a lifetime
- the power in the churning electric turbines
- the current carrying Norwegian logs to build a Cornish roof
- seeping into the tiny crack of Ayers Rock, splitting it like dynamite

I am <u>nourishing</u> and <u>draining</u>
- the morning dew that turns seeds into dates in the desert oasis
- the summer rain that swells peas and leeks in an English garden
- inside your bones and in the 'sea of marrow' so you can read this poem
- carrying the salt of the sea, the gold of tradesmen
- draining all life from the salt-pans of the world
- cutting the mountain, carrying him down his slopes
- bleeding out of the soldier, sapping his life's force
- washing the last bit of nutrient out of the table mountain in the Sierra

I am seemingly <u>permanent</u> - then <u>impermanent</u>
- the mist of a November day that hides life's continuity
- the dreams of journeys far away, sailing to distant shores
- the ebb and flow of the ocean for ever moving without goal
- the relentless drip of water in the torture chamber
- the dew on the cherry blossom, symbol of impermanence
- the primeval force of yesterdays whirlpools
- fear of the unknown, of losing oneself
- in the last out-breath of the dying

I am <u>creative</u> and <u>destructive</u>
- the medium for male and female cells to merge
- the cradle of the unborn child
- the paint depicting poppy flowers and the Medusa
- the nectar of the summer ripened peach
- the dampness of a rotting leaf, a decaying corpse
- the flood that drowns the Bangladeshi child
- the heavy water of nuclear fission

I am <u>controlled, guided as well as pent-up and explosive</u>
- the intricate system of reservoirs of Ashkloa's engineers
- arrested by dykes in the flat-lands by the North Sea
- measured in the smallest amounts in syringes in the hospital
- the sea of madness hurling the ship against the cliff
- boiling mud in the Yellowstone Park
- steam rising from the undersea volcano
- the geyser spurting forth through the earth's crust
- the force ejected from a blow hole in Australian

I am <u>crystal clear</u> - yet <u>hidden and deceptive</u>
- the mirror of Narcissus, the master's mind reflecting our ego
- the clear blue sky hidden behind the anthracite clouds
- crystal clear sharpness of an icicle, focusing perception
- the healing power, touching peoples eternal thirst
- the secret behind the unfathomable depths of mind
- the eyes focusing inwards to see the unseen mysteries
- the crushing power in a majestic waterfall
- the sulphur cloud hiding the beauty of Mount Fuji in its stench

I am <u>willful</u> and <u>surrender</u>
- will and determination forcing the floods through the canyon
- relentless unforgiving power carving giant's steps into cliffs
- the push and shove in the crowded subways of Tokyo
- the willpower of the athlete running for a world record
- the compassion and love pouring unlimited through saints
- mutual surrender when two ancestral energy's meet in orgasm
- giving one of my forms for another when I meet fire
- surrendering to the 'watercourse way'

My cycles know neither beginning nor end, balance,
wisdom and equipoise is achieved - by accepting the help of Earth;
    - by giving freely to other life forms
    - by yielding and opening myself to the warmth of Fire
    - by cleansing and replenishing myself through Air
    - by moving, always moving in harmony with all others.

As above so below; as inside so outside; as on the planet so in the body.
As all life is sustained by me, there is no beauty, no paper, no paint,
 no sculpture, no pot made without me; indeed there is no happiness,
no joy without me.

To keep these energies balanced is to keep the body and mind -
Flexible but not without integrity
still without getting stagnant
refreshed without getting frozen
gentle without getting insipid
strong without getting overpowering
nurturing without suffocating
diluting without dispersing
changing without getting lost
creative without getting spent
analysing without dissecting
energised without exploding
guided without being controlled
mindful without being secretive

clear without cutting
determined without being dictatorial
surrendering without annihilation

To keep balanced walk the middle path, attached neither here nor there.
For ultimately the water's nature is to just flow.
It is our mind that judges -
the slowly dripping water,
as a sign of peace in a Zen garden, or
as screaming pain in a torture chamber!

5.1: Contemplation of Water

Water has innumerable aspects. Hildegard von Bingen describes Water as having fifteen powers; 'warmth, wetness, is wavelike, has speed, movement, giving sap to trees, taste to fruit, greenness to vegetation, lubrication to all things, holds birds, feeds the fish, enlivens the animals through its warmth, holds creepy-crawlies coated in mucus and encompasses all.' [33]

This is a charming list, communicating the feeling that nothing exists, that is not touched by water.

Furthermore she uses a wonderful analogy: Water has an enormous treasure: salt – so have we; if we dive deep into ourselves we find consciousness.

What a lovely picture, it reminds one of Buddhist thought, which attributes Water with 'mirror-like wisdom' due to its clarity and depth. Hildegard sees Water as even 'more powerful than fire, because it can extinguish fire'.

Let's get back though to basics. In front of me on my desk, is a glass of water; in it the water is clear, I can see through it, it has no colour of its own. It fills the glass, takes on its shape; if I spill it, it adapts to the shape of the floor (Water adapts to any shape: syringe, bathtub, river, or ocean). It is given form **by that which limits it.** It is so adaptable that it appears as though it gives up its integrity, although it never does.

When the raindrop gives up its existence to become the pool, it remains 'water'; when the dewdrop gives up its existence and becomes the sap of a tree, it still remains 'water.' Our individual lives are like whirlpools in the river; their concentrated energy dances for a while - then continues with the flow of the river - finally pouring itself into the ocean. All the while water is 'playing,' nothing has changed; water **surrenders** its individual form - and yet it remains 'water,' - it merges with the bigger version of what it is already.

This aspect of water has inspired many great thinkers and philosophers to use water as a symbol for all that we are, yet need to become; i.e. Ultimate Reality.

There is a story told about one of the great Christian Sages, St. Augustine. St. Augustine went to the great ocean; he watched some boys playing with cups. He walked over to them and asked them: 'What are you doing?' The boys tried to explain that with their cups, they were trying to empty the ocean. They filled the cup, walked it to the beach and emptied the water onto the sand. They continued their feverish, but fruitless attempt with great diligence. St. Augustine said: "can you not see that your vessels can't contain the vastness of the ocean; you will never succeed in scooping the ocean out, you will have to find a different way!" The boys looked at each other, smiled - and threw their cups into the ocean. Running away happy. The childish prank revealed to St. Augustine, that only by complete abandonment, can one lose oneself in the Absolute. By becoming part of it, we can measure the ocean.

But let's come back to the glass of water in front of me! If I drink this water, it becomes part of me; it fills my veins and cells and I am its container, although not a 'watertight one.' My skin is porous (sweating); my lungs absorb and give out moisture. There is humidity outside me and lots of water (78 %) inside me in various disguises as tissue fluid, blood, lymph, spinal fluid etc. In fact I need to drink this water in order to maintain these fluid levels, in order to stay healthy or even alive. But the water in me is never pure. It not only adapts in shape but also to the needs of the host, i.e. accommodates loads of chemicals (iron, nutrients, minerals etc). Once they dissolve in water we call it: blood, lymph or bile. Equally it carries chemical waste, pollution, acid, even atomic waste. This shows water is so **receptive** that the carrier of life becomes poisonous; it can carry flexibility to its extreme.

This receptivity gives it power. As seawater it contains all other elements and thus it has the power of all of them (which explains the value given to it in some spiritual traditions). It contains the warmth of fire (without it, it would be ice). It also contains some oxygen (air), salts of the earth and, it occupies space. How then does it maintain its integrity?

Its flexibility makes it possible for water to regenerate. For example: after the water has been through my body and fulfilled its function, it leaves me filled with unwanted chemicals. It enters the ground; in earth it lets go again of those substances; deposits them on sand grains. This process of **filtering things** out is a mutual service between earth and water. Water contributes its ability to dissolve anything (good, bad - useful or not - who is the judge)? Then earth accepts the additives which water has transported, and reconstitutes it. The cleansed and rejuvenated water sinks to the deepest points in the earth layer, rests and re-emerges as a spring. This co-operation via gravity is also responsible for the moon regulating the tidal movement of oceans (man and woman might experience these as moods); or physically in our body, these 'tidal waves' can be felt in the sacro-spinal fluid.

Water in the depths of the earth - where rest and cleansing takes place - is likened to the dark night of existence; we might experience fear and depression - or positive regenerative stillness. The 'dark night of the soul' is a metaphor for the nausea of existentialism and despondency described by such authors as Camus and Sartre, or Mystics such as St. Anthony (Egypt, 251-356 AD). His biographer writes about his life in the barren desert, 'He cried, wresting himself from his seat, he leapt up as if to run from the cave, when he gasped - because there they were before him, the dark and twisted forms of demons. Were they women or men or animals? Were they creatures from some unspeakable nether region? He could not tell... ' Only later St. Anthony understood 'let us not contemplate horrors in the soul nor invent fears for ourselves... let's take courage and always rejoice... the enemies' actions correspond to the condition in which they find us, they pattern their phantoms after our own thoughts.' 34

Some other magic happens in the place of rest in the bowels of the earth: water finds other ground water; merging with the company of the like, they rise together as gushing spring, form a brook and nurture flowers! As soon as it is on the surface, Water fulfils its dharma of nurturing plants, life. Soon though, it changes shape again; evaporating through the leaves of the plant, it joins the mist of the early summer day; after dancing in the morning air it falls back into the stream. The stream gets visited by animals, they drink; thus water becomes bird, elephant and mouse. The stream receives water back from the animals and flows on, becoming a river, possibly via the electricity factory, where it becomes part of big turbines. But however many cycles there are to its life, eventually the river pours itself into the ocean – but water's journey is not finished! It merely starts another cycle; it evaporates....

Its adaptability has a purpose; it is the means that makes it possible to nourish others. Thus the second great quality of water is **to nurture**. It is used by others and then returns to reconstitutes itself - only to be used again. No surprise that water is called 'life-sustaining,' 'life-giving' even 'water of life'; due to this quality it is known **as symbol of female energy**, especially in the context of healing.

In Australian Aboriginal myth, female Goddesses or maidens guard the water-hole; they bring and harbour fertility; Ankotarinja, original man, needs to go to the waterhole to discover female beauty and wetness, in order to become 'the other.'

In another myth the Wauwalak sisters come to the well in which Kunapipi, the great mother, lives in the form of the fierce Rainbow-snake. The snake guards the future children who as spirit children live in female waters.

--- Celtic wells (still used in contemporary Britain and Ireland) are connected to female goddesses and later to Christian Saints, for their connection to female healing energy (specially to enhance fertility). Wherever water gushed forth, Anu the great mother of gods is venerated, in whatever guise or name: Bride-well; St, Anne's Well; Brighid or St. Brigid's Well. 35

--- Nymphs and healing springs were common associates in Greece and in Roman history. In the Cult of Asclepius (a great healer), water features, by association with goddesses, nymphs or even a god, became sacred. Even today in rural Greece, people will refuse to take their midday rest by a spring for fear of 'Nereids' or nymphs who might get you 'with child.'

--- In India there are numerous great rivers associated with the female, such as Ganga Mai, the great mother, and the Narmada River. It is said that Shiva was in such strenuous ascetic trance, that rivulets of sweat flowed from him and took on the form of a woman; one moment she was beautiful virgin, the next a dancing girl and even a seductress. This play of female energy amused Shiva so much that he named her Narmada (Delightful One), blessing her with the words: "You shall be forever holy, forever inexhaustible." Then he gave her to the most illustrious of all suitors, the Ocean, Lord of all rivers; she flowed, delightfully sparkling, into her lover's arms. [36]

Another of 'Shiva's locks' is Saraswati. Once a mighty river, today a powerful gurgling stream in the Himalayas, she is revered as eternal knowledge and wisdom. When I visited the little shrine by her waterfall, it was decorated with flowers, honoured by people even though none seemed to live this high in the Himalayas.

Why might wisdom be associated with Water?

Many, since ancient times thought that Water has memory! Today, the most known version of this is Homeopathy. Medicine - thought to cure illness - is diluted to such an extent, that no original molecule of the 'ingredient' is still there, yet 'Water retains its memory and heals with it.' Flower Remedies also give testimony to this. Edward Bach (1934), wrote, ' The action of these remedies is to raise our vibrations and open up our channels for the reception of the Spiritual Self, to flood our natures with the particular virtue we need, and wash out from us the fault that is causing the harm.' [37]

In 1988 the French scientist Ben Benvenista (and later Prof. M. Ennis), apparently proved that water takes up the knowledge of the medicine. Are the ancients right that water has memory? The quality of water to retain subtle knowledge is used in other ways too. Some mix salt into it for purification rites, light candles or burn incense while reciting formulas or mantras over water, claiming that water retains the 'spirit of it and should be greeted with great love and respect. Others ask the 'Angel of water' for blessing before it is drunk. This might seem 'way out,' but people like Gigi Capriolo (Cosmos Centre in Milan) support this; he assures that the waters of the Ganges, the Jordan and the well at Lourdes have the special holy vibration. As for being associated with femininity, look at the Hebrew words (writing uses no vowels) for feminine; 'nekevah,' and waterhole 'nikbah,' are almost identical words!

The Bulgarian born, French spiritual master Omraam Mikhael Aivanhov, (1900-1986) writes: 'Water is the mother of Life and we owe it gratitude and respect.... Water is sustaining, nourishing... Water is love... Let the Water flow... Fire starts with dry organisation, water starts with love....' [38]

But, you might say, water is not all only peaceful, soft, gentle, receptive and nurturing - water has also great strength and at times turns it into violence; how about excessive monsoon rains, killer floods, terrible freak waves etc. Water can carry the greatest boulders downstream! Sea levels rise and drown whole islands and continents, rivers cut enormous canyons to follow their course with unbending will and drive to get to the ocean. Rain wears down the highest mountain. Yes, and because of these aspects, water is associated with **willpower and the strength of discipline**. Here is the root of the metaphorical saying that drops of the softest water will in time wear down even the hardest stone. Water just does not give up! Why? **Its drive to fulfil its dharma** is unerring: it has to get to the next level in order to take the water to the sea, come what may. And if something is in the way, water works at it until it gets through; water, one could say, has great **determination**.

As often in life, good qualities have a down side. The danger of being adaptable is that others think they can make you their doormat! Adaptability is praised by those who want you to adapt to their ways!!! The teacher wants his pupils to adapt to classroom discipline. The ruler wants his citizens to adapt to his laws, the husband wants his wife to adapt to his lifestyle, the women wants her man to adapt to her ways of looking after the children - we often confuse adaptability with obedience or even conformity. To adapt to a situation or to requirements, or even likes and dislikes of another is to conform to the will of others; this is a common mistake under which 'Water suffers.'

A person with similar characteristics to water might well enter a relationship as a joyous creative, intelligent individual. As she adepts, to her husbands interest in football (film of crime and punishment/motor races etc.) wanting to be 'a good sport,' she gradually neglects her own interest (i.e. playing the piano).

This adaptation to the real or fictitious needs of others can reach much more serious consequences than the unwanted watching of football games. As she adapts to the husband's rhythm of day, his needs for intimacy, his needs for 'cups of tea,' his needs for socialising etc... the 'Water person' slowly might lose access to her identity. If she does not wake up and regenerate, tragedy might set in. Adaptability is helpful, but like so many things also potentially fraught with difficulties. You might want to contemplate on these questions: when does adaptability become dissolution of the self? When does adaptability lead to senseless conformity?

One of the **creative aspects of adaptability** is at the root of many myths about **shape-shifting.** It is referring to the ability to reinvent oneself, but we go beyond this in shamanic traditions. There, a human is considered able to retain intelligence and memory yet take on animal forms to defeat a certain situation, or attain a certain quality. Man becomes beast, frog becomes prince, Lords turn into stags, wizards turn into eagles etc. In Celtic lore, the Irish hero Tuan (St. Finnian of Morvilla) becomes a stag, a wild boar, a hawk and a salmon until he is born with full memory of all his previous existences - making the point that one lives in order to gather knowledge.

King Arthur is taught by Merlin to be a badger and a hawk, in order to learn tenacity and patience. Mongan, in the Book of Fermoy, takes up shapes of animals in water, land and air in order to learn the qualities of each element. [39]

The famous ballet 'Swan Lake,' is based on the Celtic legend of Aengus mac Os, the god of love and youth who falls into profound lovesickness, until he discovers that his love is Caer Iborneith, who spends most of her time in the shape of a swan. Through magic music he learns to take her shape in order to woo her.

The Celtic word for 'shape-shifting' is tuirgin: a fluid transition from one form into another (Cormac's Glossary). In a deep state of meditation we experience such transition into 'the fourth dimension,' a reality beyond the ordinary perception - the word for this state in Sanskrit is *turiya*, the words are uncannily similar.

This ability to transcend enables Water people to feel into other people, making them great healers and carers, enabling them to look at situations 'from a different perspective.' A Water person finds it easy say, to identify with the 'timidity of a mouse' and look at a problem from the perspective of the 'mouse.' She can feel the pain of a broken limb of a child, as though it happens to her own limb. She can 'shift consciousness' into the other and 'see' what they require, be it a medicine or empathy. Others, at times, might experience this gift as meddling, interference; yet I feel this 'empathy of water' is not due to projecting personality (meddling), rather to the ability of suspending one's own personality; that takes courage and training.

I heard a lovely little story: There is this little stream and it flows happily along, then it comes to a stretch of desert: " I am so afraid, if I get on with my journey, I will be absorbed by the sand." So the sands whispers, "Don't worry, just change yourself, and jump into the arms of the wind." But the fear has a tight grip on the little river; as its worry of absorption by the sand increases, it takes courage and jumps into the air, changing its shape into vapour. The wind comes and picks it up and carries it gently across the desert; at the end of the desert, at a mountain top, the wind carefully puts down the water and as it rains down, the stream resumes its course.

The stream needed to overcome its fear of losing itself, then it could shift its shape: and this is the key for continuing life's purpose. It could not have done it if it had clung to its personality. Like the stream, one has to put aside the previous shape, so that from the point of nothingness, of pure emptiness, or pure clear water one can perceive the other, unclouded by one's own personality.

This clarity, that is free from all colour, all movement, all past and present, **this crystalline clarity of still water**, talks of absence of shape or form – it is a stillness or emptiness filled with potential; being 'without shape' gives the freedom to take any shape.

This is a marked difference to the generosity of earth giving space and time to the other - **water becomes the other;** on a physical level, water becomes food, on the psychological and spiritual level, becomes the teaching.

All very well, you might say, but we live in a highly industrialised society, with high crime-rates, disrupted families, pollution, overpopulation, aggressive kids, competitive and exploiting business and more. How can being adaptable, nurturing and flexible help us in our high tech, daily lives? Here is another story:

An aggressive eleven-year old school child has frequently been reprimanded for disruptive class behaviour, but to no avail. He has even been noted for bullying. His work too, leaves much to be desired. When the parents are called in for consultation, they seem not to mind his low marks, ' he is stupid anyway, as long as he does his best, it's OK with us.' They also describe aggressive behaviour at home.

Imagine one of the teachers is a 'Water person.' She observes that in Karl's artwork he uses bold brushwork and dark colours, he does not like details. In English lessons, she notices that his reading, writing and spelling are way below average. She also notices that he gets aggravated when observed; he cannot cope with attention.

The first thing the teacher does is to give him space; she gives him little jobs to do where he can be alone, such as looking something up in the dictionary; mixing some special paints etc. Sometimes she joins him, so they can be 'private.' This way he isn't exposed and feels secure enough to make remarks about his family, how the rooms are so crowded, that he never has time or space to do anything because his brothers and sisters are always doing something or having the TV on or...

Putting herself into such living conditions, the teacher senses that in order to have privacy, he shuts off, then, disturbed in his 'cocoon,' he becomes angry and aggressive, a 'hedgehog syndrome.' Having identified his problem, the teacher can then take measures to nourish him.

She gives him bigger, solitary assignments and encourages other teachers to do the same. As the boy seems to enjoy that, he is offered the chance to do his homework in the office of the school secretary, where no one will bother. His work becomes cleaner and better, and no more bullying is reported.

Obviously the school could do nothing to improve his home situation, but by giving him what he needed his behaviour and achievements improved. The teacher acted in the 'way of water:' what is the difference to other Elements?

Earth would have safely held him in the place where he was, a low achiever, accepted it, and made it OK. to be one.

Air would have, in a very rational manner, drawn the conclusion that he needed boundaries to curb his behaviour - and if that did not work, he would have to be moved else where, a different group, school, neighbourhood etc.

Fire would have responded to anger with anger and punished him to drive 'the rebellious spirit out.'

Space would have given him the opportunity to join the sports team, because plenty of activity might get rid of his aggressive, surplus energy and 'tire him out.'

The 'Way of Water' speaks for itself!

5. 2: Associations with the Water Element

We have seen many universal attributes associated with the Water Element. These express in three interacting energy s: body, mind and soul.

5.2: a) Complementary Medicine is where most of these associations are used. First let us look though, at the function of the anatomical organs that are attributed to the Water Element: the bladder (*Yang*) and kidney (*Yin*).

The Kidneys lie just below the diaphragm, on either side of the spine; the right kidney is slightly lower than the left, the right one being closer to the liver, the left one to the spleen, stomach and pancreas. Kidneys are 'bean shaped,' about eleven centimetres long, six wide and three centimetres thick.

The kidney's function is to synthesise urine in three stages, simple filtration, selective re-absorption and secretion. The kidney consists mainly of about a million units called nephrons, some tubules and blood vessels that end in knot-like bunches of tiny blood vessels. Through their semi-permeable walls, water and small molecules pass; blood cells, plasma and other large molecules remain. This remainder is altered in the tubules and what the body can use is reabsorbed, the rest is passed on to a collecting tubule. The process of re-absorption is regulated by hormones (e.g. anti-diuretic hormone, aldosterone etc). The secreted matter (urine) is a complex product that consists of 96% water plus unwanted chemicals, such as ammonia, potassium, chlorides etc.

A large amount of water is taken into the body. Intake and output are controlled by the kidneys (messages send from the hypothalamus via anti-diuretic hormones, released in the pituitary gland). A feedback mechanism registers when the osmotic pressure is raised and instigates decrease or increase of fluids. Thus the **filtering** process of the kidney regulates concentration of various substances in normal limits.

The kidneys also keep an electrolyte balance within the body's water by regulating the sodium intake; sodium is in almost all foods, thus we take in more than we need. Its secretion is constantly monitored by the hormone aldosterone secreted by the adrenal glands. They sit directly on top of the kidneys and produce adrenalin and non-adrenalin, responsible for the **'fight or flight'** response in times of stress. This means they increase or decrease the metabolic rate, dilate or contract the bronchioles (allowing more or less air in); they instigate the constriction or dilation of blood vessels etc. in order to prepare for fight, or conversely for relaxing and withdrawing. Via this process, kidneys and adrenals are associated with fear.

The kidneys' main involvement seems to be **keeping balance.** They clean and detoxify the body in order to keep a balance of nutrients. We know the liver detoxifies and by comparison the kidney's role is more one of 'sorting' things.

The Bladder is a 'reservoir' for urine in the pelvic cavity and its size and position vary, depending on the amount of urine it contains. From it the urethra leads to the exterior world. Autonomic nerve fibres in the bladder wall trigger the micturation reflex in the brain. Micturation occurs when the wall of the bladder contracts and the internal and external sphincters are relaxed.

The main character trait of the **bladder is its adaptability**. It gathers and then releases. In a metaphorical sense we can relate this to emotions. Every new beginning is preceded by two phases; the cleaning out of the old and - letting it go! A vessel has to be empty to be filled. Old emotions, be they hurt, pride, anger, fear or rejection, have to be collected and then let go.

As we know, these organs are connected to an energy , we call **Organ-Network**; here the meridians feed and support the organs. The Water Element is represented by two such networks: the Bladder (BL) and Kidney (KI) Meridians, a system that further refines digested materials. Together they purifying all bodily fluids, thus releasing energy.

Location of the Bladder Meridian (BL):: This meridian starts bilaterally in the inside corner of the eye, over the top of the head, either side of the spine, down the back of the legs to the outside of the foot and ends on the nail bed of the little toe.

BL relates to the autonomic nervous system (close to the spine) through to the pituitary gland. It controls the reproductive functions and the uterus as well as urinary organs (collecting and excreting liquid waste). It co-operates with the kidney. The bladder is the seat (storehouse) of the emotions. If it is not functioning well, then the rest of system is stressed. [40]

Location of the Kidney Meridian (Ki): Starting in the centre of the sole of the foot, this meridian runs along the inside of the foot to the ankle, then upwards passed the inside knee and thigh to the pelvis and along the front - along the chest to the clavicle. A branch goes off along the inside of the arm, ending in the palm on the pad of the little finger.

Ki filters the blood, keeping the blood and the body, clean and balanced. The water level and the acid base balance are both maintained by the kidneys. Kidneys regulate bodily fluids.

In the Chinese system, the kidneys are seen as storing the energy of the life force (Chi) itself. The kidneys house ancestral energy and if chronic illness is present, one should look at this energy. Willpower and the adaptability to stress are signs of good kidney energy.

In Ayurveda, these Organs and their network constitute the dosha *Kapha;* here Water and Earth relate to the most physical existence. Water provides cohesion for the other elements (the body consists of 78% water). The basis of blood, lymph, endocrine fluids, urine, cerebral spinal fluid, sweat, saliva, tears, sexual secretions, breast milk - all are of course water. Imbalance in any of these leads to disruption in our finely tuned energy system and could result in any manner of symptoms, such as creaking dry joints, dryness and thirst, too frequent or too little micturation or a build up of chemicals etc. On a mental and emotional level, if there is no fluidity in our thought processes and emotions, unexpressed emotions accumulate and we become swamped with emotions; a general feeling of drowning produces all manner of fears. Conversely, we can 'dry up' and wither, become brittle and uncaring, irritated and frustrated. Cystitis might result, (irritation of the urinary system).

Overall, the essence of **the Water Element (and its meridians) is to keep things flowing and balanced.** This balance is aptly described by Cormac - the Irish equivalent of Solomon:

'Be not too wise, nor too foolish,
be not too conceited, nor too diffident,
be not too haughty, nor too humble,
be not too talkative, nor too silent,
be not too hard, nor too feeble
for: If you be too wise, one will expect too much of you,
if you be foolish you will be deceived,
if you be too conceited, you will be thought vexatious,
if you be too humble, you will be without honour,
if you be too talkative, you will not be heeded,
if you be too silent, you will not be regarded,
if you be too hard, you will be broken,
if you be too feeble, you will be crushed.' [41]

Water's quality of cohesion (keeping things together) manifests in yet a different way. Along the Bladder meridian (at the back) are special points, which are directly connected to the function of organs. These 'Yu-points' are related to the sympathetic nervous system, and in the sacrum, to the parasympathetic nervous system; these are used effectively to influence many different illnesses. The Nei Ching calls the Bladder meridian 'a magistrate of a region or a district controlling the overflow and fluid secretions which have to regulate vaporisation.' [42] Like a river who has many tributaries, he reaches the furthest corner and influences life in the most distant village.

Earlier we mentioned that the two kidneys have slightly different locations. In Chinese Tradition the function of the right and left kidney are associated with differing concepts. The right kidney carries our ancestral energy; its energy is dependent on your ancestors (genetic). It implies there is *a given* quantity and quality of energy, which *is not easy to replenish;* it is vital to conserve it by an adequate lifestyle. For example, a depleted Kidney energy from a mother (via illness or addiction), will be passed on as a low Kidney energy to a child. Since the Kidney energy is related to the endocrine system, which influences nearly all body systems, being born with such a weak energy will then affect the person's life.

Further associations with the Organ-network for Water

The Cycle: The movement of life is never still; this flow is responsible for the cyclic nature of energy. However, different energies perform optimally at different times; the **times for the Water Element** are split into two sections. The peak functioning time for the Organ-network of the bladder is from three to five p.m.; for the Organ-network of the kidney it is from five to seven p.m. On the other hand, the time of minimum functioning of the Bladder energy is from three to five a.m.; and respectively the time of minimum functioning for the Kidney energy is from five to seven a.m.

A person with the main characteristics of a Water person, might be aware of their peak energy time in the afternoon, and their lowest energy time in the very early hours of the morning (when most people are asleep; getting up early could present a problem). Conversely a Water person with weak Kidney energy would probably notice a lack of energy in late afternoon.

The Season related to Water is winter. Winter is the time of gathering, of drawing inwards to reflect in preparation for new growth. Water draws together, condenses, crystallises and as such it becomes an icy river or glacier, where what rests (from its flow) until melting time comes in spring. If one pictures the arctic continent or the eternal snow on mountain ranges like the Himalayas or Andes, one realises the power inherent in this quiet state of reflection. Even in its lesser form, the stillness of a winter's day, this is frequently associated with the stillness we call death. Yet death is nothing but a similar transitory state; now water is ice, now it flows; now the vessel has been emptied, soon it is filled with new energy for new growth. This is reincarnation.

Especially old people are frightened by the thought of this transition. Partly because of a tendency to ponder an 'unfulfilled, painful life'; they attach themselves to memories thereof and then stay either alone, isolating themselves in hopelessness or try to escape their thoughts by constant distraction. To prepare for the winter of their own life and death is so frightening to some that they need endless rounds of meaningless socialising, bingo, games etc.

Young, active people also sometimes fall prey to the same imbalance. They too need 'winter' to contemplate what is happening in their life. But all too often they drown themselves in endless rounds of parties, deafening music, even drugs – this is imbalance in the flow of Water. Such imbalances are easily recognisable, because people (young or old) positively dislike winter. Aloneness and introversion frightens them. This is vastly different from the seclusion of a contemplative who despite apparently withdrawing, stays alert and connected albeit on a subtle level.

The cold of emotional winter can lead to extremes. Ice is not just a beautiful storehouse of future energy, it has also inherent danger; slices of ice are cuttingly sharp, and used wrongly, can be weapons that kill - just like a knife. Ice is brittle and breaks, potentially drowning a person. Where isolation of winter has created such sheets of dry ice, such 'brittle-ness,' there is danger of becoming manic or insane. People who completely withdraw into a calcified state of themselves, pondering on nothing but the past, fate and isolation become depressed; they have a dangerous Water – imbalance.

The Direction associated with Water is north and spreading outward.

After the above, and considering our latitude, the north has similar associations as winter. We speak of the 'frozen north,' freezing winds come from the north bringing cold. People who suffer from the cold, who feel it more than to be expected, or people who are completely out of touch with their bodies and do not feel it at all, are showing an imbalance in the Water Element.

The north is also known for its especially crisp, clear light. The aurora borealis is another, well known occurrence of special light. Standing at the most northern point of Europe, at the North Cape (Honigsveg, Norway) the majestic stillness, a feeling of limitless expansion and watching shimmering light seemingly reflected in light, is unforgettable. And yet the North is also associated with darkness, long nights, dark feelings, long suffering, dark emotions and the fear of the unknown.

Somewhere in the stillness of our very being, we experience the two sides of life, the special light of consciousness and the darkness of material existence. This ability could be the reason why in the American Indian tradition, the north is the location of ancient knowledge, sacred knowledge and the wisdom of the Elders.

Winter and the long nights of the north have another thing in common: there is nothing we can do about it! We might prefer sunshine, daytime, or... or... but cannot change it. We simply need to trust that one day spring will come, one day light will rise, one day, day will break, one day the suffering will be over. Here Water energy relates to our **ability to trust (or not).** The fruit of trust is **a healthy detachment:** one doesn't get bogged down by details and circumstances, but knows all will change! With trust and detachment Water invites us to simply 'Be.' Being is total integrity with who you are; at any time water is totally itself yet totally willing to change – being is imbibing this state of waters, being ready any moment to change shape, to flow with what comes. This quality is why water is associated with **spreading outward.** Water can flow in any direction.

The Climate related to Water is, not surprisingly, cold. Many illnesses are created by cold or made worse by cold. Many arthritic problems are, for example, made a lot worse in cold weather - pains increase, joints stiffen. But when we speak of a 'cold person,' we are not thinking of their body temperature, we are thinking of people who are unable or unwilling to express human warmth. A mother who lacks the ability to hug, touch, warm and cuddle her child has an imbalance in Water. Many people in our society live a stressful, self-orientated life, taking no time to care much about the suffering of others. Their own stress - their aggravated kidneys and adrenals, - stop them from caring. One could say modern societies have a Water imbalance.

The Tissues or parts of the body in Chinese tradition associated with Water are bones and bone marrow. At first glance this seems surprising, what can the most fluid element have in common with the most solid part of the body? Bones, teeth, skull and the vertebrae, all are built with ever changing cells! We are a slow river; Chinese tradition even describes the brain as a 'sea of marrow.'

Icicle have a dense crystal structure, 'frozen water' is strong enough to allow a plane to land on it; similarly bones are able to sustain quite some pressure. Injury to our bones (broken bones) is said to relate to our innermost core.

There is, however, a more 'scientific' reason for this unlikely seeming alliance; the kidneys monitor the calcium levels! Osteoporosis can be linked to an imbalance in the Kidney meridian.

However in Ayurveda and Tibetan medicine, bones are classified as of the Earth Element, it seems somehow more apt.

The Sense organ connected to the Water Element is the ear, **the sense** is hearing. Apparently the first sense to develop in an embryo, while he lives in water, is hearing. Many cases of children being born with an awareness or skill that they must have heard while in utero are known. But the importance of this organ and function for the entire development of the human being has only come recently to attention through the work of Professor A. Tomatis. [43]

The ability to hear in, or rather, under water is never quite lost; the process of hearing itself, is dependent on a liquid in the ear (perilymph in the bony labyrinth of the inner ear). Symptoms like nausea, dizziness, balance problems and tinitus, point to an imbalance in the Water Element.

The Orifices associated with Water energy are the genitalia and anus. Healthy procreation depends on the condition of egg and sperm, both are cells that consist and are surrounded by water; these two meet in liquid. The condition of the ovaries and the scrotum are also related to the Water Element. The sexual act itself is dependent on fluids, so difficulties such as impotence, frigidity, infertility, illnesses of the uterus, low sperm count etc. are all linked to the Water Element.

The anus is the orifice that releases faeces which is, despite its solid appearance, 60 to 70% water, making the link to the Water Element understandable. Its activity of releasing can be linked to the character of the Bladder-organ network.

The Fluid especially noted for Water energy is urine; its service is cleansing. It is the body's agent for removing unwanted substances. The psyche too has to be cleaned constantly of unwanted emotions; stored feelings that have become useless need to be disposed of. Urine infections, (imbalances in the composition of the urine etc.) can point to an imbalance in the Water meridian. Similarly poisonous relationships, unexpressed accumulated emotions and irritation with life itself point the same way, as we aptly express, when we say: 'I'm pissed off'!

The External Physical Manifestation of Water is head hair. The condition of the hair, be it dry, split, fine, silky, curled, strong, receding, falling out or untimely greying, hair gives an indication to the state of the Water Element (disregarding, of course, racial characteristics). If the kidneys are weak, they are unable to provide energy for the furthest extension of the body. If the hair is healthy and full of bounce - so are the kidneys; if the hair is broken, lifeless, so are the kidneys; if the hair falls out, we have a warning sign that the kidneys are in trouble (i.e. chemotherapy)

Heavy metals are difficult for the kidneys to clean from the body, in fact they poison it, thus they are injurious to hair. Similarly, prolonged emotional stress, affecting the adrenals and the kidney, also could cause hair loss.

The Colour of Water is blue. It seems most obvious, but contemplate: Yes, the sea and the still lake seem blue, but water itself is clear; it reflects the colour of others. A sea is blue because it reflects the sky (when the sky is grey, the sea is grey); on a glorious evening at sunset, the sea will be golden or even red.

Psychologically, another point is worth mentioning. Water and light seem intimately connected, but water is not the sky! It is not Ultimate Reality, however apt the metaphors. Water only reflects the sky; it must learn humility. This is very significant especially on its spiritual path. [44] Water might be close to the ultimate Truth, but without humility it falls prey to illusions of grandeur, a form of insanity.

In all manner of traditions, blue is used to depict divinity. The Virgin Mary wears a blue coat; Shiva, Krishna and other gods are depicted with blue bodies or garments; Saints and God himself are depicted with a blue (or gold) radiance; mystics testify that the divine energy they saw was blue, the blue pearl of divine consciousness.

If a person has a strong like or dislike for the colour blue it might point to an imbalance in the Water meridian.

The Smell associated with the Water Element is putrid. When water stands for a long time and matter decomposes in it, it has a special stink; swamps have this unmistakable foul odour. If we can detect this smell easily on a person - then we can safely assume that, that person has a problem in the Water Element. It could be that the kidney can't remove all the debris or the urine stays too long in the bladder; either leads to rotting. The flow of the Water energy needs to be increased, so that the body will get washed more easily.

The Taste related to Water is salty. The river's tributaries have washed all the minerals, including salt, out of the earth and poured it into the sea. The sea is salted water. Too much salt in the water results in killing all life (Dead Sea and Lake Eyre). To maintain the right salt balance in the body is the task of the kidney - and also of the person. We can help the kidney by regulating our salt intake; a little salt stimulates the kidney, too much is harmful, putting stress on the kidneys. Most vegetables contain natural salts, it is therefore unlikely we get too little salt - but too much, happens easily. Excessive salt consumption can show up as darkness underneath the eyes, which denotes the state of the kidneys.

Hildegard von Bingen is quite explicit about several aspects of salty water. She mentions for instance that they 'restore the health because they take the putrid smell and rottenness of the body juices away like a soothing balm' but if we go overboard and drink this 'cleaning fluid' where there is nothing to clean, it results in ulcers. [45]

The Grain associated with the Water energy is beans and peas. **The Fruit** is dates. **The Meat** is pork. **The Vegetable** is the leek.

In individual cases, it may be appropriate to eat more or less of these if the person's intake is unbalanced. As for the recommendation to eat pork? Many cultures refrain from eating pork because the pig is an animal that reputedly absorbs toxins faster than other animals! Bad for the kidneys! On the other hand there are cultures where pork is the only meat addition to the diet, for example the Igorots of the Philippines, a strong, healthy tribe; but then their pigs are fed on water hyacinths and nettles, grown in pure mountain air!

There is however another level to look at this issue. The pig in many cultures, such as Greek, Latin, Egyptian etc. was related to motherhood and specifically to the uterus. It is referred to as the symbol of Demeter's fertility, and it is even stated 'goddesses are all great white, round maternal sows' (Ishtar, Isis, Demeter etc). [46] Tibetan Buddhism refers to one aspect of the female energy (dakini principle) as Vajra Varahi, the 'Diamond Sow,' or the 'Indestructible Sow.'

In the Chinese horoscope, the Pig is described as innocent, gullible, trustful, honest, pure, sincere, devoted, easily taken advantage of by others, sensitive and a victim, an astonishing correspondence of the characteristics of a Water person.

The Expression associated with Water is groaning. We are looking at the subconscious undertone of a voice, a sound that is almost as if the speaker is under water, drowned, in emotions and fear. Obviously if this sound is very obvious, the person might suffer from an imbalance in the Water Element.

The Sound is that of rushing; when a water person enters a room with too much of that energy, it feels like a pipe has just burst and energy flows bubbling here and there, rushing out in great gushes.

The Attitude associated with Water is the need for stimulus; it needs a task.

The Movement of Energy is one of starting up to rush. All these relate to a sudden burst of energy, the image of somebody suddenly getting out of a chair, and with a burst of energy proclaiming that they need to go to the cinema (party, book-fair, whatever) right now! The energy flow has been held by a dam and suddenly is freed. The Water person needs the stimulus of the next project, the next fulfilling idea or the next job to expand his interest; they are forever pushing themselves.

By contrast, a balanced Water person has a steady energy flow, calmly considering and following the direction that needs to be explored at the moment.

The Quality associated with Water is Will. The will is related to discipline; we need not only willpower to do things, but the discipline and clarity to carry it out. Only if we have both can we achieve our aim. Without discipline, or rather self-discipline, the will grows despotic and not only tyrannises others, but can harm.

A child ruling the whole family by its wants and wills, displaying bad temper as soon as something is denied him/her, puts a lot of strain on the family. Furthermore the child's expectations of what life 'should give it,' become false. Water might want to flow into a certain direction, but unless there are boundaries that guide its energy, all it achieves is 'going all over the place.' It floods the landscape.

To reach their aim, a Water person needs limitations, self-imposed boundaries, rituals, routines, in order to go where they want to go. In other words, they have either self-discipline - or they need discipline from the outside! This discipline, like the stimulus, is energy other than its own. The danger is that the person might become dependent on such outside discipline, even become subject to the will of others, and become a victim.

Will has the great task to guide the person to the fulfilment of their destiny. This includes the will needed to get up and start again after a knock, a traumatic event or any number of devastating experiences. On the other hand, the ultimate challenge for the Water person is to surrender its own will, deliberately and willingly to the divine, but that is a topic too complex at this point.

Suffice it to say that Water has the quality that is needed for the river of our life to reach the sea; whether a person has the determination and will, remains to be seen.

The Activity of Water is 'scanning.' **The Condition** is one of withdrawal into one's own depth and isolation, either to recoup one's energy and replenish it, or in order to run away and hide. The danger for the Water person is obviously one of isolation or of skimming over the surface, gathering fleeting impressions.

Again lets look at the special **brain activity under the influence of Water energy.** One area where the influence is more prominent (or lacking) is in the lower frontal lobes, where the sensory input for taste is processed; this co-operates with the limbic brain, especially the amygdala. Remember how an acid taste often accompanies fear! Increased activity in the amygdala is noticed in people prone to fears; traumatic memory is stored here; these people also might suffer from a tug of war inside themselves, whether to be extrovert - or withdraw.

When Water energy builds up beyond tolerance it takes on a typical **form of Aggression,** i.e. floods result, drowning what is in their wake. As Water energy is by nature emotive, more of the same is likely to drown the person in their own feelings of negativity; i.e. they become depressed. Here aggression is primarily directed against oneself – people might feel suicidal.

The Relationship of Water to the other Elements has been mentioned throughout. Following the Chen-Ko Cycle of Chinese tradition Metal/**Air gives birth to Water**; it might become obvious when we look at the chemical formula: Water has two parts of Oxygen to one part of Hydrogen.

In terms of the human body, the lung energy, *prana* (air) nourishes kidney energy, thus there is a direct link between these two energies and if the energy of the lungs does not descend to the kidneys, these starve and illness results. The relationship is one of nurturing.

Water is controlled by Earth: she can stem its flow. If earth does not fulfil its service to Water it causes chaos: here is an example. I remember such occasion: As a youngster I lived near the mouth of the river Elbe in a marshland. Either side of the river about a mile inland, were earth mounds ('dykes') to protect the village from the regular floods, which happened every spring and autumn. My family home was on the 'dry side' of the dyke. One spring moon the storms excelled themselves, the river rose much higher than usual. It kept rising into the night and then rose even more. Men were called in, lorries with sandbags were brought to fill any holes and to raise the level of the dyke; the water gurgled in the darkness with foreboding. Then sirens went off; the radio broadcast "water still rising." Eventually the water reached the top of the four meters high dyke: "Evacuate now!"

Sometime later the floodwaters won, a few hundred yards from our home the dyke burst - its gurgling powerful fingers ploughed up the land and rushed into the houses. The village had turned into sea; when the water subsided we found cows, animals and some people had died in the treetops. This example shows that when water loses its limitations; when Earth can't contain it, it becomes a destructive force.

For the human body this means that Stomach and Spleen energy, balance and limit the kidney and bladder (energy); if the former is depleted it will be the kidneys that suffer; their energy dissipated, bladder energy (emotions) goes 'all over the place.' The power of this destruction is only equalled by Fire.

The Abbess from the 12th Century pays great attention to the relationship of **Water and Fire**, and some of her observations are extremely inspired. Thus she notes 'the sun draws the inherent warmth out of the Water' sort of bringing it to the surface. (It is a bit like *yin* is inherent in *yang*); when combined with wind 'the Water rises like Fire' (hurricanes, typhoons, etc). [47] Fire is seen inherent in the fluidity of Water (without warmth, it would be ice).

In a metaphorical sense this comes to an interesting point. Water can reflect Fire (the setting sun reflected on a calm sea, making the ocean 'sun-bright.' Water thus can be like a mirror for the sun, enhancing the purest qualities of its arch-opposite. If the relationship is one of inspiration, the arch-opposites, fire and water, might enrich each other.

And finally, **Water and Space;** according to the Chen-Ko Cycle Water gives birth to Space/Wood. Taking Wood as the apt metaphor, one look into nature is sufficient to see why; as for Space? Without limits Water 'goes all over the place' - so does Space - even form (matter) only *appears* to limit Space. Sometimes it seems as though space and water on a subtle level only differ in degree, not in essence. In this context: Water goes all over the 'place' – Space is all over!

5.2: b) Association with Personality and Relationships (Psychology)

Before we focus on a person dominated by Water energy, let us look at a few psychological issues: **The Emotion** traditionally associated with Water is fear. The connection of the kidneys with endocrine glands (flight or fight response), especially the amygdalla, where fear and resulting trauma is stored, makes this obvious. The Nei Ching says that too much fear hurts the kidneys (including phobias). Even states of negative premonitions and a diffuse fear of life and the unknown are included here. Why? All fears stem from losing one's sense of self, one's personal boundaries; ultimately the ego tries to hold on to what it is. It constantly opposes change – this poisons the nature of water. Fear is like a paralysed sphincter that cannot let go of the urine and the vessel is not emptied. The illusion is that by holding onto the old, nothing new can come in, but by necessity it does! The river of life flows on regardless; in the extreme, fear becomes panic, one suffocates into despair, deep depression, even paranoia.

Just as fear is associated with Water, so is **fearlessness**. If Water energy is balanced, in tune with its own truth, change is accepted. Fear is absent.

The Manner in times of excitement or change is trembling, an obvious expression of fear. Why do we tremble? Fear makes us contract to protect ourselves. Contraction builds tension, which is naturally released by trembling. If a person trembles excessively or habitually, it indicates a problem. Trembling in people can be caused by various nerve diseases, especially those of the motor nerves, for nerve impulses cause serial contraction of motor units in a muscle, as each unit contracts. If there is any fault in the minute structures of the endings of the autonomic nervous system, trembling results. Since the bladder meridian is linked to the autonomous nervous system, the link to imbalances in Water energy is clear.

Let's look at a person characterised by Water qualities; someone with the ability to feel into other and to heal: a country doctor (or a midwife), are good examples. We are meeting him when he is in his early fifties, having served the community already for a long time. He has been able to help cure many patients and has been of immense support in emotional crisis, 'nourishing people.' He has done his job with love and great commitment; he has stuck to his ideals of serving even when it was not easy. But he is a man who can put his own needs aside, and can control his emotions well; his feelings, worries and anxieties never interfere; he is fully present for his patients and deal with their problems in an even and gentle manner.

His gentleness can not hide his clarity and directness, which some might interpret as coolness or even aloofness. Yet it is more a case of being able to focus with clear intent on his patients. He is a hard worker, who will always be there for his patients, always pushing himself, whether snow or flood he 'will' reach his patient in need. He will be there for them, even if the phone rings for the fifth time that night!

He is statuesque, well build and walks straight, purposefully and smoothly. Occasionally, especially when he is tired, and has little energy, he tends to feel his back being stiff and painful, then he holds himself erect as though he needs to be supported from behind. He has clear, open eyes, that sometimes might have a startled quality to it; and he has the habit of closing his eyes when he needs to concentrate, focusing inward. He speaks with a calm, flowing voice that in itself is soothing to his patients. His hair is fine, even thin and he has a tendency to become bold. His clothes are loose and large; he wears a great coat on his rounds to patients' homes.

He likes to relax by doing landscape paintings or by listening to soft, sacred music that continuously refreshes his spirit. He loves sitting by the river or the sea and dream - being washed by the sounds of the water. A danger for our country doctor is to just stay by the stream and get lost in a dreamy state - but with a tightly run, busy practice there is not much danger of that.

But a person does not live alone, and nothing is as important to a Water person as deep personal relationships, so let's look how our country doctor relates to others, even though we need to keep in mind that these are examples not boxes into which we can put people! Our country doctor has a wife who is dominantly characterised by the **Earth Element.** To understand their relationship, let's contemplate some aspects from the perspective of water. Entering the cycle of life for water, where rain touches the ground. At first rain seeps into earth, water feels welcome and wanted. Water loves to explore this apparently solid element, sinking into every niche and aspect. How different it is! In this fertile stage earth becomes the support and vessel that water needs in order to travel to the place where it is needed. However eventually water sinks into depths were it will join more water (meeting like minded people - a drop of water by itself 'dries -up' quickly.)

Our country doctor has found a good mate, his 'Earth mother' provides him with the boundaries and stability he needs in order to do his job; they compliment each other. In his fishing club and his professional life he finds others to share his interests.

Now, as previously, let us contemplate a conflict between these two in daily life.

Our doctor's wife is a jolly, slightly round person with a friendly smile. Together they have several children which they enjoyed watching growing up. The wife is involved in the church choir and several other village activities, which she holds together and supports just as she does with her family. Her husband feels secure, knowing that he can rely on her, enabling him to be free to look after his patients.

Even in the dead of night, or the cold of the winter, when he comes home from visiting a patient there is tea and some good smelling food ready for him - or a stern eye reprimanding him: to not overdo it.

Now recently his wife has felt the effects of the menopause, but she hasn't mentioned anything, because her husband is 'far too busy looking after the sick to take care of her.' As Earth tends to, she neglects to look after her own needs; feeling exhausted, she cancels some village activities. Since their last child left home, she felt the house was empty and cold and as her husband was out a lot, she felt left and lonely. Still she said nothing, the menopause is simply a phase all women have to cope with; 'there is nothing to it!'

One day, as the telephone rang for the third time at night to call her husband out, she reacted, was uncharacteristically irritable, and worse she overslept in the morning; her husband left without breakfast! After similar incidents happened several times, our doctor too, got irritable; lack of proper food, lack of support, lack of nurturing on either side, made him unable to fulfil his job with the same ease. Before too long, they argued about whether he could - couldn't, should or shouldn't take a weekend break. A small issue, yet they got in such a state!

When they shouted at each other they realised what they were doing and 'fell' exhausted on the couches. Our doctor, frightened of these emotions suddenly confronting him, did not know what to do. His wife was too exhausted to even be angry. For a while there was a hostile, stand off silence; then he closed his eyes to draw inside. "What is happening?" He asked himself; then he turned to his wife: "What is up, dear, I have been so wrapped up in the clinic!" He paused, and slowed down more. He became so still, the room itself seemed to slow down. Then in the stillness he felt for the first time her exhaustion, her loneliness and her confusion. As soon as he became aware of her state, great empathy, love and warmth rose in him, he went over to his wife and held her for a long time.

Later as the exhaustion and frustration had fallen away somewhat from his wife, he went to the kitchen - and for the first time in a long while made her some tea; then they talked. Both were aware that they needed each other and that together they would weather the midlife crisis.

You recognise no doubt, the way the water functions through the support of earth; how water reacts with confusion when boundaries are taken away. You see how water reacts, by withdrawing into the depths from where intuition tells where nourishment is needed, then adapts to the situation and reacts with nurturing.

In our story, the country doctor has a son who has as his dominant character the Element of Fire. How do **Water and Fire** relate to each other, keeping in mind that here we look at their relationship through the eyes of Water.

Imagine a bowl of water on your windowsill, the sun shining on it gradually warms the water; the same bowl put into the freezer, turns water to ice. From the perspective of water, it looks as though in order to fulfil its destiny of flowing and nurturing, water can not be without its 'arch-enemy.'

Yet what happens when water gets 'too warm'? It changes into a gaseous state and rises. As steam water can achieve great feats, i.e. driving turbines, moving railway engines (at worst even as a hydrogen bomb) such great power comes from the combined force of water and fire!

And yet, the bowl of water left on the windowsill for too long (exposed to the sun) will soon have no water left in it. The water has not only changed its shape (vapour) but it has evaporated; to all intents and purpose, it has disappeared. Of course, we know this is an illusion, since water merely escaped into the atmosphere in order to reconvene with other moisture and gather as a cloud filled with water.

Fire might appear to destroy water, but it merely speeds up its life cycle. With the help of fire, water runs through the cycles of its existence faster and often more efficiently, albeit not less traumatically.

There are many other aspect to contemplate, such as:

- The appropriate warmth fire gives to water has great effects; think how the golf-stream influences climates.

- Appropriate use of warm Water has great healing effects in all manner of medicines.

- We have already mentioned how fire's quality of light is reflected by water, making it into a source of light! Etc.

Summing up, we can say that although it is threatened by it, water **is dependent on Fire for its fulfilment of purpose.** Of course, this fire does not need to come from another person, but can come from within the same person, as we are all Elements, at any time.

In the relationship between a Water and a Fire person the above is important to know; they need each other – yet their extremes threaten the existence of the partner.

If the Fire person is very active, loud, demanding, aggressive, too volatile and flamboyant, the Water person gets overruled, exhausted and drained. Due to its nature of wanting to adapt and accommodate such temperament, it will change its own shape to reach giddy heights; which puts great demands on Water.

However if the couple is equal, each balanced in their own element - they might rise together and achieve great feats; they could trigger colossal changes in people and societies. Yet they must always be aware that their union could mean either losing their individual existence. In real life this could lead to 'crimes of passion.' It could cause totally irrational paranoia and possessive love that kills self or others.

Most Water people would not dream of getting involved in such high voltage Fire - they would intuit that such a relationship could explode and destroy either or both. Being aware in their depth of this potential danger, it might fill the Water person with fear. Water's inherent willingness to adapt might be curbed, purely for self-preservation, choosing to withdraw, only to 'warm' from a distance.

It is time to return to our village doctor and **his son, the Fire person.**

Sheltered and held by the Earth mother, the father and son relationship was contained; both were set limits by Earth. The son loved to play guitar and had joined amateur dramatics. His father's heart was warmed when he could see his son's performance in the village hall, he was proud of him. Now the son had left the village and gone to a college of performing arts. The father felt it was the right career move, still he missed him and fondly remembered their times together: his son playing music or reading poetry, the father relaxing.

When the son came home, after the first term in college, his father was shocked. The son's hair was cut short and stood up in bright orange colour.

He had crazy multicoloured clothes on that seemed to have fallen out of a theatre's wardrobe. From his ears dangled giant earrings; he behaved like a self-important cockerel, boasting about his college friends, being rude, arrogant and self-important.

How does the Water person react?

A person in a depleted Water state would immediately withdraw and reject the son: if you behave like that, I want nothing to do with you, I can not handle this!

A person in a balanced Water state probably lets the first few days pass contemplating his son, and comes to a point of empathising with the new sense of freedom that had arisen in the youngster; he might even accept his son's outer appearance with amusement. But he would feel concerned that the warmth seemed to have left and been replaced by obnoxious self-importance.

What was behind his son's need 'to burn so brightly?' Our doctor decides to talk to his son. As the evening draws in, father and son sit by the fireplace with a beer. The father tells his son how proud he is of his first term's achievement and how well the son is coping on his own. The son, surprised at his father's approach, feels compelled to object, letting his fire burn to challenge his Dad and he argues. "But I have not done well at all, the school paper has criticised my performance and my leg hurts and Julian said: I was not his friend anymore because I looked stupid."

The father understood: his son's attire and behaviour were due to lack of confidence! So he told him how much he missed his son's company, that he hoped that his son would come home more often. He told him he would like to come to watch his next performance in a college play. After the supportive talk the son's behaviour calmed down; on the next visit home even his hair looked more normal.

Again you might see how water's sensitivity is able to feel into the person, identify their needs and then feed their wants, even when confronted with his formidable opponent, Fire.

Having weathered the crisis at home our country doctor receives a visit in the clinic from the district nurse. She is a woman with dominant Air characteristics.

How do Water and Air relate?

For most parts on the surface of the globe, water is covered by air; air sits on top seemingly doing its own thing! But on a closer look, whatever air does has an effect on water, it causes ripples and waves, waves that affect the water so deeply that they determine the currents and flow of oceans and at times cause huge upheavals in giant storm waves.

Water on occasions is penetrated by Air (oxygen) which causes bubbles (ideas); occasionally this interaction gets so entangled and mixed up, that they foam and froth together. Water is moved by Air, which drives and motivates it to go where it needs to, pushing it even beyond apparent limits, (yet without the danger that fire poses).

In a partnership or relation between two such people, Air is the active partner; by and large water simply accepts air's pushing. Recall that at times storms whip the sea and into such a passionate or even angry reaction, that they simply have to 'thrash it out.' This 'thrashing' can be driven by passion; the high waves of fun however don't last. In the main, such struggle ends with either temporary or final separation of the two, when they each withdraw into their own energy fields to recuperate. Neither of them though, can follow each other at these times, as water withdraws into its depth, and air ascends to its heights; it means the relationship remains on the surface.

No doubt there are many more aspects between these two elements that can be contemplated, for example the similarities between the two. They share important characteristics. Both are renowned for their clarity and cleanliness; both have the ability to analyse and penetrate deeply intellectually, being creative thinkers. Yet they use this ability different. Air cuts away sharply and thus indulges intellectually, Water is more reflective, mirrors the wholeness of life. As long as both contribute their angle, they benefit from each other.

Let us see how this applies to our two fictional characters, the country doctor and the district nurse. The district nurse is a very competent organiser, she works totally autonomously, doing her rounds, caring for patients, administering medicine. She provides a lot of clear organisation and co-ordination between several clinics and country doctors; planning and time schedules are part of her main forte.

Our doctor gets on well with her, he respects her efficiency; he appreciates her clear and focused instructions. She moves around the district in a swift little car that is well known by the villagers; humour and a bubbly temperament carry her through many trying situations. Usually each keeps to their rounds trusting that both do their job well.

Last spring they were confronted with a big wave of flu, it had epidemic proportions, and the two of them had to step up their working relationship considerably; both were in high demand day and night. As the flu took grip on the community, the district nurse kept calling the doctor to step up his actions. She put more and more pressure on the doctor - but he simply 'cannot be at two places at once.' How does Water react under such Air-pressure?

When the doctor is so tired that he gets an address wrong and ends up in the wrong place at the wrong time, they both realise that a serious mistake could happen this way, and they take stock.

In a negative state, a Water person under such pressure might simply disconnect; put the phone down and contemplate on the destinies of those that have caught the virus, then proceed to do his rounds and leave the district nurse to deal with her problems.

In a positive state, Water will collect its deep resources, refocus to gain clarity and then devise a plan of increased co-operation.

Equipped with cordless telephones they could link at certain time intervals, to find where there is the greatest need for the doctor's presence. They decide together that the district nurse might benefit from the temporary use of the clinic's secretary, to help with the central management, so that the weight of responsibility is better shared.

A pattern of efficient interaction is created between the two, in order to serve where needed; both respond and adapt to the requirements of the moment.

Finally we come to the relationship of **Water and Space**. If we look at space as outer space - there is simply no interaction! However in a worldly sphere, whatever water does, occupies space; water completes its whole life-cycle within space! What appears as no interaction is - from the point of view of Water - total involvement. Yet Water is only one aggregate contained in space.

If we look at it in the Chinese context, we see easily how water permeates wood; it nurtures life. Wood and water in nature are close alleys. They are so fused it seems, they just sit 'in each others pockets,' like a 'hand in a glove.' Yet wood - in a dry state where it is without water - still has an existence on its own (furniture, building material etc.) So both descriptions of the fifth element portray it as benefiting from water – yet make clear, that they can leave water 'behind.'

Similarly in a relationship or marriage, these two have obviously much understanding and much to share. If Space can be content with limiting itself and not be distracted from the relationship, it is hugely beneficial for water – it helps water to achieve his dharma fully. Yet however close the couple appears to be, they can easily be pulled apart by the extra needs of the Space Element which 'leaves water behind.' When for example the Space person gets involved into something/someone else, the wound it leaves in the Water person is substantial; he literally sinks into the depths of despair. On the other hand, the sensitivity of Water might alert him that space is unreachable, that he is earthbound.

Let us look back to our country doctor, who has a secretary that is a person with a dominant characteristic of the 'Space' element.

The secretary is a very attractive woman, and she runs the clinic efficiently and makes the lists for the doctor's house calls. She has a way to make the waiting room appear bright and friendly, with her natural charming attitude. She makes sure there are always flowers in the room, comes up with creative ideas on how to make people more at ease while they wait etc. She is a pleasure to work with and the doctor is aware of it. As they share much of their space and time in their working life, they become very good friends, taking an interest also in each other's private life.

Because of long working hours, the secretary has little social life; and the doctor who spends many hours in the clinic talks to her ever more frequently. They share the trouble with children, troubles over nosy villagers or a lost tennis match. Over time, they realise that they like each other's company a lot and seek out time together. When the doctor and his secretary are invited to a training conference for medical staff, a close intimate relationship is on the cards. How does the 'Water person' react?

Before he even agrees to go to the conference 'Water has a think.' He really would like to be with his secretary, she makes him feel wanted and is just such an incredible, attentive companion! He empathises with her longing for a closer relationship; but if he fulfils her needs this weekend – what about tomorrow or the day after... could he afford an affair? Could he really fulfil her needs? What if she met someone else tomorrow? An 'affair' would only make her unhappy in the long run. That is - if he could overcome his own scruples towards his wife, who would suffer greatly through the 'whole affair.' His role in life is to nurture, not to inflict pain! What if his wife finds out? Suddenly fear grips his heart. Will he lose what he has got? Will he lose his wife; will his present existence come to an end? What is going to happen afterwards? He feels squashed as much by the fear of losing what he has as by the fear of the unknown he might gain. Both fear for himself and empathy for others, influence his decision to resist and talk to his secretary.

The day before they have to leave for the conference he asks the secretary to go out for a coffee. He tells her: she is very attractive, he likes her company, but he thinks that what she really needs is not a fling, but a total relationship; he tells her that more involvement could only cause pain. Space recognises his wisdom.

As water flows through all of us, so does divine energy, which encourages Water to make highly moral decisions and be aware of the unity between us. The secretary's feelings, the wife's feelings, the son's feelings all are essentials no different from our own. How can we hurt somebody that feels just like me? It makes no sense, it means I hurt or hate myself. This empathy of Water is its greatest teaching that reaches far beyond the physical, psychic or social realm. How can we slaughter an animal, cut a tree or poison a well when all of creation shares the same energy in just a different shape. Understand shape shifting from Water and you will discover it as truth!

5.2: c) Associations for Spiritual Evolution (Yoga)

The spiritual or religious inclinations of a person with dominant Water energy are characterised, of course, by Water's fluidity. The person might flow from one spiritual path, one religious orientation to another, but not heedlessly, not because of disorientation – instead they take the teachings on board, learn, assimilate them. Integrating one tributary of the river's flow after another, they are collecting spiritual wisdom. At worst they might get lost while 'Guru-shopping' or accumulating a vast body of useless knowledge – at best their river might merge with the vast ocean of divine consciousness. Now this can happen while on any path, they all lead to the one Truth. But a Water person would be attracted more to a path which incorporates non-violence, nurturing and acceptance; elements of which can be found of course in religions, but they are probably more accessible in the less organised ones.

Qualities/steps in Sadhana. The quality of water affects the Sadhana of a Water person especially; it provides the constant awareness and experience of change, of dissolution of form. Such a person becomes increasingly aware of the unlimited, infinite existence beyond all forms, time and space. The physical body and its processes, including emotions, are explored and transcended as temporary. The same goes for form of religions – they provide wisdom, but the truth is recognised as beyond form.

The path of Yoga is most suited for such a person, rooted in Karma Yoga but with the awareness that this is a step of transcending form. The person himself might be the instrument of such change, through such a person change might be initiated, be it in individuals or groups. Through water things get done, 'plants get nourished.' The Water person could be a channel for energies; furthermore we heard of water's memory - this could be used to heal, nurture, change people. The Karma Yoga, the selfless service of a Water person, differs from the Earth person, in what service is done; less physical action (organisation, nursing etc.), more sharing a state of being, even wisdom teachings. What form 'channelling' will take, depends on the presence of other elemental energies, as we are always a composite.

Similarly, the state of consciousness most relevant to such a person seems to change, it is neither this nor that, it is in transition; sometimes the person seems anchored in **waking consciousness,** other times in **dream consciousness** and sometimes in the fourth state, the state beyond. The latter however, only if the all important emotions, memory and the ability for clear thinking (which shape the waking consciousness) are transcended and recognised for what they are, conditioned personality, mind makeup. It is the fibre our dreams and motivations are made of, and we get attached to those, holding them for real and important. C.G.Jung did much work on this, even if we ban the dreams into the unconscious or the archetypal, we still have to see that they are mind made; maybe not by ours, but by the collective. For some, their dreams might even be more important than physical or mental reality; such is the stuff artists are made of.

Needs and wants arising out of dreams create desire; they have to be recognised for what they are, temporary forms, and as such they lose their value. A desire fulfilled lasts for an instant until it rises again. These states have to be recognised for what they are, then detachment grows and the bigger picture can be addressed. Water does not stay in a small pond; it expands into an awareness of the shared spirit of all that exists. Water is there to nurture, but once it has reached the ocean, it can recognise itself as a wave and with it soon, comes the awareness that it is ocean.

This dual quality of focus: supporting the physical reality (as does Earth) and the expanding awareness, is mirrored in the **energy fields and the energetic anatomy.** Amongst the five *Koshas* (subtle bodies/sheath), Water is linked to ***Pranamaya Kosha***. *Prana* has a double meaning – it refers to the breath, as well as universal life-force beyond individual forms. In both aspects, it nurtures our physical body, just like Water. *Pranamaya Kosha* refers to the subtle body that feeds vital energy to fulfil relative physical needs. To do that, it expresses in five types or 'sub-pranas.' The air we breath is the most obvious one; ***Apana*** is the downward moving energy, it works in the region between navel and rectum (excretion through bowels, bladder, uterus etc.). ***Samana*** is the power of digestion and assimilation (resides between the heart and the navel); **Udana** is the energy that uplifts, dwelling in the throat and head region (producing speech, song etc). Finally there is **Vyana** which dwells in the whole body, and circulates and causes all rhythmic contraction. [48]

Pranamaya Kosha is linked to the second Chakra for its communication between the energy bodies. This manifests and affects especially the growing child between eight and fourteen. The child, whose base needs are filled through working in the first Chakra, now opens to contact further afield; his imagination develops new worlds. A new relationship to his own body evolves with dawning sexuality. This expansion makes him rebel against too tight boundaries from parents and society. The desire for physical sensations and mental fantasies cause conflict, creating unreal images of oneself and others which can lead to negativity, low self-esteem and seeking bad company. [49] The Chakra that expresses this energy is called: **Svadhisthana**, and is associated with the frequency of 500 Htz. Its colour is a deep orange; it has six vibrant petals signifying: indulgence, suspicion, disdain, delusion, destructiveness and pitiless-ness, which are overcome when working at this level by the help of the presiding deity Vishnu (the sustainer) and his female counterpart. The animal associated is the alligator/crocodile, (associated with Varuna, the Lord of the waters). Its symbolism stands for conquering the six enemies: pride, lust, anger, jealousy, greed, and delusion.

The physical organs associated with it, are the gonads, the reproductive system, the sacral plexus and also with the whole negative side of the system of nutrition (i.e. separation, assimilation, rejection and elimination). Lower vertebrae, large intestines, pelvis, appendix and hips are also connected.

The more psychological, emotional and mental factors associated with this chakra are: blaming, guilt, sex, power and control, overemphasis on money; giving and receiving pleasure. It also questions the quality of love.

Perception and nature of information processed here concerns life as perceived through the emotions; the information worked with comes basically through pain and pleasure, joy, fear, anger etc.

The Need this energy generates is self-acceptance and self-love. In our times a lot of people still have work to do with this chakra (lower back pain!).

In the Tibetan system, this chakra is associated with the shape of a crescent and the seed syllable 'Vam'. Some of the physical Ailments associated with it, are: chronic lower back pain; sciatica; gynaecological problems; pelvic problems, problems with sexual potency and the urinary tract.

Energy fields, chakra and channels are stimulated and balanced by working with certain postures, **asana.** Probably the most ancient practice of *asana* is the practice of the *Surya Namaskara* or sun salutations; it is said that by practising it, people can become joyous, happy and content; it brings health and longevity. It especially should be done with fluidity, flowing with ease from one aspect into the next and is thus exemplifying Water energy.

Nevertheless, there are of course *asana* that especially represent the Water Element, they are those that work the related meridians - and/or are especially cooling; and bring together outer and inner breath, mind and body. Such asana are: *Suptajanullala* (simple Knee Wave); *Satangullola* (CatWave) *Pascimullola* (long Wave); *Karnapidasana* (fetus pose, also strong asana for Space energy) *Pascimasana* (Forward bend) *Sukamaricyasana* (easy twist); *Paivritasana* (twist) *Adho Mukha Svanasana* (downward dog); *Ardha Matsyendrasana* (sitting twist) etc. etc.

Previously we have touched on much that is connected to the **dharma of Water. To flow** is the prerequisite to nurturing others - in whatever way. If this is the aim, then one can not attack, hurt, or disrespect others at the same time. These two actions – to nurture and to hurt - are mutually exclusive! Here roots Patanjali's **main** ethical principal. Both *Yamas* and *Niyamas* can be summarised as 'ahimsa,' the principal of non-violence.

'Ahimsa is the supreme *dharma*, he who practises *Ahimsa* leads a life of freedom from fear. Nobody is afraid of you - so why fear them. When totally established in *ahimsa*, the peaceful vibes are so strong, that even lions, snakes or other wild animals lie down at one's feet.' So Swami Anubhavananda says; when we practise total ahimsa towards others and ourselves, the highest Yoga can be achieved.

Ahimsa as a concept has become world renowned through Mahatma Ghandi. [50] He made it pretty obvious, that non-violence does not only refer to not killing people or animals (war, crime) but extends to not having any ill feelings, no injuring words or actions to anyone, under any circumstances; a hard task! Respect and reverence for all life, is its premise. As O. M. Aivanhov said, water deserves our respect because it is part of every living and nonliving being. Giving respect to all is practising *ahimsa*. It starts with treating your child with respect for it is a unique life form with unique needs and not 'just a kid' (kid being an American slang word for goat)! It includes listening to people for that is a mark of respect to the unique life form that speaks to you. It refers to giving people the right jobs and adequate pay for their job, because otherwise it violates peoples' human dignity.

It even relates to how we build our houses and cities, how we manage our business; or small things in daily life, such as not having the radio on too loud – not venting our anger at each other! It relates to the way we drive our car with politeness rather than pushing others off the road; it relates to the tone of voice we communicate in, and it even relates to the way we look at each other.

This principle of Non-violence, in the final analysis leads to surrender. It is not assertion (believing in one's own ego) that is the crown of ethical behaviour - but service to others, surrendering one's own needs, opinions, wants and desires.

But, so I hear you object: that annihilates me, I am important too, I have rights too? Yes - remember the story about St. Augustine at the beach, watching the boys throwing the bucket in the sea. Now does the water in the bucket scream... I don't want to give up my identity? Or does the river that meets the ocean scream... I don't want to give up serving the landscape, don't want to give up my identity? In fact, does the water ever lose itself? Can it? Even when the raindrop finally reaches the ocean, it will rise to the sky to descend as raindrop!

To support our practise of *ahimsa*, we need to understand and study the scriptures, to understand ourselves - this is the practise of **swadhyaya**. Mantras should flow from our lips like a river.

The **Water's essential lesson** then, simply is one of **continual adaptation.** The psycho-spiritual question that the Water person needs to ask him/herself thus is: **'where am I going?'** When Earth answers the question 'who I am,' it can support others with no 'threat to itself'; yet because water always 'takes on any other's form ' it appears to lacks the certainty of who it is. Every time it encounters 'others' it is in danger of apparently losing itself. In order to be able to continue to serve – yet to stand in its own power, water needs to realise that it cannot lose itself! ' Where am I going?'- Only to the source that I already am. There is only One existence. The One is simply expressing itself in ever-new forms. Until Water realises this, it will suffer from not knowing where it comes from, nor where it goes; filled with uncertainty and fear, it feels, it has 'no home,' no stable point – and life is full of worries and dangers. **Water people worry** needlessly!

Contemplate: When water has become blood, is it still water? When the raindrop has been absorbed by the rose's leaf, is it still water? When the brook has become saturated moss, is it still water? When the river has become an estuary, is it still water? When the spring has become a bog, is it still water? Every time there is fear of losing oneself, then every time there is again the question: what is my *dharma,* what is my nature? This insecurity can produce insurmountable difficulties in making decisions.

We make decisions based on what we identify with. (As a mother I act like this, ...as a friend I would say this... as a businessman I have to act this way... Not knowing one's role in life or society, is one lost? If I am a rose, I have to flower - but if I am water I have to evaporate. If I am blood, I have to burn the nutrients in the cells – but if I am water, I have to leave that behind and move on? If I am a bog, do I have to flow away, or dry out and become earth? **Water is constantly uncertain** of its role, its identity and purpose – and it experiences numerous ones. It has such a rich life, doing so many different things, playing so many different roles, and they all serve merely one aim: to teach the Water person that any of this is not 'Me'; None of the roles, none of the forms have any affect on my essential nature. A high lesson indeed.

A Water person's **mental abilities** also have distinct sides. As in many other ways, water takes on 'the shape of other people's ideas' easily, it likes to explore them – it might even pursue them to an extreme; it follows arguments all the way up and down the line. Then, a new idea is taken on board, a new way of thinking or a new way of living even. For a while the **knowledge** Water has gathered can make it cling to one extreme, as if it were the whole story, but never forever! But while it does, while Water sticks to an idea or certain knowledge as if it were the whole, without reason, without foundation in truth and narrow, its knowledge is classified as t*amasic*. It is like the stage that water goes through with ice; it becomes ice, sticks to fixed ideas and fails to see things as they are; when in a state like this Water's knowledge is crystallised, limited and possibly even dogmatic.

There is another way of looking at a Water person's way with knowledge. Water goes here and there and gathers knowledge everywhere – in the process it loses its 'thread,' then it is vital that it asks its essential question: 'where am I coming from?' Otherwise, he or she amasses all this knowledge and yet it only feeds his/hers uncertainty.

Similarly **Happiness**; happiness for Water arises from doing the job asked of it, perfectly; it gives contentment. For a while Water delights in his endlessly creative job. Yet irrevocable happiness comes from finding the ocean; it is the happiness of eternal freedom. This is bliss. To reach that Water needs to 'release possessiveness and heaviness into the space of consciousness, in which alone is true happiness and abundance.' [51]

On this path the **greatest spiritual obstacle is its fear of annihilation**; he fears his skill of adaptability might end in total dissolution. Man's fears are expressed in many ways: we fear that things change - and we fear that nothing ever changes. We fear others won't help us - and we fear that others will dominate us. We fear that we have not enough to eat - and that we eat too much. We fear war, famine, over or under-population; we fear too much freedom - and too little freedom. We are afraid of life - and afraid of death. And - would you believe it, we fear that we have fears! The Water person needs to put on 'different glasses' to realise that neither the raindrop, nor the river ever give up being what they truly are. The 'river' can become **fearless**, give up its worry and rejoice when it reaches the ocean, for it becomes what it always has been! This step - is that what is described as self-realisation? Where the ego identity becomes one with the universal Self?

Can you imagine the joy of freedom, if you had no more fear! It might be worth contemplating the joy of such fearlessness. Jnaneshwar Maharaj, India's hailed Poet-Saint writes in his commentary to the Bhagavad Gita: 'Fearlessness holds the biggest place... who knows that all others are one with him through his realisation of non-duality, casts out all fear.

When salt is thrown into water, it becomes one with the water.

Similarly he who realises his unity with everything destroys fear.

o Beloved, this is what is called fearlessness. You should know that it is the servant of true perception.' [52]

The problem of fear and fearlessness is such a central issue to human life. It warrants a book in itself - yet water makes it look so simple. But how do we get rid of fears? Fear, just like anger, is basically life energy. It's natural; it's a survival mechanism triggered by real or imagined danger. Today we rarely meet a tiger walking down the street; but may be when we step off the curb we might be barely missed by a car; this is as close as we get to such physical threat. But the real threat we face is our mind, which conjures up all sorts of images and connections - the way to get rid of fear is to learn to understand and control your mind. This is... the purpose of Yoga, in all its many forms.

Meditation

The Water person like any other, benefits from the calming influence of meditation; let go of the emotional attachments; swadhyaya, chanting mantras was mentioned above – use it! Repeat 'Ohm' in conjunction with the breath, either alone or with the encouragement of a group! Be careful however, because of their 'emotionalism,' Water people's devotion could become a form of self-indulgence. They should use meditation to reduce their attachments and avoid getting caught up in the outer forms of devotion. They need to learn to go beyond the form to the formless and infinite reality. So David Frawley advises that they are 'particular good at meditating upon the eternal, immutable aspect of truth.' The awareness of water as ocean increases the space of mind; it lets us swim in wider visions.

Meditation upon the void is also particularly good. 'It can be combined with meditation upon the inner light, bringing more fire into their minds.' Their minds are prone to rest comfortably, such contentment can easily be confused with higher states of mind. Water people must make sure they stay alert; as the Zen call demonstrates: 'Attention, Attention, Attention.' David Frawley adds: 'They should use meditation like climbing a series of mountain peaks along a great journey, not stopping along the way, no matter how pleasant.' 53

Chapter Six: Invocation of Fire

> I will meet you
> I will touch you
> I will burn you
> I will destroy you
>   -out of your ashes I will resurrect you

I will meet you
A flame has no face, it expands in all directions
Agni Vedic God of fire is never the same in two moments,
Amaterasu-omi-kami, shining deity of Japan, is a reflecting mirror,
La Maue of the Igorots (Philippines) lives high in the tree to observe all,
Ra's eye ruled all corners of the world with its insight,
Odin hides his golden chariot across the firmament,
The Cosmic Christ illuminates the corners of the world,
So rest assured, I will find you.
I hide in the sparkle of a bonfire,
I tame the embers of your hearth,
I illumine your way at night,
I wax and wane as pale moonlight,
And at dawn I shower you with grace,
From the chariot, I ride across the sky -
I peer in each niche and crevice -
And when I find you, I will warm you
I will comfort you and there will be joy and happiness,
there will be lanterns, candles and fireworks,
there will be flickering lights and warming fires,
there will be dancing and merry making,
there will be passions kindled,
for since time began, there was no ceremony without me.

I will meet you
I will touch you
you feel my touch in the delicate kiss of the rays of spring,
you see my touch in the abundance of life,
you taste my touch in the sweetness of the berry
you smell my touch in the fragrance of the morning glory,
you hear my touch in the crackle of the log fire,
you sense my touch in the light of meditation,
you are aware of my existence in the light of your Self,
you hear me in the explosions of warfare,
you smell me near the ovens of Auschwitz and Treblinka
you taste me in the bitterness of raging hate
you see me laying waste the Amazon forests,

you feel my touch in your feverish body,
for I reside not only in the centre of the earth,
but also deep inside your being.

Yes, I will meet you,
I will touch you,
I will burn you,
although born from rubbing wooden sticks, I exist before all wood,
although melting her core, the earth arrests my furious flames,
although liquidising steel, my gait is stopped by metal doors,
although vaporising water, rain stops even my tiniest spark,
although I burn your body, I cannot touch your soul,
for your soul is pure, is light and as light is my-Self,

Oh yes, I will meet you,
I will touch you,
I will burn you,
I will destroy you,
as wood is destroyed to give warmth,
as chaos is destroyed to create order,
as illness is destroyed to reveal health,
as weeds have to be destroyed to make space for crops,
as ore has to be destroyed to yield gold,
as water has to be destroyed to fill the clouds,
so injustice, desires, attachment have to be renounced to grow love
so your body has to be cleansed and purified,
in order to work in harmony with itself and all else;

Fear not, I will meet you,
I will touch you,
I will burn you,
I will destroy you,
Out of your ashes I will resurrect you.
Truly is it not the same gold, whether ring or ore?
Truly is it not the same wheat whether grain or bread?
Truly is it not the same tree, whether acorn or oak?

As seeds need the sun's light and heat to grow,
You need the internal fire, 'Shakti,' that movement of life that inspires,
Sustains, purifies and guides on the path of righteousness and wisdom.

Yes, I will transform you,
So that the seed of your life's happiness can grow;
So that the Phoenix that is you can rise,
Radiant with love, compassion and eternal light.

6.1: Contemplation of Fire

There is hardly a culture that has not a myth about fire and its source, the sun. For mankind, fire has always had two strong connotations: being a great helper and a powerful destroyer. Its inherent power might have been the reason why Zeus wanted to keep fire out of reach of man, yet Prometheus, with the intention of giving mankind protection from the elements, stole the fire from the Gods and gave it to the humans. For this Zeus punished him severely, and in addition sent a flood to earth to quench the uncontrollable fire.

Some main characteristics of fire are immediately clear: it can protect, it inspires beyond control and has an arch opponent: water. But let us have a closer look:

Fire comes into existence by **friction** between two different components i.e. sticks, stones or matches on earth – and or massive colliding masses of energy/matter in space. Let's focus on the earthly version. Through friction (release of energy) a spark is created and now exists in its own right, as such it has to be fed and nourished to grow. The growth is rapid and has to be monitored carefully, for further sparks easily fly off and create new fires. The spark when growing can take many forms, not unlike water. However water takes on the form of an-other (from within) – fire **trans-forms** (destroying the form in the process)! A candle flame looks harmless enough, yet what makes its flame, is the burning of wick and wax... they give up their existence to become flame. Fire can not be separated from its burning power... it **destroys while it creates**.

The burning... is effort, is pain, is *tapasya* – yet the very destruction of the old makes way for new creation; in this it is **joyous, glorious**, happy – is celebration. Fire is never still, it simultaneously destroys and creates.

Within this, we recognise three distinct forms: burning, heat and light. There is much scope for contemplating the various forms of fire. Think about a hungry straw fire that flares up brightly, yet dies almost immediately, having devoured its fuel.

Contemplate the awesome power of wild, destructive forest fires, killing the green lungs of the planet – killing the producers of the oxygen that it needs to burn. Fire is directly dependent on and destroys its immediate source, hence transformation.

Fire, like each of the Elements, has forms that come apparently from opposite poles (i.e. the solidity of ice and fluidity are both characteristics of water). Yet fire has the most powerful extremes e.g. contemplate the flame of a candle versus the inferno of nuclear holocaust!

Out of the many aspects of fire, we will contemplate two aspects: fire in the hearth and the sun, **source of all fire**.

Let us first focus on the comforting glow of a fireplace or hearth; most of us will have enjoyed watching its gentle, dancing flames. However, rarely are we aware that one kind of matter changes, in the presence of energy, into another kind of matter. (Wood turns to ashes). In the process, more energy is generated and given off as warmth - **and light**. Light though is not so much a by-product in the strict sense, but more the visual impact of the process, which passes on information, i.e. light from a fireplace/hearth/campfire **signals safety, rest and security**.

In Greek mythology, this slow burning fire is presided over by the Greek goddess Hestia. 54 She is felt to be present in the living flame of the round fire that used to be in the centre of the home, temple and city. Her symbol was (just as in many cultures) a circle; she was worshipped not in an image or statue, but as a spiritually felt presence, embodied in the sacred fire, that provided illumination, warmth and heat. She was the oldest sister of the first generation of Olympian Gods, yet took no part in their affairs of love and war. Homer describes how Zeus gave her - instead of a wedding gift - the central place of the house, so that she could receive the best offerings.

Her Roman equivalent is Vesta; in her temples the sacred, central fire was tended by 'vestal virgins.' Her companion was Mercury, the messenger. He guarded the fire and the temple, representing the outgoing quality of the element Fire. The two belonged together yet they were not involved in each other; meaning fire does not have to go outward, **it can be contained, working inner most!**

Hestia stands for those that have controlled the wildness of fire and have learned to be able to avoid being caught up in passion of the moment. Hestia is not attached to people, possessions, prestige or power. She feels whole, warm and content as she is. Her fire is the spiritual link to others; that literally would be carried as an ember from the temple to the houses and even from the house and taken on a journey etc.

These embers were symbolic of the steady glow of the divine fire in us. The Latin word for the hearth is 'focus,' contained fire is focus, is concentrating, is being totally absorbed, perceiving things by looking inward and intuitively sensing what is going on. This perception is shared in Chinese, Indian and other traditions.

This tamed fire is very different from my second choice of contemplation.

I am sitting in front of a big 'French window'; the day is overcast yet somewhere out of my sight, is the sun. A huge ball of fire, or rather, of hot gas. Its outer periphery is still 6000 degrees Celsius hot; such heat is beyond our imagination. Its heat is the result of constant nuclear fusion. Yes, our beloved sun is a cauldron of constant nuclear **explosions.** The energy set free in these processes makes the sun 'shine.' Giant tongues of hot gas are whirled off the surface into space, much further than the atmosphere around the earth. Sometimes particles from these enormous explosions hit the earth and when they reach us they cause the beautiful lights we call aurora.

The vast temperatures we know of in the core of the earth are nothing compared to the temperatures reached in the stars and sun, where matter turns into gas and eventual dissolution into...? And yet this unimaginable destructive power is the same one that gives us life. For us this awesome power is beneficial – because it's far away! We can't see or experience the activity of the fierce, boiling cauldron; we are safe because it is exquisitely, minutely balanced in distance. A cosmic law holds us just right; a bit closer we would melt, a bit further we would freeze! An amazing insight in the delicate balance, the careful control inherent in taming the fire! For fire to be beneficial it needs to be tamed!

Fire as active energy, as light, is **radiance**. Light is the result of **transforming** one kind of matter, into another. In us such a fire also burns, it constantly transforms air, orange juice, potatoes, bread and chicken into useful oxygen, amino acids, lactic acids etc. and then again burning these with the help of oxygen, gives off energy, which makes us shine, radiating with health and vitality. The wise of India spoke of this process as the 'gastric fire.'

They also spoke of us as children of the sun, because the sun (Fire) on the physical level is the source of our existence, (a deeper insight into 'reality' than the idea of man stemming from a clod of earth). In many traditions and esoteric literature, the sun is worshipped in recognition of this:

> Dawn comes shining like a lady of the light,
> Stirring to life all creatures.
> Now it is time to kindle the Fire.
> The light of Dawn scatters the shadows. (Hiranyavarna) 55

On an inter-religious conference I met a native Shaman from the Amazon forests. He stated categorically that: there can be no life without *Padre de LUZ,* he is life. (Father of light). Christianity also frequently uses the light to describe divine truth: Christ said: 'I am the light of the world' (St. John 8,12)

> 'While you have the light, trust the light,
> The Lord is my light and my salvation.' (Ps. 27,1)

The wise of India celebrated the sun as Surya, associated with life-creating energy and timely dissolution, this was celebrated in Fire ceremonies, *Yajnas*. Surya guides us to righteousness and **inspires wisdom**; he is the eye of God, (as well as our eye), because through him, we can see the love of God and the love in each other. As such the inner 'sun,' the sun of love, is soul and points beyond the individual. Even today we say about someone we love, that the sun shines out of his/her eyes.

> Swift and beautiful are you,
> o Sun, maker of the Light,
> Who illumines all the radiant sky
> Gazing beyond the dark we reach
> The supreme Light and attain the Sun,
> The God of gods, the Light. (Rig Veda, 1.504)

The sun, due to whose light alone I can see, is itself an ordinary star - just as the other billions and billions which we see in the sky. To worship the sun as God, points beyond the physical to 'that which illumines out of itself.' The

Self-luminous is absolute power behind everything. Out of this understanding the *Gayatri* is born, allegedly one of the oldest, most potent prayers in the world:

Om Bhúr Bhuvah Svah;	Oh effulgent light,
Tat Savitur varenyam	that has given birth to all spheres of consciousness
Bhargo devasya dhimahi;	Oh God who appears through the shining sun
Dhiyo yo nah pracodayãt.	Illumine my heart. [56]

Although I chose India's Surya here as a prototype, we could look at many traditions that worshipped this radiant light as a God. In Egypt, Ra sailed across the skies; in ancient Persia, the Sun God rode in his chariot. In the northern Philippines Manaue, the Sun God lives in the treetops; for the Celts, the sun is a charioteer riding across the sky. As we heard, the Shwar, indigenous people of the Amazon, believe there is only one ultimate authority, Aruta, Padre de Luz, the Father of Light. Today in the South American Mountains, Indians still go into the mountains just like their forefathers, and worship the sunrise. During man's history some of the greatest constructions of mankind have been built to worship the sun, e.g. the Sun Pyramid in Mexico or Stonehenge in England. Furthermore, Kings derived authority for their lineage from the sun such as the Japanese Emperor (who is said to be a descendant of Amataresu, the Sun), or Louis XIV (the French: Roi du Soleil, - King of the Sun).

In modern days our 'sun- worshippers' fill the beaches all over the world.

There is another aspect worth contemplating about the sun. Yes, her instant combustion throws off light and heat, generating conditions on earth, in which life can be generated, but in the process sun destroys itself in time (so the scientists tell us). Remember what we said earlier about the candle... the wick and wax burn - give up their existence - to bring about the flame.

No wonder at the origin of ancient wisdom, is the idea of **sacrifice**! Every aspect of this earth is in one way or another fed by the gigantic fire – the giant sacrifice, the giant transforming power that is the sun. Even creatures that live in the dark, deep oceans can only exist there because the sun keeps the ocean from freezing.

Moreover a piece of plastic is not immediately recognised as 'sun-made'; yet even plastic containers are made from fossil oil (petrochemicals) which are compressed plant fibre (having stored solar energy) from long ago. Whatever we look at, sooner or later will be revealed as a form of sun energy. It brings us right back to modern science, where matter is light and light becomes matter – and that includes us!

Sacrifice always **serves new form** – it is ultimately positive, creative, life-giving. This life-affirming quality has been throughout the ages associated with love; making everything positive and good. Even though we fail sometimes to see this basic **positive-ness** of life, many mystics have see and described it:

> I am light itself, reflected in the heart of everyone;
> I am the treasure of the Divine Name
> The shining Essence of all things
> I am every light that shines,
> Every ray that illumines the world.
> From the highest heavens to the bed-rock of the earth
> > All is but a shadow of my blazing Light.
> > If I dropped the veil covering my true essence
> > The world would be gone- lost in a brilliant light.
> > > (Fakhruddin Araqui, Sufi, 1213-1289) [57]

When talking about light, the boundaries between sunlight and God-light seem to disappear only too easily. How can we understand it? We know that all we normally perceive is vibrating energy yet we see it as different objects, forms and colours because sunlight is **reflected** or refracted much like a sunbeam in a glass of water. This 'reflected light' we register, and our mind interprets and labels it according to our conditioning: green tree; red flower; brown hair etc. thus the world appears to us as millions of objects. Moreover, when our senses receive these vibrations and interpret them, this evokes feelings in us. These feelings we label according to certain frequency bands of light and as such their range is attributed to the Five Elements. What this seemingly absurd idea tells us is that everything we see is in fact vibrating light, light that originally comes from the sun.

It might seem strange to you but be assured, it is in accord with Scientists, Mystics and Poets.

The Element Fire **illumines** not just the 'objects' of the world, but our very thoughts, hearts and minds. Indeed the greatest human achievement is to be illuminated, to reach the state of *'En-lightenment,'* where we can see things for what they are... and not what label/concepts we project on it. In 'The Divine Comedy' Dante Alighirie writes:

> So dazzling was the splendour of that ray,
> that I must certainly have lost my senses ...
> o light eternal fixed in itself alone...
> > here my powers rest from their high fantasy,
> > but already I could feel my being turned -
> > instinct and intellect balanced equally
> > as in a wheel whose motion nothing jars -
> > by the love that moves the Sun and the others stars. [58]

Dante's testimony bears witness to the power of such insights, and the transformation that results. **Fire transforms darkness into light** (this is the true meaning of the word *Guru*); equally it transforms light into matter: plants, trees, animals, people etc., and yes, it transforms clay into ceramics, ore into gold and carbohydrates into diamonds, food into the muscles, flesh and energy of our bodies. Through the qualities of Fire i.e. illumination, insight and understanding, we can transform hatred and anger into love;

through Fire's quality of **inspiration,** boredom can be transformed into **joy and enthusiasm** and so on.

This transforming power of light has been called 'love,' numerous stories about the life of Saints and Sages bear witness. The story of Catherine of Sienna is just one.

In the 14th Century, in the middle of the arrival of the bubonic plague (which in its first five years killed one third of the entire European population), a daughter was born to a craftsman, the twenty-third child of twenty-five born to her parents. She was a tiny, charming child; when six years old, she walked with her brother and suddenly saw the sky open and before her sat Jesus, magnificently *dressed in radiant light.* As she stood and stared at the sight, her heart opened towards the radiant source of love.

Following this experience she had only one wish: to dedicate her life to God. She ate little and withdrew into her room, until she was allowed to join the order of 'Mantellatte' (for the cloak they wore). She followed the command of her God and began nursing the sick and dying. She did not want anybody to know about it, so she went out at night to the houses of needy families where she left gifts or helped in some small way. During this time she had many more visits of her radiant Lord who told her: "It is your duty to love your neighbour as your own self. Help them spiritually and materially at least with your good will if you have nothing else." 59

In the times of the plague this was not an easy task, for anyone. Where does a young girl get her strength from? One day, it is said, the Lord appeared again to her and reached into her chest, removed her physical heart and replaced it with his own. Catherine later wrote that the Lord had said, "Dearest daughter, I now give you my own heart and forever you must live by it alone." Her service of love to the sick and dying increased all the time. She had many visitations from her Lord. She described this time of transition in her diary: 'The One who had kindled in my heart this fire of love, kept fanning it day by day to a more consuming flame... love had grown strong as death, my heart was rent in two, my soul was set free from this flesh, but alas! For how short a time!' Soon she found herself teaching before the great minds of her world. A simple girl that had never been to any school! Such is the power of divine inspiration. Catherine became the spiritual teacher of bishops, popes and kings. Surrounded by a community that called her 'dolcissma mama' - sweetest mother, she died when thirty three, not long after having written what she simply called 'The Book;' it is 'the dialogue' between her soul and the Lord.

What would it be like, to live in an awareness that constantly perceives everything as light and love, how would we act? How would we feel? How does light taste? How do we dance with it? How do we sleep in that light, that love: we really need the experience of it! The only change is in our perception; such love could bring ultimate contentment or would it go beyond that and fill us with **joy and enthusiasm?**

What else can there be, when the fire of love burns in us? We are used to thinking of 'love' as the passionate and possessive feeling towards our lovers, partners, friends, children, dogs, cats, cars, etc. That is not the love that is meant here, because that love is created from wanting to have, hold, dominate, own – it is love stemming from our own need – ' without her/him I will die!' such love is a joke, a tragedy. Real love comes - like sun energy, free! It gives forgiveness and warmth to a child; compassion and support to a person who needs; it gives friendship to an equal and respect and devotion to those that are older and wiser. When we have love to give, we do not want something in return – we feel content, full - knowing and trusting there is enough! Such 'loving existence' seems to be forgotten by our Western society and with forgetting it, we starve ourselves of love! The consequences of this are apparent every day.

How can we forget that all through the ages, life renewed itself; it didn't and doesn't stop because we have enough - the sun does not stop shining because we are warm enough, it still gives warmth the next day, and the next, ad infinitum. The experience of such abundance brings joy, fills us with **enthusiasm (**Greek: filled with God, interpreted more freely: filled with light).

When I picture joy and enthusiasm, my mind's eye sees ***Fireworks***:
- sees an abundance of bursting, sparkling colours thrown against a dark night sky;
- or the abundance of a summer meadow overflowing with poppies, like a Monet picture; or the gurgling, laughter of a small child that totally gives itself to the joy it feels;
- or a song-bird, that sings to its hearts delight, not for an audience, but out of delight;
- or... or...

For me, joy is connected to beauty, to brightness, to lightness, to happiness, even to **celebration**. Remember how in every celebration there seems fire i.e. candles on the birthday-cake; candles on the house-altar; lights on the Christmas tree - to watch dancing flames brings joy to a room and to the hearts of people.

Enthusiasm and inspiration are the means of transformation for any type of **Creativity**; it transforms a blank canvas into a work of art, etc.

There is however another sinister aspect to fire; watch a grass fire!

Grass is eaten! But watch what happens then... finished in one place, the fire proceeds, going on to take the next bits of grass! Behind it (for the moment at least) is – devastation; and fire can't go back over the same ground – there is nothing for it to feed on; there is no going back - no past, just death.

And moreover keep watching as the grass fire reaches a path!

There might be more burn-able grass growing beyond the path, but when the fire reaches the path it dies for lack of burning material. **Fire has no past** - but also it has **no sense of future, it only exists right now.** It lives totally in the present. Contemplate it!

 What it leaves behind are minerals, base chemicals that form more earth; mix that with water and the future can begin! But fire has no own future; its future is earth!

Furthermore fire needs feeding! It can not simply 'go and get it'; it gets fed with effort... either from oneself or others.

The fire of our 'earthly love' needs to be fed, we have to do things for those we love, we have to give our support, our care, our guidance, our warmth share our light, etc. When we are 'in love' we do it naturally, we give our time and our thoughts, our unending attention to the object of our love – and if we stop feeding our love, do not talk, share, write or perform such actions anymore with/for our loved ones - love dies.

The spiritual fire of love, the fire of enlightenment, gets fed by austerities or self-discipline; the fire of spiritual love **needs food** just like any other fire, and such food means we have to give up something that can be transformed. What are you willing to give up for the fire of divine love?

What we have to give up could be as simple as our tea break, or as complex as our Ego, our future, or our Life's aspirations. We love children; we give up much time in bringing them up. We love to play the clarinet, we give up many hours in order to practise it; we love our families, we give up our own time and interests in order to have jobs, so that we can provide for them. We love nature, we give up destroying the environment. The more we love life itself, people, animals and plants – the easier we can give up our life to serve them. However little or small, however high or low - if we love it, we have to give up something for it, even if it is our fear, anger or hate! That is the nature of things; that is the law of fire.

That is the same for the love of God. Only through **renunciation,** through giving up something, can the burning transformation take place. This process has been called: **purification.** Metal ore has to give up its association with earth in the melting process so that it can become pure gold which can be poured into the most beautiful, radiating jewellery. The interdependence between purification, dissolution and creation can be easily put into practice e.g. before cutting a tree - plant a new one!

But enough of these musings let us watch some people:

It is a lovely sunny day in spring; many people are in the park. Over there are some boys kicking a ball; over here, a group of ten - or eleven - year old girls stand around. They are watched by an old man; may be he is the grandfather of one of the children. He has his face turned to the sun, he looks peaceful but alert, watching to make sure that the girls are OK. I sit beside him and watch the girls.

There is a blond girl with a green jacket that seems very energetic and cannot stand still, she hops constantly from one foot to the other, bending her knees, wriggling her body.

There is a pale-faced, quiet and very thin girl that wears a white anorak, and she seems bent over, concentrating hard, straining to get what the others are talking about, she seems to have a slight cough.

Then a plump girl stands next to the pale girl; she looks firmly rooted to the ground as though nothing can shift her, but her eyes seem very gentle as though she was pleading with the others to let her take part in the game.

The fourth girl has an extra clear, sharp face and a high forehead, she wears a long girlie skirt and a short black jacket, and fashionable blue boots, she has a very straight back, as though she is pushed to stand straight by an invisible force. They all focus on the fifth girl, a little dark-haired girl, who talks very animatedly with her hands and feet She wears red corduroy trousers with a black top. Suddenly there is movement in the group - everybody is paying attention to the small dark girl: she shows them movements, like a dance routine, that she has picked up from the TV. She is definitely in command now, she tells the others what to do, and how to move. She talks in a firm loud voice, straining for patience when they 'don't get it.' She is so enthusiastic about it, that everyone, even the plump, clumsy looking girl, tries to follow the steps.

Yet in a blink of an eye, the little dark girl turns her back on the rest and runs off, shouting "catch me;" slightly bewildered by the sudden change, the others run after her. The blond one catches her, and its her turn to run away - once she is caught, the little black girl suddenly stops in her tracks. Regardless of the fact that most of the other girls haven't had a turn in the game, she suggests that they play 'teacher and school.' "I am the teacher," she announces and, "we have P. E." Of course the others follow her various instructions to contort their body, until it becomes clear that the girl in white can actually do the splits better. That is enough! The dark-haired girl takes off her jacket and jeans; she is getting too hot and needs more mobility, to try harder. And she succeeds! In a few rounds, she is tops again. The plump girl gets frustrated with this show of physical ability, moves out of the circle and sits down on the ground. As soon as she notices it, the little dark-haired girl walks over to her and asks her to come back, "don't be sad, I will help you, I will show you." As good as her word, she tries to show the plump girl how to do it and as it doesn't bear fruit, she suggests yet another game. This time, they are all supposed to roll down the grassy bank. The girls protest: "I am not allowed," "I will get grass stains on my clothes," "I don't want to," etc. The little dark-haired girl sits down by a bush, half hiding from the girls, tired, spent, sulking. "It's always me who has to give in - give up. Why? Live is so unfair." Tears run down her face. The others find a game of their own, they do not react anymore, because: she always gets 'her funny turns!'

The old man gets up and walks towards the weeping girl, he gives her his hanky and invites her to sit with him for a while and watch the others. He is the granddad of the blond girl, but he has watched these children play for many years, and knows each one well. As she sits in the sun, with the gentle and contented granddad, the little girl recovers. He pulls out some biscuits from his pockets and gives them to the girl. When they see that, the others come rushing too, like a flock of birds. As each has one biscuit, the dark-haired has by now had her third! When finished, they all go off again to play. The little dark-haired girl suggests playing circus and all, filled with enthusiasm, follow her suggestions.

As you will be aware the girls each represent one element, and the little dark girl is representing the element of Fire. She is full of enthusiasm and inspiration, so she can lead all the other girls, even though they are of totally different character. The others feed off her ability to glow and shine. She loves to perform, to sparkle and play like the flames of a fire in all colours. She has initiative, drive and is full of ideas; it seems there is not a dull moment in her company.

She could be seen as bossy but the others do not seem to experience her that way, it is more that her boundless imagination that seems to sweep the others off their feet. There is not enough time to finish one game, when the next idea is already there, a flame seemingly turning in mid-air. But she is also compassionate, loving and caring in her interaction with the plump girl and indeed with all of them, she wants 'everybody to be happy.' She will go out of her way, even interrupt her own play, to make sure others are fine. While she is burning, she radiates fun, laughter and warmth, but invariably there comes the time, where her mood suddenly collapses. She imagines being hurt 'by a blade of grass,' she has been 'deserted and mistreated by everybody'; 'it is not fair, they will not play my game'; she is at the end of her energy; hurt, miserable, drowning in ashes, she has to retreat, sulk and even cry. Her body, mind and soul have burned so bright that it has no fuel left, she is exhausted! The body demands rest, and the mind makes up fictitious pains and the disasters of a hypochondriac, so that it gets its rest. The wise granddad has seen this so often that he understands and has help at hand: a rest and a biscuit are ready for the body to refuel. A tender word and a handkerchief help the emotions to recover and a smile warms the spirit. Thus restored, the fire energy has new fuel and is as happy as though nothing has happened. The play goes on!

The fire person will always need such a Granddad, a source from which to replenish its energy, or even just to show how to husband the energy and keep an eye on it, otherwise the fire person will burn itself out, with mental or physical damage. The 'granddad' can be any person or an aspect of their own personality, such as their faith; it can be their life partner, their teacher or Guru. But without such loving, warming guide a Fire person might become periodically depressive, buried in the ashes of their own doing.

If fire burns untamed, it kills life as in the vast deserts of the world; if fire burns too ferociously, it puts out itself, like in the firestorms of Hiroshima or Dresden; fire kills fire!

To prevent disaster, fire has to be tamed, the sun-rays are safe because they are 93 million miles away and there is the ozone layer to keep us from harm!

Nelson Mandela said in his inaugural speech in South Africa:

"Our deepest fear is not that we are inadequate. Our deepest fear is that we are powerful beyond measure. It is our light, not our darkness that most frightens us."

6.2 Associations with the Fire Element

In Ayurveda and in mediaeval Europe (Hildegard von Bingen) it is pointed out that the source of Fire is in the body is the liver, yet it expresses in the heart and the small intestines. Two further organs are associated with fire (supplementary fire) the immune system etc. and the Pericardium. Let's look how these are working in

6.2: a) Complementary Medicine

The Heart is the centre of the human organism. It governs the circulatory system, meaning it is responsible for carrying oxygen and nutrients throughout the body, producing warmth and bringing back waste products to be dealt with by the respective organs. The heart itself is a muscular sac; it pumps blood through its four chambers and into the blood vessels which transport the blood to the lungs, where oxygen is absorbed and carbon dioxide excreted; and brings it eventually to the cells. Thus the heart is constantly active; it cannot take a rest. If it stops the organism is dead within minutes. Just like a king or a 'supreme ruler' it is always in charge, always active.

The heart activity is characterised by waves of expansion and contraction, created by an intrinsic system that has no need for a nerve supply from the brain; however the intrinsic system can be stimulated or depressed by nerve impulses initiated in the brain or by some hormones. There are some nerves originating in the medulla oblongata, which increase or decrease the rate and force of the heartbeat. The activity of the heart, though not under control of the will, can receive messages from the brain that are triggered by sensory input and translated into more - or less - activity.

Apart from this central physiological task, the heart is seen in many cultures as the seat of love and other emotions. The reason is probably found in the impact that emotions have on it by releasing adrenaline or non-adrenaline.

We associate the heart with **the** soul; yet Chinese medicine distinguishes three different 'Souls.' There is the corporeal soul or spirit, (connected with the lungs and the vital breath) and the ethereal soul or HUN which houses in the liver (life-force). Lastly there is SHEN, which is Yin in character and said to correspond to the mind. It is responsible for complex mental, emotional and spiritual feelings. It receives its input from the senses, thus the events outside the body are directly related to a change in heart rate.

This last aspect corresponds to Indian tradition, where the spiritual heart is the seat of the mind and especially that aspect of mind that relates to identity, the 'I-ness.'

The second major organ of the Fire Element is **the Small Intestine**. In a manner of speaking, it is a continuation of the stomach; it is a little over five metres long and lies in the abdominal cavity. Its function is to separate out the food the body can digest from that which it can't, and move the latter on. It secretes digestive hormones, enzymes and protects against microbic infection of the organism.

The energy released here assists the heart by keeping energy and blood occupied low in the body (*hara*) in situations of anger, shock, trauma etc. Otherwise the heart would be 'flooded' by a rush of blood and exhaust itself in the effort to cope with the onrush. In severe traumatic cases, the blood might be held in the lower belly, leading to stagnation, felt as 'tummy ache' (especially with children) or as back pain and/or chilling of the legs (especially when the reproductive system is affected)

In addition to the heart and small intestines, the Fire Element is linked to **two further 'organs'** which are however not acknowledged as such in Western medicine. These two **'supplementary fires'** relate to functions known in oriental medicine as the Heart Constrictor (HC) and the Triple Heater (TH).

The **Heart Constrictor** (HC) relates physiologically to the **pericardium,** which is a set of fibrous sacs filled with fluid, providing a protective space around the heart. This is also responsible for the heart's nutrition; it is sometimes called the Heart Protector. HC in particular is said to influence the centre of the thorax, and is referred to as the source of joy and happiness.

The second major energy field of the supplementary Fire, is called the **'Triple Heater'** (TH), it has a supplementary function to the small intestine. The TH controls the energy circulation in the body and with it, warmth and heat; it regulates the metabolic activity. It is envisaged as distributing *Ki* (vital life energy) in three parts: the chest (lungs, the solar plexus and navel), the middle of the body (Stomach, Spleen, Gall Bladder) and thirdly, mainly the area below the navel (body fluids, i.e. bladder but also liver, kidney etc). 'The Triple Heater controls peripheral circulation and lymphatic flow. This means that the Triple Heater is also closely related to the skin, mucus membranes and serous membranes, which are supplied by peripheral capillary and lymphatic networks.' [60]

Both HC and TH can be understood as having the function of circulation (be it heat or nutrients), and protection. Often these meridians are the ones that 'fight off' illness or other disturbing influences; they suffer for this, being easily put out of balance.

We can observe the working of these two meridians in our bodies when flu viruses are 'in the air;' the outside of the upper arms hurt (along TH), or the outside of our calves are sensitive. The same applies when we have an acute emotional problem like a piece of bad news or an argument with a loved one. In these cases we might feel a pain on the inside of the arm or even the palm of the hand; we quickly respond by drawing our arms in.

The pharmaceutical industry has produced wristbands that press on the HC meridian to bring about a quick re-balancing, needed in cases of sea or car-sickness. Furthermore, a descriptive metaphor describes HC as a 'punch bag' for pain, trauma and shock: 'a stand-in' so that the sovereign itself (the heart) does not get hurt. The effects of 'taking the blow' on a person might be that she finds it difficult to relax, is always *en-garde*.

Together HT, HC and Triple Heater represent a person's vitality in a physical and psychological sense. They share with Fire the notion of protection, of burning and distributing energy; of separating (purifying) what can be burned (used) and what not. They harbour joy and enthusiasm, and transform stimuli received from the environment into *appropriate* internal responses. *Over reaction*, if it is frequent, over exhausts the heart; such people tend to have blood rushing to their head too easily, suffer from sweaty palms, palpitations and imbalances in the circulatory system, which can develop into more serious heart problems. On the other hand *'under reaction'* goes more easily unnoticed. Such signs as disinterest, a feeling of giving up, perpetual fatigue which can lead to depression are **signs of imbalances in HT.** If a person never laughs, has lost all zest for life, finds it difficult to have fun or express joy (even when presented with the most lovely bunch of flowers or good news) then these inappropriate response to good things in life are relate to an imbalance in HT. Other imbalances are: nervous tension, over sensitivity, poor appetite, restlessness, anxiousness, lack of memory, no will power, a stiffness in the solar plexus, thirst and speech impediments, like stuttering.

Imbalances in HC in milder forms show up as cold extremities, heartburn, insomnia, frequent dreaming and nervousness in social situations. The person is unsure of the input she might receive and whether she can deal appropriately with it. Nervousness or shyness result. In more severe cases imbalances in HC lead to palpitation, even to *angina pectoris.*

Imbalances in TH are linked to distribution. Malfunctioning will lead to headaches and dizziness, hypertension, constantly clenched fists, tight arms, signs of insecurity, sensitivity to changes in the environment, tendencies to allergies, colds and skin irritations, itching from eczema. A fight is going on between the world inside the body and the outside environment.

Imbalances in Si point to malfunctioning in the area of nutritional assimilation, causing all sorts of deficiency illnesses. It can lead to pollution or starvation, to such 'simple' matters as irregular bowel movements. Thinking is a kind of mental digestive process; thus people with an imbalance in Si energy often have difficulties in separating what ideas for them are good and what not; or who is best for them, who not; it leads to confusion. Another facet of Si, on a mental level, is concerned about 'moving' things on, or its opposite 'holding things inside.' Imbalances in this area express themselves in holding in anger, or deep sadness, controlling emotions too much. Such holding on can result in determination or stubbornness. A person with an imbalance here might be a very determined person who is driven to accomplishing things. Such a person might always want to see a situation to an end, even when it is unwise; so much so, that he/she totally overworks, suffers from headaches and eventually 'burns out.'

The Location of HT: runs from the centre of the armpit, along the inner arm, down the inside edge of the little finger. It also runs from the armpit across to the sternum, bilateral, down through the belly and surfaces on the inside of the leg along the calf between the ankle and the heel to end at the sole of the foot, circumventing the ball of the heel.

The Location of Si: starts at the outside edge of the little finger, bilateral; along the outside arm and shoulder, up the neck to an endpoint just in front of the middle ear. It also branches off at the neck through the shoulder blades, down the middle on either side of the back into the buttocks; through the pelvis, surfacing on the inside leg, going to the ball of the heel.

The Organ-network of the Heart Constrictor and Triple Heater has to do with circulation and protection, providing body heat and stimulating the immune system.

The Location of HC: starts just besides the nipples, bilateral, along the arm to the inside of the palm ending at the inside nail bed of the middle finger. It branches off at the nipple, forming a half-moon shape towards the sternum, bilaterally up the throat and down the body along the inside leg.

The Location of TH: starts at the outside edge of the ring finger; goes along the outside arm through the elbow, up the shoulders into the neck; bilateral; behind the ears and ends beside the eyebrows. At shoulder level a branch goes down the outside edge of the back, along the ridge of the pelvis and thigh, down the outside of the leg and to the third toe.

In **Ayurveda** these Meridians are associated with the *Dosha Pitta*, regulating the bio-energy involved in the metabolism and hormonal systems. Pitta imbalances can be recognised due to redness, heat, rashes, and inflammation in various parts of the body.

Further associations with the Fire Element: As previously explained, meridians have a Cycle. The time of maximum or peak functioning for HT is around lunch time from 11am to 1pm; for **Si** it is from 1- to 3pm, for HC from 7 to 9pm, and for TH from 9 to 11pm. Conversely the time of minimum function, is 11pm to 1am for HT, for Si from 1 to 3am, for HC from 7 to 9am and for TH from 9 to 11am. Symptoms of imbalances will be especially noticeable at these times. For example: a person might feel full of vitality and be very active around lunchtime or might feel extremely fatigued during these periods. Even in a person with balanced Fire Energy, there may be signs of change between maximum and minimum function. Such a person might feel that working at lunchtime and at evening (HC/TH) suits them best, but they are no good in the early morning; then they feel tired and exhausted. A rhythm like this would suit people in the performing arts (Matinees and Evening performances), or any shift-workers who can decide not to work in the morning.

The associated Season for the Fire energy is Summer, for the obvious reason it is the time of great vitality, of generous growth and abundance. Similarly in human terms, the years of family life and career are associated with it; we talk of the summer of life, with its warmth of family life, its abundance and ripening of ideas, achievements and direction in life.

Imbalances then are shown in lack of a drive to achieve, in uncaring behaviour especially towards the family and disinterest in life in general, or conversely in being driven to success, in over achievement which leads to later burn out. This is indicative of the high rate of relatively young businessmen with heart conditions.

The Direction associated with Fire is South and 'the furthest extension,' i.e. the outer circumference (we will look at that later). Fire is most potent in the South, as at least for the Northern Hemisphere, the sun is the highest and warmest in the South. The South is about the capacity to enjoy life, to make merry and celebration, Indian as well as North American Indian traditions also associate love with it. Furthermore, the latter especially associates childlike innocence, play, and laughter with it. We can just see the dancing flames playing like children, singing and dancing to nursery rhymes. It is also about the capacity to have fun, to have humour. Obviously there are people who cannot laugh, or are too serious and have lost the ability to 'be like a child.' In American Indian tradition this expresses as 'Coyote,' the trickster who laughs; it's a clowning animal of great physical fitness that leads us into illusions and teaches us that 'when you can destroy the illusion of who you are to others and be yourself, you will have restored your innocence.' [61] WOW!!! To destroy the illusion of who we are!

The person we think we are, is a construct of our own mind, an assimilation of the opinions of others. We are told that we are beautiful, ugly, stupid, clever, strong or clumsy and we live up to those opinions. Yet on deeper reflection, we will find that we are none of these! They are merely the result of conditioning! Once we cast this illusion off, we become 'innocent' again, like a child. Fire and the South speak of this process of purification into 'innocence,' into freedom!

The Climate associated with Fire is heat. When balanced in the Fire Element, one should feel good in a warm, even hot climates, contrary to that, an imbalance is present if a person dislikes hot weather strongly or desires it passionately, in fact 'can't live anywhere else.' It would be interesting to check the relevant meridians of the thousands of people who head for a better 'life in the sun.' They apparently seek heat, but what do they really miss? Do we use sunny climates to substitute emotional warmth?

The Tissue or parts of the body associated with Fire are blood vessels. The condition of the blood vessels then, can give clues to the state of the meridians, e.g. burst surface vessels in the face, especially around the nose and cheeks, or varicose veins, indicate imbalances. Blood itself is, in its various qualities, linked to all elements. Its colour links it to Fire, yet its liquidity links it to water. Hildegard von Bingen writes; 'without warmth it would not be liquid, without being liquid it would fall off like small scales.' [62]

The Sense Organ is the tongue; its association with Fire might surprise us, yet in Oriental diagnosis the tongue is seen as a miniature picture of the whole organism, with the heart as ruler of the whole organism. The colour, texture and general appearance of the tongue is correlated directly to the condition of the heart. Furthermore, the surface of the tongue is looked upon as a map representing the whole organism. Here is the origin of the practice of tongue scraping in the Orient, where the plaque is scraped off the tongue, just as we scrape it off the teeth, in order to keep the heart healthy.

Hildegard von Bingen's opinion differs, for her and for the Ayurvedic tradition the sense organ of seeing (eyes) is linked to fire.

The Sense related to Fire is Speech. Effects and modes of unclear speech, too fast or too slow speech, a lack of willingness - or the constant need to express oneself verbally, indicate imbalances.

An old lady in her eighties told me that she still needs to study (at colleges and university etc.), so that she always has a topic to discuss with people. Why - I asked - does she need the constant talk? Her answer: "Talking to people, always having something to exchange with people, attracts people to me; that is a very important source of human contact, in fact it is my only source of warmth, yes, talking, exchanging ideas, for me creates human warmth. No, even more, talking creates warmth inside me." Once there were no people to talk to... she literally died.

Here is a case of somebody who attempts to balance an obvious problem by exercising the Fire energy in the mode of speech to generate warmth, which for some unknown reason could not be generated elsewhere. Speech has in many traditions been known as special transforming power; it brings thought or ideas into manifest form. The creation myth in the Judeo-Christian tradition starts with: God said 'let there be light... and there was light!' (Gen.1.3) And St. John has it, that 'In the beginning was the Word, and the Word was with God, and the Word was God.' (St John 1) Similarly a Japanese story tells about the priest, Kuya, who speaks *mantras* (spiritual verse) and each one forms manifestations, in this way creation literally emerges from the words coming out of his mouth. Furthermore the Australian Aboriginals say in the Djanggawal, the creation story of the Dreamtime, each Ancestor gave an original cry of 'I am,' followed by 'I am Snake, Cockatoo... Crocodile... Honeysuckle... Spinifex... ' And so each of the ancient ones put his left foot down calling 'I am... (name).' Their naming created the waterholes, gum trees, rivers and salt pans. This first act of naming goes on and on all over the world until the present day and is revered as the most sacred part of the Ancestors song, that created the world.

The Orifice associated with Fire is the outer ear, because like the tongue, the ear represents the whole body. Imagine a human embryo upside down with the earlobe being the head. Acupuncture points for the whole body are found here, thus the ear represents the realm of the supreme ruler, the heart.

The Fluid connected to Fire is sweat. The Yin and Yang symbol each hold the opposite in their centre as a tiny seed. I see sweat in this way, as fire producing its opposite pole.

The External Manifestation linked to Fire is the complexion. It is not the skin as such (which holds in and limits), but that which goes beyond the body, its radiance, its appearance and tone. This circumference or furthest extension of a person glows like an invisible circle around him/her, just as the rings of flame around the wick of a candle. Some people glow with inner light.

The Colour associated with Fire is red. Even though fire itself has many colours, red seems dominant. Red is passion - is lifeblood (which of course has also reverse connotation: spilt life, bloodshed and war). Maybe for this reason, in Ghana red marks sorrow. At funerals, the family as well as the deceased are clad in red cotton clothes called *Kobene*; for the 'destructive force' has been victorious, transforming the physical Life to the other realms.

On the other hand, in Japan and India, red denotes happiness; the bride wears red, and special gifts are wrapped in red; red signals the joy to give, the joy to receive.

In other parts of Asia, red symbolises independence and courage, the courage to be active; passion is spiritual power, holds the drive to create! In India temples painted red are dedicated to *Shakti*, the creative energy per se, the revered goddess, the *Devi*. She, called *Sri*, is dressed in flowing red robes. Red flowers are offered to her; she is said to be the fire that purifies the spirit, she is also known as *Kundalini. Maha-Kundalini,* the spiritual energy, raises us to the supreme awareness of consciousness, a symbol for active grace, abundance and wealth. Thus the colour red has in many parts become a way to honour the creative energy, and that not only in India - temple gates in Japan (*Tori*) are painted red or have a red roof, columns, flowers or sculptures.

In Central and East Africa the colour worn by the Masai and Samburu is bright red. They wear this colour because it mimics fire and thus the wild animals fear it.

Red has become the colour of safety for the owner, warning off others. How well this works can only be appreciated if one has seen the vast expanses of grey, green savannah, seemingly endless and then many, many miles away there is one bright red dot - a lone Massai with his herd of goats!

In the American Indian tradition too, red is the colour of the South.

A person who has a passion for the colour or an acute dislike, has an imbalance.

The Smell associated with Fire is a definite, unmistakable smell of scorched matter. **The Taste** associated with Fire is bitter, Fire needs stimulus, coffee, tea, chocolate, all grilled or burned foods have such a bitter flavour as does alcohol (Beer, Gin etc). Extreme likes or dislikes for this taste point to an imbalance.

The Grain that is associated with Fire and best serves it, is glutinous millet.   **The fruit** are plums. **The meat** is lamb, t**he vegetable** cabbage. These must be considered carefully. It may be appropriate to eat more or less of these foods if they are neglected, or have been indulged in.

The Expression associated with Fire is laughter, which shows as a subtle undertone of everyday speech, a constant giggle or simply humour. Appropriateness is here as always, the key. An endless joker is just as much out of balance as the always serious person; yet nothing is more heart warming than open, joyous laughter.

The Sound of laughter is like crackles of the fire, and sometimes like fireworks.

The Attitude associated with the Fire Energy is one of receiving, and in a lesser way, control. Receiving is used in the sense of taking in, and holding in the centre. In the extreme this can become obsessive control. So far we have associated the HT with receiving input from the senses and Si with receiving food, ready for transformation. But to be receptive, i.e. open to receive, has much wider implications.

Life energy in Chinese Medicine is divided into two complementary Energies; *Yin* represents 'the receptive,' thus HT is a so called a *Yin*-Meridian, yet at the same time the heart is the supreme ruler, holding all things together in the centre (implying control). Without control fire 'goes wild.'

Fire is constantly feeding itself on what is presented to it, what it can receive. Fire cannot by itself 'go out and get it.' Left alone, it starves, dies down. This means fire is in a constant state of receiving; it lives without planning, without preserving the past. For the Fire, the past is wasteland, the future is not yet 'consumable.' This is of great benefit if one wants to understand a Fire person; she/he needs constant confirmation, needs to receive constant attention, trinkets, applause, food etc. It is no good saying: make a plan... get your own... the person can't and won't. Thus people dominated by their Fire Element are often thought to be irresponsible and indiscriminate; out of balance they have a hard life!

On the other hand, the much loved philosophical concept of 'living in the now,' is very tempting for them; however to be successful with it, they have to make it a conscious choice, not just allow it as a default explanation to justify behaviour.

The supreme ruler, the HT, has to exert some measure of control from the centre. He has to control his servants, the sense organs, and receive their service. To receive means to surrender all control of wanting to 'get it,' or of 'I can do it myself,' or 'I cannot trust anybody to give it to me,' or 'doing it anyway.' Receiving requires an openness and trust that the universe it will provide; a far cry from manipulation!

Such control needs self-knowledge, and thus explains why **the Movement of *Ki*** for the Fire Element is that of meditation and deep thinking. In order to allow us to be receptive, we have to be able to become still ourselves. Our very persona, our *Ego*, has to stop shouting: Me, me, me; our brain, our mind that we are so proud of, has to give up its grip, and decide on a path of non-doing; only then can we be empty enough to receive. Obviously meditation is the tool for such a task.

The Fire Element holds deep spiritual energy, therefore it is not surprising that **the Quality** associated with it, is that of 'in-spiration,' of spirit. 'The heart takes the spirit and the divine Grace and gives it a home.' [63] Hildegard writes that man gets his feelings of sensitivity, his longings, his devotion, from Fire.

The human being is seen with an inherent striving towards a healthy life energy and even a longing for something higher. Being alive means constantly changing energy; it strives towards a healthy, balanced state.

When input comes, it disturbs but immediately triggers the wish to be integrated, transformed and adjusted to health. This is the constant throbbing of the Movement-of-Life, in a physical sense, in a psychological sense, and even in a spiritual sense. Life constantly tries to realign, to fulfil the longing for a higher energy, a higher unity with the ultimate aim of re-merging with its essential nature, the divine Self.

If this longing in any of the three levels is destroyed or lacking, then the result is disorientation, desperation, illness, a state of joyless-ness; we say: the heart has gone out of a person. The result of it is that the life energy gives up, *Ki* collapses.

From the above said it is clear, that religious frenzy, despotism and simple over-indulgence is just as much due to an imbalance in the Fire as rejection of anything spiritual; the latter is total denial to fulfil that longing for health and balance.

Some people thrive on being sick. Hypochondriacs use their illness to feed their e*go* in order to manipulate others. The child screams because something really, really hurts! (A finger got stuck in the hole of a soft blanket!) His screams bring all adults to her/him and thus he receives the attention needed. Behind such behaviour is a sense that life itself has let him down; there is a need to know 'somebody cares,' a deep longing for love, longing to know that there is a heart ready to embrace him.

Imbalances could also show themselves in an everyday way, by lack of inspiration, a drying up of ideas, a loss of sparkle.

The **Activity of** Fire is perpetual transformation. We have considered that above. However let's look especially at **the brain activities** of a person dominated by Fire energy . First it needs mentioning that fire energy has a higher frequency than the first two elemental energies. It means that it vibrates higher i.e. its general activities are more pronounced (or especially feeble). They are especially noticeable in the Temporal and Occipital Lobes; vision and speech are important; there is great need for external energetic input, people tend to be extrovert and have an especially good (or bad) long-term memory.

What happens when this 'Fire energy' builds up...? When it reaches a state beyond tolerance for the individual it simply blows up! It explodes; it is felt by others as **Aggression.** When Fire can't contain itself any more, when a Fire person has reached its largest expansion (tolerance level), just like the fire in nature - it reaches a stage where it is starved of available combustible material and oxygen - then it destroys itself! This form of aggression is probably the most dangerous; either 'fiery-people' damage their health (heart) and destroys what they want to achieve – or it drives away the people they love or worse damages others.

This prods; Eknath Easwaran to say: Anger is inherently its own punishment. [64] Physical forms of aggression are most prevalent and dangerous in this group.

The relationship of Fire to other Elements has been mentioned here and there but let us summarise:

Fire gives birth to Earth. The ashes that fire leaves behind, the minerals and molten waste, make up the earth. A volcano's slowly cooling lava, weathering over thousands of years, will become fertile soil.

Fire controls Air. Fire consumes Air, in its extreme it means total annihilation, the Ozone layer problem is a loud witness. Or from the spiritual realm: intellectual knowledge has to be totally surrendered to be transformed in higher knowing; for it to evolve it needs a quantum leap.

Water and Fire have a two-way relationship; in one way water controls fire, yet water sets fire free from the urge of self-destruction, via the limitations it provides. Water is to Fire, like the North Pole to the South Pole; neither can exist without the other. Without Water, Fire would implode.

When I was a younger woman, I drove through the Nevada desert in an old car. The fan belt broke and the car overheated. To press on, to reach the next village I poured the drinking water into the car. In these conditions it lasted but a few miles, and the next village was 60 miles away! Now I had no water and no transport. Thinking I might hitch a lift, I walked and soon collapsed with dehydration; vultures circling above me, was my last conscious awareness; luckily I was found by a ranger patrol. Apart from learning about my own foolish actions, I had a powerful lesson in the relationship of Water and Fire, outside and inside my body. Without the limiting influence of water, Fire is deadly!

Wood/Space finally is the mother of Fire. It gives birth to it and from there the cycle ends, or rather begins again. Via the cosmic sun - fire reaches earth. Through friction, the sparks of fire are born. With the spark of inspiration, the world of ideas is born. 'The sages looked for an analogy in nature and found fire, which though highly amorphous, is nevertheless possessed of great energy that inspires change. From Fire, the cycle moves on to a more solid, grounded state...' [65]

6.2: b) Association with Personality and Relationships

Now let us recollect what Fire teaches us. <u>On the gross level</u> there is the actual manifestation of fire, which we experience as pleasant warmth or healing heat giving safety, providing energy for growth and bringing happiness; then there is the light of fire, which illuminates giving knowledge. Combination of these make for the following attributes: its creative, inspiring; enthusiastic, prolific, quick, active, powerful, full of vitality and transforming – and equally it spreads easily, is in constant need of nourishment, driven, passionate, volatile, explosive, consuming, irresponsible, indiscriminate, potentially unstoppable, destructive. We have heard that transformation from the destructive fire to the warming hearth-fire, or to the celebration of life is achieved by discipline.

And there Fire <u>on a subtler level</u>, it teaches us loving kindness; talks of sacrifice, of purifying ourselves, of devotion and enlightenment.

Now contemplate how the above attributes come together in a **'Fire person.'**

They might be someone small, rather petite in stature, with a small pointed head, small but strong hands and feet. They might appear rather wiry; 'fit' with an upright, dancing walk; On the other hand they might not walk in a straight line, because they would always be something that catches their eye, distracting them.

If the **Fire energy is balanced**, the person will be full of vitality and of a happy, joyful disposition. The creative force in him/her will be boundless, displaying a colourful array of talents. The person might find it easy to talk; eloquence can be one of their many assets. They like doing many things at once, which can give the impression that they are without co-ordination; but they do not lack co-ordination, its not their body that is lacking but it is their mind that gets easily distracted.

Yet such a person might be especially warm to others, might be amusing and inspiring to her peers and the community, provide a happy home and entertainment for her many friends. She would be a person with seemingly limitless energy that leads an active life, her intimate relationship would be characterised by warmth and passion. One probably finds her/him amongst the performing Arts, where constant stimulus feed his/her enthusiasm, unlimited imagination and abilities. In order to have constant and rich stimulus they need people; in fact they might be terrified of being 'left alone'- it feels to them as though the whole world has forsaken them – 'nobody -loves –me,' and yet the loving mother or friend is next door!

Especially when they are in the 'state' of ashes and exhaustion, they find it difficult to 'ignite' themselves; they might withdraw into themselves, become recluse and cultivate their 'dream-world' from which they can re-gather themselves.

In relationships they tend to be rather unstable, because once a friend, lover or partner is familiar, they might experience a lack of stimulus. They then have to leave and go and search elsewhere; hopefully in a book, or a hobby, but quiet likely in an endless chain of love - affairs.

This behaviour pattern can be broken if they learn to find the love and stimulus they look for in themselves, in their own imaginative and extremely creative personality. Fire people more than most other types oscillate between highs with love, affection, great happiness and joy - and destructive depression and isolation (into which they put themselves) when feeling neglected. If they do, they tend to look to chocolate, coffee, alcohol or even drugs in order to maintain the constant stimulus their body needs. Because they are so active, their body burns the food they provide quickly and the body runs out (burns out).

 This condition leads to extreme exhaustion, which over prolonged periods of careless living will actually lead to heart disease, angina, and heart attacks.

The Emotion related to Fire energy is joy, which brings with it the counterpart of sadness and pain. It's in the nature of life that all temporary emotions come to an end, sadness of departing, of 'moving on' follows.

Too much joy is as hurtful as is too much rage, or too little joy. Those who live a life in constant search of excitement in order to find constant happiness are prone to too high blood pressure, or to heart attacks, for these are the ways of the body telling us to take be more even, to take it easy. This constant search for sexual exchange is a sign of our time fiery times; sexual stimulus is followed quickly by boredom; real commitment is out of the question, because the next person, the next situation might provide more excitement. The result is an unending stream of unfulfilled relationships that leave people empty, their energy is drained; they feel desperate and humanly exhausted as in an emotional desert.

The Manner of reaction to **times of excitement** or change is melancholy, a difficulty in parting. Before we can move on, we have to say good-bye to that which has no more use (Si). Imbalances here show as melancholy; in a fire person this gets exaggerated as one would see on the stage, in a burlesque show. Reactions are 'theatrical': i.e. the loss of a glove might causes a colourful display of maddening grief by a flamboyant film diva; which in turn might results in firing a servant, or calling the fire brigade. We all have come across such artists; unable to measure their emotions they become lonely and 'burned out.' We hear of these people because they are in the 'limelight.'

Imagine a musician of classical music, in his mid thirties, in full swing. I choose the image of classical music because we associate it with spreading joy and light to people; it sparkles and relaxes others. The musician in our story is basically a kind, gentle man with a radiant, all embracing personality, he is cherished by many. He is of a physically small stature, but very agile. It is his own voice, as much as his piano playing, which built his reputation as a musician! He enjoys leading the local orchestra; he loves to inspire others to play there best and to invent forever new ways of playing with harmonics. When he conducts, he seems to sparkle; his body, although immensely focused, becomes like fireworks; music seems to burst out of his every pore; at times he seems to disappear into being sheer energy.

Of course he has to work very hard, he has many practices and performances often late into the nights, and many social engagements. He keeps up with all these demands, by drinking many cups of coffee and nibbling chocolate whenever he can. He is aware that this is not good for him but the 'drive to do,' the enthusiasm for his work - is so great, that he has 'no time to eat properly,' life is simply too exciting for him, he wouldn't wish to miss anything.

A person does not live alone, how does he relate to others?

As in the other cases, we will first see how fire and earth relate to each other. Fire warms the earth from the outside by way of the sun, and from the inside by way of magma (molten earth, a mixture of fire and earth).

In the Chinese Shen-cycle, Fire is regarded as the mother of earth. Thus fire generated planet earth, and it still nurtures and warms it. Fire is also the instigator of any creativity happening on earth, filling it abundantly with manifold forms. On the other hand fire (inside) is given boundaries by earth; to be freed fire has to tear, rip, or violate the earth (volcano). This mutually limiting quality is used when forest fires, oil fires etc. are dammed/suffocated by earth.

There is, as always, an optimal point of balance in this relationship. Then earth does not get too warm so that it can do its job without turning into useless burned out desert, and fire gives just enough to support life without running wild.

From the point of fire, earth is its creation, it feels responsible for it, and maintains it, but it is also always afraid that earth might be limiting it, might stop its movement, might encroach on its space, might interfere.

Any relationship or marriage between two people with the dominant characteristics of **Fire and Earth** mirror these. Fire has it in its nature to love; it even encourages love, warmth, lightness and joy. However, Fire might think: 'I am always the one to give and initiate actions, suggests all games and provide all stimulus!' Fire gets quickly tired of that role, 'if I don't do something, it will never happen.' When tired of Earth person dragging her heels, s/he will quickly look elsewhere for stimulus.

Even when Earth warms up, it is a long way from Fire! But its stability is necessary to give a Fire person a base from which to 'flare up,' a stage from which to perform. Earth's lack of involvement makes such a partnership difficult, yet it does happen, for at its core earth, is in total union with Fire. For that to happen, earth needs to dominate (like the earth crust enveloping its centre). A lasting relationship can only succeed, when the Fire person surrenders to the Earth person, hard to imagine!

But let's see how our musician is doing.

The conductor of the local orchestra has a very good friend; in fact they have been friends since they were together in the school orchestra. The friend is a percussionist, the drummer of the local orchestra and a good one, with a fine sense of rhythm. The conductor in his past and present has been travelling a lot and led quite a chequered life, but wherever he was; he knew he could rely on his 'best friend.' The drummer by contrast never lived out of town, but he understood about the rhythm of life, the cycles of human behaviour, the ups and downs that affect all people. He was a family man, with a lot of common sense and understanding. He liked his high-flying, creative, restless artist friend, because his company was full of ideas and surprises and he had a good heart.

Several times, when the conductor was devastated over newspaper critiques for his performance, or when yet another of his love affairs turned sour, the drummer friend had to 'hold' the conductor with his earth wisdom, stabilising his volatile friend.

But as in any friendship, sometimes the relationship got stressed to its limits:

The orchestra had played very successfully in a neighbouring town and all players went home afterwards (in high spirits) by coach. Immediately after the conductor reached his home, the phone rang. His agent told him that an important, prestigious concert abroad was cancelled; the organisers had changed their minds.

Our performing star slammed the phone down, went straight to the coffee pot and had a large mug of strong coffee, adding a big dram of whisky. The stimulus, of course, did nothing to calm his indignation, instead it made him more angry.

He paced up and down the room; how could they do this to him! Unfair! What did they think they were doing! Suddenly the room seemed too confined, he needed to go out and talk to someone. Totally impulsive, regardless of the time of night (2 a.m.) or the cold wind (without coat), he stormed out to see his drummer friend. He rang the doorbell, long and repeatedly, fuming with indignation and anger! Finally his pal opened the door - sleepy and shocked.

The drummer was not pleased, being pulled out of bed and afraid his children would wake up. Still he still asked his friend into the kitchen. As soon as he sat down, the conductor collapsed into self-pity. He was tired, his anger had worn him out; the fresh air had cooled him down; seeing his friend was enough! He wept, feeling cold and lamenting about life's injustice. His friend had a family to support him; could sleep and 'poor old me, they don't even want my music.'

His friend felt far from fortunate, he needed his sleep - this 'night performance' was uncalled for; this really went too far, what if the kids woke up!

Fire and Earth are like mother and child according to the Element circle. Here Fire behaves more like the raging goddess *Kali* (the 'dark' side of the creative energy, Goddess Shakti). The 'role of the child' is held by a grown family man who has a strong Earth; because he is strong and stable, he is able to hold his family and his friend, giving boundaries to the Fire, which is rapidly collapsing.

The drummer puts his hand on the shoulder of his suffering friend, expressing support and empathy, 'dear friend, we all know what an excellent musician and superb conductor you are; life will bring other opportunities.' When that does not have much effect, he simply says: "Pull yourself together - you can sleep here in the guestroom tonight; we have all had a long day and are exhausted. I'll talk to you tomorrow."

Boundaries are set and the Fire person is given the opportunity to rest and recover. Fire knows on some level, that his friend is right, and sheepishly gives in to such direct clear instruction. He knows if he goes home now, he would probably sit up all night and feel miserable, lamenting his fate, and tomorrow he will be worn out.

The next morning he profusely apologises to his drummer friend and family and tries to make up for the inconvenience caused, and generously invites all for dinner, where they can enjoy the stories of his latest adventures.

Fire can not solve a conflict with 'Earth' out of its own temperament. Left to its own, it will cause devastation; it will burn itself out and take 'Earth' with it via arguments and anger, creating a desert! To solve a conflict, it relies on Earth's density and resistance to put up boundaries and mellow its destructive tendencies.

Now our conductor has a mother who is a Water person. The mother is an artist, in her own right, a poet. How do the classical antipodes **of Fire and Water** relate (looking at it from the perspective of Fire)?

Deep down in his own heart, Fire loves Water; it is in its nature to love and many Fire people especially love swimming, having a shower, sitting by the water - or playing music with the fluidity of flowing water! But, let's look a bit closer:

Fire illumines the dark, deep waters makes them transparent and keep them from freezing over; Fire heats water to boiling point and evaporation. On the other hand, Fire is extinguished by water! Fire's light rays get redirected, fractured by water into something most beautiful: the ray becomes a rainbow!

Fire can share a mutually enriching relationship with a Water person, because it gives warmth, gives love, light and enjoyment to the other.

Fire enjoys the cool, clear wisdom of the Water person; Water teaches, Fire enlightens.

Fire challenges and aggravates the Water person to the point of anger and hate, where the Water person totally loses its 'cool,' and boils over.

Fire is afraid of the power of the Water person, whose calmness can cause Fire lose its vivaciousness, its zest for life.

Fire gets redirected, channelled, by Water to use its energy in constructive ways, ways where the inherent talent becomes manifestation, i.e. art.

Now add to this the power struggle between son and mother, then we have a very difficult relationship indeed. Yet one that is potentially rich, for both partners are inherently creative. Fire's ideas and enthusiasm can be nourished by Water's ability to unfold ideas, making them real. Water's calm refreshing qualities can be welcomed to balance and soothe the extremes and burns of Fire. This requires two people, balanced and aware of the dangers of going to 'extremes.'

The Fire person rightly fears somehow getting squashed if the Water person is strong in the relationship; Fire will react with extreme outpourings like a Fire spitting dragon: aggressive, acrid and domineering, potentially exhausting itself in his constant defensiveness. The actual positive aspects of the partnership, like sharing ideas, lightness, flexibility, joy and warmth will be lost.

The inherent depressive tendency of the Fire person can be brought out, if water is drowning the fire.

Yet Water can also benefit Fire: remember the quality of redirecting light beams! At times Fire spews out its energy in useless little fires; then Water can help to focus, directing the sparks into a skill where they can lead to great success.

For example: Water can encourage the musician to discipline himself to practice playing music, the dancer to dance etc.

It is clear that the relationship between our musician and his mother is not an easy one. Of course the musician loves his mother, but especially when the musician was growing up (and his element weak and unbalanced), the relationship was fraught. Yet as he got older and stronger, a balance seemed to grow. He had been a delightful child, filled with a sunny nature and an obvious talent for singing and making music, much to his mother's delight; it warmed and inspired her. Sometimes they enjoyed doing things together; she wrote poems that he would set to music. But these moments were rare because the child would easily withdraw from the strong mother, even sling anger and abuse at her simply out of fear of her power, and sometimes he would even lash out without reason. In the teenage years their relationship was stretched, so that both sometimes wished they had nothing to do with each other. But always mother had encouraged practising his music and it paid off, as his talent grew. He achieved high standards, even excellence, and enjoyed fame; music gave his life meaning, focus and even stability. Now as grownups, they can share fertile and mutually appreciative moments.

But as the tendencies of mothers in general and Water-mothers in particular surface, conflicts arise. When his mother tried to introduce him to marriageable girls in order to settle and calm down, he blew a fuse and they had a 'mega fight.' How can such conflict between Fire and Water be solved?

If the Fire person is off balance he will just scream and shout at his mother and probably slam the door and just 'go somewhere else for a while!'

But if both are mature and have learned that extreme reactions are useless, then Fire might appeal to Water's clarity and wisdom and try to illuminate her. When the Fire person 'sparkles and dances' before her, warms her and enchants her, the Water person simply has to accept his 'light.' Mother might understand that his career, his freedom, needs him to shine without family obligations. He might even convince her that if he radiates enough light and warmth, it will warm her too.

Fire people often have a brilliant mind; he also might try to transform the issue of marriage into an intellectual battle of wits with the clear minded Water person, which both might enjoy and either could win! In the end, in such conflict between a Fire and Water, the Fire will always try to dominate, to burn brighter and be more - and he will be successful! Water will have to give up or dry up!

As we proceed through the cycle of the elements, we need next to look at the relationship between **Fire and Air** (from the perspective of fire). Almost by definition, fire can not exist without air. Oxygen is - at least on earth - the medium that makes ' fire into fire.' It is the catalyst without which there is no fire. This speaks of a relationship of highest dependency.

All know how Air (wind) can wipe fire into frenzy and drive it to ever greater heights, be they creative or destructive.

But there is more to this relationship. Fire, as we know, has different forms. Of the three: light, warmth and flame, the burning flame is what needs oxygen; light and warmth are different. Whether the wind blows or not, the sunlight will reach the earth! Light needs air not so much to fuel it, as to filter it and direct it. Warmth exists in a sun warmed stone, or the thin earth crust on volcanic land; warmth is there whether wind or not, but the wind helps to distribute the warmth.

So here we find that different abilities of air serve different states (or forms) of fire.

The relationship has always a certain amount of dependency in it, but if fire is tempered into light or warmth, air can provide additional benefits: it sets ever so gentle boundaries, and it distributes the heat, so it cannot build up into destruction.

Air has also the potential to diffuse Fire's energy by channelling it towards a goal. It is less effective than Earth or even Water, but it takes heat into a different direction.

Now we can transfer this into human behaviour.

Our eccentric musician, totally dedicated to his music, might lose all sight of ordinary life. He could be so consumed by rehearsals, practices and concerts that he gets no sleep, no rest, no food and eventually suffers from 'burn out,' heart disease or something else? He needs an organiser that tells him gently when to rest, when, where and how much to perform to look after his business etc. What better than to have an agent that has the qualities of Air.

Such an agent or manager could in fact be at the same time his wife or partner. Such a relationship no doubt is potentially very close; they share life and it is exiting and fulfilling. The Fire partner totally relies on the Air person and Air happily supports him. Of course there are also difficulties.

Fire is given to temperamental bursts; jealousy is part of this. Since Air is extremely fond of Fire, but by no means considers Fire as its only source of interaction, Fire might have a problem with jealousy or envy, which can indeed destroy the relationship. (Air is not only there to feed Fire, but also for people to breathe, for earth to dry and loosen up, etc). Fire might react to competition with total possessiveness, growing out of his/her great need for the close 'fuelling' interaction.

On the other hand, when Fire becomes too powerful, too dramatic and flamboyant and over the top with emotional reactions, it might be the Air partner who in the most natural and gentle way can curb this destructiveness. He/she might either withhold support - or filter out the most vicious rays (or tantrums). It does this by simple distraction. Because of the high dependency, the Fire person will probably accept criticism from Air more easily than from anybody else - not that it will ever accept it easily! Air can help by distracting Fire with its 'own weapons'; it can move lightly, illusively and freely skipping from here to there, so that the heat is taken off; a gentle way for regulating fire's heat

So from the point of view of Fire, a partnership with Air is close, passionate and exciting, and limitations are brought gently and with love. A desirable relationship from this perspective - unless Air whips Fire into a frenzied straw fire that burns itself out in minutes and then leaves - or, Air finds another Fire to ignite and dances somewhere else and leaves!

Fire also can be in such a frenzy that it sucks up all the Air: it annihilates itself, as was the effect of the bombing of such a town as Dresden or Hamburg, (even Hiroshima), where the fire storm was so great it used all the air, suffocating itself. When Fire is left by Air, only ashes remain. It is a tragic loss for Fire. Fire likes to play games with any one of the other Element personalities, it likes to dance from one relationship to another, but when Air does treat it with the same disdain, the flame goes out! The experience might be so traumatic that Fire refuses to be ignited again.

If Earth leaves Fire - fire will bath in its abstract glory, free of restrictions.

If Water leaves Fire - fire will sigh with relief; no more fear of annihilation

If Air leaves Fire - fire dies, physically, mentally or spiritually, it loses its spirit.

If Space leaves Fire - fire knows it is only temporarily, Space will be back.

But lets return to our Conductor. He has an agent that is dominated by the character of Air. Of course it's a woman. She is straight, clear, elegant and extremely efficient. She knows exactly what our conductor needs and how to get it for him, be it a concert review by the right person, be it a prestigious concert hall, be it a new orchestra to work with, or a holiday on a remote island were he can recuperate. She is totally dependable; they have worked together for years and have proved to be an excellent team. She fires his career and he inspires her life, in fact she feels almost like a successful artist herself, through identification with him.

They refrain from having a sexual relationship only because they both know that they could not handle such passion and it would take over their lives completely; so they fuse their passion in the pursuit of excellence, of building a brilliant career.

Nevertheless there are conflicts. The musician's love for his music, love for the audience, love for his friends, all make him into an exuberant person that is much sought after. When he is in town, both agent and musician are constantly asked to attend dinners and prestigious social events, at times especially organised for the celebrated Maestro. In one such spell of late nights, mixed with performances and obligations, our conductor caught a particular nasty and fierce attack of the flu. He certainly could not stand up in front of a crowd of people to perform. Just that night, when his body was feverish, there was a grand, prestigious charity gala concert. An opportunity he would never want to miss, nor could he afford to miss, from the point of his career. How will they solve the problem?

If Fire is totally unbalanced, he might do something very stupid, like taking lots of fever suppressing drugs, put his tuxedo on and go anyway; probably collapsing in the middle of the 'show' and ending up in hospital.

On the other hand, in a more balanced state he might call his agent. She comes over and they think together, what can they do? Sheltering him from his destructive urges to go anyway, she manages to convince him that this is not a good idea. She knows him long enough and well enough that he listens to her and trusts that she only wants what is best for him. What she thinks is best is always close to his own heart - this is the key to their relationship.

As they mull over what to do, she has the idea of letting the first violinist take his place, leading the orchestra. But in order to still be present and not lose out on the chance of making an impact on this grand occasion, he would make a message on tape: a small speech of praise and gratitude and wishing success to all present. Then the agent, as his representative, would give out the prizes he was supposed to hand out to various dignities. She could perform this task with style, and the crisp clean elegance of an Air person.

Air and Fire do not really have conflicts with each other, the only conflict possible is: that Air leaves! Fire can not leave Air, from its own vantage point. If Air leaves Fire it simply would be the end of Fire.

If our conductor did not have such an efficient, sympathetic agent, he would not be able to climb his career as he does; he would not be able to focus on his music as he does, because there would be too many other problems to take care of. Remember the Granddad with the fiery dark-haired child that played in the park? The Agent could just as well be such Granddad! Fire and Air-people have a natural close relationship, they are excellent at it, because they 'think together,' they 'feel together,' they exist together.

Fire and Space have a similar relationship. Fire can only exist in space. That goes for the big fires such as the sun, the moon and the stars - and planets; and the small fires, from the candle light to the nuclear explosion, all happen in a certain space, or even space time continuum.

If we think back to the Chinese tradition of this fifth element, it is just as obvious, for fire resides as potential in wood, just as it burns inside space. Space/Wood is the mother of Fire, as the Chinese Shen-Cycle of the elements tells us, it nourishes and supports it. Fire can do what ever it wants, it can burn and die, can sparkle with joy or rage with anger and hate. Space is not really bothered! Space has an infinite capacity to accept these temperamental outbursts of fire. Balanced Space-people are totally tolerant people; not even fire's gift of warmth is needed by space. Space (contrary to everybody else) has enough power and energy to do without fire. This means that the favourite game of the Fire person - that of manipulation and blackmail for the price of warmth - is useless towards a Space person.

From the point of the Fire person, that makes Space almost boring, it does not lend itself to friction, to arguments, to enthusiastic challenges, space does not ignite, it loses the thrill for the Fire person, there is nothing coming back! Imagine a thousand-ton burning meteorite - a massive ball of fire - sails through space as though nothing has happened.

In a relationship or even marriage between a person dominated by the characteristics of Fire and one characterised by the element of Space (or Wood), an interesting scenario unfolds. It is as though two people live side by side. Quite possibly they share the same interests, yet they are neither competing nor stimulating each other. Even when we think of fire and wood in real terms, wood surrenders without pain or fight, it just burns under the influence of fire. If in this partnership, the Fire person is well-balanced and warm, gentle and loving, the partnership can be harmonious indeed; the Space-partner will receive the warmth and love and mirror it.

Since space holds so much - in fact the whole universe in himself; it will have plenty to stimulate Fire's insatiable appetite for excitement, fun, love and creativity. The Fire person can let off as much steam as it wants, can be as enthusiastic as it wants; the partner will not set boundaries - Space has not got the willingness to limit fire. The Space-partner will allow Fire all the flamboyant, attention seeking behaviour Fire craves and let him/her dance to exhaustion. In fact, in his vast kingdom, Space might be busy elsewhere and not even notice that Fire totally exhausts himself.

Such 'modern' freedom holds the danger that both partners might lose sight of each other, both having a 'great life,' parallel and independent. Such independence can mean, especially for Fire (always in danger of excess and running wild), that without control from outside it will experience disaster. Mind you, this might not be the end of the relationship, because Space holds Fire even in these devastating times. The Space-partner will always be there for his fiery friend and partner, in whatever role.

Fire can depend on Space for support, for nourishment and for shelter. Just as with Air there is dependency here, yet the difference is that Air fuels Fire, it 'makes it burn'; Space lets it burn if it wants to. There is much less active involvement!

Now let us see; the father of our conductor is still alive and he is a Space person. The father likes going to his son's concerts, but afterwards retreats with his pipe into the armchair and does not say much about the performance. In his heart, he might be even proud of his son. He certainly loves him, but the world of music is foreign to him. In his day he used to be the head of a big company, there were many different parts to running such a multi-faceted business, but music - as far as he was concerned was only part of relaxation, not the real stuff!

In his spare time, he is rather more a golf man, himself. Of course he never has put a stone in his son's way - he would not dream of preventing him to do what he really wants to, but, then, what 'does he know, about such extravagance.' The father has indeed encouraged and helped the child musician with generous tuition, contacts through his old boy's network, a word in the right ear here and there; this kind of help is more his style. It has slightly changed, now that he is retired he has more time and listens more and more to recordings of his son's music, and indeed enjoys it. Sometimes, when convenient, he goes to a performance, but enjoys the society of music lovers as much as the music itself - of course he meets several business friends whenever he does go!

Sometimes he does not see his son for months, but it doesn't bother him too much, his son's lifestyle is not his own. He prefers to go for a walk in the brisk morning air, needs to move and do his own thing. He thinks it's crazy to have agents that tell you what to do; he always has been totally his own boss, only telling others what to do.

The town has built a new concert hall. The inaugural concert is held on the first of May. Many dignitaries are invited from all over the country. Our conductor has been asked to give the first performance in this hall on this auspicious occasion. He admits to being honoured, and in his heart of hearts he is flattered, delighted, yes thrilled about it and convinced this will be his star performance; the best evening ever! Since it is his hometown, he will finally make his father really proud of him!

Rehearsals are under way, florists have been instructed to abundantly decorate the hall, and most exclusive cards for invitations have been printed in golden lettering and sent out. One of these cards is sent to his father. Unfortunately, on the 1st May, his father has an International Golf Championship! He is convinced that nothing can be more important than his participation in the game! How do Fire and Space solve their conflict from the perspective of Fire?

Well, where his dad is concerned, the musician is very sensitive. He loves his father dearly despite his apparent aloofness and disinterest. The musician has grown to understand that his dad has a life of his own. He accepts that they are different, yet he still feels very close to his father. When he is in a balanced state, his love for his father and the closeness is just there in the background; but when he is in a state of need, the distance of his father causes him grief. The slightest criticism or even humorous remark is taken to heart and felt as rejection; Fire immediately feels then a withdrawal of support and is 'mortally wounded.' Why, he then wails 'does his father never support him,' understand him, love him etc. He blows the situation totally out of proportion. The day he learns that his father has decided to attend his 'international golf match' instead of his special concert, is a black day indeed for the conductor. He feels rejected, unloved and downtrodden; the little boy in him wants his father so badly to be part of his glory, so badly to show that he is good and loveable. So first he is stunned with shock, then he cries in his study for a while, then he flees into his music and listens for a while. As he settles down, and the feelings of the little boy are pacified by the music, he takes charge again. Maybe there are ways around this situation, and if not - well it is Father's choice and Father's loss! So he decides to ring his father.

Father explains that he would of course like to come, but the tournament is important to him and such an opportunity might not present itself for him at his age again. He describes the match and where it is, and the golf course and the people. Bored and still disappointed, the musician listens and reluctantly accepts. Then, suddenly his brain kicks into gear, a spark!

Did father say the tournament is in Par - that means a town an hour's flight away. If the tournament is in the daytime, on both days... if Father took the plane, rather than drive; if he would present his father with a plane ticket...? If? Maybe both their wishes could come true. And so they embark on working out the details, both relieved that they did not have to let go of what each wanted.

In relationship to Space, the Fire person is always inventive and can transform situations, it has plenty of sparks flying through space, so hopefully in a conflict situation one such spark will help to make Fire and Space find a solution. Both are willing, yet Fire is the one that needs to make it happen - for Space won't.

6.2: c) Associations for Spiritual Evolution (Yoga)

Fire is the most used symbol in the language of Yoga, in fact one speaks of Yoga itself as Fire. In the practice of Yoga or any *Sadhana,* we offer our life and mind to the fire of transformation; the Sanskrit word for fire is *'Agni,'* meaning the transforming force. The drive to advance, evolve, especially on a spiritual level is inborn in man (albeit neglected) – this drive itself is the 'transforming power.' There are many aspects to this, only a few can be highlighted.

Qualities/Steps in Sadhana. Fire in Sadhana expresses as the burning power of love, and the fire of knowledge; when both merge on the highest level, the goal is achieved. Being filled with the transforming power of love and devotion in India is called Bhakti Yoga. By totally identifying with the object of love (God, Guru or beyond...) one loses one's ego; such fire of love purifies, bringing about a state of light, delight and ecstasy - called bliss or Ananda. Such divine love is found in all major religious traditions. It was there in ancient Greece as agape, it is the essence of Christ's teachings, is pinnacle of Sufism and is at the centre of the Buddhist tradition etc. etc. Love for the Divine has its root in man's own heart, it is a divine treasure buried deep inside man; once released it is totally absorbing, it has not even words to describe it.

This absorption can be experienced through any aspect of nature; nature's beauty and magnificence triggers unattached enjoyment. The 'real' appearance becomes unimportant, for what is seen, is seen through the eyes of love. This love does not see the object through its critical faculty, there is no judgement, only awe for the splendour of divine creative energy. From here the 'furthest extension,' the highest goal is reached, human potential is fully realised, man becomes pure in spirit and the world can be enjoyed for what it is - a play of energies; the goal is joy, pure and eternal bliss – Nitya-ananda.

The second facet of the spiritual fire, the fire of knowledge, burns away, destroys all ignorance. By using the mind, one penetrates into the mysteries of existence. All veils of conditionings are destroyed, are seen as temporary and unreal. Finally nothing remains bar the insight that there is no person, no ego, no witness of the process of life even - there only is the workings of pure creative energy, in ever changing forms – yet herself formless, beyond all concepts. From the ashes of destruction of all ignorance, rises the highest insight. 'Being' rests in the witness-state of pure spirit, from where the world can be enjoyed for what it is - a play of energies; the goal is joy and eternal bliss – Nitya- ananda.

As for the level of consciousness? Fire is the power of transformation; yet this transformation does not come via our doing. Hidden, like in deep sleep, in the depth of consciousness the gates of the fourth level of consciousness, Turya, the state of bliss and the Beyond are opened – this stage is only reached through grace. The agent for that transformation is divine grace.

Now let's come back to a lower level of considerations. We have talked before about our identification with the physical body and the persona, and that these consist of different **energy fields;** lets look at their quality and the relevant **energetic anatomy.**

The energy field connected to the Element of Fire, is the **Manomaya Kosha,** (Sheath of the Mind). It is maintained by Prana, through the chemical soup prepared by the Annamaya Kosha and its **gastric fire.** Here various 'moods' are created, mental frames of the 'I-consciousness'. There are nine different moods (*rasa*) that are played out in the drama of life. The mixture of these emotions and moods of *rasa* gives individual character to the *jiva* (personal soul). But let's stay with the gastric fire. There are seven such fires recognised in the Five Koshas.

The first is the digestive fire (*jatharagni*), particularly working in the small intestine (meridians!); the second is *pranagni*, (burning power that turns oxygen into vitality).

The third fire is the fire of perception (*manasika agni*), the mental fire transforms sensory input into ideas, thoughts, etc. The fourth is the fire of discrimination, (*vijnaagni*),that uses the thoughts and ideas and transforms then into intelligent insights and understanding in wider concepts, beyond.

The fifth is the fire of love (*ananda*) which expresses in the un-evolved person as desire; the sixth is the fire of consciousness (*Chid-agni*); it is ultimate self-knowledge, where the seer sees the entire universe as his body. The seventh and final fire is the Fire of Being, *Brahmagni;* it is self-consuming reality, all existence is permanent, self-transforming fire.

When the divine, creative energy works in the *Manamaya kosha*, the third body associated with the Fire Element, it expresses through the **Manipura Chakra**. This is situated at the navel area, and 'physically relates to the small intestine and the heart (the Fire Organs). It is energetically related to the liver '(closely connected to Fire/*Pitta*)'. [66] When it especially works here, the person mainly lives at the level of the mind. He/she identifies with the mind; she might be striving for better education, trying to hold up the values of a given culture and is concerned about mental and social attitudes of a society.

Manipura, the third *chakra* is associated with the frequency of 520 Htz., the colour red and has a fiery red triangle in its centre; it is surrounded by ten blue petals symbolising ten mental modifications (*vrittis*): spiritual ignorance (*avidya*), thirst, jealousy, treachery, shame, fear, disgust, delusion, foolishness and suffering (*dukha*). The petals also symbolise the ten *pranas*. Indian wisdom associates it with the right nostril (*Pingala nadi*) the sushumna and the seed syllable 'Tram' or 'Ram' and 'pham.' The deity at its centre is Rudra, and his female counterpart. The physical organs associated with it are: the abdomen, stomach, upper intestines, liver, gallbladder, kidney, pancreas, adrenals, spleen, middle spine and the epigastrian and solar-plexus. The more psychological, emotional and mental factors associated with it are: mental activity (*Manas*- mind), knowledge and will-power. The qualities that have to be purified here are hatred and treachery, fear and intimidation; the digestive fire has to be purified (in more than one sense) and trust built. Therefore, self-esteem, self-respect and the ability to take care of others is cultivated here; the responsibility for making ones own decisions is learned.

The Navel Centre is also, in some traditions, associated with the element of water, in the sense of transformation and 'assimilation of subconscious material' and as such with a white disc, symbolising a reflective quality.

Perception takes place on this level mainly through intuition; once the lessons are learned they give a wider perspective, a vague sense of knowing on the sensual level; from here intent and motivation are developed. The Need this energy generates is for understanding ourselves- and others clear and rationally.

In the Tibetan system, it is associated with the Tibetan symbol of Buddha *Ratnasambava*, who symbolises generosity and giving spiritually and materially. Physical ailments caused by malfunctioning on this level are:

arthritis, gastric and
duodenal ulcers/cancer,
pancreas/diabetes/ingestion/anorexia/bulimia/liver
dysfunction/hepatitis and adrenal problems.

The young person between the ages of fourteen and twenty-one is said to be working on this *chakra*. They want to be in tune with society (fashion), are arrogant yet demand respect from others. Their Ego is strong, they know... and express their personal power. The ego feels proud to be able to control. However the aim is to achieve a more realistic sense of self, more stable and honest relationships with others and the environment.

Practising **Asanas** can help on this path; but asana (posture) can never be alone, it is always accompanied by the breath. When the breath is especially used to 'fire' the body to give it energy and heat such as by using the ujjayi breath, then any posture works with the Fire Element. This is especially so in Pattabhi Joi's Ashtanga Yoga. The heat generated though is not just used as such, but is instrumental in purifying the body, serving literally by burning up impurities and toxins. When controlled breath is used to stoke the inner fire, the quality of transforming and purifying is uppermost.

In a way one could say this process of detoxification is the main reason of practising asanas (other than the meditation postures). The fire of Yoga on a physical level transforms matter into purer and purer existence, until - as the yogis of the Tamil Tradition of South India believe, eventually the matter can be transformed into spirit. An alchemy takes place where physical body becomes a 'golden body,' which is 'almost pure spirit' and as such then chooses a material form according to his will and purpose.

This might seem far out, but the foundations for it, practising asanas that especially work on the Fire Element is very real, the asana chosen can either work on increasing or balancing fire. A*sanas* with a strong emphasis on Fire are those that open the Pelvis and thus strengthen the *bandhas* (muscular locks to preserve energy), and those postures that exercise the fire meridians. (By bending backwards, HT, HC and TH are exercised (see meridians); postures that mainly work on the inside legs/arms (intense forward bends and intense twists) also are related to Fire. This we find in: *Halasana* (Plough), *Dandasana* (both these also have strong Earth), *Urdhva Dhanurasana; Urdvakapadasana, Parivritakapadasana, Parsvaikapadasana, Urdvkonasana* (all sitting postures with strong legwork); *Utthita Hasta Padangusthasana* (standing legwork); and of course *Virabhadrasana,,* the various variations of the warrior pose. Most *asanas* work on several Elements.

The *asanas* are of course only one aspect of the eight limbs of Yoga (Patanjali); before any of these can be successfully practised one needs to purify one's behaviour. This aspect of the fire of Yoga refers to the ethical code, the *Yamas* and *Niyamas*.

From contemplating the nature and teachings of Fire, we recognise two of their maxims: **Aparigraha** and **Ishvara pranidhana**. The former refers to the abstinence of avariciousness. Fire needs to learn the meaning of 'enough'! Not to need 'more than is essential.' Thus stop its greed and desire; anger and frustration only rises when we have not been able to be, get, or do what we want. Even gifts should be abstained from - as they only bind us to the giver.

The latter aspect refers to 'devotion or reverence to God.' If you are aware of this dimension, then there is nothing left except reverence for God - then 'no more is needed.' The connection between the *Yamas and Niyamas* here are very clear. Once there is devotion, service and love expand to what we call universal love – you could call it supreme energy or simply the 'Lord' itself, as does Mechthild of Magdeburg,

> Lord, your glory pours into my soul;
> like sunlight against gold.
> When may I rest within You, Lord? [67] (12th Cent. AD)

So how can we sum up the **Dharma of Fire?** The dharma of fire is to burn, to transform one 'thing' into another. Transformation began before time; what was the original 'essence,' the dharma that is continuously transformed – irrespective of time and space? Today finally science agrees with a notion long known to the wise - that this original force is some form of consciousness - but this is all we can say about it, although Quantum physics has probably come closer to the Mystery than any other explanation. [68] To understand, we have to be able to penetrate the interdependence between the forms (matter) and the eternal formless (spirit) or as it is called in 'Yoga speech,' *Prakriti* and *Purusha*. There is nothing we can say about the formless, as soon as we do, we give it form. But what we can do, is recognise *IT* in *Prakriti*, in form. See God in his Creation, and celebrate this wonder, with all our being; that is devotion. Isn't it also the dharma of fire to celebrate and 'be joy'?

For this knowledge has to expand beyond the activity of fire.

Knowledge related to the Element Fire is mental knowledge, it 'sees in all beings various entities of distinct kinds as different from each other, know that knowledge as *rajasic* (passionate).' (Gita XVIII/21) The Bhagavad Gita here refers to those people whose mind is dominated by Fire's intellectual fervour. Their mind runs especially here and there, clinging to sense perceptions; they are easily caught up in opinions and judgements. The Ayurvedic *dosha* addressed here is *Pitta*, ruled by the passion of action; action power is another word for transformation. People get caught up in their individual achievement and success, often regardless of means and method, and forget the aim: insight into **the unity** of all existence.

Happiness characterised by Fire and Air, arises from movement and passion. 'That happiness which arises in our bosom when the appropriate world-of-objects comes in contact with our sense organs is indeed a thrill that is nectarine at the beginning, but unfortunately it vanishes as quickly as it comes, dumping the enjoyer into a pit of exhaustion... this contact cannot be permanently established; for the objects are always variable... and changing... No man can FULLY enjoy even the passing glitter of joy that the sense organs give him... it gets unfortunately tainted by an anxiety that it may leave him.' This sense-orientated happiness does not last. (Holy Geeta XVIII/38) Fire has the capacity though, for much deeper, lasting happiness. It can taste the '**joy of being**,' that joy is the bliss of man's destiny.

Meditation can be a 'god's end' for people dominated by Fire energy, it can calm their inherent anger and aggression, their need to 'get on doing this and that' and their ability to concentrate can be put to good use. The danger is they want to achieve something here too – they have to learn to relinquish all control, and become **receptive**, this way they can expand their hearts and minds. To meditate on forgiveness, compassion and love is a great help. To surrender to the divinity of their choice is the ultimate Meditation for these people.

What than can we learned from meditating on Fire? None can say it better than this ancient prayer from the Aboriginals of Australia.

> 'May the fire be in our thoughts, making them true, good and just.
> May it protect us from the evil one.
> May the fire be in our eyes.
> May it open our eyes to share what is good in life.
> We ask that the fire protect us from what is not rightfully ours.
> May the fire be in our ears.
> We pray that we may hear with a deep, deep listening so that we may hear the flow of water and of all creation.

And the dreaming, may it protect us from gossip and things that harm and break down our families.

May the fire be on our lips so that we may speak the truth in kindness, that we may serve and encourage others.

May the fire protect us from speaking evil.

May the fire be in our arms and hands so that we may be of service and build up love. We ask that the fire protect us from all violence.

May the fire be in our whole being, in our legs and our feet enabling us to walk the earth with reverence and care, and to walk in the way of goodness and truth and be protected from walking away from what is truth.'

To think that this is 40,000 years old, makes me want to close this book and stop immediately writing it; with humility I capitulate, for there is nothing I could add.

And yet, I continue - why? Because the prayer also asks for a deep, deep listening, that we may hear the flow of the water and all of creation - and that we may serve others. May I serve you, may this help us 'to listen to all of creation.'

Chapter Seven: Invocation of Air (Metal)

I am the invisible order of the cosmos
-Rita, the cosmic law and Satya -Truth.

Out of me 'ritu' is born, the seasons - and
'ritual' your performances of respect,
respect for the harmonious functioning of nature.
You know the law!
You know what is needed, in your ancestral soul!

That knowledge rides on my breath,
I record it in all that is ancient,
ancient like the stones and crystals,
the record holders of the past
they carry the history, that gave you birth
they store the truth you contain.

I am the breath of your vitality
I breathe the supreme force of life into you
I have unrivalled power to sustain
thus honour my breath,
honour breath
I am the wind you feel on your skin and
I am the intellect that lifts you to great insights
As both I rise to where the gods reside,
I bring the gift of intelligence,
just as that of sweet fragrances
rejoice, all beings in my delight
rejoice.
I descend as storm to the earth by the grace of the gods
tremble, all beings, before my power
tremble

I, storm and thunder am the love-call of the mating dance with earth
I re-energise the Great Mother, so that life may continue,
so that the rains may feed her body.
Yet despite my power I am invisible

I am the invisible order of the cosmos
Rita, the cosmic law and Satya, truth
- storms are followed by delicate stillness
- turbulence is succeeded by quiet
  - chaos put into order
  - abundance is succeeded by scarcity
  - growth follows decay
  - autumn follows summer

I am autumn, the time of farewells
- leave the clatter of accumulated riches,
return to your soul
- leave the chatter of your monkey brain retreat into
- your interior, sink into your roots
- leave the exterior gloss and paint,
- collect your resources

I am Manjushri, Buddha with the 'Sword of Wisdom'
- leave the frenzy of a business persona
prepare for hibernation, slow down
- leave your distractions and illusions
contract, contract into the purest substance
- leave your self-important theories and values
crystallise into 'the salt of the earth'

It is a time of farewells, for then you realise,
- that I fuel the fire of self-inquiry, revealing the Self
- leaving the self in constant flux;
realise
I am the invisible order of the cosmos
Rita - the cosmic law, always accompanied by Satya-truth
- as holding is accompanied by letting go
- as ripening is accompanied by decaying
- as expanding is accompanied by contracting
until these antipodes come together,
they themselves have antipodes,
each to its own nature
each to its own truth

Thus I am truth, right action, right dharma.
Encouraging each thing, animate or inanimate in the entire universe
To follow its own dharma
its own 'suchness,' its own truth
To find your own truth, you have to be in touch with your soul
acknowledge your soul and do not hide,
hide behind rules, regulations and principles
preconceptions, judgements and other similar
calcified structure of armour

But - Rise above them, cut through them,
Let go, Let go, Let go
then, surrender - to me
me, Rita, the cosmic law
me, Satya, the Truth.

7.1 Contemplation of the Element of Air (Metal)

Air - such an elusive substance; Metal such solid one, what can these possibly share? According to Vedic thought, the gross state of energy called Air is the penultimate element of creation and dissolution, Space being the most subtle.

Air is already so 'thin,' most of the time we are not aware of Air - the eyes can't see it; our ever greedy tongue can't taste it; our oh so discriminating nose can't smell it etc. Children think that there is nothing around us - having no awareness or concept of this elusive substance – and yet it's the substance that **connects us** with all other things. Imagine we paint the air yellow, suddenly our whole perception would change - we would 'see' that we are connected to everything else - outside and inside. Even more astonishing - what was a minute ago air in you (the cat, a cow or a bird) - is now part of me! It is not surprising that this Element is connected with the communication. (Communication as associated with 'Metal' becomes clear if we remember how semi-conductors, copper wires etc. are a vital ingredient of instruments of communication).

'Air' has different consistencies. Air in its most dense state is where it touches earth, and only here, it supports life - after that, it thins out through various atmospheric strata into Space.

Here is a curiosity: Within the Chinese writing, the symbols for Air and Metal are very similar; in addition the written Character for 'Element' in Chinese means phase, movement and path. Together, it seems that the 'path of Air and the Path of Metal' are similar! How ever odd it may seem, there are surprising parallels:

When Air is compressed/cooled, it solidifies with substantial weight (re: ice/Metal). Metal on the other hand is easy to melt and although not gaseous, it becomes liquid; so both substances can change shape, narrowing the gap.

When melting down metal, various substances are separated out. The rubbish of the ore floats away, leaving the pure metal; similarly when air gets heated in the lungs, the rubbish of other gases such as nitrogen oxygen is breathed out, leaving the pure oxygen for the body to use.

On a winter's day, or a clear crisp morning, air seems to cut into your lungs - such sharpness is associate with a metal implement, such as a knife/sword!

Metals naturally occur as a mixed substance, ore! Air is a mixture of gases.

This might suffice.

Keep in mind that different cultures have different ways to express themselves. The form changes; the content remains the same. I will use 'Air' for describing the fourth Element.

Now, let us experience and contemplate this illusive Air. Take a minute, sit up straight, relax your mind and breathe in. Note the coolness in your nostrils; breathing in more air, feel how your ribs expand, then how your belly fills up. Become aware that air has volume, it expands your body. When the lungs are fully filled, then for a fraction of time there is stillness, then the ribs sink, the lungs deflate and the substance passes through your nostrils again. This time we can feel the warmed air - the substance has changed. If you are sensitive, you might feel a rush of energy through your system, the air intake has changed you!

The original air we took in, consisted of oxygen, small quantities of carbon dioxide and a lot of nitrogen and other rare gases (neon, helium, krypton, radon etc.) and loads of water. Only some of this is kept and used. The air we breathe out contains approx. 5 % less oxygen and an increased amount of carbon dioxide (0.04% to 4%). [69]

The consistency of air changes with every breath a living being, man or microbe takes on this planet. We take out oxygen, plants mainly take out carbon dioxide; microbes mainly take out nitrogen (converting it into proteins). Thus **by responding to others, air constantly changes.**

What happens actually happens when we breathe? There is always some air in the lungs and into this reservoir a wave of 500ml of air rushes with every breath, mixing with the old. Imagine the lung as a tree: the trunk as the throat; the bronchioles the main branches, the alveoli are the leaves on the tree, which are surrounded by blood vessels that bring de-oxygenated blood. The higher pressure of the oxygenated blood makes it seep through the walls of the blood vessels, (descending into the lower pressure area); blood then transports it to wherever the body needs it. On the reverse journey, the pressure of carbon dioxide is higher in the blood vessels than in the alveoli - so it seeps through from vessel to alveoli in order to return to be breathed out.

What we perceive as in-breath, change, out-breath - is really no sudden, no distinct 'change' at all, but a sequence of small movements. Lesson No. One: 'Change' does not happen all at once, it is a **process of small movements** where little bits are continuously left behind! 'Change' is thus a fluid pattern, a rhythm. What we originally saw as a big change, turns out to be a **reoccurring process of leaving behind,** (like a mountaineer leaves the valley behind when he climbs to the peak).

This Movement, or **wave of change** and interaction, goes through the many layers of Air, which we call the atmosphere. The first layer is the troposphere, here air becomes increasingly thinner, so that on high mountains, there is barely enough oxygen in the mixture for us to breath, and it gets increasingly colder.

The next layer, the stratosphere has even thinner air and contains a special layer of oxygen called the ozone layer. As one layer merges into the next (stratosphere to ionosphere, to exosphere) the air thins out so much, that eventually where the earth's atmosphere becomes space, only a few molecules of hydrogen and helium float about. Air has changed so much, it loses its identity!

The strata vary and change depending on the time of year, latitude and activity of the sun and so on. Warm air nearer the earth raises and cools as it moves up and away. In this way Air is constantly on the move – this is why

'Air' in most cultures, (especially India South America etc.) is almost synonymous with 'Movement.' In Tibetan and Ayurvedic medicine, this Element is at times called Wind.

Let's look closer at these Wind-movements.

As we look at a world map, we can see a pattern of obvious rhythm to these movements of air. In the Southern Hemisphere, the 'Trade Winds' follow a certain pattern triggered by the flow of the 'Westerlies' (other winds). In the Northern Hemisphere, the swirls of the Northern 'Trade Winds' and the Monsoon determine our summer and winter weather. They work like clockwork: for half a year, they blow from the North-east, the other half from the South-west. Unfailingly in June they bring, for example, rain to countries such as India. The ' **burst**' of the monsoon can be forecast from year to year almost to the exact day.

Normal movement of Air we merely experience as a **gentle touch** – but in storms, tournedos and hurricanes, it becomes a brute force. Air as each of the elements has a scale!

We might experience air, not only through its volume, but its weight. A bucket full of air weighs about as much as two sheets of A4 paper, but consider the height of the atmosphere, then you will realise that a heavy weight is on your head (at sea level 15lb on every square inch) - why do we not get squashed? We always have air inside us to create counter pressure. As the weather changes, the atmospheric pressure changes and so does the pressure on our head! (Headaches!)

It seems obvious that **change and movement** belong together, they give a constant **rhythm of renewal and 'good byes'**; a rhythm of creation and dissolution. Marcus Aurelius (Roman emperor and stoic philosopher 121-180 AD) writes:

Is anyone afraid of Change?
> Why? What can take place without change?
> Can you take a bath, unless the wood undergoes change?
> Can you be nourished unless food undergoes change?

Can you not see, that for yourself also, to change is just the same, and equally necessary for the universal nature? [70]

The severity, the suffering (or excitement) we experience in change is not inherent in what is happening, but depends how observant we have been to 'see it coming' or whether we are able to see the larger picture; this is the **Wisdom** attributed to Air in many cultures.

Wisdom is also attributed to 'Metal'; metal and stones are considered 'record holders' by American Indians and Celts. Why? When we find these, they have been around and changed over and over in a period of millions of years; they have experienced devastating changes and great upheavals so that we can read from them earth's history; going a bit further, one could say: they store knowledge. Ever heard of the Japanese meditation practise of: 'listening to the stones.' Minerals, Metals, hold earth's memory; they are calcified knowledge. And yet calcified knowledge is dogma – the grossest, most inert form of wisdom! In 'element-speak' one could say dogma is the Earth of knowledge!

Although Air is characterised by movement into many directions and levels, that movement is by no means erratic, as we have seen by 'the winds,' it follows a certain pattern: from warm to cold, from higher density to lower density, from in-breath to out-breath, etc. It moves in never-ending, smaller and larger cycles. The cycle of breathing is a relative small cycle - but if we remember that all life breathes - we understand there is 'breath within the breath,' continuity in cycles within cycles! Each breath takes only what it needs - the rest flows into others. Our lungs only absorb as much oxygen as we need – the rest is passed on for others to use what they need. We can't take more breath than we can use nor can we exist with less than we need - this is being **responsible.** Responsibility means, we have to be conscious, to see, observe, be aware of the needs of ourselves, others, of situations and the environment and we have to <u>respond</u> appropriately. To respond appropriately means to act adequately to the situation as a whole, not to react according to my own wants and wishes. **Action not re-action** is appropriate to a certain situation. If, for example we breathe in more than we should, we hyperventilate, our body system gets defunct. The same applies on many levels: if we take more electricity than the kettle needs, we burn a fuse; if we use more resources of our environment, it too will burn out etc. Responding to our body's, family's or society's need, means taking appropriately - no more! Much of the world's ills, such as pollution, radioactive and chemical pollution, the death of our 'green lungs' (the forests of the world) etc., all come from ignoring this principle. Ignoring it makes us ill, poisons body and mind! <u>Inappropriate wanting</u> drives to inadequate response. Even if our body says, 'I need rest' or 'I am full,' we drive it into ever more stressful situations, because our mind decides we need another fridge, car, house, business, lover etc.? Air teaches us to act according to a situation, with **knowing, with intelligence!**

The trouble is, we are not sure what it means 'to act responsibly'; too often we equate it with fulfilling expectations of others (calcified cousin of response-ability); expectation to meet standardised requirement of a certain culture, family or person. Appropriate action follows the invite in a unique moment to a unique situation; it comes from a point of freedom and love; is **always Now!** Calcified patterns mean we have handed over our power to follow somebody else's decision!

One aspect frequently forgotten: we have **responsibility to ourselves!** If I do not rest or feed my body adequately, I will be too sick or weak to look after my child.

Or: the powerful motivation to do, to achieve, to strive will no longer be appropriate to the body's changing demands in times like puberty or old age. New laws apply!

Or, psychological or spiritual responses need to be appropriate e.g. a youngster's mother dies. This is a massive change. He needs to be allowed to grief; sorrow needs to be felt; the vacuum that arises needs to be acknowledged, these are the demands of the psyche. Furthermore, death and its nature as part of life, needs to be understood, talked about, and knowledge embraced by accepting ones own mortality; that is the demand of the soul. And then - only then - there are the demands of other family members, customs and society to consider. If the needs of the whole being, body, mind and soul, are not responded to, those changes that have not been treated responsibly, will soon hurt, poison or damage the person. They will, in one way or another, 'clog the drains,' and upset the wheels of Change!

Yes, responsibility has its point of reference always **in the Now,** neither being caught up with the past (let go!) nor of the future (don't worry), but act appropriately to the situation now!

There still is more: adequate response to the moment depends on trust. Trust that there will be air again for the next breath, that there will be enough food! But if we do not let go of the first breath, we cannot find out, we suffocate with the previous breath. We have to let go and trust there will be more, that there will be help coming at the right moment, that there is always a new cycle of change coming. Because this change is the nature of life, **to trust is to know life**, to understand the movement of life, is to live in Trust.

Looking at the cyclic nature of breath, another insight is revealed: 'Cyclic means it comes again and again! Just like we celebrate our birthday again and again, just as the sun turns at her highest point again and again etc. etc. Such reoccurring events and behaviour become rituals. The ritual follows a certain stimulus just as the winter cold comes on the back of certain easterly winds. The ritual than reminds us, celebrates the underlying connection. This aspect i.e. regular reoccurrence, is what has led the Element of Air to be associated with **ritual (**Rita; Sanskrit for cosmic law). Air teaches us to listen and to observe re-occurring patterns; they are **cosmic laws and they reveal universal truths.** Rita and Satya (Truth) are like two sister attributes of the Element Air.

Truth is probably the most elusive aspect of Air. Because of Air's clear and transparent nature, it defines objects clearly. Look at a clean sharp sky, when the air is pure and reveals stars with precision! The landscape seems cut, revealing sharp contours. Air is so clear when impurities, dust particles, have been 'washed out.'

This 'washing' process happens in the mind through the tools of the intellect; by using **discrimination** - illusions and delusions get cut away. Under the **power of discernment,** wisdom and truth, the good and pure get separated from what is coarse and primitive. Truth is revealed?

What is this elusive 'truth'? Most people would admit that 'truth' is if you say, Water is wet! 1 km equals 1000 m! Sure all this is 'true,' yet: Water to a fish does not feel wet at all; and 1 km is 0.621 miles! It depends how something is phrased; 'truth,' even 'scientific truth,' is relative; it changes according to the viewpoint, the times one lives in, the state of science. It changes because life changes. And yet we argue endlessly whether something or somebody is right, whether this or that is true. Air alerts us, saying, when you look for truth, you actually look for somebody who looks through the same 'glasses' as you! So **be alert and stop pretending** is the first step to truth! Use discrimination and wisdom to stop seeing what you want to see - or not seeing what you don't. Take off the glasses that condition how you see!

For example: We reassure people they are all right, because we are afraid of their anger; or: we savour unhappiness, because it assures us people's pity; thus we do not have to change ourselves.

Many examples could be given; we are geniuses in masking the truth; we have an enormous talent to self-righteously fool others and ourselves to avoid using our mind to face the truth. We are, in other words, masters of delusion. We cling to our pet projections as though they were gold. It is this delusion that we have to cut away with the **sword of wisdom** in order to see clear. It is this, which the Element of Air encourages. However self-inquiry is not an endless mud-raking that pushes waste from one point to another – Air is clearly asking us to face our tendencies such as delusion, blaming, infatuation, laziness etc. and... let them go! But it seems we don't want to! Lord Krishna had a conversation with one of his disciples about the nature of suffering. The disciple asked the teacher: why do you not change the world - take all people into heaven? Lord Krishna answered that people do not want to go! He asks the disbelieving disciple to find out for himself, and ask whomever he meets. So the disciple goes for a walk; the first Being he meets is a pig.

He asks, "Oh, Pig, if you knew a beautiful garden, a heavenly place would you leave your miserable existence as a pig?"

The pig said, "Sir, will I find refuse and filth and swill there to eat?"

"No," says the disciple, "but you will have food that is extremely delicious and a big garden to play in."

The pig answers: "What could possibly taste better than garbage, what garden could be more wonderful than this mud in which I wallow all day with my young ones? No sir, I am not interested in your heavenly place." So the disciple returned to his teacher, who waited with a knowing smile. [71]

The truth is we do not want to clean up our act; we do not want to move on; how incredible!

Finally, let's contemplate one more aspect of Air. Imagine you are sitting in a garden and you become aware of the Air as a moving substance (not unlike water) around you, imagine you could see this substance. In the warm summer breeze you observe air coming to you, parting to flow around you, then continuing through the garden. It comes to a few hydrangea bushes, lifts up a bit and swirls down again taking a few dry leaves with it! Your garden is on a slope and the Air-flow increases its speed and it takes a bit of dust and dry earth with it, as it hits the windbreak to your vegetable patch. There it gathers its strength, rises up and the force of momentum takes more leaves; then it jumps over the windbreak, pushing hard against the bushes that make up the windbreak. The effort rips some more leaves off, little twigs swirl and dance with them in the back-flow behind the windbreak. As soon as air is back on even ground, it drops the debris. It continues as though nothing has happened.

As air moves, it constantly touches and picks things up! Then it lets go of what it has gathered! At times, this might take some effort but Air has no alternative; it is in its nature to move and let go! In this way Air is forever ready to change, it reacts appropriately, then lets go!

The big lesson Air teaches us here is: to live according to what is required in the moment, to act without preconception, without <u>arrogance</u>, to learn to respond clearly and spontaneously without being attached to our past clutter; then we become truly alive, in the NOW. When being ever present, there is no need to cling to the past loves, hates, concepts, ideas of ourselves and others, no need to hide behind our <u>delusions</u>. We can take from the world what we need in the moment to sustain our life, rather than constantly feed our <u>desire</u> to have even what we do not need.

If we can learn to act in the moment as Air does, we can let go of our worries that entice us to armour ourselves, build walls of safety for imaginary protection. For the walls we build to keep us safe, equally keep energies of love and help, even 'the universe' out! We become lonely! Air teaches us to 'ride the wave of change,' let go! Meister Eckhardt, prominent mystic, prophet, feminist and philosopher writes in his theology (via negativa) of a path that he calls, 'letting go and letting be.'

When one has learned to let go and let be
Then one is well disposed
and he or she is always in the right place whether
in society or solitude.
But if one has the wrong attitude
one is always in the wrong place, whether in society or not.
Now one who is rightly disposed, has God within one -
in actual fact in all places, just as much in the street
and in the midst of many people
as in church, or desert, or monastic cell.

Even man's highest goal - his union with God - is dependent on this one principle. So why are we so afraid of letting go of change? Life changes anyway... it cannot be any different!

'For the will to be free, it needs to let go
and return to its prime origin.
For the intellect to be free
it must become naked and empty
by letting go to return to its prime origin.
Think of the soul as a vortex or whirlpool
and you will understand how we are to
sink eternally from negation, to negation ...
from letting go, to letting go,
into God. [72]

7.2. Associations with the Air Element

Hildegard von Bingen points out that the element Air is the animating 'enlivening' power for plants, animals and even stars and planets alike! She forges a link to water, as it both brings dew and circulating movements to all that grows. She also links it to the mind as ratio/rationality saying that Air carries the warmth of Fire to man's mind, mentally and spiritually stimulating him, an incredible insight (way ahead of her times) as breath stimulates the movement of the spinal fluid through the spine to nourish the brain!

A similar stance is taken in Ayurvedic medicine, where Air is linked to stimulating movement. It plays an important role in the Dosha **Vata**, as elemental Partner to Space. All these, including TCM, connect the lungs and large intestines to this Element, for their activity is moving and expelling.

7.2: a) Complementary Medicine

To begin with, let us look at the anatomical organs, for they carry their own revelations. Yet, let us not forget that 'each organ and bodily function... is only a physical manifestation of a spiritual quality that was inherent in your soul when you joined the earth at your conception.' [75]

The Lung is the first and last sign of the activity of life; there are two wings to our lungs, one on either side in the thoracic cavity. Each lung is cone shaped, the right lung is divided into three lobes, the left into two. The lung is invaginated into a sac called pleura; the function of this fluid filled sac is to protect (like a punch bag) and to ensure smooth movement of the lung. The lungs are composed of the bronchi and smaller air passages, alveoli, connective tissue, blood vessels, lymph vessels and nerves. The expansion and contraction of the chest occur due to muscular activity – via the intercostal muscles and the diaphragm; partly voluntary, partly involuntary. The intercostal muscles and the diaphragm change, reduce and enlarge the chest cavity, and with it change the atmosphere inside to lower pressure. This stretches the lungs and with it, the pressure of the alveoli and the air passages is reduced, drawing air into the lungs in an attempt to equalise the pressure. This is inspiration; when the muscles relax, the process is reversed and there is an elastic recoil of the lungs, resulting in expiration. Due to the tendency of gases to move from higher to lower concentrated areas, the Oxygen moves from the alveoli to the blood. The inspired air consists mostly of Nitrogen and other small amounts of gases, yet 21% is Oxygen; 16% of the expired air also is Oxygen, thus each time only a small amount of Oxygen is retained. Carbon Dioxide is originally only present in small amounts - 0.04%; on the out-breath it is 4%, so a larger amount is expired. The Oxygen enriched blood moves out of the lungs via various ducts and is collected in the pulmonary veins in order to be fed into the heart.

Voluntary control of breath happens when speaking, singing or during special activities, via the cerebral cortex. Involuntary breathing is controlled from the nerve cells in the brain stem, and are activated after a short time of holding one's breath.

The second organ that relates to the Element Metal is the <u>Large Intestine</u>. It is about 1.5 metres long; it begins at the end of the small intestines, or rather the caecum, and ends with the rectum and anal canal. It forms an arch around the small intestines and lies in front of the abdominal cavity. It has the same basic four layers of tissues as all parts of the alimentary canal, with slight modifications. The 'stuff' it receives is fluid; one of the functions of the large intestine is absorption of water in order to concentrate the matter to an appropriate consistency. Mineral salts, vitamins and some drugs are also absorbed into the blood capillaries here. The large intestines house a large number of microbes, which synthesise vitamin K and folic acid. They do not have constant peristalsis like other parts of the alimentary tract, but at intervals a strong wave of peristalsis sweeps along the colon, called a mass movement. In an adult, the external anal sphincter is under conscious control, involving various nerves and reflexes. Repeated suppression of these reflexes or over-control may lead to constipation. The excrement consists mainly of water, but in addition, contains large amounts of fibre, dead and live microbes, cells, fatty acids and mucus secreted by the large intestines for the purpose of lubrication.

It seems apparent that both organs, lungs and large intestines, are organs that constantly move, they provide exchange between the outer and inner world. Both take in matter (be it air or prepared food), refine it and eliminate that which is not needed. They eliminate that which cannot be used!!! They let go of the useless! What would happen to our homes, cities and society if the waste products were not removed? We would sink into rotten, stinking matter and eventually die of disease and poison.

I will never forget Batavia, the old Djakarta, a former Indonesian capital where previously the Dutch had maintained an open channel sewerage system. Several years before I visited the town, the original channels - through lack of maintenance -had been clogged up, they had become a stinking swamp. People used the sidewalks as toilets in order to keep their houses clean. Consequently the roads were deeply covered with human excrement. It was baked dry by the sun, but when it rained, I was walking literally ankle deep in human excrement, an experience too horrible for words.

If waste in the body is not removed in a timely way, it results in swelling, stiffness in the shoulders, asthma, bronchitis, pains in thumbs and the chest, malicious boils and other skin diseases, headaches, mucus congestion and general symptoms of poisoning.

A similar process happens in our mind. We take impressions of the external world through our senses into our mind – refine and assimilate that which is needed and wanted – and release the rest. The activity of the energy field of lung and large intestines thus reaches into our mental and emotional life. If we do not let go of outlived patterns and attitudes, old hurts and emotions, our bodies will similarly congest and react with depression, melancholy, withdrawal, unrealistic expectations etc. resulting in disappointment, lack of determination, negativity and emotional poverty. Why - because such holding on means that we always react to already past patterns, and consequently do not live in the present. We need to recognising old patterns and to let them go. Or... with Plotinus:

'Withdraw into yourself and look. And if you do not find yourself beautiful yet, act as does the creator of a statue that is to be made beautiful: he cuts away here, smoothes there, he makes this line lighter, this other purer, until a lovely face has grown upon his work. So do you also cut away all that is excessive, straighten all that is crooked, bring to light all that is overcast, labour to make all one glow of beauty and never cease chiselling your statue, until there shall shine out on you from it, the godlike splendour of virtue, until you shall see the perfect goodness established in the stainless shrine.' [73]

The two meridians or Organ-networks associated with the Metal Element are the Lung meridian (*Yin*) and the Large Intestines meridian (*Yang*).

The Location of the Lung Meridian (LU): Runs along the clavicle, along the inside of the arm down to the thumb (bilateral, of course); in addition, one branch goes along the trachea, another down from the hollow underneath the clavicle along the side of the chest, through the belly, and surfaces on the inside back of the leg, then down to the sole of the foot.

Imbalances here show as skin disease, lung disease and psychological conditions mentioned above.

The Location of the Large Intestines Meridian, (LI); Starting at the nail bed of the index finger, it runs on the outside of the arm, across the shoulders; along the throat to the flare of the nostrils (bilateral). And again, on the outside edge of the back of the legs to the sole of the foot, ending at the ball of the foot.

Imbalances here show as all manner of bowel problems, but also skin problems and all manner of psychological problems with 'letting go.'

In Ayurveda, the Air Element is associated with Vata (Prana). Vata show lack and imbalances in either Air or Space. It is the most subtle dosha and 'is normally involved in most physical maladies, because being closer to the source of energy, it is easier to unbalance... Vata, like the other two humours, is inherited, so that a person may be prone to certain Vata disorders unless preventative measures are taken. By this, Vata is also a constitution, with a proneness to certain diseases.' [74]

The Cycle. The circulation of Life's energy creates the meridians' Life Cycle. The time of peak activity for the Lung Meridian is the early morning, between 3am and 5am. Note: the key to meditation is breath; since earliest times, spiritual teachers and masters have recommended these times to meditate. In Hong Kong coming home from a party, I used to find people doing *Tai Chi Chuan* at 5am, when the air is still and life energy purest: these hours before dawn are known as the brahmamuhurta, the time of the Lord.

The optimal time of activity for the Large Intestines Meridian is from 5am to 7am. Many people have the habit or the need for bowel emptying when they first get up in the morning. On the other hand, late afternoon, between three and five o'clock, we often feel tired and need a nap because it is the time when the lungs have their lowest time of efficiency. This is followed by the time of least activity for the large intestines, another good reason for a rest. A person feeling without energy in the early morning and late afternoon has most likely an imbalance in this energy.

The Season associated with this energy field is Autumn, in a literal sense but also the autumn of life. In medieval times, the ages of man were divided into seven different stages, linked to seven planets. In modern times, the psychologist Erik Erikson has designed a model of a life cycle where he sees twelve stages. The Indian tradition speaks of four stages of the sanatana dharma (the eternal laws). There the stage of birth and student years is followed by the stage of the householder, followed by the stage of the 'forest dweller,' followed by the stage of the renunciate (*sannyasa*). Hence the third stage, the 'autumn of life' is the time after the children have left home and man retires to contemplate. With a longing for solitude and silence and released from the obligations of family and job, the 'forest dweller' can devote his time to contemplation, scriptural studies and meditation.

Medieval Christianity also mentions four stages of life. The first refers to the *common* ordinary stage of family life, the second is *special,* people start to reflect on the 'why and whereabouts' in life. The third stage refers to *the singular*, a stage where one is called to focus on what is essential. The last stage refers to the *perfect* and points beyond death, to enlightenment, be it in this life, or thereafter. 75

Thus 'Autumn' refers to the stage where one should concentrate on what is important. In western society at this stage, people tend to let go of commitments, move to a smaller house, focus on leisure time to pursue interests they previously have neglected; they might even start to wonder what gives meaning and purpose to one's life?

In nature at this point, most fruits have been harvested, yet some still are to be reaped. Likewise a person's experience and knowledge might be gathered and stored in paintings, books or letters. I am reminded of the grape harvest in Germany. Most grapes are harvested in August and September, yet some very special good varieties are left on the vine in order to be touched by the first frosts. This crystallises the sugar and concentrates the juice to make a special, highly appreciated, wine called *Eiswein* (Ice wine).

The trees and plants prepare for winter, e.g. trees draw their sap inwards, sink into their roots, slow down their metabolism. Animals prepare for hibernation, either by storing food within their own bodies (bears) or storing nuts and grains (squirrels). Likewise people turn inward, sort themselves out, deal with/clean up old problems and fears, so as to prepare for the last phase of life. A person looks more and more at what is essential, on their true dharma; on his/her own 'such-ness,' their own truth.

And yet this goes hand in hand with one last glorious show of colour. The beauty and luminosity of a Vermont (North Eastern USA) or Canadian Autumn; or the colour nuances of a Japanese mountain landscape in autumn, are beyond description. Similarly the inner riches of a person's life might be summoned up at this stage in a display of talents never seen before; they may reveal insights and visions of great beauty - finally discovering and displaying what it is all about!

People, whether young or in the life stage of Autumn, who display signs of being unable to concentrate on the important; unable to identify outdated circumstances, relationships and life patterns and let go of them show an imbalance in this Element. Time as much as energy may be wasted on petty issues, resentments or outlived habits and reactions, if they are not cleared out.

The Nei Ching says, 'The three months of Fall are called the period of tranquillity of ones conduct... soul and spirit should be gathered together in order to make the breath of Fall tranquil; all this is a method for the protection of ones harvest... Those who disobey the laws of Fall will be punished with an injury of the lungs.' [76]

People who look towards the past, or want to cling to the present in order to prevent the future, show an imbalance in 'letting go.' People who dislike the season of Autumn, who leave their fruit to rot, or have difficulty in conserving their energy also suffer from the same imbalance and might display such physical signs as diarrhoea and constipation, or a feeling of being sick after meals, even vomiting. Their body/mind is unwilling to gather and absorb what is nourishing to them.

The Direction of Air/Metal is the West - or down and inward, easy to relate to the above. In our society the direction of the West reminds of the setting sun - the transition phase between day and night; the dusk where images soften and contours are mellowed. This is a time of immense colour display - just like autumn and in the same colours too! This is time for preparation for the night, the time of rest and regeneration. The time of sunset is a symbol of closing down.

In the tradition of the North American Indians, the West is linked to a cave, or the womb. 'The womb is a place where all ideas, as well as babies, are nurtured and given birth... The West is the 'looking within' place from where we must first understand our natures... if we understand that the spirit of all other life-forms dwells inside our bodies, we begin to understand that we can look within to feel and know the answers (we need).' [77]

The West is the direction of introspection, and - the potential of the future. The cave, the womb, the time after sunset: all hold the germ of tomorrow. But to enter tomorrow we have to let go of today! We were the future generation to our parents; the fallen fruit of this season provide the fertiliser for tomorrow's seeds. This is the law of the Cosmos (*Rita*).

Originally the concept of medicine in the *Nei Ching* was limited to geographical China. The West thus referred to as Western Provinces, and its people live on hills exposed to wind and fertile soil, thus they are described as eating 'good and variegated food and. they are flourishing and fertile.

Hence evil cannot injure their external bodies, and if they get disease they strike at the inner body.' [78] In a strange way, that still applies today. We in the western, so called civilised countries have ample food. We live in an environment that is affluent. Here diseases that stem from hunger or natural hardship are rare, but diseases that strike at the inner body are prevalent. These are heart disease, stress related illnesses, cancer, AIDS, also mental illness, depression and other unseen disease that destroy the soul, such as the deterioration of values, morals and social standards. These 'inner diseases,' these 'diseases of civilisation' often result from the inability of Western man to be in touch with cosmic laws, with the inability to tune into various phases of life, or even the soul. Introspection, contemplation and meditation are frowned upon and replaced by the analytical, secular dimension. We are distracted by images and artificial needs forced on us by those to whom we have handed our power (political, industrial and social magnates); we become slaves. That which can empower us, introspection and self-inquiry, remains neglected. Has 'the West' lost the ability 'to be West'? Lost the meaning and willingness to live according its own wisdom, its inherent sense of Being?

The Climate associated with the Air/Metal Element is dryness. If we think back to the activity of the Lungs, we recall that air, when reaching the lungs is actually saturated with water vapour. This enables the cells, surrounded with the alveoli, to engage in the exchange of gases. If we think back to the Large Intestines, the matter they receive is fluid and one of their major tasks is to extract water. Both organs need water to function; lack of water then stops Lung as well as Large Intestines from doing their job. This is mirrored in nature. Matter does not rot in the absence of water; it just dries out. Dryness is a sign of imbalance. If somebody doesn't like dry climates, has very dry skin, suffers from a constantly dry, thirsty mouth or too hard stools (constipation); they probably have such an imbalance.

Furthermore, this Element relates to exchange with the outside world in general, thus dryness appears also in other ways. An artist's creativity can be 'dried up'; somebody being sarcastic has a 'dry humour.' After a tragedy has hit us and we have wept a lot, we feel 'dry inside'; even a person as a whole who adheres to facts only, is described simply as 'dry,' because he lacks an emotional, moist response.

The Tissues or part of the body linked to Air is the skin. This is described as the largest organ of our body and as the 'third lung.' The skin is both, consisting of the epidermis, the top layer and the deeper layers (dermis); the uppermost always consists of dead cells that are constantly rubbed off by clothes etc. The active cells have as one of their functions the process of internal or cellular breathing.

The upper skin is the boundary between the moist environment of the living cells of the body and the dry atmosphere of the external environment. Underneath is a layer of collagen and elastic fibres, containing sweat glands, hair follicles and sebaceous glands; oily substances are produced by the latter, keeping the skin soft, pliable and waterproof. It also contains sensory nerve endings, which react by reflex action to unpleasant and painful stimuli. When the skin is intact, it also provides a barrier to invading microbes. Furthermore it is the major organ of heat regulation.

Thus the skin is considered an organ that erects and protects the boundaries with the environment (including the sense of one's own and others' personal space). This organ-network is related to keeping one's energy contained so that one does not encroach on others, and others' energy does not encroach on one's own. People who can't set boundaries for self and others have an imbalance here.

Furthermore skin symbolises the spiritual quality of keeping inner and outer worlds defined, yet together; a great Sufi Masters says:
'Whoever has the outer law without the inner reality has left the right way.
Whoever has the inner reality without the outer law is a heretic.
Whoever unites the two of them has realisation.' [79]

Skin is said to mirror the state of health of the Lung and in eastern and western medicine it is acknowledged that skin diseases such as eczema, scaling or other skin eruptions often accompany illnesses such as asthma, bronchitis, coughs etc. On the other hand, skin diseases such as acne, dermatitis, boils and skin eruptions that appear during puberty or later in life, are seen as a way of the body getting rid of unwanted substances, just like the Large Intestines eliminate unwanted substances. The role of eliminator thus makes the skin part of this energy field.

If skin is a symbol for our relationship with the world/people, then skin problems might refer to repelling, rejecting that world around us. Are we revolting against what life presents us? We express our insecurities and problems through our skin. We blush with embarrassment, we redden with anger; we erupt with angry skin sores; we peel or flake in trying 'to shed our old skin.' Skin is dry, because we withdraw inside, not letting enough fluid to the surface to keep the skin alive. One might well ask, is there nothing like simply having dry skin? And the answer has to be 'NO,' if we believe in the interconnectedness of body, mind soul. Behind a layer of dead skin we hide outlived patterns, old habits we can't let go of. This might apply especially to such skin diseases as psoriasis, hives or rashes?

On the other hand - is our relationship with our environment smooth, permeable and a well nourished ground for exchange, are we receptive and flexible in all interactions; if so, then our skin is also most likely smooth, elastic and flexible.

The sense organ as well as the orifice connected with this energy field, is the nose - pretty obvious! Difficulties with the nose often have a direct link with the Lungs, as well as with the Large Intestines. In fact one of the most influential tsubo, or energy points of LI is directly in the groove at the flare of the nose. The nose is like a gateway through which the air, the life-giving energy enters. Wide-open nostrils speak of a generous gate, a free and easy exchange of intake and giving out of that energy which animates all life.

The Chinese say the lungs house one of three aspects of the soul (see Fire). Po, is the corporeal soul - once it leaves, death results. Similarly in the Indian tradition, *atman*, the joyous self, lodges in the heart, *jiva* the individual, ethereal soul in the liver and *prana*, the animating spirit in the lungs. 'It is closely linked to the body and could be described as the somatic expression of the soul... breathing can be seen as the pulsating of the corporeal soul; ...on a mental level the corporeal soul protects the individual from external psychic influences. Some people are easily affected by negative influences; this is due to weakness of the corporeal soul.' [80] This makes the nose the entrance hall to our innermost being. This is well recognised in Yoga.

There is also another aspect of the nose. The nose releases mucus, unwanted germs and tissues that block the airway. In a metaphorical sense, at times when we feel disappointed, powerless or disillusioned, hopeless and frustrated - we might get a runny nose or even a cold to rid ourselves of whatever is bothering us, or our soul. Thorough cleansing of emotional as well as physical accumulated waste from the sinuses can happen through the nose. Thus people with permanently blocked noses, polyps or chronic nasal congestion have an imbalance within this energy.

The sense associated with this energy field is smell. Particular smells often trigger good or bad memories and associations. An inability to smell can be a particular way of blocking off experiences (congestion), of being unable or unwilling to let go of the associations with that smell. Conversely, people who open their minds to the soul or the heart often experience an improvement in their sense of smell, a new link, a new awareness has been established. Life is full of smells. Think of a flower that is not just beautiful in itself, but it gives us pleasure to smell it. It provides an extended awareness of beauty, of life itself. In this way, as we develop our awareness, our nasal passages can be opened in the widest sense to the 'smell of Life.'

I remember well once when I was sitting in a room and suddenly the room smelled very strongly of burning human flesh, very acrid. No one else in the room smelled it; shortly afterwards I heard the news: all over central India funeral pyres were burning thousands of earthquake victims. At the point in time when I smelled it, I knew nothing of an earthquake!

The Fluid that relates to this Element is mucus. Most of the body's eliminations are accompanied by the excretion of mucus. It is the transporting lubrication of the body and vital for elimination. A dry throat and nose, cough, a tickle in the throat, point just as much to a lubrication problem in the respiratory system as too much mucus, with constantly oozing sinuses or dripping noses. The same is true for too dry faeces or certain forms of diarrhoea.

External physical manifestations attributed to this Element are the skin and body hair. The body hair, whose follicles are embedded in the skin, has a close link to the skin and thus is useful as an indicator for the state of the skin. It is said that unusual amounts of body hair or the lack of it (within reason and considering racial and cultural background) indicate whether the lungs are in splendid and flourishing condition. Ohashi explains this with the link the hair outside the body has with that inside the body, such as the cilia in the oesophagus and digestive tracts as well as in the lungs and intestines. Excessive cilia indicate mucus accumulation.

The Colour linked to this Element in TCM is white. White is really a combination of all colours (which might be the reason why some link it to space). 'The spectrum of colours which makes up white light, ranges from the short violet and blue waves, through green, red and orange waves to red waves, which are the longest that the eye can detect.' [81] We speak of white noise, describing random sounds across the spectrum of all frequencies. Both organs of perception (eyes and ears), register this quality of collecting, gathering things as white. This word 'white' has from here found entrance into our every day language and is used to describe objects made of alloys (white metal) of a grey colour; it is a slang word for being honourable and square (white person); it describes a variety of fish (white fish). This gathering mode is taken to extremes in cosmology, where we have 'white dwarfs' - (stars that 'have a mass similar to that of the sun, but are only 1% of the sun's diameter, consist of degenerate matter... packed... together as tightly as is physically possible, so that a spoonful of it weighs several tonnes).' [82]

White is a collection, (as air collects leaves). How come we talk of white as pure, as minimalist? When we focus on the sum total, it becomes One! One is pure, not yet cluttered by the richness of individual aspects. White as purity refers to a state before – hence some societies associate white with virgins, virtue, and sacred spaces- others associate it with death. Either way it has a quality of being without individual attributes, empty. After what was said above it is not surprising that in the Indian traditions, white is the colour of Shiva. He holds all: creation and destruction, as well as the interval. White ash, from his sacrificial fire (Yajna,) is applied to the forehead; such white streaks of Bhasma are a sign of devotion and surrender to the divine consciousness, the Truth!

In Buddhist tradition white is associated with the Dhyani Buddha Vairochana whose body colour is white and Akshobhya whose radiance is pure white to symbolise mirror-like wisdom.

In Chinese medicine, nuances in facial skin colouring (taking into account racial variations) are used for diagnosis. A white shading of the skin points the prudent observer to an impaired function in this Organ-network which is not fulfilling their role of purifying, condensing, absorbing and eliminating.

The Smell connected to this Element is rotten. As with the colour, the smell of skin (or person as a whole) is used for diagnosis. Large Intestines and the Lung energies, when inefficient, leave matter too long, thus lazy elimination allows matter to rot. Illnesses such as tuberculosis and other infections have distinct rotten smells, as is often stated in the description of war hospitals in fictional literature. The smell of rot is a smell of decomposition.

The Taste associated here is that of pungency, referring to strong flavours such as cheese, curry dishes, peppery dishes and in general, spicy food. People particularly liking or disliking such food, have most likely an imbalance in this energy. These foods are said to open the pores and improve the circulation of saliva and mucus, a desire of the body to help itself in the removal and elimination process. On the other hand, one should not eat too much pungent food, for 'if too much pungent flavour is used in food, the muscles become knotted and the fingers and toenails wither and decay.' [83]

The Grain indicative of the Metal/Air Element is rice, **the Fruit** chestnuts, **the Meat** is that of the horse, **the Vegetable** is the onion.

These are foods that are said to have a specially balancing effect. Rice is a grain that easily absorbs moisture and also, when eaten with the husks (brown rice), carries a lot of fibre encouraging the movement of the bowls, helping absorption, condensing and eliminating. Chestnuts are a water carrying vegetable and as such lubricate; thus they are beneficial to both meridians. I have no idea why horsemeat should be beneficial, unless its toughness provides fibre and bulk.

Onions are rich in water and its sharp gases penetrate the nostrils and bronchioles, stimulating their activity, as we have all experienced when peeling onions - with watering eyes and dripping noses. They clean the air passages. An old house remedy is to make onion tea when children have bronchitis, or even to burn onion skins in the room, helping bronchioles and the general respiratory tract.

The Expression associated with this energy is weeping. The ability to weep and express one's feelings easily or conversely, the inability to weep (suppressing such emotions) is connected here to a quality in the voice; a kind of whining, that 'should be accompanied by tears.' Some people always speak with a whine; it even accompanies joy and happiness. This sound in the everyday voice gives a clear indication of an imbalance in the Large Intestines and Lung meridians. Equally some people have constantly watering eyes, or an expression in the eyes, as though they are ready to cry at any time, indicating a need for support of their Air/Metal Element.

The Sound linked to Metal (in TCM) is that of cracking. Metal is sensitive to heat and makes little cracking noises when it expands and contracts. Once lungs have held the air for too long - they literally burst with a big howl - or crack - to release the pressure. The sound of bursting/exploding could refer to a person whose internal stress has built up too much, (suppressed emotions have reached such intensity) they 'crack up'!

The manner, in times of excitement or change is that of coughing (a way to 'crack open'), and nervous scratching. Both the above speak of attempts to release unwanted substances - either physical or mentally - or, for example, a need to get rid of frustration, a need to let go of one's feelings (Eczema is a sign of attacking oneself!).

The Attitude associated with Metal is a deep breath, a sigh of relief or resignation.

The Movement of Energy here is yawning. Again a tool to hide feelings. Feelings are nothing but energy, which flows between body, mind, spirit and environment. When we experience loss of a loved one, or a cherished dream, we immediately generate energy to address the loss. Unfortunately we are not taught how to react to this 'rising energy,' instead we are raised to resist the feeling of movement of energy, then the energy gets stuck. It remains in our body and seeks for ways to 'come out.' When that energy is not allowed to disperse it can lead to mental neurosis/or physical disease. Unpleasant things happen all the time: a tragic loss, an accident, the way a teacher spoke to us or, even the sound of the voice of a dominant father etc.; experiences are unavoidable, but how we deal with them, depends largely on ourselves. A yawn is a slow way of controlled, hidden release. 'I have to get rid of it, but I will disguise it!'

Conversely, deep breathing, sighing and yawning all can also be signs of a need for (rather than too much) energy. A lack of the vital energy of breath can create the spontaneous desire for a deep breath, followed by a sighing of relief. Similarly yawning can express the need to move stagnant air quickly.

The Quality connected to this Element is - Vitality. The Oxford Dictionary describes vitality as none other than the vital force, power or principle as possessed by living things; the principle of life. The word itself means life: vitae; (a Sanskrit name for Shiva, the highest principle of life, is *Vitthale* (pronounced vital). The breath is what makes us vital; we exist as living breath. Swami Chetanananda writes, 'The breath you are usually aware of is nothing more ... than a form taken on briefly by the Breath of God. That is why we practise focusing on our breathing...You see, there is only one thing behind the appearance of many things, and that one thing is the energy of Life itself... Its pulsation vibrates at different rates, giving rise to the appearance of different forms... it is all still one thing.' [84] Vitality and breath are inseparably linked on all levels. Incorrect breathing, shallow breath, a-rhythmical breathing, wheezing and so on will affect the vitality and lead to illness.

The Activity of the Air/Metal energy is that of analysing. In Buddhist art the Buddha of Wisdom, Manjushri, is depicted with a sharp, gleaming sword, with which he cuts away all, that is irrelevant. Moreover, Manjushri embodies 'the transcendental knowledge that death is ultimately an illusion and that those who identify themselves with the ultimate reality, the plenum-void (*Sunyata*) of their inner centre, overcome death and are liberated from the chains of samsara.' [85]

Manjushri cuts with his sword even death, being called 'the Ender of Death.' The sword, made of clear, refined metal, stands for a sharp mind that not only takes apart or analyses (cutting up into smaller and smaller bits to look at), but sees even further than the bits, to the pure essence. Such inquiry reveals the unity of all and thus is 'the death of Death.'

The Condition/activity associated here is that of inhibition. In the wake of what has been said about blocking out emotions and experiences, it is obvious that such a person would appear inhibited. A person that has no intimate friendships finds it difficult to relate to people; his inhibitions could affect all aspects of life. It might be related to the **brain activities** itself. Where Air energy is dominant (or especially slack) it shows in the areas of touch and communication. Noteworthy activity is observed in the unemotional frontal cortex (abstract thinking) and the posterior part of the frontal and parietal lobe. Such people tend to be very clever (analytical) but introvert (living in their own ivory tower); their ability to store process knowledge, evaluate memory is often limited to physical data, focused on technical often mechanical knowledge showing more (or less) activity in the putamen etc.

As we know, **Aggression** is always the result of energy build up; imagine that Air energy builds up to an intolerable level. Drastic changes in air pressure result in violent movement, storms such as typhoons bring devastation; within the centre though, there is some deadly calm, some clear eye readying itself for the next violent movement. If we relate that to a person dominated by Air characteristics, we look at a person usually clear headed and rational, a thinking, intellectual person. If this sharp, clear, unfeeling energy builds up without release, it will reveal itself by violent outer movement (storming out of a conference room!) with clear deadly contempt for the opinion of others – inside the person. Aggression might also express itself by trying to force the opponent to see one's point of view, or by treating others with silent disdain (sarcasm or damming irony).

The Relationship of Air/Metal to the other Elements is, as for all the Elements characterised by two sequences, the *Sheng* and *Ko* cycle. In the Shen Cycle Metal/Air is a mother to Water. Tradition suggests water springs forth from a rock. However, implications are that Air nourishes and replenishes Water, anybody ever having had a fish tank knows how important it is to have oxygenated Water (only then does it support the fish). If we take the issue deeper, we see that Water is a combination of Hydrogen and Oxygen molecules; Air shares (chemically speaking) its most vital molecule with Water).

Furthermore Air without humidity in the lungs, is useless. The gas exchange within its cells could not take place without the air being enclosed in water vapour. The same is true within the work of the Large Intestines: water is absorbed, but also used as a lubricant (since faeces is 70% water).

Air supports the action of the cerebrospinal fluid, a central part of the body's system, through breath. 'The Breath of Life - this pulsation - moves through your spinal column twelve times a minute. The breath that you are aware of, is nothing more that the gross manifestation of this pulsation.' [86] Their relationship is one of help full co-operation.

Looking further at relationships with the other elements, the Chinese *Ko Cycle* has Metal(Air) controlling and limiting Wood; the action of an axe or saw (sawing of a tree trunk) vividly illustrates this. If the Lung and the Large Intestines do not supply the blood with fresh oxygen and nutrients, the gallbladder and liver have nothing to process. Their relationship is characterised by control.

If we expand this, then Air is supposed to control Space... a much less easy metaphor. Where there is apparent Space... Air rushes in (Vacuum), but control?

On the other hand Metal/Air itself is controlled by Fire. Metal thrown into fire will melt and although it will not perish for a long time, it will lose its form and capacity to act. Even more so, Air gets used up by the burning process and completely vanishes – as one can see when a candle in a jar is extinguished by simply putting a lid on it. ...Without the heart, the work of the lungs is unthinkable; yet an overactive heart can damage the capacity of the lungs. Lung and heart depend upon each other, the blood alone is useless to the rest of the body; unless the blood carries oxygen in sufficient quantities, the body is not healthy. They exist in mutual dependency.

Metal/Air itself is the child of Mother Earth. The vital Air of a consistency we can breath, depends on the close interaction with Earth, and what happens on it; too far removed, the oxygen is not sufficient for life to survive. 'The lung extracts the Essence from Air, combining it with the essence from food sent by the spleen, distilling it into the pure, correct *Qi* of bodily life.' [87]

7. 2: b) Associations with Personality and Relationships

> 'Right now you are a bud, tomorrow you are a blossom.
> Right now you are a small plant, tomorrow you are a tree.
> Right now you are a tree, tomorrow you are not at all -
> this is the basic dharma, the true nature of all'.

So said Swami Chidvilasananda, in March 1995. It sums up beautifully, Air's emphasis on Change and Movement; it brings out Airs' challenge to constantly look at the now and letting go of the rest. It calls us to live in the present, each moment new. Many proverbs express this link: 'Wind blows cobwebs away'; 'Fresh air cleans more than a room'; 'Good news travels on the wings of wind' etc. On the other hand, we speak of foul air, stale air and people 'being in the doldrums' (geographical areas where the air is nearly still), when they are depressed and their life has become stagnant.

Psychologically we can say that Air challenges us to ask a fundamental question: What do we need to let go of, what do we need to leave behind in order to progress, or even just enjoy life. Spring does not stay eternally as spring - it lets go of itself in order to become Summer. Summer lets go of itself to become Autumn etc. - there can be no life without change. Yet we hang on to all sorts of things for dear life!

There are the clothes we haven't worn for years; the baby shoes, teeth, teddy bears etc. of our grown up children - but do we part with them? Do we let go of cars we need no longer because we live in the city where there is plenty of public transport?

More important, do we let go of relationships we have outgrown, with honesty and no regret? Do we let go of our children when they have grown up? Do we let go of our pet ideas, concepts, images, limitations etc.? Do we let go of our anger, fear and pride? Do we let go of our prejudices, outmoded behaviour patterns, or even our calcified persona, in order to live life afresh?

In the above poem: if the bud would hold on to being a bud - it would never become a blossom. If the blossom would hold on to its beauty, it would never experience being fruit, seed or tree.

What could a person be like that is strongly influenced by the above issues and tendencies?

A person with dominant Air characteristics could be someone who is either broad or slim, but certainly with a 'barrel chest.' He tends to have a tight pelvis; is rigid with suppressed emotions; pushing the chest forward as a brave front, showing the world that he 'can cope – no one will succeed in getting to me.'

He holds himself especially straight, upright like a Prussian officer, a soldier with a stiff neck, and walks contained within himself. (If unbalanced in the Air element, a person would walk with rounded shoulders, heavily burdened by his responsibilities). His quiet self-contained countenance might give the impression that the person is shy, but when spoken to, he speaks with a clear, precise voice, almost clipped and he impresses others with his clear thinking. He is a person of pale complexion, and often has taut, dry skin. He is immaculately dressed, elegant even and extra clean, he would pick off any fluff from his suit; his hair is well cut, maybe even severe.

He likes order and precision; when asked about a topic or business, he talks as though he knows exactly what happened or is about to happen, he can give precise, detailed descriptions of structures and sequences with his sharp mind. It is for these abilities and skills he is liked in the business world; he would probably have a job as an accountant, computer scientist, analyst, researcher or manager; he might also be an antique dealer, collecting something or other.

Lets make our Air person into a systems designer or manager for a large international computer firm, with the hobby of collecting tin mugs!

In a positive state of energy he is well liked by his colleagues; he is well organised and methodical. He can cope with the ever-new challenges of his demanding job and achieves much, (possibly even for humanitarian benefit). Even when there is a hardware problem he is willing to help by taking things apart and putting them back together with a sense of order and purpose. As a child he might have played with a 'Meccano' set (or other technical toys).

In business meetings and conferences he stands out, due to his ability to analyse and keep focused; he is a defender of principles, providing a structure for others to work with. He cuts through arguments, coming straight to the core of the problem, or sums up discussions in a serene, unflappable manner, cutting through all ambiguity. He appears emotionally uninvolved, remaining aloof; thus it is easy for him not to mix business and pleasure. He keeps his family apart from his working life, but (as in his job) he expects the family to work to schedule. He is committed to the family with integrity and reason. He has a keen eye for stark, austere beauty: that's why he is passionate about tin mugs.

He dislikes all conflict and disorder, expecting life to be agreeable and sensible. Since others don't always conform or have the same high standards and principles, he judges them 'unworthy' and, not willing to give his principles up, he covets his own authority and expertise, withdrawing into his own company. Yet even he himself might at times not be able to meet his high standards, he gets disillusioned and disappointed; at this point he might resort to self-punishment or to installing order by force, sacrificing pleasure and spontaneity, even intimacy.

These tendencies, aggravated by stress, could lead to skin problems, breathing problems or illnesses of the digestive tract. Psychologically such a person might find it difficult to balance or express feelings, especially grief, holding on to memories of loved ones, past loves, past memories etc.

In fact the associated **Emotion** with the Element Air is Grief.

Grief is a stage of transition, it is a necessary part of saying 'goodbye' – of letting go – in order to be free for the new. This applies to many situations. We have to grieve and indeed accept that we miss things or people before we can let go of them. For example, we need to accept that we miss our old home, past job, grown up children or the friend who moved away, before we can really look forward to the new. Most cultures have rituals for these changes; they usually include a set period of solitude (to come to terms with whatever is taking place). Our own rituals, birthdays, weddings and funerals have always an element of grieving; why else do mothers cry at weddings, why else do we celebrate with our friends on the night before a wedding. We have farewell parties to let go of the previous year, our parents, children, our friends or - the dead.

In these celebrations we remember the shared times, we reconcile feuds, try to let go of problems and express our feelings for the person (places, situations), we tell them about our love for them and wish them well. We face our loneliness, we acknowledge the emptiness they leave in us, and then we let go of it, to be filled again with the new. Each step has to be taken, each is as important as the other.

When my father died (I was fifteen years old), I knew he was dying, he had been ill for a long time, but because of the circumstances I was not able to tell him that I loved him and to say 'goodbye' to him. The pain of that unexpressed grief stayed with me for thirty years! Obviously the most important grieving is connected to the loss of a close relation or next of kin – and people who have unfinished business here, might be unable to face 'goodbyes' altogether. They might refuse to grieve, pretending that the other person did not die etc. This leads to severe emotional 'constipation' and probably they will need outside help.

When a death occurs in a family, the etiquette might demand not showing emotions. In this case, one does not cry (exerting self-control) displaying a behaviour pattern suggesting 'I have to be strong, I can survive, I'm all right Jack.' This leads to suppressed anguish, sorrow and grief that clogs up the system of emotional flow, (through clogged pipes nothing flows) and eventually leads to withdrawal, even depression, physical illness in the respiratory systems or the bowels. Furthermore, 'extreme grief is injurious to the lungs.' [88] Similarly the roots of extreme post-natal depression, diseases occurring after retirement (especially skin diseases) and depression that causes pathological illness (i.e. after the children have left home) might well lie in the inability to grieve and then to let go. Healthy grief is transient.

But back to our Manager: he feels in charge of his life and his emotions, has no need to show them to anyone; he likes 'holding in and holding on.' Any sign of illness he shrugs off, "I can't complain thanks, everything is fine," or: "no doctor please..."

Behind this, is a great ability to cope with structure but not with emotions. Sympathy is pushed away; "do not come too near, I can't deal with emotions so I have to cut you off." There is fear of breaking down or letting 'the side down'; or denial, "this is not happening to me; it can't;" "I refuse to believe it, see it or respond to it." The person in the negative Air energy state, protects himself behind a personal armour, from where nobody can convince him otherwise. Consequently such people become isolated and prone to depression, a point from where it is difficult to surface again.

Before we go on, again a warning. Do not put friends, family or self into boxes like the above; we all have some characteristics of all elements. The examples throughout are caricatures, simplifications to invite the reader to contemplate how the tendencies of the elements can be used to understand life and our selves.

Now **a person like the above, does not live alone – so how does he relate to others?**

In the first instance let's look at the relationship between **Earth and Air**. We recall: that Air and Earth have only intimate contact where Air touches the surface of Earth; from there Air thins out, leaving Earth behind; Air moves over the Earth without much involvement.

However Earth provides hurdles as stimulus for Air. Air is not too bothered though what stimulus Earth provides, it has a whole kingdom to play with. A mountain is a significant 'hurdle' that Earth can put in Air's way; it means Earth puts forth its own truth to challenge Air's move. By stating its own nature, wishes and wants, Earth literally says: 'I stay here, I can't be different.' In this way Earth 'dares' Air to act appropriately i.e. change its course. Without this challenge Air finds it difficult to move on. Air needs stimulus via heat (Fire) or obstacles (Earth). Thus the Earth person is important sources of stimulus. Yet once on the move the Air person leaves the Earth person behind, mainly unruffled; interacts with her/him only occasionally, almost as a by-product (dust, sandstorms). Earth becomes a kind of backdrop for Air.

If there is a partnership or marriage between people dominated by characteristics of Air and Earth, it will not be easy. Earth will provide limited stimulation in everyday life... but it might not be enough for Air... and when Air wants to move the mountain, to stimulate Earth, it needs considerable energy - and still might be defeated! Air might sooner or later run out of 'steam,' tire of having to be the active part; then even when Earth drops a mountain in the way, it just has to wait for Air to react in its own time. The interaction between the two relies on the skill and willingness of the Earth person to put herself in the way of Air. There is no way to hide between Air and Earth. Lies and deceit do not work in this relationship, clean fresh, sharp Air will immediately detect any dishonesty and the Earth person is not able and willing to play the Air person's dancing games. Air might try it, but Earth will not stand for it. Only a solid, honest response can foster their interaction.

Mind you, the world of Air is so much bigger than the sphere where it matters, what 'mountain the earth puts in its way.' And here lies the problem of such a relationship. Potentially the Air person is seemingly so vast, so powerful, so extensive and elusive, that the solid, contracted, heavy Earth has little chance of 'measuring up' to the Air person, unless it finds its value on a different scale. If it comes to pragmatic issues, manifestations and every day living, the **Air person has only a flimsy dance to offer to the strength of the Earth person**. A working relationship between the two has thus to be based on a balance found in mutual acceptance of vast difference; only then can a partnership or marriage between these two enjoy any positive interaction and growth and become more than coexistence.

Let us look at that manager of a computer firm - in his job he is effective, honest and hardworking. He is abreast of all new developments in this fast changing business world, and not only in his field of expertise, but also with the needs of his clients. His firm is run like a tight ship where everything is clear and ordered, everything has its place. His junior partner is an Earth person. His junior partner is a gentle, solid and generous chap, who is liked for his subtle humour and friendliness. He likes to take his time and slowly work his way through the various jobs; he also likes his lunchtime and rest. The secretaries and co-workers like him because he is patient and does not judge their work harshly, rather supports each one in what they do.

Together the two heads of the company make a good team, they have build a company that flourishes on respect and co-operation.

Recently the junior partner has been taking extra long lunch breaks, which makes the work on his desk pile up, soon some letters get delayed and a few chances of efficient response missed. When a decision actually is made too late and due to this a big client withdraws his business, the manager has to be informed.

How does the Air person in a *negative* energy state respond?

At first there is a feeling of resignation: let him be, it is just the way he is, I can't be bothered right now to disrupt my life's routine. I need to finish my own project. But as the magnitude of the 'mountain' sinks into his awareness, he knows he needs to deal with the situation; after all, he is 'responsible' for this company.

He shuts himself in his office (builds a wall around himself) and starts to ask questions. Why has the partner taken extra time? Was it necessary? What damage did the action actually do? What can be saved? Should he talk to the client etc.

After he has peeled away layer after layer of the problem, stewed by himself and established what he thinks is the truth of the matter, he calls his colleague. The colleague comes to the office and with a sharp eye for analysis, the manager goes over all the questions again with his partner. As it turned out, the partner has discovered a fascinating book; he started to read it during the lunch breaks and gets so absorbed in it, that he simply forgets time. The Earth person is not worried about it, this is just the way it is. The manager however is shocked - it would never occur to him to neglect his duty; he has been back in the office at 2pm sharp all his working life. He is unable to understand, but recognises how different the junior partner is.

Helpless, he clasps his fingers and asked the partner to be punctual in future and to 'somehow make up with the upset customer.' For weeks he checks that his partner is punctual, clings to his mistrust, unable to let go; he feels more than ever that the business rests on his shoulders; bending low, his shoulders even tighter.

An Air person in a *positive* state, due to his sharp observance and clear awareness would have known that his partner came back late from lunch in the first few days and straight away 'called his truth,' and the situation probably would not have escalated. As soon as he had his chat 'man to man'; he would feel the mishap is sorted out and left behind, forgetting as soon as the partner walked out of the office, and able to focus on new demands.

You might think this parable simple and obscure - and I encourage you to find your own opportunities, to see how these two Elements relate. Observe, trust your insights; you will gradually encounter the wisdom of the cosmic laws.

We turn now to observe a relationship between **Air and Water.**

At a quick glance it appears that air 'sits' on water, just like on earth. After all, water covers most of the planet and air surrounds it all. It is said that the oceans get their movement from the wind (well, tides are actually caused by the moon) and waves are the obvious proof. Wind drives waves from the tiniest ripple on the almost still lake to gigantic surf waves; waves splash with such force against the shore that they get totally infused with air to form spray: a water-air mixture whipped into frenzy. Furthermore, air penetrates deep into the domain of water, (carried by fish and mammals) so that gas bubbles can be seen to rise out of great ocean depths.

With the help of heat, on the other hand, water rises and mingles with the air. Air itself contains sometimes more than 90% of water, and we know already, that only moist air can it be absorbed through breathing. Air and water have great affinity.

For a partnership or marriage that points to a close, sharing relationship, that can even have its passionate moments (foam). Air and Water-people like to spend time and space together. Problems arise in their relationship mainly for two reasons: in higher spheres, air can exist quiet happily without water (or in deserts)! Air does not need water, on the contrary if air gets too saturated with water (clouds) it gets too heavy and has to let go of water (rain). And secondly: independence sits well with Air, she is quiet happy to be alone; and when she moves too fast, water gets left behind; its heaviness frightens Air; scared of being slowed down, it drops Water and 'runs.' If the Water person gets dominant - or too interfering - the Air person simply moves to other parts. In a relationship, this can mean quite literally - they move out of the home or environment; this is part of the basic law for the nature of their interaction. If two people sharing these energies want to make their relationship last, they have to work on balancing their act. The Air person needs the Water person to stay fresh, moist and beneficial to others - and the Water person needs oxygen and movement for its task. However 'still air' is of no use to water; they have a parallel existence.

They are good - if they maintain a balance. Air needs to be light, to be able to rise up; water has the tendency to sink into the depths, this is so physically and psychologically. Unless they limit themselves they will go into opposite directions.

Our Manager of the Computer Company has an employee, a woman of similar age, who is responsible for the computer graphics, animation and other artistic endeavours needed for the advertising side of the business. She enjoys her job and has many creative ideas that have become invaluable to the company. She has actually pioneered a new layout incorporating new photographic material. She is well known in her field. Her success is appreciated by the manager, but when she suggests changing the image of the company to accompany more of her artwork, he sees it as a threat to his own endeavour and calls a staff meeting.

In a clear, crisp manner he portrays the problem and lays out his interpretation. If the company incorporates the new ideas, they need to cut down on other business; her section in the company will become too big.

The Air person in a negative state goes on to say that he does not want the company to change, it runs well the way it is and if the woman colleague does not like it, she can leave. They can thrive without her, possibly even expand. He puts to her the options of letting go of her plans - or leaving the company.

Most of all, the manager fears the change, but also he tries to influence truth and uses his sharp intellect to cover up the threat he felt from the woman becoming 'too heavy.'

An Air person in a positive state would look at the colleague's proposal in detail, enjoy the new stimulus, acknowledge the good points – may be advise not going that fast. A slow, integrating policy might be more advantageous to the business and he can give the woman a limited period to try her ideas. After working side by side for a time, it might become obvious that their ways have to part into two different companies, each going into opposite spheres.

The relationship between **Air and Fire** is startlingly different. Immediately we are caught up in dynamics. Right from the start Air and Fire work together. Air is needed even with the tiniest spark; it is only a question of time how passionate their venture becomes. Aware that we look here at the relationship from the perspective of Air, it is hard to separate the two.

Let's go back to the old example: a burning candle in a jar extinguishes as soon as we put the lid on - moreover it becomes difficult to open the jar afterwards - why? Because inside is a vacuum left by the consumed air; i.e. both suffer!

If allowed, Air fuels fire, they create incredible passionate colourful and warm and loving interactions, yet once air is all consumed by fire, the dance ends in death. The Greek myth of Icarus demonstrates this. Icarus wants to fly (be carried by air) and he builds wings like a giant bird; he succeeds in flying; he is ecstatic; he flies, higher and higher, which also means closer and closer to the sun - Fire. As his wings are held together with wax, the sun melts the wax and he falls to earth, to certain death.

From ecstasy to annihilation! If he would have been content with less... flown at appropriate distance to the sun, he could have ridden the currents of the air forever. Moderation and discipline is the key to such a relationship- yet that is almost asking the impossible from these two!

A moderate draft on a coal fire provides the comfort of home fires... when we open the chimney flap, fire will burn faster; if we take the fire out of its restricted place it will go wild! Equally, sun warms air and air rises creating wild currents throughout the world, a major influence on world climate. In a larger picture, all metabolism of all living beings are dependent on successful interaction between these two elements; what a potential!

Well, how does this kaleidoscope of colour and passion apply to Air and Fire people that are in a relationship, partners or married?

Obviously they have a great time. They make each other rise, shine and shimmer. They help each other grow and transform; from that perspective there could be no better partner for Air than a Fire person. Yet for all the stimulus, and wonderful, varied interaction, there is danger. From the viewpoint of Air, it needs a double dose of responsibility; it must be acutely watchful, aware at all times that the Fire person does not flare up and destroy everything. Even though totally besotted, the Air person must be vigilant that he doesn't lose him/herself in the passion of the Fire person. He/she must retain some distance, space, integrity, privacy etc., otherwise he/she cannot give/fuel the fire and the Fire person will move on or 'die.'

With prudence Air could find the ideal partner in the Fire person; he/she keeps Air moving, keeps the Air person forever fresh, moving constantly into new adventures; stopping him from getting stale, stagnant and attached. The Fire person keeps Air entertained, amused, and inspired, on their toes, ready to roll away from gathering dust over yesterday's dreams!

You will not be surprised if I suggest that our Manager of the Computer Company has a woman employee who is flamboyant, pretty, witty and ever so lively - and that her ideas sparkle and inspire the manager. They spent more and more time together, at first at business meetings and conferences, then privately. They get on 'like a house on fire'; in fact they get on so well that he thinks of sharing his private life with her too. But there the problem starts. As they become more closely involved, their relationship strangely enough, seems to lose its sparkle. The manager begins to feel worn out from the many late nights and is thus not able to pay the same attention to her or his company and the business is suffering.

The Air person in a negative state would try to keep up the pace. He is attached not only to this – 'his' woman, but sees in her the culmination of all the chances of being loved throughout his life; he is afraid of changing the relationship for fear of losing her; he can't let go! He is also afraid of letting go of the business, so he works even harder to compensate. Serving both, he is exhausting himself. Meanwhile the Fire person will start to cast her eyes around and look for a new relationship, getting bored with a <u>tired</u> partner. As he can not see the truth of their relationship uncluttered by his past, he cannot respond clearly to the changes. Eventually the Fire person would probably leave him and his business.

An Air person in a positive state would see this coming, due to his clear perceptive mind, set boundaries, separate private and business involvement and make absolutely clear where his priorities lie. In terms of the company they can share business and meetings, but leave any private feelings out; come the weekend they could have an intimate, but exclusively private relationship. Clarity and precision has to rule! With care, those weekends can remain always fresh and new, which will satisfy the Air's need for movement as much as the Fire person's need for inspiration and excitement.

In the long run, they would probably be wise to choose between a business or private relationship. But then real life is not that simple for we have always tendencies of all five Elements and you can imagine how that complicates the issues described!

Finally we contemplate the relationship between air and the fifth element. What can we observe of **Air and Space** (or wood) in nature?

At a first glance we might fall prey to the illusion that space and air are identical; after all, what separates me from the window in front, is both space and air. Really <u>two</u> things separate me from the window, because air fills space so completely we are usually not aware of it! Why - because they seem to share attributes, (transparent, subtle, movement, potential change, etc. etc.) They share much, yet space is so much vaster than air! We are forgiven for seeing the two as one; in the Indian philosophy space is gross and subtle. It is the gross space which is the element we deal with here, it is that which contains life-force, *prana*. *Prana* is also air. There is a second aspect, subtle space as infinite potential. Infinite potential carries the 'juice ' (*rasa*) of becoming.

This creative juice brings forth creation and is much more than 'just air.' It ss like the sap in a tree which is the source of later fruits. It links Space and the Chinese fifth Element of Wood. Space and Wood thus encapsulate the idea of ultimate creative potential. That potential includes the creation of Air, thus Space has the ultimate authority and Air finds it easy to dissolve into that, it forgets even to fight for its own integrity; it loses itself - it thins out, it dissolves; there is no more air in outer space.

How do these aspects (and others) relate to a partnership or marriage between people who represent these Elements? The Air person is happy and grateful to surrender and share its space with the Space person. S/he is at ease and satisfied and finds security in the Space person as well as enough initiative and movement to fulfil his/her wants and needs. Air is simply not enough for the Space person to express his/her fast potential, and different interests. Air can go through enormous trouble, all sorts of trials and attempts, s/he can literally loop-the-loop, yet it will not satisfy all of Space's needs. (Similarly for Wood to prosper, s/he needs sunlight, minerals and water and air; Air alone simply isn't enough).

In a relationship between an Air person and a Space person, they would be advised to cultivate and foster other aspects of their personality, so that they do not depend on each other for their needs. The Air person has to learn to let go of the partner enough, so that he or she can follow their own interests.

Let us return to our manager of the computer firm and see how in a conflict situation, people of these two Elements would behave. Our manager has a daughter. She is extremely gifted and has many talents. She is clever, intellectually gifted and bright; she draws well and is an admired painter; she loves sports and spends much time with judo, tennis and games; she loves to dance and party as well; but also makes time to read and write poetry. She is an inspiration for many people in her enthusiastic and versatile personality. She likes to do a bit of this and a bit of that and can really not be tied down to any specific career. Her father, our Air person, greatly enjoys her company and when the child was small he responded to her stimulating ideas and moved with them - from a sports match to a reading competition, from a painting class to horse riding. The daughter was tireless; had abundant energy. As the daughter gets older, the Air-father feels she should focus on one or two things, and should take up one thing as a career and do it 'properly.'

They have a long talk and in his clear manner he explains the pro and cons of careers in all the different layers of talents she has. The daughter does not want to listen! To decide on one career - no way! How does the Air person solve the conflict?

In a positive frame of mind of a person with the dominant character of the Element Air, he would appeal to her intellect and meticulously go over the theories again and again, hoping that one aspect will catch her attention. He would also listen carefully to her counter-arguments, why she should not limit herself at this point in time. He would try to direct the conversation to the practical, denser, more grounded aspects of daily life, hoping that where they share earth, they can meet.

Finally, after many arguments he accepts that she is intelligent and mature enough to choose her own profession; he dissolves his own objections and respects her decision and lets her go to do her own thing; even if - it is the other side of the world. When appropriate they will have contact again; he knows that Air will always be one important aspect of Space's life.

In a negative frame of mind, the father would insist that the daughter stayed at college in their hometown and pursue one specific career; he cannot let his little girl go. He wants to be with his daughter - holding on tight to the good times they used to have, bringing this up in every conversation. He might be so worried at the possibility that she could leave his life that he gets quite ill. He might try to manipulate her by pointing out she is such a good hockey player that she could become a sports teacher; it's a solid career and he would even go to her games! If only she would stay and do something sensible.

In a negative Air state the father would not be able to see his daughter's truth - that she is different from him and could not stay in one company, school or college - there is a world beckoning her out there! She has to go - - and she does. It would break her father's heart; he'd lose his little girl and the grief would stay with him for a few years. Because he would be unable to let go, he would live focused on the past, looking at photos, talking about memories, regretting forever that he let her go.

In a positive state the father has a challenge, can he let go enough, so that he can move on himself to create his own new patterns.

7.2: c) Associations for Spiritual Evolution (Yoga)

The most important aspect of this, must be the parallel between Air (*prana*) and life energy, p*rana*,. Air - for all living forms - is a vital essence, meaning living things do not exist without Air. Yet *prana*, life-force, is more than Air; how? It's the life-force that uses the air; this close liaison is called the cosmic breath or Chi/Ki.

We heard earlier that in Ayurveda, imbalances are considered to cause illness, and the imbalances are related to the Elements and *doshas* (Vata, Pitta, and Kapha). The three forces in a positive state are three vital essences Prana, Tejas and Ojas – the vitality behind Air, Fire and Water.

All three are wholesome and involved in renewal and transformation. We cannot go into the science of it here, suffice it to say Air is one of the vital essences – and as such it is more than the physical combination of the gases we breath in. '*Prana* is more than breath. It is more than the creative power of semen or the force of motor nerves, more than the faculties of thought, and intellect or will power.' [89]

Although more than breath – breath is the active symbol for these forces of life. In Tibetan, the wider term *vayu* is preferred, because as such "breath penetrates into the toes and fingertips, and rises through the hollow of the spinal column up to the brain," so says Lama Gangchen. P*rana* links the outer and inner world in such a way that it creates a rhythmic dependency between the body, its parts, the environment and the world, the cosmos. What *prana* stands for, in all its complexity, is much too complicated to explain here in detail.

We looked at life-force in the context of the nourishing Water and the warming/transforming fire; here we look at it in the context of Air and its movement, which affects especially lungs, skin, large intestines, speech, thought and - cosmic consciousness. This more general *Prana* is said to express in different forms (some mention ten modes, most work with five); they are:

Apana is stimulated by deep belly breathing, thus refers to belly; it stimulates the excretory force, expulsion through bowels, bladder, uterus, perspiration. When the excretory force is disturbed, symptoms of illness can result. As the breath expands and contracts, the sacrum thus moves the spinal fluid, it is also important in the movement of Kundalini.

Samana refers to the influence of breath in the region between heart and the navel; it is the digestive and assimilating force that makes food into useful energy. It is seen as active in the entire body - for example, Vitamin D is absorbed through the skin. This vital force is said to cook the food and separate its nutrients from waste, thus is responsible for growth and nourishment. Abnormality in this results in nervous diarrhoea, intestinal colic, spasmodic and nervous retention of urine, constipation etc. and their further consequences.

Udana dwells in the throat and head region; it is 'energy that uplifts,' that enables the production of sound in the form of speech, music etc. It causes contraction of the thoracic muscles, thereby pushing air out through the vocal cords. All physical effort requires strength, the strength of *Udana* rests on the larynx, the upper part of the pelvis, all joints in feet and hands.

Vyana relates to the pulse of life that co-operates with the diaphragm. This pulse governs the whole body, always circulates; all rhythmic contraction take place because of this force. It governs the process of relaxing and contracting, voluntary and involuntary muscles. It governs ligaments and nerves, peristaltic. It is involved in the opening and closing of the eyes; ears, neck, ankles, nose and throat are said to be the abode of this force. Fibrosis, sclerosis, atrophy, and muscular pain are the result of disturbances in this force.

The link between life-force and air is obvious.

There is an old story told (Upanishads). According to it, the mind, breath, speech, ear and eye argued amongst themselves about who is the most important. To solve the dispute, they decided one by one to leave the body, and assess which one was least missed. Speech left - the body, although mute, lived happily on; the eye left - the body, though blind lived happily on; the ear left – the body lived happily on; the mind left - the body continued, albeit unconscious. Once *prana* left, the body died and all others lost their strength.

Clearly *prana* won... it gives energy to all others. The moral of the story: if we control *prana*, we control all, *prana* is the boss! Yet *prana*, even as the enlivening gas, is the energy of consciousness, the creative power of the universe, that energy which has been called Kundalini, Shakti, the great Goddess, the creative power per se etc.

When we look at **Qualities/Steps in Sadhana** in this context, we can simply continue: a strong vitality is obviously important for spiritual practices. The strength considered here comes from surrender to the divine and the cosmic life-force. In Indian tradition this strength is symbolised by the monkey-god Hanuman, the son of the Wind who surrendered to the divine in the form of Sita and Rama. He can overcome all sorts of hazards, because of the control he has over the senses and the lower vital urges.

The practise of controlling the breath is called *pranayama*. It is believed to purify our body and give us strength. It is one of the most central yogic practises, it's the fourth of the eight aspects of Yoga.

Prana–ayama means the 'expansion of the vital force,' but equally it can be understood as 'the retention of the breath'; in both cases, the point is to practise to enlarge our capacity to take in vital energy - and with it to heal body and mind. It enables us to gain power over the mind and senses. The mind and its power is closely linked to the Element Air, it is obvious then, that purifying, controlling and directing (strengthening) the mind is a powerful association. Behind the working of the mind is the power that drives it, we call it intellect. The intellect then, helps us to penetrate the delusions and illusions we have about ourselves and the world, and enables us to let go of those aspects we don't need. This is the highest level of working with this energy field. It comes together in the question we looked at earlier: **What do we need to let go of**, what do we need to leave behind in order to progress on the spiritual path?

Ultimately the intellectual awareness enables one to let go of the firm identification with the body itself - we realise 'I am not only my body, not even a mind, conditioned by many influences – but I am.' When we are in deep sleep, there are no attributes, we are neither mother nor child; we have let go of all roles and concepts – so surely, as for the idea of spiritual advancement in the four levels of consciousness, the Element of Air must belong to the deep-sleep state. We let go of every identification; what remains is only the 'I am' – the notion that we exist!

We find this mirrored in many aspects of **the energy fields and the energy anatomy relevant to the Air** Element.

The *kosha*, energy body associated with Air, is the ***Vijmnamaya kosha*** the sheath of knowledge. What is meant here with knowledge has little to do with what we call 'factual knowledge,' but knowledge that reaches beyond the sensory perceptions. It is the seat of the *buddhi* (intellect) and *ahamkara* (I-consciousness). The mind presents the phenomenal world to the intellect, which has recorded all that happened in the past and all that is possible in the future. The individual consciousness, intellect and ego are all time bound. Only pure consciousness, the Self, is beyond time, is continuous, everlasting and resides as a core within its own sheath *(Anandamaya kosha)*.

When the main activity by the vital energy is focused in this sheath, it also works on the **Heart Chakra or *Anahata***; (positioned in the middle, between both lungs/sternum), the person has reached an important switch point in spiritual evolution. At first a strong sense of Individuality, ego-identity develops here, i.e. 'I as a person, mind and body, am different from you.'

Consciousness gets strongly polarised into 'I versus you,' or an awareness of 'I' and 'not I.' In this 'hub,' in this centre of the body, lies the root of all

Duality. Being aware of the 'Not I' (the other), makes us aware of our differences from others; our individual consciousness (jiva) latches on to the lower energies, playing games with itself, such as 'my mind' versus 'your mind', my body' versus 'your body', my daughter, my house, my car, my country etc...

In the lower three Wheels of energy/and energy bodies we are bound to the worldly existence, where we are very close to our animal nature, bound by survival instinct, by animalistic needs and ego tendencies. Here in the Heart *Chakra* we gradually recognise that we have a choice - to stay on that road, or choose a different path, the path to a more conscious, less limited life.

This *Chakra* is a sort of road-crossing amongst these lower four *Chakras* (connected to the body) and the three higher ones, connected directly to *Prana* (in its cosmic sense). That upward path begins here and it dawns on us, that there is a higher self, *Paramatma*. A person centred here might become an inspiration for others, who find peace and calm in their presence. In the course of one's life, between the ages of 21 to 28 years, one vibrates in the *Anahata Chakra,* becoming aware of one's role, actions and life's goal. Self-confidence grows and might lead to following the spiritual path; then one begins to realise the truth beyond words.

Surrender to a Guru helps one to restrain from running after the outer interests of the world 'like an antelope' (wandering purposelessly here and there). [90]

Let's look at more details about this *chakra:*

Anahata, the fourth *chakra*, is associated with the frequency of 570 Htz – and the colour green. It is seen as having twelve petals containing the letters kam and tham in a soft pink. It is associated with love to all human beings and openness to life, hearing of divine sounds (*nada*) It is the residence of the individual soul, (*jivatma*). It is considered the hub, the centre of man, as here the personal identity is establish as different from others (I versus Thou). The presiding deity is *Vayu/Isha or Rudra* (different names for Shiva as) the Lord of Air mounted on a black antelope... swift as the wind, and his female counterpart.

In its centre is a six-pointed star, consisting of two overlapping triangles. One points upward, symbolising *Shiva*, the male principle. The other triangle points downward symbolising *Shakti* the female principle, creating a distinct divide and balance between the three lower and the three upper *chakra*.

Physical organs associated are: heart and the heart plexus, the vagus nerve, circulatory system; lungs, shoulders, arms, ribs, breasts, diaphragm, thymus gland.

The more psychological, emotional and mental factors associated are: dealing with love versus hatred, with resentment, bitterness, anger, self-interest; loneliness, commitment, forgiveness, and compassion; openness for life.

Perception and nature of information here is via love and the need to be loved. This energy generates the focus for everything.

The Need for love and loving interaction is obviously at the core.

The Tibetan system associates the shape of a hexagram, the colour grey-blue, the sound HUM, and the Tibetan Buddha Akshobya who is a is symbol of integration. Physical ailments are: congestion in the heart, heart attack, heart failure; valve problems; asthma, cardiovascular diseases, lung cancer; bronchial pneumonia; upper back; breast cancer.

The Dharma of Air, there cannot be any doubt, is that of Movement which constantly brings change. We observe it as falling and rising, as in and out, as coming and going, as sowing and reaping, as life and death, as creation and dissolution; expansion and contraction – this gives a constant rhythm: a coming and going we know best from inhalation and exhalation. It is perpetual change - there is nothing to hold on to, nothing that is defined, all 'fixeties' are an illusion. The movement moves through ever large cycles, breathing in and breathing out - as the breath of one gigantic Being breathing in and breathing out. Thousands of years ago, wise ones made a Hymn: **'Homage to Breath,'**

> Lord of All, O Breath your power is our life,
> All life you support.
> As wind you blow with terrible force...
> All beasts praise you. They too rejoice,
> Knowing you shall give them strength
> All the plants rejoice, with tender breath they hail you
> For your gift of fragrance and sweet life!
> Oh dear Breath!
> Like a father his beloved son, you clothe all beings.
> Truly, you are Lord of All!
> (Artharva Veda.XI.4)

That Movement includes the phase of 'letting-go' as an absolute necessity.

In Patanjali's ethic laws for *dharmic* life (*Yamas and Niyamas*) he speaks of *Satya* (Truth) as the second necessary maxim, and recommends *Shava* (cleanliness, purity) as the activity that corresponds. We have talked about these earlier; it remains for me to affirm, that through purification and cleanliness, whether on a physical or mental level, health is supported.

Our lungs clean the air we breathe by separating those gases we need and those we don't. Air itself needs to be cleaned of 'stuff' such as dust, seeds, tiny microscopic animals, bacteria, pollution and water.

Similarly our mind needs a sharp intellect to clear away the unnecessary clutter; the need for cleanliness and clarity implies letting go of the impure.

This 'letting go' has become the central issue of many teachings, from Christianity to Yoga and oriental medicines, to ancient and modem mysticism and Eastern and Western psychology. *Manjushri* is Buddha portrayed with a gleaming sword, which he uses to cut away all impurities, especially stupidity, misunderstandings, and ignorance. The root of his name is *Mani* – is Sanskrit for 'mind'; he symbolises discrimination, that ability which like a 'sword' of clarity and wisdom cuts away ignorance and cleanses our personal mind. This is a universal attribute of Air no matter whether amongst American Indian, Patanjali, Buddhist or... in the Yoga Vasishta, where it says:

> The mind being curbed
> with its senses and organs focused on the Self,
> there appears a bright light before it
>> and the apparent world fades away...
>> The imaginary world recedes from view
>> and falls like a withered leaf...
>> The intellect, cleared of the cloud of illusion,
>> which veiled the deluded mind,
>> shines as clearly, as the vault of the autumnal sky. [91]

'Air' as a subtle element works on clarity and wisdom; thus wherever Yoga is practised with wisdom, a wisdom that leads beyond the mere physical practise of *asana*, there this Element is at work. It is an energy that constantly urges us to become lighter to not get bound by matter; it lets us ascend. Similarly in any posture we practice, there is knowledge, 'know how' but there also needs to be the mastery that lets us forget the 'how to do it' and simply float up with the *asana*, be at ease with it, light and ascending. Transparent, without the heaviness of striving and willing, of forcing and pushing - but light as a feather drifting on a warm air stream.

Nevertheless, there are of course certain *Asanas,* which specially work on the Air Element. All inversion postures, are said to work on the Air Element, and then of course there are those that stretch the Air Meridians, i.e. expand the chest and work the arms. *Arhalasana; Ardhapindasana, Ardhasarvangasana, Vrksasana, Trikonasana* etc. most of these of course work on other Elements too.

Knowledge It has repeatedly come up that the Air Element is linked to knowledge; but knowledge has a different slant for each of the different elemental energies. For Air (and Space) knowledge is predominantly *sattvic* – this means it is that knowledge which tries to integrate, harmonise, see the bigger picture – it is knowledge that goes beyond projections of the mind to seeing things 'as they are.' In the Bhagavad Gita *sattvic* knowledge is described: 'one sees the one indestructible Reality, in all beings, the undivided in the divided, know that knowledge as *Sattvic* (Pure).' (Gita, XVIII/20) [92]

This is of course tied up with Air's quest for Truth and universal laws. Once Air recognises the world as mere forms of the One Vital Power, it can let go of all distractions and focus on itself (the changeless immortal Self that is its origin).

Similarly **Happiness** in this context has a subtle quality; it comes from inner harmony and peace 'born out of purity of one's own mind, the peace and tranquillity, the joy and expansion, that the mind and intellect come to experience as a result of their discipline and contemplation... the gladness of the heart that well up in the bosom of a cultured man, as a result of his balanced and self-disciplined life of high ideals and divine values of life.' [92] (Holy Geeta, XVIII/37)

Meditation

In many traditions the most frequent recommendation for Meditation is to focus on the breath. The cyclic rhythm of breath is like a gateway to experiencing the movement of existence. But focus on the breath reveals not only movement, but a 'space in between breath'; this point is a powerful point of stillness.

This stillness plays a great part in Buddhist Meditation, especially Zen; it's the core of all emptiness and with it the womb of all form. Stillness in between breath has been compared to the zenith of the sun; it's the vital 'turning-point.' For one instance there is 'neither this, nor that'; one can witness - from the outside - the ever changing movement. Much as a mountaineer standing at the peak can see both: where he came from - and where he is going.

But as the example shows, we have to stop and stand back if we want to see 'change;' we can neither be caught up in the past nor the future; the process of change needs us to let go – let go eventually even of this the vantage point. The 'I Ching,' Taoist book of ancient Chinese wisdom and divination, writes:

> After a time of decay comes the turning point
> The powerful light that has been banished returns.
> There is movement, but it has not been brought about by force...
> The movement is natural, arises, spontaneously.
> For this reason the transformation of the old becomes easy.
> The old is discarded and the new is introduced.
> Both measure accord with time, therefore no harm results.
> The idea of return, of turning is based on the course of
> Movement, which is cyclic, and the course completes itself [93]

The 'Turning Point' is Now; in the now, the mentally agile Air person can harness their 'abundant mental energy for meditation, which for them should be like the flight of the eagle. They must let their mind soar without losing focus.' [94]

Chapter Eight: Invocation of Space (Wood)

In me all else exists,
Not the smallest particle exists apart from me.
In me all else moves, yet I do not.
In me all changes, yet I do not;
In me all takes form, yet I have no form.
From me all takes its place, time and marking,
Yet I am beyond place, time and meaning.
As above, so below; as inside so outside,
I am total integrity;
Contained within myself as myself.
In this I seem apart - just like a mighty tree
Standing aloof on the top of a hill,
Gazing far over all lands.

In me, as in the tree the most powerful sap rises
- the sap of continuous creation, the greening power
As tree I am nourished as much through my roots
- the roots, that reach deep into the bowels of the earth,
- the earth, that provides me with water and nutrients,
As I am nourished through the crown of my leaves
- leaves that reach into the limitless sky,
- sky that provides me with water and sunlight;
Thus I am a bridge between heaven and earth
The bridge between matter and consciousness,
The bridge between Man and God
A bridge whose feet rest either side of life's turbulent river.

The turbulent currents of Life happen within me-
Yet simultaneously they bends me this way and that
I stay steadfast in the most violent storm
Rooted in what I am.
Through wisdom, acquired in rings-of-years;
I know "I am That" - no form,
Yet producing all fruits in accordance with the seasons;
Into this "I am"- I withdraw to rest and gather strength.
I have the foresight of creation
In me cosmic laws have left their timeless blueprints
Accordingly I create each cell of new growth
To fit the vision of the species
One leaf, the same as another;
One oak the same as another
As womb of creation or giant tree
I am a host to many creatures;
the wise owl sleeps peacefully in my branches,

The robin builds its nest and the insects feed under my skin
The bees enjoy my blossoms, the squirrel feasts on my fruit,
The fox hides behind me, and deep hidden in the apex of my trunk,
Lies the coiled serpent,
Protecting me, protected by me,
To be awakened one auspicious day.
The shy violet enjoys the moisture dripping off my leaves,
The weary wanderer seeks my shade,
The children dance their nursery rhymes around me
It is not that I need them but they need me,
For I emit the oxygen they breathe.

I have been worshipped by most primitive man;
I have been worshipped by most venerable sages.
I draw forth faith from within you,
For I am the mirror of your own divinity
Forever reaching to heavens for divine light.
Faith's energy is boundless, how else could
I nourish the tiny acorn to become the mighty tree?
How else could I bring lush, rich freshness to wilted shrivelled people?
How else could I nourish the heart's intention to become light?

In my most subtlest garb - I am brother of consciousness.
I am the Spirit of the tree, I am greening-power in motion.
I am the Spirit of Creation, nothing can manifest without me
I am the Spirit of steadfastness, without me no direction is safe
I am the Spirit of Man, his nature being divine energy.
I am the Spirit of Being - I am what I am.
I am the Spirit of Energy, I am the Life.

8.1: Contemplation of Space

The elusive subtle nature of the fifth Element is mirrored in the many labels it has been given, although its meaning remains the same. It is named Ether/Faith (in some Indian contexts); Wood (Chinese), Nature (African), Great Spirit (American Indian), and Cosmic body of Christ (Medieval Europe), yet the most widely accepted label is probably Space, so we will work with that. All labels try to capture three aspects: the subtle state of this Element, its importance as life's essence and its source connection in the Mystery of the Divine. These will reveal their knowledge in due course, but here just a few thoughts to each label:

Ether, according to the Hutchinson Encyclopaedia, is either a colourless, volatile inflammable liquid used, for example, to sterilise and clean wounds - or a hypothetical concept introduced to explain some of the properties of light.

The former, ether as cleansing agent, has strong links to the liver and its organ-network (relevant to Chinese Medicine and Ayurveda). The word 'Ether' in Ayurveda has diverse meanings, such as: 'sound,' or 'root' radiation and 'that which does not provide resistance.'

Here we come closer to the second point: The more subtle qualities of light reach beyond the Element of Fire, deep into spiritual realms, meeting the label of 'faith.' Pure Vedanta, the oldest and probably the original source of qualifying the energy in five elements, at times uses this stage as 'faith.'

Looking at the second label **Wood**, it relates to the biological life-force, (just as does the label **Nature** – and is symbolically represented as trees.

The third group of names abstracts even further focusing exclusively on the intangible essence or **Spirit**.

In several ancient traditions there is talk of the <u>tree of life</u>; this concept seems to marry all three aspects: Wood (tree) Space and Spirit. According to Sankara, one of the most respected ancient Philosophers of India, there is - **a botanical tree (Pipal tree, Ficus Religiosa)**, which has been chosen to ' represent the entire cosmos, because of its creative meaning;' it is called *Aswattha* . Sanskrit syllables carry great meaning: *A – swattha* means 'that which will not remain the same till tomorrow;' in other words, the tree indicates the ephemeral, the ever-changing world, of phenomena. In the Bhagavad Gita (Chapter 15) this tree is described as having its roots 'up' in space, in the most subtle dimension 'that contains all phenomena,' and deriving its sustenance from Beyond. Its leaves and branches speak of spiritual growth and the knowledge that leads to a noble life, enabling the knower to reach Self-realisation. [95] The plurality of worldly existence, including the human experience, is allegorically pictured as a fig tree arising from and sustained by higher energies – even consciousness. Similarly Space (just as the tree) is 'that which gives accommodation to all things' (Sanskrit: *Akasa);* it is the potential and womb of all phenomena, yet in its pure state, is consciousness.

Now let us contemplate what we can learn from **'Wood'** as described in the Chinese tradition. Imagine a majestic tree standing on a mountaintop; spreading its branches in all directions, it has a commanding view, allowing an extended vision. This superior vision enables us to see beyond illusion.

At the same time, the tree (as well as man), exposed to all weathers, being pulled by winds this way and that, must be firmly rooted! There are two sides to this: yes the tree can bend, but it is bound to its location. Similarly our roots nurture but limit us. When they keep us from moving on, vision and opinions are narrow and blocked. The blocks prevent the sap of life from flowing, stunting growth. Eventually a tree where the sap cannot flow (for whatever reasons), withers and dies; out of congestion, illness arises! To heal this, the rising sap has to be strong enough to find new ways of expressing life, cleaning the blockages, freeing itself from restrictions and relaxing back into the original task. The latter is synonymous with surrendering to the all-embracing principle of higher unity, where we become part of a multi-dimensional living organism.

Trees (Wood) have a unique feature, called geotropism. Normally trees grow upwards for two reasons: firstly, they grow towards the light. I remember a narrow valley in the Grampians of Australia where the trees grew horizontally, at a 45 degree angle to the slopes instead of straight up, in order to reach the little light that was let into the centre of the canyon. Wood always stretches *towards light – and against gravity.*

However, a tree also grows towards the force of gravity; they have a special ability to tune into the earth magnetic field with their roots; thus *a tree stretches in two opposite directions,* or into all directions (re: multi-dimensional space).

Trees stem from seeds (ancestors) and produce seeds; they are 'parent-plants.' The seed contains a complete blueprint of what its fruit is going to be. No cabbage seed has ever grown into a bushel of rice. The seed with its inherent plan - or its morphogenetic field - is put into the ground *carrying its karma.* There the earth protects it, so that it can germinate. For this process to begin, the environment has to be just right for that individual seed in order to make the quantum leap from seed to seedling. For some plants it takes decades, for some days; for some it takes fire (to crack open seed-pods), for some it takes water; for some it takes sand, for others rich humus. Why and how these needs are shaped, depends not only on the environment for which they are destined, but is also determined by knowledge held from the past. (The collective knowledge held is referred to as cosmic knowledge, eternal knowledge or... the Akashic records).

From the start, the seedling has a very special relationship to its environment; the conditions for its development are crucial. Initially it has its own potential to grow roots, (a measure of wholeness and independence) but soon the seedling requires dependence on others i.e. sunshine, rain, nutrients in the ground, shade, wind, adequate space etc. (it has to establish links between its inner needs and the outer world). Once a young tree, it further needs to respond to its environment with flexibility, needing to bend in strong winds, otherwise the high demands could snap the trunk. To remain flexible it needs adequate water to dissolve the nutrients provided by the earth and to fill the cells with sap, hence its dependency on water. Without water it will dry out and shrivel up or break at the next encounter with wind, animal or man. When dry it also easily falls prey to fire, whether it wants to or not.

Some trees, old and sturdy trees like the Redwoods, and Mahogany, can actually survive fires not only while green and living, but also when dried up, or cut. The reason lies in the density of their cell structure, which does not allow the oxygen the fire needs, to penetrate. One could say these are so strong in their integrity, so true to themselves, their 'tree-ness' and conviction, that nothing can touch them. Some of these trees are three thousand years old!! Branches can be cut off, the trunk be sown off, and still the sap is so strong that it makes new growth, new shoots, eventually a new tree.

It helps a young tree to grow up in a group; they provide shelter for each other. But eventually they will outgrow this arrangement and need space.

Trees compete for space and light. If they have not enough they wither. Let us assume our young tree survived and his companions made room for him, then it grows stronger with each season. His branches will stretch in many directions, some bigger, stronger, longer, some smaller, shorter, weaker. Some of these branches will die. In the winter, the sap will retreat to the centre of the trunk, or the roots, to avoid the frost. In order to prevent severe damage, the sap retreats, avoiding a damaging confrontation, with icy winds or drying frost. This withdrawal from the harsh winter attacks might lead to branches dropping off, yet as long as the centre stays untouched, 'unimportant' shoots can be sacrificed. **The tree renounces aspects of lesser importance while maintaining faith and trusting that spring will come** again; or that after a dry period it will rain; or in the case of endless rain, that the sun will shine again. And when spring comes, he sees his faith rewarded. With confidence and vigour he produces new shoots, leaves, branches, flowers and fruit - only to withdraw again in the autumn into himself to integrate last summer's experience. In this way, he builds time after time more rings around him, gathering strength, ready to green again in another spring. The tree grows stronger as long as he maintains enough flexibility to sway in the wind, yet stays firmly rooted in the ground. This says something about measured existence, not wanting what cannot be yours! Accepting life as it is.

In this way his roots grow too, reaching deep, like the anchor of a ship, while his crown reaches high into the sky with a canopy of leaves that soaks up the sun and rain. Once old and established, he has a beautiful vista over wide rolling hills, a view over life as it proceeds, unattached, contained and peaceful.

His peace is by no means egotistic; he gives generously and selflessly to others. Even though the earth and environment provide for his needs, in exchange he gives oxygen, life-sustaining energy abundantly, to all that live. Generosity is one of his characteristics, for not only does he give oxygen (vital *prana*) to others, but eventually sacrifices himself to fire. But all along he gives small necessary gifts to those friends that need, providing a community for others. All sorts of animals and birds live in his branches, live in him or off him; he supports plenty of life unperturbed.

The tree can protects others throughout blizzards, droughts and floods because his roots are firmly planted and his energy is self-contained; he is not bothered by little guest creatures (from bug to bird), they live according to their nature, as he does to his. He loves them, is even grateful, for their droppings are of some benefit, fertilising his earth. He might even share his version/vision of life with them.

One day the woodcutter comes and decides it is time to cut the tree. But even then it takes the tree trunk a long time to dry out or decay. Eventually, when wood is ready to be used, the natural beauty of the tree is still recognised; its spirit, its legacy, can still be appreciated and enjoyed by people who own the wooden furniture for hundreds of years. Yet some of the tree will be cut into logs and burned in the fireplace; but then the tree always was aware that it carried fire intrinsically in himself. In its wisdom, Wood knew and accepted that finally transformation comes into pure energy, into pure spirit.

Now **to contemplate Space,** how can we? Its vastness seems prohibitive. To talk about space is like talking about infinity - there seems to be no limits for our mind. And that's it: Space has no boundaries; it is infinite (in place and time). This grandness is hard to grasp. Looking at the night sky, we see billions of stars, planets from near and far, and yet what ever we see is, of course, the tiniest fraction of space; it belongs to one family of stars we call the Galaxy! Recently I heard someone say: 'we used to think there were a million galaxies, well these days we know there is a galaxy for every grain of sand on this earth.' The nearest Galaxies to us are the two Magellanic Clouds, they are 180,000 light years away. One of the biggest Galaxies that have been studied so far, is one called M87; it is a million light years across and 50 million light years way. [96] These numbers go beyond our comprehension beyond even imagination - and that goes too for what goes on in it. But in all its grandness, we must not forget that space is still an object of our perception, something we can study, analyse – it is 'beyond us' only because of our limited view of reality.

On one hand there is the vastness of space – one the other, each grain of sand, each blade of grass is filled with space! How is that? Every phenomena, a gas-explosion on the sun, Mars, Jupiter and other planets or blood-cell in our body, has potential and manifestation **in space and of space.** Less than one billionth of the human body is material; the rest is space!!! [97] This incredible complexity is not without order; stars follow a certain life span, the earth has a certain life rhythm. A plant has a certain structure, as humans, we have a certain life cycle, so does our skin and cells; creation is not chaotic. Richard Dawkins, not without humour, says, [98]

"Nature, it seems is the popular name, for milliards and milliards and milliards of particles playing their infinite game of - billiards and billiards and billiards."

Space generates out of itself, particles that come together in certain, seemingly innocent objects – and then something happens; the phenomena or object – acquires the ability 'to self-replicate, the object is able to use the surrounding materials to make exact copies of itself' (Dawkins) and bingo! We have structured manifestations.

Space does not only contain all that exists, but it contains all, even before it exists - as well as all the laws according to which it exists; a matrix for future potential - ad infinitum.

It is awesome to think that not only all solid matter, the desk, the chair, the computer all, around me exist in space, but the potential for this book exists in space as well, in fact the blueprint is already there even before I write it. It exists as ultimate potential – even our future grandchildren already exist potentially in space!

It gives a totally new understanding to the age-old argument between predetermination and free will. It suggests that, the potential for all sorts of actions are mapped out, yet all options and all consequences are included! Mind splitting! The blueprints are there, and we with our will make manifest – yet only that which is already possible. As always: both 'sides' of the ancient argument are right! Eastern philosophies have maintained all along, that past patterns (karma) hold present choices.

If space contains not only all matter, but also all potential - then **space contains time,** by virtue of containing the sequence of events between potential and manifestation. It makes Albert Einstein's suggestion of a space-time continuum obvious. Space, that includes time, has not only as we assume in everyday life three, but four dimensions, or as scientists of today would have it, not only four dimensions but n-th-dimensions. [99] Space is truly unlimited. Can we stretch our minds to understand and feel the above? Normally we look at objects, see a table and perceive it as a solid object. This way of seeing things, is called in modern physics the 'middle dimension' - the way of everyday life, it is a useful way of looking at things. Yet we know from modem physics that objects are not really like this, they are not only made of small bits of matter, but these atoms consist of even tinier 'things.' If we imagine one tiny atom of our table to be magnified to be as large as the dome of St. Peter's Cathedral in Rome (the largest Cathedral), we would see that really the atom is huge empty space (just like the Cathedral). In it a grain of salt and a few specks of dust (nucleus and electrons) are flying about! – Wow! [100]

My desk is really masses and masses of microscopic space filled with a few free floating, minute particles – and so is my hand on it. Wow! Of course mystics have seen this along; their awareness is so finely tuned that they live in this extended awareness; this other dimension is called *turiya*, is the 'fourth dimension' which reveals the essential emptiness, or the seeming void of things. *Mahayana Buddhism* accepts this empty space as the true 'Body of Being,' *Dharmakaya*, ultimate essence – that we are.

In the old *Vedic tradition* too, there is the notion of space as emptiness, *mahakasa* is the great space, where 'nothing' exists and simultaneously all exists, divine consciousness. When the focus is not on emptiness, but on consciousness – the source of all potential - then space is called *cittacasa*, or ultimately *cidakasa* .

In emptiness, vibration of energy is 'motion in space.' And that is all there is! Now comes the odd bit: what we perceive as the world is only those frequencies which our limited five senses can register and thus deem as existing – to the rest we are 'blind!' And yet there is a whole universe of moving energies out there. So to talk about 'space' as such is only referring to that which we can register or imagine; there is much about space, due to human limitations that we cannot qualify, we can't say much about - Sages call this 'pure Space.' Once pure space is 'polluted,' it contains the energies that include us! The purity of the innocent space-body is what is described in the Guru Gita (Skanda Purana) Verse 64:

I am everlasting, self-luminous, taintless and completely pure.
I am the supreme Ether. I am immovable, blissful and imperishable.

This is our original nature, to become aware of it and sink into that pure space; in Buddhist and Vedantic tradition it is seen as the bliss of emptiness. To focus on that pure inner Space becomes a tool to unblock and free us from our 'complicated, narrow, boring and limited reality.' The '*Rishis*' explored the inner space through meditation, and called it *athma bodha*, the house of *Atman/Brahman*. They also knew this must not be confused with the Ultimate itself; it is still an object of observation i.e. still limited by our perception. It is *Akasa* – perceptible, it is that space which contains phenomena, belonging to the *Mahabhuta*.

Space, just as each Element, has this quality of pointing beyond itself to its divine origin: Earth points to the creative goddess, Water reminds of the flow of life itself. Fire called us to witness the God-light and with Air we are aware of *prana*, the vital essence, breath of life. Now Space adds the void filled with divine potential. With this, Space as well as 'tree,' calls us to expand our perspective beyond place and time:

High upon Sacred Mountain,
With unrestricted view,
The clarity of vision
Comes to us anew. [101]

This expanded vision challenges our intelligence – we have the potential to achieve anything in life? The potential is there before we even take a 'step,' moreover our mind knows, even our brain knows any idea already before 'we' do - yes - and it sends out a message to the body, muscles etc. instructing them what to do. Before action, comes knowledge, comes intelligence, comes vision. All of nature acts from the source of such innate wisdom. Before setting out to seek a new job, a holiday destination, a new motive to paint, or a new direction in life, really before doing any job, before planning a city, before raising a child - the idea, the vision, is always there. Only once we have this 'vision,' can we harness our strength and find the right tools to do the job! Only then can others join in and help us to 'get where we want.' Space has in itself the 'ideas' even before the start of evolution.

As above so below, we need such vision too. When stuck in life we ask, 'what shall I do? Where shall I turn? What am I supposed to do with my life?' In these situations Space offers its wisdom: A lettuce does not produce carrots; similarly each of us has their own potential. To find our potential, to find the vision that is ours, we have to look into ourselves, into our inner space, to reach the unformed potential, our most powerful source! This process is called meditation. If we quiet our mind, eventually we will hear our own inner wisdom, showing us the right path.

Different traditions have different ways of doing this. Tribal people, under the guidance of a wise person, are often sent into remote locations, such as a hill top, and asked to pray, fast and meditate for three or four days. In the more urban environment, we might choose to go on a retreat. A businessman, needing an insight into his business deals, might just lock himself in the office for a while. Whichever method we choose to reach our own inner wisdom, we need to know that it can be reached, because it is already contained in space! The question is not whether we can access it, but **how to shut out all other interruptions and babbling of our mind, so that we can see the vision, hear the wisdom. This is the path of Yoga.**

The next problem we have is, we do not believe what we hear, we have little faith, do not trust our own wisdom. Space teaches us to respect our own inner wisdom. It is there, call it Higher Self, Soul or Intuition! Inside ourselves, inside our mind we have Space containing all the wisdom we need. With this inner wisdom-space, we are 'plugged' into the universal Wisdom-Space, universal mind or consciousness. The guidance will come - we just need to respect it, trust it, and not doubt it.

Space does not doubt itself: 'Oh, maybe this oak tree doesn't look right, maybe I better give it some blue leaves;' Space trusts its integral knowledge, respects its own decision.

Once we have learned to respect our inner wisdom we know that the same is in every being and thing. If inner wisdom is in the Space that is me, how can it not be in the Space that is you? So I need to respect your Space, the tree's Space, the house's Space, the earth's Space etc. Space containing **wisdom, divine wisdom,** (remember 'divine' = 'beyond the limited human being') is **sacred Space.** Sacred Space needs to be **treated with respect** and awe - have we not seen earlier how awesome space is?

Each creature is by nature 'sacred Space;' each being needs respect, no matter what kind, creed, shape or colour. Treating these with respect means not to allow others, or yourself, to abuse them in any way, not allow ourselves to violate sacred space: [102]

Treat 'every-thing,' person, animal and plant with respect. Treat every thought, idea, concept, religion, and philosophy with respect.

Treat everything, form or formless with respect, it will change our way of being, our whole life! It will affect how we build our cities, how clean we keep our air, whether we have enough room to live – or parks to relax in?

It affects our relationships too - how about our friendships? Are we possessive towards our friends, partners or children? Do we give them enough space, enough distance to do what they feel is right? Do we allow enough support and space for other beings to develop their full potential? If we would give people such quality space they would have no need for drugs, no need for fights and over-reaction, no need even for harmful stress.

Finally: do we give ourselves enough space to relax during the day, sacred space to be with our own inner self to grow emotionally, energetically and spiritually?

Let us summarise: Space/Wood is an energy-field with certain characteristics. It is all-pervasive, spreading into all directions, known, unknown and yet to be known - including time. It contains an enormous, creative potential generating out of itself all phenomena. It does this with intelligence, holding all phenomena in an ordered way. It contains the door to infinity and is laden with divine intelligence; it's the vehicle that carries Chit (Consciousness) into all existence.

This expansiveness is there also in the interaction with other Elements; i.e. Space holds within itself the most solid and dense matter (from the earth to black holes) thus is the bridge between matter and consciousness. These qualities are also inherent in the symbol of Wood or the 'Tree.' It is 'rooted' in the seed of their predecessors and contains a plan/vision according to which it unfolds; it lives in respectful partnership with others and its environment; it strives for light (higher needs)and is also grounded. It appears to be a bridge between heaven and earth. A tree is flexible; can endure real hardship, has trust and faith in its own existence and might still be admired after its death - or be immortal!

8.2: Associations with the Space Element

The meridians linked to the Element of Wood/Space in Chinese Medicine as well as in Ayurveda are gall bladder meridian (*yang*) and his sister the liver meridian (*Yin*). First let us focus on the bodily function of the organs after which the above Organ network is named, for their functions reveal some worthwhile lessons.

The gall bladder is a pear shaped sac attached to the liver by connective tissue. It acts as a reservoir of bile. Bile is secreted by the liver and consists of water, mucus, bile pigment, salts and cholesterol. The gall bladder has a lining, which adds mucus to the bile and absorbs water, concentrating the liver bile 10 to 15 times. By contraction of its muscular walls this is expelled and passed via the bile duct into the duodenum (part of the small intestines). Fat and hormones secreted by the duodenum stimulate this. The workings of the gall bladder can be summed up as being a reservoir; substances flow in and out; they are like an 'upright official who excels through his decisions and judgement' [103] Such official, a magistrate is the acting power of a general, similarly the gall bladder controls the amount of bile (including some hormones) that is expelled, thus influencing the nutrients and their distribution around the whole of the body.

The Liver is the largest gland in the body, weighing between 1 and 2 kg. Its importance is hidden in its very name, which has the same root as life. It is situated in the upper right part of the abdominal cavity. It has four lobes, a right and left one, each in the front and back. Various structures enter the liver (portal vein, an aorta; sympathetic and parasympathetic nerve fibres), the hepatic ducts carry bile from the liver to the gall bladder and lymph vessels. The close link to gall bladder is obvious.

The functions of the gland are numerous; it's an extremely active organ. It breaks down amino acids, into new proteins and waste (uric acid). It converts glucose to glycogen in the presence of insulin. It converts fat; it produces heat due to its high metabolic rate. It secretes bile. It stores vitamins (B_{12}, A, D, E, K and water soluble ones) and minerals (iron and copper). It synthesises vitamin A and nonessential amino acids, blood clotting agents, etc. It detoxifies drugs and noxious substances. It metabolises ethanol (in alcoholic drinks). It inactivates hormones (insulin, glucagon, thyroid and sex hormones).

To sum up this complex job one can say: the liver processes nutrients, and stores them. It produces heat; it cleans and detoxifies, it destroys or converts unwanted substances. In the Chinese theory, the liver is the general or ' military leader who excels in his strategic planning' [104]. The liver decides (what the gallbladder puts into practice) what to store, what is needed, what to dispense and how much; what is poisonous and must be cleaned; when more hormones will be needed and how much. The prime task of the liver is keep the overall purpose 'in mind,' assuring the movement of bodily substances is smooth and effective; maintaining even-ness and harmony throughout. From the above it is understandable why these two energy fields are linked together and linked to Wood. Wood metabolises nutrients, sunshine and water according to its inherent blueprint, with vitality and vigour. It stores some in its roots and some such as Chlorophyll, in its leaves. It works to a hidden blue-print/vision and the actions mirror that. Using these skills appropriately will create balanced growth. A person who uses his resources and mental abilities appropriately, neither erratically nor exhaustively - might display even-ness and harmony in body movement, mind and emotions.

A person suffering from erratic mood changes, shortness of temper and lacking emotional equilibrium might have an imbalance here.

Imbalances in the activity of the gall bladder (GB) and liver meridians (LV) might result in various forms of migraines. Most likely the liver energy gets out of hand and rises much too fast into the head and cannot assure appropriate supplies to the eye, ears, or brain. Arthritis results, if the element fails to neutralise acids and other poisonous substances. Menstruation problems can arise if the liver cannot discharge the necessary blood evenly to the uterus at the start of menstruation, it will cramp and period pains will be experienced; also there may be a disturbed sugar metabolism. Inappropriate bile release will affect the peristalsis of the stomach and intestines and thus can produce interference in the assimilation and elimination of food; constipation can be the result.

This might effect the personality, its clarity of vision, thought and decision-making - leading to a disability to make appropriate judgement. On an emotional level, GB imparts the power to make decisions, LV the power of planning and carrying them out. Dissonance between these two functions may result in action without discernment, without appropriate consideration - or an in ability to actualise decisions leaving the person in a state of feeling 'there is no way out.'

Location for the meridians related to Space/Wood : **The Gallbladder Meridian (GB)** starts at the outside point of the eyes, wriggles along the side of the head, down the neck, around the shoulder-blades, curving right into the side of the body, going along the side of the body and leg as a 'trouser seam' would, right down to the ankle and the fourth toe.

Its **task** is to distribute nutrients and Ki and balance the overall energy through the internal hormones and digestive enzymes. 'It decides courses of action such as which part of the body needs the energy.' [105]

Location of the Liver Meridian (LV). It starts at the outside edge of the big toe, runs along the frontal inside of the leg (along the shinbone) up to the groin. It surfaces on the outside of the chest and goes up the neck. At arm level, a branch goes off along the side of the arm, ending on the palm side, up at the top of the ring finger.

> 'While life itself depends on our lungs, heart and circulation to bring oxygen, warmth and nutrients to all cells of the body, the liver provides essential support to all these processes. It stores nutrients and energy for physical activity. It is involved in the formation and breakdown of blood and filters toxins from the blood. Its job is to keep the body full of vigour...' [106]

In Ayurveda, **'Ether' or Space** is the most difficult element to come to terms with. It is part of **Vata** (as is Air) – yet seems to have strong links with Pitta (Fire). On the one hand its said to have cold and dry attributes (Vata) yet 'it also has a potential energy which, when released, can 'radiate' and become totally different from its previous qualities.' [106] However the physical organs and meridians are the same as in the Chinese system. In classical Ayurvedic texts, the functions related to Vata all have something to do with movement, activity, vitality and breath.

Further Associations with the Organ-network for Wood/Space (For the purpose of simplification, I use ' Wood' in this section, as it primarily relates to complementary medicines/TCM.

The Cycle is, as we know, a bio-energetic clock. The time of peak functioning for GB is 11pm to 1am, and for LV the maximum working time is 1am to 3am. Conversely, the time of minimum function is 11am to 1pm for GB and 1pm to 3pm for LV. Symptoms of imbalances will be especially noticed at these times.

A person with the main characteristics of Wood Element might find that his peak functioning time is in the middle of the night! Late morning, early afternoon, he feels low and tired. This is a potential 'problem,' but people adjust their life to being a night person or - they might use the sleep time for creating and decision making. This sounds intriguing? I am sure, if we learn how to work with our subconscious and use our dreams, a lot of creative work can be accomplished. The result? One wakes up with a host of ideas, ready to put them into action. Some work does itself 'overnight'! This is useful with emotional adjustments or problems: after a good night's sleep we feel different! On the other hand, even a person balanced in Wood Energy, might face slight fatigue over lunchtime, which will be made worse by having a large lunch; Liver and Gall Bladder-organ-network will not be of much assistance to the digestive process. A rhythm like this suits entertainers, craftsmen or business people are able to 'take siesta.'

Each Element in the Chinese tradition has **a host of correspondences.**

The Season associated with Wood is spring, the time of new growth. Greek mythology associates Persephone with spring, she is married to Hades, God of the Underworld and periodically allowed to come to the surface of the earth, to be reunited with her mother Demeter, who is summer and brings forth fruit and grain for humanity to be nourished. (She goes into the underworld, i.e. sub-consciousness or sleep, or dream, and awakens in the morning with fresh ideas.)

Spring is power coming alive, is the greening power Hildegard of Bingen calls *Viriditas,* the germinating force. The energy of spring is intimately connected to creativity. If a person loses the ability to grow or to bring new concepts into their life, if a person does not allow himself to grow new roots or shoots, or in the extreme loses interest in life itself – has an imbalance in the Wood Element. Furthermore, if a person has symptoms that get periodically better or worse in the spring, they too have such imbalance; as does a person whose elasticity in muscle tone gives way to tension or stiffness. Dullness or rigidity of mind indicates the same, some people dry and shrivel up inside! They lose their sense of purpose, their spirit, 'the soul is the freshness of the flesh, for the body grows and thrives through it, just as the Earth becomes fruitful through moisture.' [107]

Spring as we know it, is abundance breaking out in the presence of moisture; the Chinese must have had this in mind too. However having lived in the tropics I am aware of the limitations of this metaphor and frequently use the term 'greening power,' which has a wider application.

The Directions associated with Wood are East and upwards. The sunrises in the East, the day begins from the East; dawn heralds a new beginning. All these relate to beginning and creation, to new growth. It is obvious how this relates to a person: if a person finds it difficult to tune into new phases in life, or to accept new ideas, their Wood Element is out of balance.

The second concept of moving upwards relates to the movement of sap. Here is a direct link to the five *pranas* of Yoga. *Udana–prana* carries energy upwards (more on this later). Imbalances in rising energy can be observed as flushes; such a person might also have raised shoulders and hold their neck and head stiff when imbalances are prolonged. A Wood person can be recognised either by a posture that is too 'upright' or because it lacks the energy to uphold the posture, and thus appears withered and sunk.

I feel there is another concept hiding behind the 'upwards' movement. People of the Wood Element forever seem to strive higher and higher - they need a challenge to do their best; they are always searching, always reaching out. Imbalances show when this ambition gets out of hand and the connection to the earth is lost by moving upwards to the stars, by reaching for the impossible or conversely have no ambition, no interest in reaching up.

Reaching upwards is also related to spiritual growth, it expresses itself in the interest in philosophy, the expansion of faith and the ever-present drive to explain the mysteries of life. This movement upwards denotes the longing of the soul to achieve the union with the divine consciousness and is part of what makes us human.

> The American Indians see in the East, the Door 'that leads to all other levels of awareness and understanding; one example is the artist's creativity... the second ... is healing and transmuting poison... The third is in knowing how to properly use and exchange energy...' [108]

The Climate associated with Wood is windy. In oriental medicine, wind is considered a powerful force, which can injure a person's energy. 'Wind is the cause of a hundred diseases.' [109] Wind of course is air, is *prana* - the vital breath, the life-current that flows through all.

A person suffering badly from the effects of external/internal winds has an imbalance in space energy. The East wind in particular, might make people with a strong Wood tendency very bad tempered or even ill.

The Tissues or parts of the body associated with this energy, are the tendons, ligaments and muscles, they make movement possible and hold us together, governing suppleness and flexibility; they remind us of a young tree bending with ease in the wind. It is understandable that rigidity, stiffness, tension, cramps, spasm and certain types of paralysis may all be caused by an imbalance in the Wood Element. There may be spinal problems, even over-flexibility, looseness of joints, in fact a kind of floppiness in the general body stance. The joints themselves deserve special mention, since it is ligaments and tendons, which hold them together and make 'them' work; their condition and consequently all mishaps with joints, including arthritis are governed by this energy. Wood people tend to have a lot of physical energy (like the tree) - or indeed a marked lack of it, thus physical exercise is especially beneficial for Wood people, it frees the energy trapped in joints, muscles etc.

The Sense Organ connected to Wood is the eye and **the Sense** is sight. The quality of vision, clarity of purpose, planning and decision making is connected to sight, literally and metaphysically. Blurred eyesight, short or long-sightedness, blindness, astigmatism, distorted vision, cataracts, eye strain and pain, how eyes adapt to light and any other eye symptoms relate to Wood Energy. The ability to see clearly through a problem, to gather and sift information with one glance, the ability to really see - grasping the essence of something, all this is connected. Obviously any blocks in such matters are due to Wood imbalances.

The Orifice associated with the Wood Energy is the eye. The eye is actually an interesting organ, the process of seeing is fascinating. We see only in the presence of light. Without light we do not see, yet whose light helps to 'see' dreams or visions? We can see clear pictures in our mind, yet without participation of the organ of seeing and with self-generated 'light.' R. Sheldrake suggests we share an electromagnetic field, inside and out. This would explain why for some people, when they close their eyes – there is darkness; for others there is light; different intensities of the electromagnetic field?

The interior of the eye is dark! However it reflects the light that hits the outside objects. The eye is thus more of a mirror, than an autonomous organ. All light comes from the sun, thus the sun is the one that actually 'sees everything.' This makes it quite clear that there are two aspects involved in seeing: the actual seeing and recognition of the seen. The seeing of the eye has been linked with the sun since time immemorial. In Malay the sun is called ' Mata Hari,' meaning the 'eye of the day.' Some traditions thus link the eyes to Fire/Light, rather than to the second aspect, the recognition of the seen, the clear perception, the clear understanding of the seen which is an integral part of making decisions. This second aspect is especially relevant to the Wood/Space energy. Having clear vision and foresight, as well as being able to interacting adequate and efficiently with the world, is a quality of Wood energy.

An imbalance in Wood is indicated when the eyes show tension which prevents them from taking information in; they might be experienced as vacantly staring, seeing without seeing; or the opposite, they might be too open and receptive, taking in without selection and being overwhelmed or over-stimulated.

The Fluid connected to the Wood Element is - tears. This does not mean that just because somebody cries they have an imbalance, although with excessive tears this may be so. Tears in this context refer to smarting or conversely unusually watering eyes. Crying is one way of cleansing stagnant energy or rather getting rid of excess energy. On the other hand, dryness of the eyes is often encountered when the person is very tired and stressed; 'the general' is overworked!

The External Physical Manifestations of the Wood Element are nails, hands and feet. Thus the condition of the finger and toe nails show when the Liver is in splendid condition. Cracking, discoloration, splitting, peeling or ridging of nails all is indicative of a Wood imbalance. The condition of the hands and feet of a person may give further clues: do they look thin and brittle, do they look overly swollen, fleshy, too wide, flat and as though there is too much weight on them? Do they look strong, adequate in size and well maintained?

We use the feet to step forward in life. So feet that are well equipped for their task, point to a person with a strong sense of purpose and determination, actively going where they want to go. On the other hand people with lifeless, weak feet may tend to lack a firm footing in life, they may even 'drag their feet.' Sometimes one sees feet that seem to have a lot of tension in them, in such a way that the toes seem to grasp the ground. This usually denotes an imbalance in Wood, since LV and GB run along the first and the fourth toe respectively, on top of the foot. The big toe is indispensable for balance. When the toes curl inward, then the owner might have a very rigid outlook of life and resists changes, or is desperately trying to maintain a link to the earth, its roots; it is something we find amongst people who have been uprooted.

How about the hands? Now here is another complex feature to observe. Although few people see each other's feet, we all see each other's hands.

From the hands as well as from the feet, one can gain an overview of the body. Why? Hands and feet are said to have nerve-reflex points and zones that are connected to the whole body. For example there is the fleshy part underneath where the fingers (or toes) root, which is, in part representative of the lungs and chest. There is the inside of the tip of the thumb (or big toe) which is representative of the pituitary or master gland of the body etc. Condition and sensitivity of such areas give clues to the state of wellbeing of the related organs.

The hands as such, have also strong connections to the heart and circulation because of the central position of HC that runs straight through the palm of the hand and to the top of the middle finger. And furthermore, HT and Si (the meridians of heart and small intestines) both run on the outside ridge of the hand along the little finger. This can be understood as a special connection between the supreme ruler (see Fire Element) and his general (Wood).

Most meridians have endpoints on the hand and feet thus they represent the whole body energy. Rough patches, gnarly joints, rough nail-beds, flexibility or stiffness of fingers, thick, worn skin; all are indications of the state of the Wood Element and the relevant areas of the body. For example: a thickened stiff joint on the index finger points to arthritis, but the arthritis manifested itself on the finger that is connected to the energy field of the large intestines. This asks for investigation of the large intestines, or the mental inability to let go! Hands and feet can not only reveal intrinsic imbalances in specific locations, but also the state of the Being as a whole. This 'reaching further' itself is characteristic of the Wood Element.

The Colour associated with the Wood Element is green. (In other cultures, especially when connected to Space, it might be white or very light blue). It is interesting to note that in some cultures this is the colour of the *heart chakra* (ruled by Air, the companion Element in Vata/Ayurveda). Both heart and liver are revered as the seat of the soul or spirit. The latter is ultimately life-giving energy, 'greening-power'!

As often the case, there is more meant by these associations than can be expressed in words. Energy that manifests as sap in the tree, providing lush vigorous growth, is green. This colour has been used in mythology and legends to depict the splendour and virility of heroes and gods; e.g. the Indian Goddess of abundance, Lakshmi, wears a green blouse, the colour of healthy vegetation, of chlorophyll. Green is also the colour the Indian bridegroom often wears, a sign of the abundance of seeds, of greening-power. The personification of male fertile energy in Celtic tradition is simply called the Green Man. A person who always wears or surrounds himself/herself with green may be feeding an imbalance in the Wood Element, or may be (consciously or not) trying to right it.

The colours of the other baser elements (blue, red, yellow) are primary colours; the fifth Element is represented in a colour combination: yellow (earth) and blue (sky) (mixed becomes green). White - the other complex colour - represents Air (Metal); the fourth and fifth elements are linked in

Vata; both are subtler energies, more about combined potential than differentiation. Subtler still, they are recognised as two primordial prerequisites of creation – Space and Motion.

The Smell associated with the Wood Element is a rancid and offensive, 'goatish' smell; the dictionary describes rancid as 'smelling like rank stale fat.' This points to the idea of food gone off. At the root might be a defect in the working of the liver to help digestion.

The Taste associated with Wood is sour. The origin here might be found in decomposing plant matter, which goes sour or even starts to ferment. Fresh fermented leaves or grass are strongly acid, thus wood soil is often acid and acid-loving plants such as rhododendrons, azaleas etc. thrive on it. Someone who either loves or detests sour, or vinegary foods, or conversely has great cravings for sour food may have an imbalance in the Wood Element. **The Grain** associated with Wood is wheat. Wheat allergies are increasing in the West; has our liver been effected by all the pollution of progress (pesticides, fertilisers and genetically modification)? Is our indulgent way of life poisoning us? A point worth investigating. **The Fruit** ... is the peach. The peach in Chinese culture is a symbol, for long-vitae. So if the gallbladder and liver are kept happy it bides well. **The Meat** ...is chicken. **The Vegetable**... is mallow (mallow is a plant of the Malvaceae family, like the hollyhock, which is not commonly associated with food in the West). As with the sour taste, these must be approached carefully. It may be appropriate to eat more or less depending on one's practice to reach a balanced intake.

What needs also to be carefully watched is the intake of stimulants and relaxants. Tea, coffee, sugar or alcohol in excess are not good for anyone, but the person with a strong Wood Element will feel its adverse effect sooner. Wood people tend to over-indulge especially in alcohol, which has a negative effect on the Liver and easily throws the Wood Energy off balance, resulting in nervous energy and uncoordinated movement, destroying the harmony of Life. We will now look at some correspondences with less tangible concepts.

The Expression associated with Wood is shouting. Shouting is a release mechanism for anger. People that shout a lot, (or conversely find it difficult to use their voice) might have an imbalance. Yet shouting relates not only to extreme expressions but also to a quality of the voice, a tone of voice that always sounds like 'a general' on the parade ground, no matter what they say, or how it is meant when they say it.

The Sound associated with Wood is that of crashing, which is self-explanatory. Just think of a falling tree! It also suggests the bursting force of spring, of plenty - or too much energy. People like that might walk into a room and it is almost audible. Sound is especially relevant to Space, as its only sensory attribute. We can neither see, taste, touch, or smell Space - but Sound, the original vibration of creation, is its permanent attribute (singing of the cosmic spheres, Ohm). Sound carries through Space, even gets amplified... echoes, thunders etc.

The Manner in times of excitement or change associated with Wood is that of control. The obvious connection is the function of GB and LV as the instigators of actions, through planning, judging and deciding, and their correspondence with muscle, tendons and ligaments that enable physical and mental control. Someone who shows rigid control in times of stress, or loses all control and physical co-ordination and panics, shows an imbalance in Wood. In a less extreme situation, such people might feel the need to take over, become bossy - or conversely feel insecure, bump into desks and tables, drop objects and find their vision becomes poor – they have no control.

To exert control can become manipulation. This can be observed in children - if they feel powerless, they resort to manipulation of emotions, events and people.

Control is a well-known aspect of any Yoga; Yoga is controlling the mind via the practice of concentration and meditation. Control here does not simply mean dominance, but the mind should be trained, guided like horses in front of a chariot. Such one-pointed concentration is seen as the gateway to the Self - its focus realises the enormous potential humans have (once they let go of their ego)!

'In the Bhagavad Gita, Arjuna says to the Lord:
"Impetuous, stubborn, violent and fickle is the human mind,
I believe that to restrain it is as hard as to confine the wind."

The Lord answered: "It is true the mind is fickle and hardly anyway controlled yet by untiring exercise and practice it is yet controlled." ' [110]

The Attitude associated with the Wood Element is Irresolution; one simply doesn't know which way to go - this way or that? **The Movement** of *Ki* is Vacillation. Both have a parallel in nature - the tree bends tree this way and that! Destiny deals us blows that make us swing in different directions, opportunities present themselves for this path and that. Planning and decision-making incorporate the act of choosing a path or a direction in which to proceed. An unbalanced Wood person cannot decide which way to go; she/he constantly changes his mind; furthermore he might blunder ahead in one direction without considering the options – then change. This is a person who cannot decide what food to order in a restaurant, what job to take, what cause to support etc.

In a positive state, such a person might explore many directions in Life in all sorts of ways, like having many professions, travelling many countries, getting involved in many causes etc.

On the other hand, somebody who walks rigidly in a straight line, follows one interest all his life, sticks to one holiday resort all his life and lives in one place, eating the same food etc., lacks in the energy necessary to explore Space. To achieve balance in this state, the joy of self-control has to be discovered.

The Quality associated with the fifth Element, the world over, is 'Spiritual.' As we have seen, the Chinese did not see the body and the soul as separate entities, but rather as two equal sides of the human being. The tree is abridge between earth and sky, man and God. Hun, the soul housed in the liver, gives direction to our lives by striving for a greater sense of purpose beyond the everyday material existence. It urges to find sense and meaning in this existence.

In a negative state, lack of this energy shows itself in the complete absence, and loss of interest in such matters.

The Faculty associated with Wood is active awareness. This not only relates to the ability to look in all directions, but also the ability to have an overview, to see what is needed and to keep in mind a vision: all these need active self-awareness. One needs to be aware of what is going on in life outside and inside oneself, be it physical, emotional or spiritual. When we cultivate detachment, a witness emerges in us who can observe with suspended judgement. Meditation cultivates this higher faculty.

People who display either no awareness, or awareness to the point of hypersensitivity, then show an imbalance in Wood energy.

The Activity following awareness is - implementing. It is linked to GB and LV, providing energy for action. Implementing goes beyond making plans – it carries them out! A person that cannot carry out their plans, or on the other hand, has too many plans, or implements inappropriate actions without planning, expresses a Wood imbalance.

The Condition associated with Wood is one of 'arousal.' Arousal, just as the ability to express anger, relates to rising energy and its opposite - withdrawing. In a balanced state, Wood is able to handle both arousal and withdrawal appropriately, one in spring, the other in winter. Just the same, a Wood person can deal with highly charged situations; potent, intense times occur at certain intervals for a purpose – and are followed by periods of rest. However, a person with dominant Wood energy, should be aware of his/her susceptibility to addiction, be it to highly charged situations or stimulants in general e.g. a business tycoon who lives off constant excitement, exhausting his energy, keeping abreast of fatigue by using 'pep-pills,' coffee or even cocaine. Conversely the very quiet, withdrawn person whose enthusiasm cannot be aroused by anything, is just as much out of balance.

Let's consider what **brain activities** are involved. The above might be due to imbalances in the reward system of the dopamine trail (so that the rush of pleasure is reduced). Dopamine excess causes hallucinations, uncontrolled speech, euphoria etc. and too little causes lethargy, meaninglessness, cravings and addiction etc. Dopamine releasing cells are distributed throughout the brain in well-defined pathways.

These, the dopamine trails are especially well defined in the frontal and mid-brain.

Furthermore Space energy, i.e. spatial awareness, is especially influenced by activities in the Temporal and Parietal Lobes and comprehension of speech (frontal cortex) – rather than speech itself. Meaning is important here more than the word.

There is also poignant activity in the area of sound; people tend to be active listeners (be it to music or word); they comprehend - through intense active listening – or they might deny their 'inner tune.' Such people tend to be introvert because they listen to the meaning behind things; they might be scientists, meditators, mystics or great visionaries, idealists and humanitarians.

Can there be aggression in such people?

Aggression and Space on one level are almost contradictory to another, as Space is generative potential per se. There comes a point of a 'big bang,' potential destroying one galaxy – yet simultaneously creating a new one.

If we have 'too much space' (time or place) - we start doing things, we fill it with something 'new;' it might be just 'for the sake of doing something,' it might be frenzied, senseless activity without purpose. The traditional Chinese symbol Wood shows how growth can produce wild shoots, cancerous growth (such as briars on a rose!) These sap the plant, destroying what was there before. Aggression within Space expresses as chaotic growth, as breaking cosmic law, as dehumanising activity. In its most extreme form we might say that Hitler's 'politics and his final solution' are the result of such intense, frustrated creative energy, (denied Artist) which resulted in the most de-humanising, destructive activities. Space swallows itself - the black hole appears, sucking life into itself.

Less extreme, a person with the characteristics of Space/Wood might store their emotions until they explode into a burst of activity; acting - for the mere relief that 'doing something' provides - regardless of sense or purpose.

The Relationship of Wood to the other Elements has been mentioned throughout the text where appropriate, but let us summarise. In the **Chinese Chen-Ko Cycle** Water gives birth to Wood; like a mother, it provides nourishment and fulfils the intrinsic needs of all. It seems an obvious sister to the all creative, life-sustaining space, as it spreads into any available Space on earth!

When we look at the **Vedic Creation Wheel** – the obvious limitations of this become clear. Water and Space are far apart. Water is not subtle enough to rise to the heights of Space, much less even be its 'mother.' Look to the horizon - where ocean and space melt into each other - what an illusion it is! Water 'thinks' it is a close ally to Space and it seems real, like a mirage! To ascend to such subtle heights, water, like all other elements, has to go through profound transformation; it has to give up its identity!

How about **Earth and the fifth Element**? As the root of a tree, Wood certainly controls earth in its vicinity; in the manifest body, the function of the liver bears witness. If the liver does not detoxify the body, the body will perish. On the larger scale, farming techniques today constantly exhaust the earth. It can only flourish if enough Wood energy is there to clean our environment of all the pollutants.

On an even bigger scale Space holds Earth, controls its orbit, and with it all that happens with Earth. However subtle space is, it holds the most dense element and looks after it; it controls its destiny!

Metal/Air has, as we seen, the closest link to Wood/Space. In the Chinese Cycle it seems to be a 'negative' relationship - a metal chainsaw cuts a tree! Yet the cut wood becomes building material for something new! The cycle of creation within Space never ends. We know that Air, (storms) kills trees but also is vital to its growth. Air and Wood co-operate in the oxygen cycle when it concerns the livelihood of others.

In Ayurvedic medicine, as Vata, Space and Air have similar effects; so they can reinforce each other's benefits or lacks; in the latter, they might even destroy each other 'by overheating, causing dryness (as in deserts) and aggravate... the nervous system.' [116]

Fire is acknowledged as the child of Wood or Space. Both contain the potential fire; Wood in the Chen Ko cycle is mother of Fire – and in many creation myths Fire energy is there as the first-born of Space.

8.2: b) Associations with Personality and Relationships.

What might a person look like who is characterised by these attributes? As previously, these characteristic descriptions are gross simplifications – their purpose is only to help us understand tendencies – not tools for 'boxing people.'

According to classical descriptions, people especially influenced by Space/Wood-energics are often tall with a light physique; but even when short, they appear tall because of a very upright posture. Their musculature might be poorly developed; their hair thin and at times curly. True to the all-pervasive nature of Space, there is much variety here and thus this is a most difficult 'portrait to paint'!

One thing is sure, these people are very creative. We have seen that the fifth element holds past, present and future potential and constantly creates new forms out of itself. Just the same, a person blessed with this energy has many abilities and consequently often many different careers! He doesn't just have infinite potential for new ideas and things but also is able to execute them, making him a confident person, bold, committed and powerful. Under the positive influence of this energy, a person might less prone to limiting habits and blocks than others; he might be wise, even enlightened.

Conversely, a person of such unlimited potential could also suffer under the freedom, drifting through life without boundaries, without discipline, respecting no laws, having no commitment and as a result end up hurting her/himself. It could be somebody who can't make any decisions, because there are too many choices and the energies pull this way and that; how does one choose if all options are equal? To such a person this road is just as attractive as that; there is no preference to render this direction 'better' than the next. Without limits, boundaries and preferences, choice becomes a nightmare, causing total confusion – rendering him not only ambivalent but ineffectual.

Furthermore, in this state a person might be sticking to an unfulfilling job, deciding to 'grin and bear' the old routine, withdrawing into a state of 'I can't do it anyway! There is no point, I am too small, too stupid, too fickle to ever achieve anything.' In such cases the potential lies wasted, the person becomes torn and depressed. For her what the neighbours say, what her parents/friends do is dominating and paralysing her own life.

On the other hand, in a positive state this energy might open a person to go beyond the ordinary animalistic life and become immensely spiritual. Of course a lack in this sense of the sacred could trigger the opposite, i.e. having no respect for higher aspirations, seeing nature as pure matter, there for the taking; a materialist and nihilist. For example, a ruthless company manager, who cares only for profit, who walks 'over dead bodies' and knows no scruples could be said to be lacking in Space characteristics.

Leaving the baser energies behind, Space challenges one to lead a noble life, through honesty and discipline, as for example by control over our mind and body. Such person aspires to the highest human goals and could become a great humanitarian, a Saint.

But even here lie dangers; if appropriate discipline gives way to the rigid discipline of a control freak, the person becomes hard, dogmatic and cold, living by dominating his own heart and feelings as well as other peoples' minds. A person driven to such tyrannical and reckless use of manipulation, might show a character less like a chivalrous knight, and more like a dark, demonic and evil warlord.

Space, we said, has vision – has a wider perspective which generates ideas but also leads to planning and implementing dreams. People characterised by this aspect of Space, often are Visionaries/Pioneers. They are people who are drawn to the unknown, either to explore or to fill it with their own ideas, concepts and castles. They are highly imaginative and have a quick mind that is not bothered about details, daily routines and accounting, but they are free, at least in spirit. They can 'fly.' They look at the general, the overall usefulness of a plan; they sum up a whole theory in a few words at a board meeting! They might 'direct armies,' or use their ability to influence the course of humanity. Their life is not to be limited by pettiness, by withdrawal into safe niches, or cosy family or individual concerns - they live for the betterment of humanity. Such people have foresight, they see the consequences of actions before they happen; they learn lessons from past failures; they see the wisdom of the ancestors and respond.

They can see for example what calamities the long-term use of chemicals causes; they can see how misuse of Earth's resources will affect the future generations, their view is not bound by time and space! Their task is to protect the children and the future children! The American Indians say you shall not do anything that affects the children of the seventh generation! That is thinking from the point of Space.

Such people have the ability to foresee present and future needs and trends and thus the survival of a company, the wellbeing of a nation, even the survival of the human race is in safe hands with them. Such an extraordinary person has not only the ability 'to fly him/herself' but to do so for the good of all.

A vital point needs to be made here! The extraordinary Space person can 'fly high' because he/she has made the 'ultimate sacrifice' - given up self-

interest! Space just is, it contains all other elements having no more
'individual little niches' for himself. A person of such calibre, having given up
the ego, acts from a total different level than the other elements. Space can
'fly high' precisely because of having given up 'being manifest earth;
nurturing water; transforming fire and life-providing air.' Such a person is
the rarest indeed, the most highly evolved amongst human beings!

Returning to a more usual level of people, let us look at the domineering
emotion that would characterise an ordinary person influenced by the fifth
Element.

The Emotion related to Wood/Space is anger. As with the quality of
'arousal,' these refer both to the powerful rising sap, shooting up 'to reach
the branches.' What if this flow is barred? The rising energy hits a wall, gets
frustrated. Anger is one such frustration. It comes from spoiled plans, from
obstruction to the blue print. The Being cries for help, indicating that the
Movement-of-Life is frustrated, needs to be freed, so that energy can flow;
the accumulated blocked excess energy needs to go somewhere. If it can't, it
'explodes.' Anger thus is a natural valve, a positive sign of abundance in
'rising sap.' Channelled into growth, it provides the courage to act;
frustrated, it isn't allowed to reach it's goal! An angry person will benefit
from physical exercise to prevent the penned up energy from harming the
Organ-Networks. If a person has difficulty expressing themselves, the rising
energy will be stored in muscles and tissues. Such holding patterns show
particularly in people's jaws, pelvis and hips.

Let's imagine a journalist who is under the strong influence of Space
energy; she works for the travel section of a big Magazine. She is a tall lady
with good muscle tone. She has a square face and a sallow complexion; thin
lips are set in a strong jaw, she wears glasses. Her shoulders are often stiff
with tension and drawn together; she walks with long firm strides and
appears to move with elegance. Her voice is firm, her mannerism is decisive,
she knows what she wants in life - be it in general, from the person she
interviews or even from her superiors.

She is highly motivated in her job, driving herself hard to fulfil her
commitments and meet deadlines. She constantly reaches out for more
assignments; she is happy with much less comfort than most people and if
necessary will climb a mountain-ridge, live with tribal people, or chase after
an astronaut! She does not think of making things easier for herself, but is
willing to 'drive all the way' just to get *that* story, to make *that* idea work!
Once she has achieved her aim, something else will have to enthuse her.
There seems no end to her ideas, no limits to her energy.

She is highly individual and thus easily breaks traditions, family ties and
conventions - she needs to be free. She inspires others with her confidence,
ambitions and dreams; she knows she can overcome all obstacles. However
knock-backs do happen, especially when she outdistances people. They
cannot follow her many flights and high standards.

At times she gets fatigued; when exhausted she becomes nervous,
irritable and uptight. Occasionally there comes a point where she feels she
can not cope with one more single thing! If this happens in a relationship,

she ups and goes; if it is in a job - she cuts it off! She knows she has reached her limit!

To re-gather her strength and balance she has learned to meditate. As she sees it, she does some exercise for her physical body and meditates to give her mind a rest. This 'coping mechanism' has worked well, it has softened her harsh exterior, and helped to find a balance within herself from where to draws new inspirations for life and work.

How does she relate to the other elements? How does **Space relate to Earth?**

Earth exists in space, like a fish in water. Space is above, around and in it; there is an intimate connection. Space has definitely the 'upper hand,' yet it does not hold Earth tight; it allows earth to float unencumbered within the limits of its orbit. Space does not force Earth to do anything; it allows Earth to do its own thing.

Space is limitless - Earth is bound by its own gravity, solid and staid. These two seem light-years apart from each other, making it difficult for Space to understand Earth, yet aware of their difference, Space knows that Earth is OK in its own, particular way. This detached relationship benefits when both explore their inner nature; Space respects Earth for being one of its finest creations; Earth gains inspiration, realising that space is part of each of its particles. With this new awareness they meet in 'sacred, Space.'

How would a relationship between two such different people be?

On the earthly plane, they could benefit from each other: one from the grounding effect of the other; one from the freeing and expanding way of the former. Space in its abstract and limitless nature, needs the confines and solidity of Earth to make its ideas manifest, just as much as Earth needs the door to more freedom.

The 'Space-journalist' has a daughter, who has dominant tendencies of the Earth-element. The mother needs constantly new activities, new people; there are always new horizons to explore. The daughter likes her own company, she likes to stay home, rest and read; her social activities are limited to occasions when she can help others.

At the time of our sketches, the mother is in her early fortieth and single and the daughter is in her late teens. During much of the last years the daughter has managed the home by herself, which she enjoyed, while mother was off on various assignments all over the world. Recently the mother showed signs of strain and over-work, she decided to take time off. For mother and daughter, sharing the home is not easy, their expectations and daily routines seem miles apart.

Despite being 'home' mother was still constantly meeting people, telephoning; going to the gym etc. When she came home and saw her daughter curled up on the couch in the same spot as a few hours ago, she despaired about this Youngster – who 'should be out partying!' Over a lengthy breakfast they found time to talk. The mother, desperate to do something 'together,' suggests they share the time of exercising and meditation. The daughter agrees;

after one such session the daughter tells her mother, that she would like to become a Buddhist nun! The mother is horrified, her only child 'shutting herself away and contemplating her navel!' How do Space and Earth **solve the conflict?**

After the initial burst of anger our Space-mother has time to think. She loves her daughter dearly, always let her do her own thing, what right has she to interfere now? She has brought her daughter up to the highest moral standards, what is there to feel sad about if her daughter strives for the highest human goals? She reasons: her daughter will have the security and sense of community, which she will enjoy and Space-mother can not give. But Space-mother is also terrified by the thought of the single-minded focus that will be required; for her there is so much to do, invent, create, taste and enjoy?

Earth-daughter points out that for her, it seems there is plenty to do in monastic live. It is not all study and prayer but a lot of work to do for the good of people. In true Earth-fashion the daughter points out, that one has to find peace in one's centre first, before there can be peace in the world.

But mother is unwilling to give up - she suggests that before the daughter makes the decision, they should see some other countries and aspects of life. The daughter agrees to the idea, but only for a limited time - and if the travels include some sacred sights! Once the idea is born - Space-mother is off; she calls her magazine and puts forward the idea of running a series of articles about the holy places of the world. Within minutes her mind brings forth pictures of how and where they can travel. She will show her daughter the world, and - if after that she still wants to join the nuns, well so be it!

You can easily see that Space's unlimited capacity creates concepts which are limited by Earth's will to manifest; Space's acceptance allows Earth to fulfil her own destiny. Space cannot say, 'NO,' however absurd it might find the potential idea. Conflicts are solved by Space providing possibilities; then standing back, it lets Earth be.

Normally the Journalist travels with a photographer dominated by the element of water. How does **Space relate to Water?**

Space allows Water, with its fluid nature to follow it; where they meet, they have a very close relationship, operating in the same dimension and time. They fit hand in glove; Space leads and Water follows like a pair of classic Ballroom dancers. As soon as Space has a new idea, a new concept, Water follows suit, taking on the idea and feeding it and making it bloom. As long as Water can keep following, there is no discord - but... there is no water in 'outer space!'

Looking to the Wood image, the story is similar. Acorn, seedling and tree, all stages of wood rely on water to nourish it; without water, they wither, dry and die. A powerful union! The Wood/ Space character might behave with arrogance to all others, yet is pliant and soft in the presence of water.

For such a relationship to flourish, the honours lie with Water - if it can follow the dance of Space - all is well; if water dries up, gets exhausted, it is either its own or Wood's end. In any relationship between these two, it is clear that the people will share many things, interests and often beliefs; they even display the same characteristics. Due to Water's adaptability, they might seem like 'two peas in a pod.' Water might even make the Space person be less aloof, more lenient and understanding of others; just as the watery sap of the tree allows the tree to bend in the wind (dry wood breaks!).

Conflict arises when the Space person is tempted to loftier heights where 'nobody' can follow not even water!

Let's get back to our journalist and her photographer. Wherever she travels, the photographer goes; she digs out the story, chooses the sights to explore and the countries to go to. She tries out the beaches, the food, and the excursions for her magazine. The photographer follows in her footsteps, yet he does not just follow. He is very adamant about what he photographs. His choice can make a report interesting and successful or boring. Without the photos, nobody would read about the countries about which she reports. They work together, as a team they are successful.

But there are times, when the Space person's imagination runs away with her. When the photographer heard about the recent project, he was not interested; it does not happen often but this time they argued: should the report be on the main religions, or on the culture? Should they try to assess what the various sights have in common?

The Journalist, influenced by her daughter, tends to want a general spiritual angle, the photographer a more cultural angle. How do they solve the conflict?

Space feels tempted to let the photographer do 'his thing'- either that, or she could even sack the photographer and push ahead with her own plans. On the other hand, she wants to do a good series, not least for her daughter's sake, and she knows the photographer's tendency to take over. If his photos become more important than her story, the magazine might reject her story and just settle for a photo reportage. First she tells the photographer that she respects his interests, and that his photos are excellent, then she tells him about her true motivation for the trip and appeals to his understanding. She succeeds in painting such an interesting picture of a spiritual quest, linking it to ancient stories such as the search for the Holy Grail, that she inspires him. Eventually he finds a challenging angle: the *simplicity and beauty* of sacred spaces. (Water reflects, mirrors space, just as the sea mirrors the sky.) Space solved the conflict by resisting the temptation to withdraw into the angry solitude (I will do it on my own), and instead pulled the Water person up to her own heights.

And so we move on to Fire. How does **Space relate with Fire**? There is much to contemplate; here are only a few pointers: 'Fire' as in the suns, moons, stars and planets, are strewn throughout space; they follow much of their own path in cosmic space. In our world, space contains equally the three forms of fire, and there is no difference to Space whether the sun shines, flames hungrily devour and transform much of space's creation, or the warmth of a hearth fire is attended, stoked or left to die!

Again, Space is characterised by two aspects; all activity happens within it/through it yet it is not involved. The two come together when Krishna talks to Arjuna in the Bhagavad Gita about detachment; it does not mean not acting - but being detached from the fruit resulting from the action.

This also comes together when the fifth Element is seen as 'Wood,' because Wood actually holds the action of Fire in its 'belly;' it makes fire and yet it gets transformed in the process. It is as impossible to envisage Wood being uninvolved in Fire, as it is to have Space without creation - and yet Space stands apart, aloof with dispassion, just as tree aloof on a mountain top. Action and Non-action are contained in Space.

A thirteenth poet Saint of India called Jnaneshwar, talks about these two aspects in his 'Nectar of Self-Awareness,' as the play in a marriage between Shiva (the motionless) and Shakti (the active).

'These two are the only ones, who dwell in this home, called the universe.
When the master of the house sleeps, the mistress stays awake,
And performs the function of both.
When he awakes, the whole house disappears, and nothing is left...
While he sleeps, she gives birth, to the animate and inanimate worlds.
When she rests, her husband disappears....
Two lutes - one note; two flowers one fragrance;
Two lamps - one light; two lips - one word,
Two eyes - one sight; these two - one universe...
They are as mirrors to each other.' [111]

Space Absolute and its creative energy, the fire of transformation, belong together.

In a relationship between a person characterised by the element of Space and a partner characterised by Fire, there is lively and passionate interaction. It can be like the above relationship between Shiva and Shakti, with much love and closeness. As long as Space stays calm in the background, uninvolved, letting the Fire person take the centre of the stage, the Fire person can create a universe; she can live a flamboyant, active life.

Trouble starts when the Space person does not remain in the back ground, but wakes up, is in his active creative, driving role. Then the two will have much conflict; they will be like warriors invading each other's territory, and eventually destroying each other with their inherent fire, passion and anger.

A relationship between these depends on the intensity of their tendencies and the ability of Space (Wood) to be detached!

Our Journalist has a boss, who is dominated by the characteristics of **Fire.** He is a vibrant person, with many ideas, great influences and power. He likes to mingle, making contacts in the right social circles in the arts and marketing world. He is an eccentric with choleric outbursts and needs to have everything done to his command, pushing and manipulating others *to serve just that 'all-important' idea he has in mind now!* And has forgotten in a few hours! His sparks do catch other people's enthusiasm though and once left. they carry out his ideas well. Due to his contacts and other people's diligence, the magazine is a success. Yet when he heard about our journalist's announcement that she would write a series on 'Holy Sights;' of course he blew his top: It doesn't fit into the magazine! No-way would he run that!

How can the conflict be solved from the perspective of the Space person?

The Space person in her wisdom knows that if she gets involved in an argument about it, they will just have a shouting match which will end in both feeling drained, getting nowhere. So the Space person decides to let her boss be cross and steaming by himself. She hopes that given time, he will cool off.

Meanwhile she prepares a synopsis and a layout for the first part of the journey. She focuses on a holy sight that might interest the majority of the readers. They probably are Christians at least by birth and holiday in southern Europe. She sketches a visit to Assisi in the province of Perugia, Italy, including a visit to Gubbio, home of St. Francis of Assisi, who was in 1979 proclaimed by John Paul II as the patron Saint of the ecologist movement. This contemporary connection, the peace walks and international inter-religious conferences they host, makes this a place of interest.

A week later she presents her synopsis to her boss. He catches fire and joins in, looking up people she could interview there especially on the inter-religious aspect.

Space can not solve the conflict with Fire by entering into battle, but by being creative and with that, giving Fire fuel to unfold.

We move on to the last element with which **Space interacts, that of Air.**

From the vantage-point of Space, space and air are almost too close. On our planet one could be tempted to think, that where there is space, there is air. In fact air dissolves into space in the higher spheres. As far as we know, life-sustaining air though is only wrapped around earth and not other planets. For space in its cosmic regions, air is merely one of many substances it holds and thus space by and large, is not too bothered about this rival. Only once we look closer to the ground, does the rivalry seem to matter.

As you might recall, in the Chinese system this element is named Metal and the rivalry between wood and metal is symbolised in the axe that cuts the tree. The cut wood however is not the end, (as it is with fire; total annihilation); wood often survives such cutting and sprouts anew; even dry wood continues as furniture or building material for possibly hundreds or even thousand of years. Although Metal is a threat to Wood in this 'down to earth level,' it does not mean the end of its existence.

Returning to the original metaphor, the relationship between Space - and Air seems to have two aspects; they are almost identical yet with this very fact they are prone to injure each other. How? By reinforcing the same tendencies. Both Air and Space can escape; becoming aloof and uninvolved – they dry up, retreat into isolation. It's a fine line- where such detached focus becomes saintly – or mad.

However in every-day life we could find just as well that the opposite is true; for example: that Space unaware of its grand purpose, gets glued and lives in symbiosis with earth, water, fire, and air. Due to this close symbiosis, Space-people are in danger at times, to forget that they are the space *behind* and he/she might imagine to be fire-/water-/air- persons themselves. The intensity of such life- could lead to a 'burn out'- space collapsing on itself! Space person does well to remember it is the stage on which the others play! She holds the potential for all plays!

It is interesting for a Space person to explore: being true to her dharma in both, its grounded-ness (in the manifest earth) and its limitlessness (that it can fly). It is responsible for exploring the vision but it needs to bring it back to serve other elements: - such is the nature of a Boddhisattva; a Buddha that after enlightenment decides to 'go back to the market place' and help others in this world to find their way. To fulfil its potential to learn, to aspire to greater heights is the Space person's birthright.

But let's return to the relationship between two partners, exemplifying the element **Space and Air.** A Space person in <u>its ideal state</u> with an unlimited ability to gather knowledge and wisdom; with unlimited potential, creative and tolerant is on a similar wavelength to Air, but 'one step up,' one spiral higher in the evolution of mankind. This is what brings these two Elements in Yoga and Ayurveda together, into one humour (type, Vata).

A couple in marriage or partnership characterised by these two elements might have great understanding for each other. But, as easily happens in such closeness, there might be rivalry and envy on the part of Air and disappointment, frustration, even anger for Space if it can't reach its own potential; then Space might retreat too far for Air to share. On the hand Air might prevent Space from going beyond all concepts – even the intellect, so cherished by Air. Space then might just step out and do his/her own thing, knowing full well that in the final analysis, nothing can come between them.

The journalist has a brother dominated by the characteristics of the element Air. All their lives, they have been close. Unlike other families, they experienced little sibling rivalry; instead the various shocks and traumas that accompany any life have moulded them closer together. They each pursued their own life and career, yet always have a heartfelt and close interest in each other; even though they might live half way across the world from each other. Time has passed.

The journalist, together with her daughter has visited several sacred sights. Through the contacts they made and the places they visited, the journalist did not remain unaffected. She deepened her meditation practice and began to explore her own spirituality. She meets her brother on a stopover to yet another destination. As they talk on the first night, she tells him about some of the revelations and experiences that she had in these places. Her brother is horrified, what nonsense, what totally dreamy nonsense is his sister talking about! 'It is just so unreal': visions of golden inner light and seeing light rising out of shrines and elephant statues drinking milk; this just does not happen!

It does not make sense, it cannot be explained, his intellect refuses such scientifically impossible 'stuff.' He used to think his sister was clever, but this nonsense? He works himself up into a state of disbelief, maybe hidden envy (could it really be that she sees these things and I don't). He whirls around like strong winds rising to a storm but the Space person just listens, uninvolved and unperturbed by so much wind. From the brother's point of view she is frustratingly quiet - this makes him even more upset. In the eye of the storm, the sister retreats to go to bed. Disharmony and conflict remain!

How can they solve the conflict from the Space person's perspective?

Air and Space share the domain of the mind, intellect and knowledge play a great part in their closeness (and occasionally create conflict). Space can use this shared ability or retreat into non-involvement; she is leaving again soon, it does not really matter to her. She knows in her very heart, this conflict will make no difference to their fundamental closeness.

The next day, the sister goes into town and visits a bookshop; she finds two biographies of spiritual masters that seem to have witnessed similar phenomena to herself; she buys the books and gives her brother a 'leaving present.'

Much later, when the row is long forgotten, it surfaces in a conversation that the brother has really enjoyed the books and looks forward to the next visit and talk with the sister.

Let us recap: how would this conflict have ended if the brother had been an **Earth person**. He could have dug his heels in and told his sister stubbornly, that he did not like such airy-fairy stories, they are not solid truth, and it makes no difference whether other people write books about it or not.

A **Water person's** reaction might have been: oh what a brilliant idea! Maybe there is something in this, if other people empathise with it? Maybe I should try to follow your idea and read up some more about these phenomena.

A **Fire person** might have been less than pleased about being pointed towards her/his own ignorance! The books only serve to support the sister's experience, not helped his understanding - thus he would have indeed become very angry and continued the fight of the previous night, bringing up several other circumstances in their lives where the sister 'pretended to know more.' Hurt pride, jealousy of the sister job/education/ parental favouritism etc. all sorts of buried resentment might have fuelled the fire .

Let's leave Space.

Potentially each **Element also relates to people, that are like him/herself** dominated in character by the same element. These meetings will be either like looking in a mirror, or showing a different facet of the same element. There are countless variations of the theme. But let's just have the briefest, simplistic preview.

Assuming that an **Earth person meets another Earth person,** both are reliable, hold and support others. They would feel like sisters. However, if one of them is characterised by a negative Earth state, being egocentric, unreliable and totally absorbed into their own health, possessions, body, interests, etc., rock hard and with total lack of compassion, sympathy or interest in others, such an Earth person might feel less than a sister, and more like an alien.

A Water person in relationship with a Water person, might be mutually supportive, nourishing, and be great companions. If you add water to water, it mixes well. Due to its ability to feel into others, a Water person might even be safe enough to be able to feel into the dark sides of their own character. In this way, even a companion that shows a totally different aspect e.g. ice or vapour, would still find empathy and understanding; because of water's adaptability and flexibility, there could always be shared interest.

As for **Fire meeting another Fire person**, who knows? They could increase each other's flame and enthusiastically share their ideas and spur each other on, albeit if the fires get too big, they would starve each other of the much needed oxygen and destroy each other. Two closely involved Fire people are unlikely to last long.

As for **two Air people relating** with each other? Can you add air to air? If you do, they share existence with little change; neither enriching - nor taking from each other. Air and air just lose themselves into each other. This might be a relationship without challenge, stimulus - and without tension, simply two people beating with one heart.

Two Space people? Well you can not add space to space. A relationship between two Space people is a relationship with unlimited creativity and noble aspirations, they would work together onto some greater cause to serve the world. The idea of spiritual communities where people help each other to strive for the highest, has meaning here, as has the relationship between Guru and disciple, between teacher and student. Young trees flourish in mutual support and protection - each one to their own karma. Thus dharma will grow; some will grow taller than others, yet all will evolve.

Leap clear of all that is corporeal,
And make yourself grow to a like expanse
With that greatness which is beyond all measure;
Rise above all time and become eternal;
Then you will apprehend God.
Think for you too, nothing is impossible;
Dream that you are immortal...
Find your home, in the haunts of every living creature;
Make yourself higher than all heights,
 And lower than all depths...
Think that you are everywhere at once...
That you are in the womb, that you are young,
That you are old, that you have died,
That you are in the world beyond the grave;
Grasp in your thoughts all this at once, all times and places,

All substances and qualities and magnitude together;
Then you can apprehend God. [112] (Hermes Trismegistus)

8.2: c) Associations for Spiritual Evolution (Yoga)

Qualities/steps in Sadhana here directly to the sanatana dharma, the eternal law. This law is a law of evolution, where consciousness unfolds from matter which inherently carries its seed. The various states of knowledge and awareness on the path of evolution shape creation. The simplest level is determined by the need for food and reproduction followed by the need for shelter and protection; leaving these gross concerns behind, we evolve towards self-awareness and God-realisation (when matter realises its divinity and merges back into it, the perception of the world changes).

The power that drives this change is linked to one of the *pranic* powers, *Udana-prana*. It is the friend to be cultivated by all *sadhakas*, (students of Yoga). As the perception of man and his world changes, awareness of a common origin grows. It is like a wave becoming conscious of being part of the ocean. Yet evolution is still ahead, namely to see that all is 'Water,' that all forms are manifestations of one energy. From this higher vision, all phenomena lose their individual attraction; the viewer develops equal vision. Like Space who contains all of existence in itself with dispassion, so does the highly evolved Space person see all phenomena as nothing but divine consciousness.

With this, all poles of opposites disappear; there is neither fear nor joy, neither black nor white, neither male nor female, neither old nor young, neither past, present or future. These categories simply are not 'seen,' the physical manifestations have become irrelevant and with it the ordinary process of life - the world as others see it - holds little meaning. The ever-creative nature of Space or the 'upward' nature of Wood energy is still there, but the only interest is to push ever deeper into the frontiers of spiritual awareness through spiritual practices, meditation and contemplation. In time, even these become futile, only surrender remains. 'Thy will be done'! Being has surpassed Doing.

Grace is shared through mere existence; self-effort has lost its power.

For a while the tree accepts its role of just being, even sharing its insights with others, for the benefit of all; ultimately burning alone will free the embodied pure energy.

As for the **level of consciousness** of this energy: it is unlimited; in its purest form, in its highest attainment it can only be t*uryia*, the fourth state of consciousness, beyond normal planes. As the contours that divide are wiped away, the universal alone is. There is no discriminating awareness of the physical, there are no more ideas, dreams or emotions. Awareness is from within the unified whole; 'I am the Universe;' *Aham brahmasi*; mere existence.

This is the goal of our spiritual journey; we start with self-discipline, but will be taken there by the grace of the Divine. The end state is the Union called 'Yoga,' or *Kaivalya*, a state free from all fetters. During this journey, Kundalini, the evolutionary force hidden within us, unfolds our spiritual potential. When it comes closer to its goal, it works on our 5th energetic body – the **Anandamaya kosha,** which signals the home of 'the Self,' that which is undaunted by pleasure and pain, is non-dual cosmic consciousness – is everywhere. It sort of hides in this last sheath behind the other surrounding sheaths. Mind you, even *prana* cannot reach its core, only *chitti* - pure consciousness - is able to experience this eternal bliss.

Gradually we work towards this energy through the unfoldment of the upper three *chakras*. It starts with the expansion of awareness from 'I' to 'We' in the **Throat Chakra**; 'I-awareness' gradually loses the bond to the individual 'I,' becoming inclusive; 'I am part of one humanity, part of one existence,' 'I share divinity with you.' This is liberation of the 'Ego-bound I.' This is freedom. Once our whole being has understood that 'I am not the body, not the emotions, not the intellect – but pure consciousness' then one starts living in harmony with all others. Not anymore bound by individual perception, we are no more 'different.' A wiser level of existence evolves. As we get established in the Throat Chakra, it is said we make our home in the *atma bhoda* (the house of *Atman*). But to be truly home, grace has to lift us to the **Ajna Chakra;** only here we are established totally in this shared reality, we live immersed in the knowledge of the divinity of all.

Only few people ever go beyond this point. Once spiritual energy, *Kundalini Shakti* reaches the **Sahasrara**... nobody knows what that is like. We can not comprehend it, we cannot share it, and the people who live in it can not communicate it. How can a 'body' know... how it is to be pure Spirit?

Let us look at a summary of these chakras: The Throat Chakra, **Vishuddha**, is obviously attributed to Space, meaning it holds in itself, the other four Elements. Classically it is represented with a deity having five heads, each for one of the Elements. It is said that after this fifth Chakra the influence of the Elements ceases. The fifth *chakra* is associated with the frequency of 630 Htz and the colour blue or smoky purple. It has sixteen petals. Its presiding deity is Sada-Shiva or Panchavaktra Shiva (five elements/ energetic principles (tanmatras); and his female counter part, also with five heads depicting the five senses). The Chakra is located in the neck, at the carotid plexus.

Physical organs associated are: thyroid, trachea; neck vertebrae; teeth; gums; oesophagus; parathyroid; hypothalamus, cervical ganglia and medulla.

The more psychological, emotional and mental factors associated with it are: the choice and strength of will; personal expressions; to follow one's own dream; personal power; addiction, judgement, faith and knowledge and the capacity to make decisions. Perception and nature of information is through hearing and speaking- through words or music. A sense of self is built in society via assimilating knowledge and talking (teaching); also a more refined sense of smell and taste develop.

The Need generated here is to develop alignment with the divine will, leading to commitment to speak and follow the truth; especially to discover ones personal truth.

In the Tibetan system, this chakra carries the symbol of a semicircular bow, the syllable 'Ham,' and the shape of a white circle. It is associated with the Buddha Amitabha, the embodiment of discriminating wisdom of inner vision.

Physical ailments due to the malfunctioning of this chakra are: a chronically sore throat; mouth ulcers; gum-problems; scoliosis, laryngitis and thyroid problems.

Ajna, the sixth *chakra* is associated with the frequency 710 Htz and indigo blue or a luminescent bluish white. It has only two petals and its seed-letter is the primordial AUM. Instead of an Element it is associated with the *Mahatattva* (*buddhi, ahamkara and chitta*, meaning the great mind that holds intellect, I-ness and thought-related activity). The deity is Shambhu, a form of Shiva and his female counterpart. Or Andranaishvara (a half-male and half-female Shiva) symbolising the end of duality. The location is between the eye brows, by some described as the Medulla plexus/pineal plexus.

Physical organs associated are: brain; sympathetic nervous system; eyes(especially the left), ears; nose; pineal gland; pituitary gland,

The more psychological, emotional and mental factor associated with it are: the capacity to visualise and understand and learn from your and others experience (self-evolution); feeling of open connected-ness with the world; generation of unlimited ideas and the ability to carry them out; visionary facilities and emotional intelligence.

Perception and nature of information perceived is through 'hearing' and seeing revelations, visions.

The Need generated here is for the experience of divine love, spiritual energy and ecstasy.

In the Tibetan system, by and large *Ajna* is linked with the crown chakra; the seed-syllables are 'Ham' and 'Ksam' (or So-ham).

Physical ailments encountered through malfunctioning of this chakra are: brain tumours; haemorrhages, neurological disturbances; spinal problems; learning disabilities; seizures.

Sahasrara, the seventh *chakra*, is associated with the frequencies around 750 to 1000 Htz; the colour is luminous white and the 'element' is the 'light of pure consciousness.' It is said the fifty letters of the Sanskrit Alphabet are inscribed twenty times on its thousand petals. Inside this chakra is an inverted triangle (the symbol of Shakti) and the seat of Shiva, transcendental consciousness. It is the house of God, the soul's place to rest and live in unconditional joy. Together with the 6th *chakra,* it is associated 'with 'the blue flaming drop,' the *bindu*, the symbol of the element 'space' or 'ether.'

Physical organs associated are: The entire being within his skin; the pineal gland, the upper brain, right eye, cerebral cortex, and the cerebral spinal nerve system...

The more psychological, emotional and mental factor associated with it are the integration of the whole personality; the ability to trust the divine completely, having high ethical and humanitarian values, selflessness; living in expanded consciousness governed by divine inspiration.

Perception and nature of information happens simply by internal knowing, even of universal concepts. There is no more Need generated here, as one lives within the divine, the universal mind.

In the Tibetan system, Lord Vairochana embodies the 'wisdom of the Universal Law,' he is embraced by the 'Mother of Heavenly Space.'

Physical ailments, disturbances and malfunctioning here, cause: energetic disorders, chronic exhaustion and extreme sensitivity to light, sound and other environmental factors.

Here, in the *Sahasrara*, in the thousand petaled Lotus, the union of *Shiva and Shakti*, of the Absolute and the Serpent power of *Kundalini* takes place, finally leaving the other six centres behind.

It is said that normally people around the age of 30 start to be influenced by the **Visuddha Chakra**. (Keeping in mind that due to a much shorter life span in ancient Indian society, this was the penultimate phase of life) The fifth *chakra* aspirant seeks knowledge that is true, beyond limitations of time, culture conditioning and genetic code, however his main problem is doubt and a negative intellect. The study and practice of Yoga brings self-mastery. The planet ruling the *chakra* is Jupiter, making the person working at the level of the fifth chakra, interested in studying scriptures and ancient knowledge. This accords with what was said about the Space person. [113]

The *Ajna Chakra* person realises that he/she is an immortal spirit in a temporal body; they have cosmic knowledge and can generate scriptures; their mind reaches a state of undifferentiated cosmic consciousness. He has become stable, true in: 'I am That.' He cannot slide back on the spiritual path, whereas at the level of the fifth *chakra* we still can; therefore it is important to keep practising Yoga. [114]

In fact, it is more vital than ever, as the Yogi is nurtured by *sattvic* energy - that harmonious, wisdom energy that is a mixture between Space and Air in their most subtle, beneficial states.

When **practising any asana**, our focus should be turn inward (not on how it looks, how it compares to others etc.), turned to the sattvic inner world of stillness at the core of our Being. We tune in to our spiritual heart, into the space within the space, where 'I' is pure; is 'the hub of the universe;' where I can witness the pulse of consciousness.

There are **asanas** that especially lead us to this *sattvic* energy. Sitting postures are good, especially those that create strength and stillness in the lower abdomen like *siddhasana* (lotus pose) and *virasana*. Any *asanas* that keep the spine supple (forward and backward bends) are helpful e.g. *Karnapidasana* (fetus pose; also Water Element) and spinal twists like *matsyedrasana* are good as long as the breath remains full. Standing postures that emphasise strength, stability and calmness are good, developing patience and concentration (also *Urdvabadakonasana*; Cobbler pose). Space people should practise *asanas* gently, with plenty of rest; their minds to be kept peaceful (*Savasana*.).

Asanas are of course only one aspect. We have referred several times to Patanjali, whose ethical principals, the *Yamas and Niyamas,* are a basic must for any spiritual seeker. The fifth Element of Space is linked as we know, to detachment, and so two of Patanjali's recommendations for a spiritual life relate here: **brahmacharya** (celibacy) and **tapasya** (bringing bioenergetic forces and mind under control**).** *Brahmacharya* primarily refers to students of Brahman, those devoted to study the highest truth and *sannyasins* (renunciates). Celibacy has a reason that has nothing to do with morals... the *udana–prana,* the upward rising energy, draws up the sexual energy and converts it into prana, prana that becomes a powerhouse for spiritual development. Yet Celibacy has here also a meaning beyond abstaining from sex, it addresses all our hidden desires and indulgences. Frugal diet and a moderate amount of sleep for example, keep us alert – but not invigorated and tempted for indulgent life. It assists the same path as non-injury, truth and discipline, and thus in the latter sense is relevant for anyone, be it householder, student or monk! It asks us to **household our life energy**!

In the *Niyamas* Patanjali asks for 'tapas' austerity. *Tapas* literally means heat, and the meaning is applied to mean especially that heat which occurs doing the practices of yoga. It is said that heat is generated by the friction between mind energy and heart energy; e. g. when our senses are not allowed to have what they want, through mind control. This is also called the 'fire of yoga,' which burns up impurities in our body that keep us from experiencing inner wisdom.

If we find this portrait of the Space person daunting, then keep in mind that our evolution is akin to a helix, an ascending spiral; we cover the same compass 'position' again and again, but hopefully on a progressively higher level. There are many different levels in which the elemental energy fields influence our evolution. On a simpler level than the above portrait, spiritual aspirations might express in someone's discipline to go to church every Sunday, that too is *tapasya*. A person going on a fast - to sponsor a good cause – that too is *tapasya,* i.e. restricting the wants and wishes of the senses. Even refraining from low self-esteem by using affirmation, is tapasya (using a mantra to control the mind). Refraining from a beach holiday - and going on a pilgrimage instead - is 'giving something up into the fire of yoga.' We normally say such 'sacrifices' make us better people. Well this is the same in any spiritual context, no matter what creed or religion; such self-control cleans inner space, removes the blocks in ourselves that keep us from higher insight and wisdom. Why? Because they chip away at the ego and open us to see the 'sacred We.'

Earlier we talked about turning within to hear the voice of our own wisdom! What stops us hearing it, is the never-ending chatter in our mind: we think about the shopping, about the kids in school, about the bill that needs paying, about the dust on the chair. If nothing else, then the mind goes on about the knee that hurts, the tickle in your throat, the back that feels tired etc. etc. One of the hardest things in the world is to let go of that chatter. Only if we control this chatter can our mind be quiet and we can connect to that stillness in which we can hear the inner wisdom.

This control over our mind is the Yogic practise of **Samyana,** the collective word for the last three steps of Patanjali's eightfold path. The way to control the mind, is by practising concentration, meditation and 'meditation over prolonged time,' (*dharana, dhyana, samadhi*).

To control our mind is to practise austerity; ' *tapas*' is to prepare our mind to let go of the constant occupation with that which our senses desire. This precondition for 'mind-control' is called *pratyahara*, the ability to withdraw our senses within ourselves, and forsake reacting to and desiring all manner of things (fourth step of Patanjali's eight limbs). And really we have no choice; if we want to hear the wisdom of our Soul, we have to practice *tapasya, pratyahara and finally samyama*. But the key to all of it is tapasya; it is kind of the training ground of everyday life; encouraging us to give up things that prevent us from reaching our potential as human beings.

There is a common misunderstanding that mind-control or detachment means poverty – either of mind or of material or spiritual wealth. This is not so! Neither does it mean to give up action. A king can be detached from his wealth – just use it as necessary; a warrior can fight – just doing his duty; a mother cares for her child - just fulfilling her role. Think! Space is detached - yet all the actions go on within it. It is detached yet holds all the wealth, all the power and action of the Four other Elements. The secret is to enjoy – but not be influenced by it! A king that has wealth and does not cling to it, for his own gain, can serve his people much better. A fighter (like Arjuna in the Bhagavad Gita) can act appropriately to protect others - and a mother that looks after her child with love, yet without suffocating the child's own ambitions, enables the child to truly grow into its own power. Detachment gives freedom – gives joy; enables others, allows wisdom to grow. Space is a supreme example of this.

Knowledge within the Space person is sattvic in character 'one sees the indestructible reality in all beings, the undivided in the divided, know that knowledge as pure' (Bhagavad Gita; XVIII/20). It is like looking at a picture and being aware of both, the painting and the canvas; such 'equal vision' can truly appreciate the beauty of the created, it reveals all there is to know! In esoteric literature there is talk of the *Akashic* records (*akasa* = space) a so-called library of wisdom. Accessing it, we access the universal mind, or as the Catholic Sage Teilhard de Chardin says, we access the Noon–Sphere which holds all cosmic knowledge. [115]

Happiness derived from Space energy is a subtle happiness of inner peace. 'Born out of purity of one's own mind.' ' The peace and tranquillity, the joy and expansion, that the mind and intellect come to experience as a result of their discipline and contemplation... the gladness of the heart that wells up... as a result of his balanced and self-disciplined life of high ideals and divine values... ' [116] (Holy Geeta, XVIII/37)

The Question Space challenges us to ask: the lesson it provides?

Spiritual evolution is like going to school and learning various lessons. Once a lesson is learned, a quantum step can be taken to the next class. Each element with its wisdom helps us to learn certain lessons by asking us questions. Earth asked: Who are You? Water asked: Where are you coming from and where are you going? Fire asked: Have you completed your transformation and celebrated? Air asked: What do you need to let go, leave behind? And Space /Wood asks us: What is your true purpose? Once you can answer this question go out and live it, do it, that is all there is!

Somehow we seem to get stuck with this question more often than with the others. All through life we hit points where we ask, what's it all for? What is my purpose? Indeed Richard Dawkins goes as far as to say:

'We humans have purpose on the brain. We find it hard to look at anything without wondering what it is 'for'... The desire to see purpose everywhere is a natural one in an animal that lives surrounded by machines, works of art, tools and other designed artefacts; an animal moreover, whose waking thought is dominated by the personal goals. A car, a tin opener, a screwdriver and a pitcher, all legitimately warrant the 'what is it for' - question. Our pagan forebears would have asked the same questions about thunder, eclipses, rocks and... Today we pride ourselves with having shaken off such primitive animism but the old temptation comes back... when tragedy strikes: why oh why did the cancer/ earthquake/ hurricane have to strike my child? The illusion of purpose is so powerful... homo sapiens is a deeply purpose-ridden species.' [117]

It is, as though we imagine we have been given a purpose by our designer just like a tin opener has been designed for a purpose, yet we have forgotten it.

We incessantly enquire about our purpose, surely for one reason: because we want to be assured that what is happening is appropriate, is right - right for what? We don't trust ourselves, we need to hear confirmation that we are right because we have forgotten who we truly are, forgotten even, what is right. Right to fulfil our destiny, our potential? From where do we need this outside confirmation? If space contains all, the question and the answer both are contained in us! Space, might as well ask, 'how are you doing in fulfilling your potential?' Do we know our potential? As a human being can there be any other purpose, than becoming fully human?

In one way we are animal; an animal needs food, shelter, reproduces etc. - yet we are human animals. What makes us special is our mind. To become fully human we need to realise the potential of mind to see a greater perspective.

Each one has inherent, the capacity to become fully what he/she is capable of.

But what is that? Our minds are brilliant 'fibbers,' they invent a 'purpose' for which we then can strive: become a great engineer, a great poet, father, mother, thief or actor! And we keep thinking in this mechanical mode, confusing roles and technical performances with our true purpose, our true self! Our mind truly limits our perception. It has us identifying ourselves with being a parent, a friend, a spouse, a professional, a speaker, a listener, a company director, a bricklayer, etc.

We forget that we are on the one hand 'merely players' (as Shakespeare had it), and on the other hand, we are the script (life, energy, consciousness) - and the script writing. We have also existence 'off-stage' - who are we when we are not performing? The real question is - **who are we when we are our true selves?**

The secret of that can only be revealed in the space of our own inner wisdom. Only there lies the answer of total truth, total honesty. We have to dare to look through our own mask, our 'persona.' Is it possible to be aware of that true 'Me'? Once we have seen this true face of ourselves, even if it is for one second, we will never forget who we are and what our true potential is. Remember - Space includes everything; there is no hiding; total honesty is required by Space. Space reveals all.

I remember when I was a child, and my parents brought me up to be 'good' and honest. Yet at the same time I was told: 'You are too honest, if you always tell the truth, people will put you into a mental home, they will think you are mad, one cannot always speak the truth.' The truth meant here was the kind of 'truth' which might become uncomfortable to the self and others.

The Indian greeting with folded hands in front of your heart is called 'Namaste.' Ram Dass, so I was told, wrote this beautiful interpretation of 'Namaste.'

> I honour the place in you, where the universe resides
> I honour the place in you of love, of light, of truth, of peace.
> I honour the place within you, where if you are, in that
> place in you,
> And I am in that place in me, there is only one of us!
> An honest reaction to another has to come from that inner space,
> where we just are, naked! Honesty comes from that sacred inner
> space, where there is no pretence.

Amongst the Tibetan Meditation Symbols, the Dhyani Buddhas, the Buddha for 'Space' holds a mirror; the mirror itself is empty - yet it reflects everything. Space is empty and clear and yet it reflects all. Space itself is pure, is just potential, yet as it is said in Zen Buddhism: it is 'filled Void.' The Avatamssaka Sutra says:

> You should train your mind to be pure like Space.
> By abandoning thoughts, discrimination and clinging to cognition,
> you will enter the Buddha realms with a mind like Space.

The more complex our life is, the more difficult it becomes to be honest. Country folk used to live a simple life; honest faces, open eyes, generate a feeling of being totally trustworthy. Why? Because they have nothing to hide! They do a day's work, they help people when they can, and they do whatever is appropriate. I watched a gardener, and the honesty seems represented in the straight, strong pulls with which he moves the garden rake. No fancy playing, no unnecessarily rests, no looking for distractions, just him and the rake and the ground, total, clear unadulterated union of being and action. As our lives get more complex, this simple direct union is not so easy; we think we have much to lose with our fancy interactions, pretend reasons, avoidance tactics etc. Many demands are made upon us and the more we have to accommodate, the more we have to bend this way and that to accommodate it all. And so we lose sight of our own worth.

Those who do not fall prey to the above pitfalls, live a noble life. Toward the end of the great Indian story, the Mahabharata, Bishma, the ageing king, describes the noble life, the life of virtue:

...be truthful and above reproach, self-restrained, humble and righteous...

...he should surround himself with men who share his noble qualities...

...Malice should have no place in his heart... Self-restrained is sacred.

Its fruit are nobility, calmness, contentment, faith, forgiveness, simplicity, humility, reverence for superiors, benevolence, compassion for all creatures, frankness... [118]

Living out a noble life, is that fulfilling our potential? In our daily lives, do we live a noble life, when we are consistently truthful and honest, when we see to issues as they arise promptly, when we put in an honest day of work; when we give the right quality time to our loved ones? Do we live noble lives when we allow ourselves time for our own spiritual practices and rest; when we tend to the needs of our bodies with food and sleep in the best way possible?

The noble qualities of heroes of a bygone past surely only have relevance if we ourselves aspire to them. A noble life is longing and working towards the highest, a cherished ideal in mediaeval Europe amongst the chivalrous quest for the Holy Grail. The Knights like Galahad and Percival show that the greatest battle is to defeat oneself, - this is 'tapasya,' the ground where Indian sages and mediaeval heroes of Europe meet. Even Chinese thoughts join in - when the absolute formless power of Tao, becomes a specific form, it is called Te. Te is the inner power of a thing or person that gives perfection of personality. The highest potential of each being is revealed in the written Character of 'Te.' This symbol has three parts: the first one means as much as: flawless, perfect, without deviation, the second is the symbol for the human heart, and the third is a symbol for walking. 'Te' becomes a symbol for the answer to the question of our purpose, our raison d'être. [119] Out of the Absolute Space, the TAO, arises our individual form Te, which has a perfect, flawless heart to walk with.

As the American Indians say, we need to 'walk our talk.' Or 'to walk and act from a perfect heart,' and that seems to have little to do with the roles we play of being a plumber, a wife or an artist, and more to do with allowing the perfect divine energy, that lives in our heart, to express through us.

Space shows us the error in our thinking. It tells us that it does not matter whether we are a writer, shoemaker, mother, or husband. It is irrelevant whether we are a teacher, a poet, a president or a pauper, a computer technician, a nurse or a Guru; it is not the roles we play that are important, it is not the achievements we gain which is our purpose, but <u>how we are</u>.

All grandeur, all ego-trips can be cut out. The vision that space holds for us is to fulfil our potential by achieving the highest aspirations of a human being, and history is full of such noble men. Socrates was such a noble man, he was tried and executed in 339 B.C. because he did not believe in the city gods and is said to have misled the youths of the city with his philosophy. Indeed he was renowned as a man of fortitude and courage. He was also known for living the truth, for being true to himself; he was known to be even-minded and for having great self-control; he was dressed summer and winter in the same thin clothes and walked barefoot. Plato described for us Socrates' speech (Apology), in front of the court at his trial:

'Someone might say: "Are you not ashamed, Socrates, to have followed the kind of occupation that has led to your being now in danger of death?" However, I should be right to reply to him, "you are wrong sir! If you think that a man who is any good at all, should take into account the risk of life or death, he should look to this only in his actions, whether what he does is right or wrong, whether he is acting like a good or a bad man. It is not difficult to avoid death, gentlemen of the jury, it is much more difficult to avoid wickedness, for it runs faster than death." ' [120]

Meditation

Meditation for people that are especially influenced by Space energy has to be on the peace and emptiness of the mind. None symbolises this better for me, than the following prayer from the Metah Sutra. [121]

Peace to all beings, may all beings be well and happy and free from fear.
Peace to all beings, whether near or far, whether known or unknown,
Real or imaginary, visible or invisible, born or yet to be born...
Within and beyond imagination, in the world of ideas,
In the world of memories and in the world of dreams...
Peace in all elements, of earth and air and fire and water, fulfilled in space.
Peace in all universes, from the smallest cells in the body
To the greatest galaxies in space, peace and light rising.

PART III
RESTORING THE BALANCE
IN THE ELEMENTS

WE HAVE rediscovered the five energy fields of the Movement of Life which man has been aware of throughout time and cultures. Man has used this knowledge for three main purposes, one, to understand himself and his environment and secondly to ease his suffering, be it mental or physical – and thirdly, to satisfy his thirst to explain his existence. The first two aspects work with the physical plane of existence; wherever an element is unbalanced over a long period of time, it leads to suffering or dis-ease. Man's suffering and illness can be redressed, by re-balancing the elemental energies. It is this aspect we will address first. Secondly we looked at the mental and spiritual plane, where balancing takes on a different role; it becomes a step for man to realise his potential and thus find his place and purpose in existence.

Life is energy on the move, thus 'distortions' occur naturally with every wave of incoming energy, all experiences from taking a breath to being struck by a falling brick, from being confronted by an aggressive word to twisting one's ankle. Distortions happen constantly; a person is healthy when she has the ability to regain equilibrium quickly. Health is the relative ability to bring back balance.

In ancient China, the doctor was paid as long as he was capable of maintaining a person's health. If the person under his care became ill, he would not be paid. If the sick person happened to be a high official or even the emperor, the doctor might well be killed, for he had failed in his job! The focus being on a preventative life-style, that re-balances.

Under the influence of Western science, the body is seen as a machine, health care is for fixing the part that <u>appears</u> to be ill. If thoughts are energy too, then such focus on illness might actually create illness. Indeed, in highly civilised countries with technically very advanced medical systems, actually more people are sick than in other nations. For example Americans '...have more doctors, more dentists, more and better equipped hospitals... and a greater supply of food than any other nation, yet we still are, by far, the sickest nation in the world.' [1]

We are what we think; having become what we thought,
  Like the wheel that follows the cart-pulling ox,
  Sorrow follows evil thought.
And joy follows a pure thought... (The Dhammapada) [2]

Observe your reaction when shocked: Yes, fear makes you hold your breath; we become scared of breathing out, scared of what might happen next. Now if we repeatedly experience such fear we condition ourselves to withhold our breath. This habit leads us to the symptoms of an asthmatic person. Asthma feels like suffocating.

To relearn to breathe out, one needs to ask, what are you afraid of? There are two aspects to be considered, and both point to imbalances in the Water and Air Elements.

1) To release this 'holding on to fear,' one needs to understand that behind all fears is the fear of annihilation. 2) I hold onto MY life, not 'life' but mine! Mine means owning it; to own something, there needs to be two – one who owns and something or someone who can be owned. Thus owner and owned are seen as separate; in the fear for our life, we postulate that 'I' and my life are separate! Then the question comes: who is this 'I' that owns my life and can lose it? This illogical and irrational thought is our most common fear, underlying all others, such as fearing to be separated from my family, my house, my body! All because we feel separate from life itself!

The asthma sufferer or anyone in this position would do well to ask him/herself, who suffers, what dies, what is annihilated? In the constant Movement of Life, the Elements are in permanent transformation and re manifestation. Who is holding on... and onto what? We are constant change! One physical state of body and mind changes into another; what 'dies' cannot be the life that is housed in that body - only the temporary house changes. If I am not the form, but life itself - 'I' cannot 'die.' Wow! There is nothing to fear, because death does not happen to 'Me' and yet this existential fear is the deepest imaginable root of all other fear.

Giving up this fear is balancing the Water Element - or balancing the Water Element will lessen the fear, which in turn then allows to breath freely! Let go of the fear, exercise breathing out and asthma might well disappear.

So really balancing the Elements means to re-educate our bodies and mind, this is why, again and again, ignorance is mentioned as the cause of all suffering. To restore balance one has to recognise and unlearn patterns that distort. In our example about asthma, allopathic medicine would prescribe inhalers, which merely give a chemical shock to the system so it breathes differently. It does not re-educate the system, the situation appears again a few minutes later and possibly the inhaler himself becomes the root or addiction that reinforces a disturbed lung energy pattern. Instead of curing the illness, it is reinforced - suffering continues.

You might well say – 'it's not that simple,' a virus infection happens, a baby might have leukaemia, a good person gets multiple sclerosis, cancer etc.? If the above thesis that illness is based on distortions in the energy fields is right, then healing happens through balancing these. For balancing we need a holistic worldview, to see that everything is connected to everything else, that we are not separate from life. Just think about how many people are involved and growing, producing and getting the bread for the sandwich on your plate! Try, it will show you once and for all how connected you are in an enormous, complicated *Web of Life*. Each event, each individual, each illness is embedded in the entire universe, past, present and future; we cannot isolate any bits, just like a drop of water cannot be isolated within the ocean. The Tibetan Yogi Milarepa sings: 'Accustomed as I've been, to meditating on this life and the future life as one, I have forgot the dread of birth and death.' [3]

How life is linked to past, present and future, and all else is speculated upon in the theory of *karma*. The energy field I call 'my present existence' is bound into ever changing energy fields beyond my present awareness. We accept this when science talks of genes; we accept that genes get passed on from one generation to the next. Modern science tells us we are all linked to all females that ever existed via the mycondrial gene in the DNA! Matter is energy, genes are energy patterns, energy flows, is movement connecting everything. The law of mutual, continuous influence is called the law of karma. These influencing patterns cannot start just with my present existence. It is said we incarnate with subconscious memories and patterns from previous lives. Now how we work with these patterns, what we learn from them determines our destiny. *Karma* is where we come from, propelling us towards destiny.

Considering illnesses then, is looking at patterns of interference in this life, yesterday or 'yesteryear' or in some cases, probably even to patterns affecting us before birth; or even in a previous life. Undoing such patterns or distorting habits and restoring balance in the energy fields varies in the effort required, opportunities taken and success achieved. Obviously a habit fallen into a few months or years ago is easier to unlearn and replace with new behaviour, new thinking or new attitudes, than unlearning or healing distortions that are years old, or even a lifetime or several lifetimes old. A smoker that has smoked a few cigarettes can give up relatively easily. Somebody who has smoked for twenty or thirty years will find it much more difficult to unlearn that habit.

It is nearly impossible to unlearn or heal patterns that are older than this life. They simply have to work themselves out, just as a stone thrown has to land! However much we try to heal ourselves, there are limits to what we can achieve. Our limits can however be affected by something I call 'Grace', or the love of God. Grace comes from an altogether different source; it is pure divine energy, which carries no elemental patterns, it is pure love and comes to us for no rhyme or reason. It is said, that if we are fortunate enough to meet a fully realised person, a Guru, Saint or Avadhuta, that their pure energy can erase our energy patterns; such is the compassion of God. Like the compassion of the man who forgives, regardless whether the person deserves it or not, so divine compassion just washes *Karma* away, like we wash clothes. It restores life for no reason at all. Grace is the source of Earth's abundance - it just is. Without this grace our attempts to heal ourselves are limited, limited not just by the depth and veils of *Karma*, but also by the complicated pattern of the many levels of life's interaction. Yet we must put forth the effort to re-educate the energy patterns in body, mind and soul. How long does this take, how far is it to relative wholeness? The answers are shrouded in each one's destiny, but we must embark on the path - just as the Hoopoe bird describes in the 'Conference of the Birds':

'Before we reach our goal,' the Hoopoe said,
'the journey's seven valleys lie ahead;
How far this is the world has never learned,
For no one who has gone there has returned -
Impatient bird, who would retrace this trail?
There is no messenger to tell the tale.' 4

The path depends on our state of mind. There is a story told about Rabbi Meshulam Zusya of Annapol, (eighteenth century, Poland). He belonged to the Hasidim, a mystical branch of the Jewish Community. One day two men came to Zusya to ask him about suffering. Zusya sat in his chair, smoking a pipe and asked them what they wanted? They explained and Zusya just laughed. Eventually he said:

"I am afraid you will have to ask someone else: I have never experienced suffering." The two men were confounded, they knew Zusya was extremely poor and often very ill. They left pondering their experience; one said: "There is a man who accepts suffering with love. He accepts it wholeheartedly, as God's will."

Then the second man, after a long silence spoke: "I think, my friend, that it goes deeper than that. Zusya is living in such a state - the joy to which we all aspire - that he was only speaking the truth just now. Truly, he has never experienced suffering." 5

If we live in a state of awareness, in 'the joy to which we all aspire', where all creation is One, then there is no suffering, what ever happens to us. There might be pain and misfortune, poverty and illness but we will not get attached, thus not suffer. This is not only 'looking at the bright side of life' - it is to be the bright side of life. Many sages wrote that suffering and pain are caused by two aspects: ignorance and imbalance in the Five Elements. The solution then is twofold, to become aware and work to balance the Elements.

Chapter Nine: Balancing the Earth Element

LONG standing patterns and distortions of the Energy field we call Earth, can be observed in the posture and the habits of a person. As we saw previously, the relevant meridians basically run down the front of the body and legs. Imagine a puppet where these lines are strings and they are contracted, pulled too tight, the puppet would bend over from the hips shoulders rounded, head pulled down towards the chest much like a caricature of a perching vulture. If the strings were too loose, 'empty', the puppet would sag together like in the caricature of 'the couch-potato,' never upright, sliding further and further.

Such a person might walk with a slight inward shuffle, such as can be observed in old people. This is described as 'an apraxia of gait, which is characterised as a slow, halting, short-stepped, shuffling or sliding gait. ' [6] In fact, the feet might be dragged, as though 'sticking to the earth', or people might appear as though on their tiptoes, cut off from the earth.

In a person with strong balanced energy, focus comes from the centre, their belly. They stand poised strong and stable, as mentioned earlier in context of the *Hara*, they have presence.

Imbalances can also be noted through seemingly innocent habits, such as rubbing the fingertips nervously over any surface, or against the thumb (the Spleen meridian ends on the inside of the index finger! rubbing it stimulates or sedates that energy). For a similar reason people might habitually rub their cheeks, the side of the throat, or even the lower rim of their eye socket (working ST meridian).

9: a) Balancing Earth in General

Now the question arises what can we do about it. In ancient times sages healed 'by the grace of God'; they transmitted the essence of life to the sick, much as Reiki-Healers today. In Healing groves marked out by stones, the ancient medicos were priests 'not a human, but a divine physician' or 'therapeuts. They were 'attendants of the cult and served the god by carrying out prescribed rituals.'[7] Later, temples were built with either sacred incubation chambers or holes in the ground where people descended into the earth itself to be cured (*catachthonioi*). The cure was envisaged to happen through the energies of the place, or through the appearance of the goddess associated with such a place (Asclepius, Diana, Gaia) in a dream. [8]

Hippocrates practised in these traditional sanctuaries which were always near springs and groves, (as can still be seen in Celtic healing traditions in Wales, Cornwall and other places in Britain). The actual treatment consisted of ritual purification and of people sleeping on the Earth in the innermost sanctuary (or on a couch, called clinic!).

How different it is in the present world. 'Grief, calamity and evil cause inner bitterness... there is neglect against the laws of the four seasons 'the elements and the environment; people have lost faith, thus 'minor illnesses are bound to become grave and the serious diseases are bound to result in death. Therefore the invocation of the gods is no longer the way to cure.'[7] So explained Ch'i Po to the Emperor of China thousands of years ago. It sounds like it could have been said yesterday. The Tibetan Buddhist teacher T.Y.S. Lama Gangchen explains that 'we have caused overwhelming outer and inner pollution, the decline and misuse of natural resources... resulting in... violent crime, drug abuse and ever increasing body and mind sickness... we all possess a precious human body; if we use it negatively, we can contribute to our personal and planetary suicide. We can choose to go from darkness to darkness, from light to darkness, or from darkness to light or from light to light. The choice is ours.' [10]

Healing the Earth Element in us will affect each other Element in the body and in turn earth itself. Each creature has its own adequate Earth - so your Earth is different from mine; your needs are different from mine and they are both equally good; we are ONE in many forms. Stop judging hold and support each other as one!

The first step is to get to know your own Earth - find out who you are, what your needs are; then find what you can do to ensure that you fulfil your potential? In nature, Earth needs to be ploughed over, dug up, opened up - to let the air in; it needs to be watered to provide moisture for growth; it needs seeds that fulfil the need to create many abundant forms; it needs the sun to warm the earth. In other words Earth needs to work in conjunction with the other Elements; but what is it you need from your Earth mother? It might be as little as a mudpack or as much as defending your rights. The Earth-goddess has many faces, from life giving mother to giver of learning and wisdom, to upholder of the laws and their defender as warrior and destroyer.

I have a friend, who whenever she feels down, simply lies, spread-eagle fashion on the ground. Others recommend walking barefoot on grass, beach, even stones. In parks in Singapore I found especially reserved areas for walking bare-feet. Another simple way of getting in touch with earth and replenishing your earth energy is gardening; get out of your head... into your garden!

When the Earth Element itself is ill, then not only all else will be affected, but serious disruption of the energy flow is at stake. In order to heal the Earth, recall that stomach and spleen are involved in digesting. To heal earth energy, a sensible diet is adamant. What's that? The quality of food in our times is generally low, it is mass produced (artificial ripening, long transportation, refrigeration etc), with loads of chemicals (fertilisers, insecticides, herbicides etc.), then often processed (irradiation, freezing, additives excess use of oils and sugar etc.) and consumed with little care and attention. On top of that, these days we are confronted with genetically engineering food which adds all sorts of genes (i.e. fish and pig genes are now added to tomatoes!) So it is almost impossible to get 'good food.' To balance earth energies it is even more important than ever to eat fresh food and as healthy as possible.

Food itself can be a healing agent, especially when it contains 'a mixture of essences of heaven and earth in proper proportions' (referring to *Yin* and *Yang* foods), and are eaten 'during the season having the closest affinity to the affected organ.' [11]

Medicinal Food is chosen for the effect and qualities it has, that are similar to the energy field 'Earth.' ' A cooked yam is yellow, moist, soft, slightly sticky and sweet. Yams are considered excellent food for supplementing *Qi* and strengthening the Spleen and Stomach. Because they are so nourishing and digestible they are a good food for relieving weakness, fatigue and building tissues.' [12] In the same sense, other vegetables like pumpkins, potatoes, carrots, turnips, millet and rice are recommended.

In the same way, late summer fruit should be chosen, especially those that fit in texture, colour or shape (round, yellow, soft) such as apricots, pears etc. as they are ideal for balancing the Earth (shape, colour and taste, are linked to Earth). Minerals are very important for the Earth, (they constitute a large part of it); we too need them in our diet. Since all vegetables contain minerals 'all vegetables enhance the stomach and spleen and pancreas function. Particularly helpful are collard greens, which are rich in minerals and calcium.' [13] How important these are, I experienced one year in India. I stayed for a prolonged time in an ashram (monastic environment). As advised, I drank a lot of water, as the heat of the day made me sweat a lot, especially during work periods. I got weaker and weaker - the water, although in itself important, washed out important minerals. Eventually an Ayurvedic doctor suggested adding ionised minerals to the water; I drank loads of such water - in 24 hours I was fine!

As a herb, dioscorea root, which is soft and starchy, could be recommended, as it replenishes *Qi*, as well as other herbs such as astragalus and poria; and if the Earth meridians need warming, fresh ginger, cardamom and even rice wine should be used in cooking. In general, it can be said that extremes of either a very *Yang* food such as salt, eggs, red meat should be avoided, as well as extreme *Yin* food. Yin foods are chemical additives, sugar, spices, stimulants (carob, coffee, strong tea etc). , alcoholic beverages, tropical fruit, tropical vegetables, cream, yoghurt and milk. The balance should be around a diet of (fish), cheese, even more grains, beans, seeds, vegetables, nuts and fruit (the latter three from the climatic area where the person lives).

To heal Earth we have to consider the many different levels of our energy system. The ST/SP network does not only relate to the physical but also to the emotional and spiritual. The base level, the physical manifestation of Earth energy (ST/SP) has to call on higher levels of energy (e.g. the emotional or spiritual). The power to heal one's Earth comes from the spiritual centre, the Higher Self. How can we do that?

The North American Indian tradition has a way that combines several levels. They suggest we go on a 'vision quest" to a power place.' The person is sent under the guidance of a Medicine Person, to find a remote but very special location, where the aspirants feels the power of the earth; there he fasts and prays for three or four days. Some people walk a long time to find such a place - some walk literally (or metaphorically) a lifetime to find such a place. Jesus went to the desert or to the sea, Buddha went to the Bodhi Tree, Abraham went into the wilderness, and Merlin went into the crystal cave in Wales (UK). Once we have found our place of power 'the attention of Mother Earth is directed to that spot, and energy begins to flow to that area, the Earth Mother is there to nurture and give solace to that person 'or a vision, direction or healing.' In learning how to find an individual Power Place it is important to walk the land until we feel a drawing within us to an exact spot. The keynote is trusting one's feelings and then being quiet; when our Earth connection is strong, we come to at-one-ment with the Clan Chiefs of Air, Earth, Water and Fire'[14].

The reader might think this totally impractical: just imagine that one million Londoners go walking into the countryside to find their power place, to heal their stomach ulcer by lying on the ground dreaming! - Ridiculous! Yes, well said, but strip away the form and go to the essence. What is the wisdom behind those traditions? To spend time out of the routine of ordinary life, quietly, alone, not distracted by anything else, in order to get in touch with our inner core energy. In that totally quiet space our own inner Self, our life-essence can focus on healing us, or communicating with us. The Self can only speak in that stillness - or rather we can only hear it in that stillness. There it can tell us what is wrong with our lives and how to redress it.

This, in essence is meditation! We do not have to go around the countryside, but the countryside can be in us! We can stay at home - calming our minds - and merely looking inside, seeking the centre of our being. We will realise that the energy of the Earth is the energy of our Self. Well, I hear you say – 'fine, but what about my stomach energy, my ulcers, my wasting muscles, the lumps in my breasts, my infertility, my lack of energy etc.? Listen... to what you say! 'My' ulcer? Are you identified with the body that has the ulcer or what? Find out who you are. Sooner or later you will get in touch with the original creative energy that you are. From there healing will take place.

Even conventional medicine uses meditation these days. 'Research has shown, for example, that even the most elementary meditation practice, repeating a *mantra* or focusing on one's breath, tends to have a beneficial effect on the immune system, and it improves such conditions as hypertension, angina and arythmia, high cholesterol, anxieties, stress, chronic pain, phobias and addictions.' [15]

Meanwhile more practical help might be sought. Obviously treatments like Shiatsu, Acupuncture, Zero Balancing and Spiritual Healing and Reiki focus on balancing energies. The Nei Ching recommends, 'these diseases are most fittingly treated with breathing exercises, massage of skin and flesh, and exercises of hand and feet.' [16] Massage can easily and professionally be obtained, including Rolfing (a deep tissue massage). Foot Reflexology or

Hand Reflexology are freely available. Maybe you need to change your job! Hands are used therapeutically in jobs such as a potter, practising crafts like papier-mâché, weaving and spinning; simple things like gardening and cooking are not surprisingly connected to the Earth Element.

All too often I have heard: 'this means I have to totally change my lifestyle - I can't do that!' or 'Isn't there some medicine I can take?' - Nothing happens without the will to change, old patterns get just more ingrained. But even that is an earth problem; when people have lost the energy to take charge, they rather hand over to others; they have lost their core. So for these, activities should be suggested that kindle the spirit of movement, of adventure, of doing. Reflect, you might discover a lot of patterns that have to be re-thought, re-educated and adjusted so that your body gets what it needs to heal your Earth Element.

To heal our Earth is to heal our Being. We need to change focus to reconnect with, and/or rebalance ourselves with the ground from which we originate and which we are. 'Man draws life from the Earth, but his fate depends upon Heaven. Heaven and Earth unite to bestow life-giving vigour as well as destiny upon man, (to be) effective one must first cure the spirit.' [17] To sum up, the way to heal the Earth is to renew it from its own core, which is its source. A person that has Earth as their main characteristic might find this means that the purpose of their Life is to find that Source, that centre of being. By implication the greatest fear or danger for such a person, then, is that of getting lost. And yet, we and that centre are one:

'We are the mirror as well as the face in it.
we are tasting the taste this minute of eternity.
We are pain and what cures pain
We are the sweet, cold water,
and the jar that pours.' (J. Rumi) [18]

9: b) Balancing Earth on the Mental and Spiritual Plane

The wisdom teachings of the world tell us that we do not need to be 'victims of biology or psyche!' nor of our circumstances. We can make fundamental changes in our selves, and the most powerful tool we have for change is our mind. But what is this elusive 'mind.'

To understand its working is vital... there is no understanding ourselves without it. **So let me tell you a story:**

A toddler sees a flower and mother explains in a gentle voice and with a supportive smile: "Isn't this is a beautiful rose, smell it! Ah how wonderful!" The information, given in a safe and caring manner, makes the brain release some dopamine... and as a result the child feels good. It feels good because mother was kind and smiled when she used the word 'rose' and as a consequence of the released chemical, a pleasant sensation is caused. Next time the child sees a rose, the mind re-members; goes back to a sort of filing cabinet where the previous associations are stored, pulls out the 'file' the pleasant feeling returns - it is happy. Every time another pleasant encounter comes with roses, the impression in the mind is reinforced, like a groove in a CD.

Another small child spots lovely colourful things in the garden and toddles over to them; stumbling into the rose bed he grabs a stem pricking his hand at the thorns. It screams in pain. Mother comes out, stressed at having to attend to the screaming child, and shouts: "Stupid! Can't you pay attention; these are roses, they have thorns. Can't you see! Look how filthy you are, I am too busy to clean you up now!"

Anger and frustration is written on her face. The child feels his own pain, and sees the angry face of mother; a chemical is released that makes it feel miserable and sad. Just as in the first case, an imprint is made in the child's mind, like on a CD. This time the imprint is: roses hurt, are bad and dangerous. His brain is getting programmed to release chemicals inducing a feeling of misery and danger whenever he sees a rose.

Both experiences are stored in a filing cabinet we call memory. Both experiences carry certain energies with them, which also are recorded in the filing cabinet. This base information shapes base vocabulary, the meaning and associations we have with each word (with is, by itself mere sound)! And this association is what determines how we see 'a rose' in the future. This association between words and feelings remain valid connections for the rest of the life. (Unless some reprogramming is done, which is extremely difficult).

Basically everything we think and experience enters our brain via the doors of the five senses; we hear, see, taste, touch or smell the world - then what happens? You can imagine any time we see a rose, we want to repeat the pleasant experience we had! Our mind creates desire; in fact left to its own devices it runs wild - seeing ice-cream, we want ice-cream; hearing praise, we want more praise; tasting chocolate we want more chocolate etc.

In the same way our mind and the nucleus in our cells (which holds memory) store negative associations and trauma and so the mind constantly creates its own monsters, fears and insecurities, which then stop us from living and, most important, from enjoying life! Again an example:

A little girl falls off her bike and badly scratches her knee. Mum takes her to the doctor, the knee is treated – and heals in no time. But does the mind forget this? NO! Twenty years later, when the girl is a Mum, and her own child wants a bicycle, she first refuses to buy one, then nervously watches, with misgivings every time her little tyke takes the bike out for a spin, because, "He might be injured, by this monster." This is how our mind works, creating grooves of misery; and we hold on to them 'for dear life' - until they destroy us.

Billions of bits of information are thus stored in our mind, and with anything we come across, some of these are reactivated. Moreover, the bits of memory triggered are split for processing in various areas of the brain (colour here, shape there, smell there etc). to be checked against existing bits of past recordings. Then the 'bits' are put together again – meaning what we become aware of is 'what matches personal previously stored knowledge!

The implications? We don't perceive what is there, the reality - <u>but our own reassembled version.</u> Meaning whatever we understand of anything is determined by what we have understood before! <u>Our perception is in fact projection!</u> Much like a fly spitting his saliva on the food first, before it can suck it up. Yes – we know only through what we already knew; learning happens when something known, falls together in a new way! Aha!

Because our experience is shaped by the energies of the Five Elements, our mind is influenced by them. Pure mind is consciousness, the original energy - yet as soon as it becomes manifested, it is tinted by the five energies, which throw the mind here and there. This mixture of congenital dominant influence (Elements) determines the nature of the projections of our mind, thus we see the world through the limitations of our own mind! That's why it is said:

Wake up to perception, stop projection!

Perception comes from a pure mind, a mind that is uncluttered with the old personal 'stuff', it is alert, perceptive and able to act always fresh, always present, NOW.

The way to such a 'pure mind' is - first to recognise and observe the actions of the mind, then to balance the various energies that dominate it and then with detachment leave the reaction patterns behind - thus we evolve to pure consciousness.

That is the aim. But how do we get there?

The first step is self-awareness, and we can see how that fits into Earth's question of: 'Who am I?' To find the answer, we have to watch the actions of the mind, which we can do anytime we sit sill. We can observe how fragments of thoughts constantly shoot through the mind (in the endeavour to sort and interpret). Literally, electric impulses shoot across the corpus callosum (gap between our right and left brain-hemisphere) frantically trying to catch up with the sense inputs. This 'rush-hour traffic' creates confusion! What comes in cannot be properly decoded; the mind is jabbering, no clear thinking is possible. Our perceptions of the world get distorted.

This is what Patanjali, the father of Yoga and sages through all ages saw hence the advice that the only way out is to discipline the mind. Thus the practise of Yoga is 'to control all modifications of the mind ' (Yoga chitta vritti nirodhanah, as stated in the 2nd of the Yogasutras)

As long as the mind is not disciplined, it constantly distorts your energies, paints one mad picture after another; it fills the world you live in with fear and worry, dragging you down, tying you to these self-created projections! Then you panic and look for refuge in something, that 'supposedly makes me feel good!' Would it not be better to control the mind in the first place? But how?

The issue of mind control follows Earth's question of finding out 'who we are.' It is especially relevant to the role that the **Earth energy field plays in our mind.** Where Earth energy in particular influences the mind, there is a strong link to the genetically encoded memory i.e. the caudate nucleus and limbic brain. On the dopamine trail, this stimulates action and planning memory on a basic survival level; it is a very old part of the brain, which stored that memory which helped our ancestors survive.

It means that the projections through which the mind sees its world are bound to the primitive survival of an animalistic nature. The world is threatening and we need to protect ourselves. This was mentioned in the context of the *Muladhara Chakra* and the *Anamaya kosha*. Earth energy tries to secure survival on the material plane, it believes that possessing material things will provide the security he/she craves. It validates its experiences, things and people according to whether these provide confirmation and security or not. It does not see what is - but merely whether what is there helps to provide mental and physical security. How to get out of it?

We need to realise that the projections **put on the world,** are due to past patterns.

As long as we identify with the body, we have to face issues on an animalistic level, looking for shelter and safety. Once we realise that there is something else that chooses body and life, then we know that we exist whether food and shelter are provided or not. There is no need to worry and be insecure for 'when this body was born it was born without consulting me. That mighty law by which it was born, will keep it going for the purpose for which it was born. If it falls off, never mind, let it go!' [19] Understand this and there is no worry about food or security; the body's need to be here has its own momentum. When the answer is found to 'who am I', one is secure. Once the question is answered beyond the identification with the perishable physical body and its roles, Earth finds stability and security in knowing 'I am, who I am.'

One more point about the mind influenced by Earth energies. Watching the thoughts becomes tiring; the mind is lethargic and tends to 'drop off', go to sleep. The lack of stimulus inherent in the solidity of the Earth makes her mind lazy, it needs to have stimulus – using the mind to control the mind can be helpful. We can use a phrase (mantra) or text, to get the mind used to obeying us - rather than us dancing to its erratic tune. It is yogic practice to recite a chapter from the Bhagavad Gita or other Scriptures by heart for this purpose.

Chapter Ten: Balancing the Water Element

THERE are old pictures of young nymphs or goddesses pouring water from one jug into another, from one chalice into the other. It needs a skilful, smooth movement that takes care that nothing gets spilt, that the same amount is given and received - one into the other, the other into the one - a steady, timeless flow. To move too quickly would let too much water flow, it would spill, or cause damage to the container; to move too slowly will interrupt the flow. Balanced Water is marked by fluid continuity.

Balanced Water has a further aspect. It is equally accommodating towards poison or medicine, both dissolve un-judged - but the effects are different: one is detrimental, the other healing and purifying. Water - like its opposite Fire, purifies and cleanses. Fire does it instantly (in its extreme, as instant combustion - a powerful cleansing by transformation, in the vein of alchemy). Water does it gently, by diluting and diluting further; then it transports the unwanted away. Patiently, through continuous work (washing!) it achieves transformation. While Fire, with one inspired action, can change a situation, Water has to work at it. There is one exception - in the presence of the right fire, water instantly changes into steam!

In order to balance Water Energy, there are three pointers: 1) maintaining an even, steady flow of energy in the related meridians and organisms. 2) using available energy (especially kidney Qi), appropriately measured; and 3) ensuring the purity of energy suited for its cleaning task (again especially in the kidney-organ-network). For example, when 'the kidney becomes blocked from fats, salt, cholesterol and stress, the amount of Qi that reaches the organs and lower back is diminished.' [20]

When the ancestral energy in the kidney-organ-network is weak and of poor quality, the slightest misuse (stress, diet or illness) will have a more severe effect than on people with stronger constitutions. When emotions such as fear, melancholy or insecurity are experienced by the body over prolonged time, the back tenses up along its length and BL/KI contract and it will cause the backache so common today.

The posture of a person can reveal whether a person has excessive, contracted Water energy, or its opposite too little, or even poisoned Water Energy. The Water meridians both run either side of the spine and down to the heels. Imagine the meridians as strings of a puppeteer. If he pulls the strings too tight, we see a puppet with its head pulled back, chest pushed forward and out, with the pelvis and coccyx pulled back, the legs apparently stiff from behind. The weight rests on the outside edge of the feet and heel; with the hard front shown to the world, such people appear to 'dig their heels in,' inflexible and uncompromising. They might appear outwardly strong, pushy, achievement orientated with high ambition and occupying much space.

By contrast, if the strings on the puppet are collapsed and too loose (for lack of Water Energy), the front of the puppet collapses; not held upright, it seems she is 'without a backbone,' giving the impression of being without conviction and inner strength.

There are other little habits that show a Water imbalance: Having a low centre of gravity, when unobserved, such people might stand with their hands on their sacrum, or indeed rub their sacrum. They appear as though they lack support from the back, physically and mentally (which might be due to lack of support while growing up). They feel tired in the back from constantly striving to hold themselves up.

Such people might rub the sole of their feet, especially the centre of the cross-arch where we find the start of the kidney meridian, which the Chinese befittingly call 'the gushing spring.' They might also be seen running their fingers over the centre of the scalp, seemingly massaging the Bladder meridian; or indeed they might rub the inner corner of the eye, where BL starts. Children sometimes sleep with thumb in mouth and index finger resting or rubbing on the inside corner of the eye.

Water people might always choose to sit in a corner with their backs to the wall, or on the edge of a seat, and find it hard to explain their feelings. Their eyes might be shifting around the room, avoiding close eye contact, or their eyes might gaze, look startled - full of fear; they might plaintively look for support.

Recognising Water characteristics in posture, gestures or in illnesses is one aspect, but what can we do to **balance the Water Element in general?**

10: a) A Look at Balancing Water in General

How can we encourage healing in the Element that itself contains healing capacity? The latter has been recognised by man in every culture since ancient times; Goddesses and figurines connected to Water cults have been found in south-east Europe dating back to 6000 BC. [21] Celtic pagan traditions share ancestry with Hindu India; in both cultures we find sacred sites built around stepped wells, healing baths and hot tanks. Later, temples or even Churches are associated with such wells.

Although one finds the like throughout all of India, my favourite spot is Ganeshpuri. It is a village north of Bombay, in the Tansa River Valley where such water tanks have been and are, used for both sacred, ritual bathing ceremonies as well as for the village bath. These 'tanks' are right next to a Shiva temple that is a step-down temple, where the symbol of Shiva (*lingam*) is bathed with the sacred waters naturally dripping from the ceiling. The temple walls and the air too, are dripping with moisture even in the dry season; the steps down into the tiny area are slippery and wet. It feels as though this holy place is actually built into a hot spring. Water, spiritual energy and fertility seem inseparably woven together to generate the feeling of potent energy.

Although we are familiar with the sprinkling of holy water in the churches, to sprinkle blessed water on our head in order to dissolve and clean out the stagnant energy blocks and impurities might be less familiar.

Even more strange appears to us the drinking of bath water of a holy statue (*murti*) or person. Yet this is exactly what is done in India after *Abishek*, a most beautiful sacred ceremony where statues are bathed with precious substances such as milk, honey, coconut water, oils and perfumed or pure water, under the incantation of V*edic mantras*. The ceremony is performed with such love, such devotion and with such unrivalled care that the bathing itself is not only an act of worship, but the worshipper itself seems to be transcended by it. The 'bath-water' is afterwards shared out amongst the worshippers to impart healing for body mind and soul.

This and many more practices are there to restore the quality of one's own Water Energy - be it from Indian temple tanks or holy rivers like the Ganges, or from sacred waters around the globe. E.g. France (Lourdes), Polish, Spanish, Scottish, Irish, and Cornish wells, all bear witness that water and sacred ritual have been linked for more than 5000 years.

Water is at times also considered to be the door to 'the Otherworld.' 'This 'Otherworld' seemed to have been thought of (not only) as 'another place', but also as a state of consciousness,' [22] a place infinitely more alive and beautiful than this world and bathed in light.

'When all is done, will you sail with me in Pridwen, my ship?
Will you come with me, to the silver-circled castle
at the back of the North Wind, where there is peace between the
stars and apple orchards grow?' [23]

Water also plays a major sacred part in other traditions from the American Indians to the Incas, to Africa and to Australia. Most might be familiar with the tradition of Roman Spas, whose legacy we still find all over Europe. Baths are taken in hot or cold mineral springs and/or the water is drunk to cure various illnesses. Often the same water maybe recommended for external or internal use, either because it is full of health-giving minerals, such as sodium, calcium, zinc and others, or because of its purity. Hydrotherapy often accompanies such cures, and for centuries has included: alternative hot and cold foot-baths, pack-wrapping in wet cloths or sheets, compresses for inflammation and to lower fevers, steam to inhale, hip-baths or even jets to rinse the bowels in colonic therapy. Today water births can be added to the list. Most of us will have experienced saunas, being sprayed or sluiced by water jets (many homes nowadays have Jacuzzis), or under-water-massage, be it by bubbles or human hands. Hardly anybody takes a bath anymore without adding aromatherapy oils of one kind of another.

Prominent figures like Priessnitz of Bohemia or the Dominican Dr Kneipp in Austria, or Dr Gully in England, built on the belief that water is capable of curing every disease 'by dissolving the diseased matter and enabling it to be expelled from the body.' [24]

Seawater is the last to have come within the field of modern medicine. I remember as an asthmatic child being taken to the special healing places, where salt water was run down walls built of twigs, about five meters high. The air was saturated with fine spray to be inhaled; the patient walked slowly and with measured steps and expanded chest for deep breathing around such 'Salinen', or even spending time sitting wrapped in blankets, within feet of the dripping water and reading. This process has the same nourishing effect for kidneys and lungs as living near the sea. Hot and cold baths of salt water, swimming, gentle exercise or relaxation in pools or the sea, even bathing in hot sulphur springs are all part of common experience today.

Other less 'watery' ways can be used to help the Water Energy of the body. As with the other elements, traditional ways of complementary medicine such as Acupuncture, Shiatsu, Massage etc. can be successfully used. To increase the flow and soften the character of Water Energy listening to music, dance and art therapy and all manner of slow exercises such as Tai Chi and slow Hatha Yoga can be recommended. Exercises that stretch the back of the trunk and legs are especially to be recommended. But equally and less straining is just sitting by a waterfall, listening and/or contemplating a still pond or a clear lake, listening to the sound of falling rain. Tuning into the lashing waves on a beach also helps to balance Water; it flushes out and dilutes the impurities of the emotional body.

To drink too much liquid though, overworks the kidneys and then they tend to tire easily. A person with swollen areas below the eyes is showing such fatigue; the kidneys cannot cope with the amount of water. It is even worse if the person drinks a lot of toxins and stimulants, such as alcohol or tea and coffee, which tend to colour the 'bags under the eyes' into dark rings; increasing dark areas signal severe illness. It would be good to eat a diet that does not put so many impurities in the body (that they need flushing out) so that the kidneys do not have to work so hard!

What then would be good to eat for a person with the main characteristics of Water? Foods are chosen here for their ability to enhance the functioning of the kidneys, such as beans and salty foods (small amounts stimulate their work); barley and buckwheat in terms of grain; all sea vegetables support the kidneys. Foods are also chosen for supplementing and regulating moisture. Illness caused by the Water Element is often connected to cold – thus warming food is essential to support the kidneys, such as ginger root (as spice, tea or vegetable), garlic, chilli, mustard seeds, coriander and cardamom seeds. Kidney energy is a limited resource, so to replenish its essence, dioscorea root is recommended, as are rehmannia root, black fungus and other mushrooms and the cornus fruit, all found in Chinese herbal shops.

It is especially relevant to conserve and manage our kidney energy because of their role as 'vaults in which the inheritance of the ancestors is stored.' [25]

TCM has it, that the amount of life energy available to us is connected to kidneys and their condition; we have been dealt an unidentifiable, but limited amount of it by fate, nature or God; we should look after it. If we mistreat it by eating the wrong diet (too many refined foods carrying chemical toxins, fat, cholesterol, too many salts etc). or use too much of that energy by leading a harmful lifestyle (excessive sex, too much stress, continued fear and excitement/shock), it will suffer! A dangerous lifestyle, abortions, misuse of drugs or abuse of our bodies in any way, will irreversibly deplete the Water Energy and an untimely death will follow.

The body is the servant of our spiritual growth, through the body alone the soul can learn in this school of life, through the body alone lies our ability to evolve, to grow towards greater understanding, to higher wisdom. Thus it is important to keep the amount of Water Energy in a steady and even flow; in fact it is said that the origin of Yoga is to prolong the body's life to fulfil our spiritual purpose. 'Understanding and protecting the body are acts of spiritual mastery.' [26]

Ways of extreme austerity (ascetics) are just as damaging - as are extreme pursuits of sensual pleasure; both misuse the body's resources, both damage the ancestral life energy. Hence Buddha's advice to follow the 'middle path'; balance is inherent in the Water Element. 'He who sees 'the waters' only as a colourless material liquid with certain physical properties will surely fail to know what that word really meant... He who... neglects or even despises the internal physical structure of water and does not bother to study its properties will equally miss the point.' [27]

10: b) Balancing Water on the Mental and Spiritual Plane

Water energy is especially activating the lower frontal lobes, where the sensory in put of taste is processed. Furthermore it triggers strong activity in the limbic brain, and the amygdala where fears originate, where traumatic memory has its core.

A person dominated by Water energy views the world through 'glasses tinted with fear.' Coming through from the limbic brain, it is almost a sister aspect to Earth; both are related to the ancient memory of the species, both are connected to physical survival. Where earth wants to build security, Water is not sure whether it is 'fight or flight.' However it is more inclined to do something about it 'although I might not know what.' Even though this might be strong and noticeable - or latent, in the unconscious, such a mind is constantly occupied with 'trying to find solutions.' Problem solving is top of the list and the mind does not rest until it found a solution it finds satisfying. It doesn't really matter whether it is an appropriate solution, but it 'is my solution' – and it may change any time. It is the right way, profession, idea, partner etc. now... but two years later there is another 'right solution.' When the water gauge sinks to a different level, solutions get challenged; it is difficult to hold on and so 'Water' drifts into the next issue.

Water contains 'the movement of life of the airy element and the gravity and consistency of the solid' [28] which makes it difficult for a Water person's mind to know where to go, what to do? With no clear direction it gets lost in its own fluidity. This seems nowhere more obvious than standing on a sheer cliff of any coast, when mist draws in, touching the land, erasing its contours and smudging the limit between sky and sea.

Such dissolving of boundaries confronts the mind of the Water person with its own greatest fear, which is to dissolve, to be extinct and meaningless. To balance such existential fear the Water person seeks to protect itself, by seeking to give meaning to their lives, by seeking constantly new jobs, friends, religions or explanations. It has constantly to justify to itself or others its thoughts, actions and beliefs. 'Someone somehow must have the answer!' must be able to give meaning to solve 'my puzzle' - (flight or fight) of running away - or running towards? Is there an answer?

In the Vedas, Agni the God of Fire is portrayed as the 'Son of the Waters'! [29] In the Chinese tradition, Fire and Water belong together like Yin and Yang. Amongst Celtic and Germanic traditions there is a celebration where the sun is reflected in a bowl of water, to symbolise just that.

The search of the Water person is for its completion, is striving to give form to the ancient awareness that Fire and Water belong together. He/she searches for the warmth of Fire, the confirmation of light, the experience of its opposite pole. In order to fulfil that dream, Water has to control himself; self-discipline is of prime importance. It has to set boundaries; classically speaking, these come from **Earth**. As a dam, Earth channels Water to flow towards its destiny; a disciplined life will channel Water's energies. Water needs to learn from Earth, to stay in one place, in one profession, in one relationship - then it can follow its dream. Its dream is to reach the ocean; there it can ascend to the light! Light (height) and darkness (depth) both need to be experienced as one entity. Water and Fire are essentially one. By embracing its opposite pole, Water can heal its ultimate confusion; realising life is simply One, the split into the duality of coming and going, of fear and security, of male and female, good and bad, is healed.

The fretting **mind of a Water person can be balanced** as soon as it discovers the divine unity of all; then fear and trauma can be released. There is no more fear!

No more fear!
There is no getting lost, for I am the direction;
There is no loss of purpose, for my life is its purpose;
There is no hunger and thirst, for life will feed me,
There is no sense of failure, for what needs, will be achieved;
There are no missed opportunities, in God's perfect time I am there.
What is the use of being afraid, if fear has no object?

Svetaketu, in one of the teaching stories in the Upanishads, can help us to understand. In his search to understand the nature of reality, he is told by his father to place a lump of salt in some water. The next day, of course, the salt is dissolved in the water; it lost its identity, permeating everything. Once a wave identifies with the ocean, individuality is lost, but totality is gained. What then is left to fear? There is nothing that is different, nothing to be afraid of; for 'That art thou', Svetaketu. [30]

How though, can Water get to the point where it can leave behind the fears and worries that shape the working of his mind? A practice suitable for Water is to focus especially on chanting divine songs; the chant is 'music for the ears'; as water flows, so does music! Chanting or making music nurtures water; the focus of prolonged and disciplined chanting/praying sets the boundaries that Water needs. Chanting with love and devotion keeps the focus on the goal which floods the heart with love, which, in turn gives security (the grounding Earth) and prepares surrender (undoing duality). The fire of devotion will warm the cold of fear. The focus on the chosen object of devotion will exclude other thoughts, will purify the mind of patterns of fear, trauma will melt away. So let the discipline of regular practice and the unconditional love of the divine, heal the worries of the Water person's mind, so he/she can arise above it.

There remains one very particular point to make: the activity that goes on in the mind influenced by Water energy is of a certain nature. It flows! Let us say the sensory input is a rose, yet the mind does not stay there, it flows of into memory lane: the rose reminds me of my mother's garden; she also grew peas; I wonder who tends that garden now, will they also grow roses... etc. etc. Of course we all suffer from this kind of mind, but the Water person even more so. One way to control this kind of mind is, to trace back the thoughts. Direct your focus to unravel the thought, sort of read the above backwards. This way, thoughts are traced to their source and eventually the mind will give up the habit.

Chapter Eleven: Balancing the Fire Element

ONE of the most well known images for 'the essence of Fire 'is that of Shiva Nataraj, God dancing surrounded by a ring of flames, creating the world out of sound and movement (vibration and energy). Yet he dances on a corpse; creation and destruction are one. Some see in the corpse, a demon - the dance of creation is a dance of transformation! While the activity goes on, Fire plays on the surface, purifying, in its core transforming.

Under the surface of our outer skin we find the tiniest blood vessels, they give us a rosy glow. That radiance has its roots deep within. From deep within the body, energy is supervised and held together by the heart. In many traditions the heart houses soul, houses awareness, our self-perception, and our higher moral and spiritual faculties. When we speak refer to the 'I', we point to the middle of the chest, the heart (re: heart chakra). The sense of 'I' is, in Indian thought, part of the mind, giving thoughts and perception a unique angle. From the mind in the heart, true communication happens, from here we shape our human identity, our personality; we shape how we see ourselves.

When the personality has a balanced Fire energy it shows in the posture. Remember: the two major Fire meridians flow from the upper frontal torso deep into the belly and resurfaces at the back inside of the legs (HT and HC). The other two, (Si/ TH) flow along the clavicle, down the shoulder blades and descend deep into the pelvis, resurfacing in the frontal inside of the legs. They run almost diagonally through the body, crossing deep inside the belly. If we imagine these meridians as the strings on a puppet pulled too tight, the body folds in the middle, appearing as though the legs are drawn up towards the chest, opening up the knees like an 'o.' Conversely when these meridians are too slack, the body appears as too loose, without substance, not holding together.

There are other simple ways to identify Fire imbalances: broken vessels on the skin, especially in the face, bluish coloured lips, nose and fingers. People might have the habit of crossing their arms over their chest, (like hugging oneself) or cupping their elbows while doing this (unknowingly holding core points of all Fire meridians). Furthermore people with Fire imbalances might rub the side of their neck (stimulating the meridians). Another observation is: people hold their left hand with their right, the right thumb in the left palm, rubbing the centre of the left palm, much like a pipe-smoker when crumbling their tobacco. (The palm is a vital point for the heart-protector, HC). Sometimes one sees people sucking their little fingers, like a baby would suck a thumb, subconsciously stimulating both main Fire meridians. Many gestures of devotion, such as folding the hands so that two palms (centre HC) are facing each other; greetings where the palms are touching, or even bowing the head to the heart (*chakra*), point towards the Fire energy.

Gestures such as beating the chest, crossing the arms in front of the chest to hide the heart (or indeed the opposite, such as opening the arms wide to embrace somebody, taking him/her to the heart) draw attention to the Fire energy. So does sitting with one leg crossing over the other. This common practise is not only restricting circulation but also the energy flow of all Fire meridians (HC, HT, SI and TH).

Emotional imbalances of the Fire Element shows in people who have a volatile, restless disposition, or on the other hand might suffer from overwhelming fatigue due to stress, shock, trauma or simple exhaustion. Constant need for attention or distraction, disturbed sleep, as well as total withdrawal from the world and fanaticism, are disturbances of the Fire Element.

What can we do in order to help balance the distortions observed in postures and gestures, in behaviour and illness? **How can we balance Fire Energy** so it warms without burning, gives light without blinding, is steady and tranquil without feeling bored, is responsive to what life gives without hunting after each opportunity. How can we entice Fire Energy to be its best: joyful, happy, content and celebrating life? William Wordsworth described the state beautifully:

'With an eye made quiet by the power of harmony, and the deep power of joy, see into the life of things.' [31]

There are as always the outside agents that can help, such as Acupuncturists, Shiatsu practitioners and all manner of therapists and energy workers, who might help us to re-educate our body energy. There is however much we can do ourselves.

11: a) A Look at Balancing Fire in General

Tai Chi has been recommended by cardiologists for patients who have or are threatened with heart disease; palpitations, angina or hypertension. Tai Chi is a gentle exercise that puts no strain on the heart, yet strengthens the circulation and enriches life energy; the same can be said for some forms of Yoga exercise, as well as the Makkaho exercises [32] advocated by Masunaga and Ohashi. Another home remedy worth mentioning might be that of rubbing your skin vigorously in the morning when you have your bath or shower, with a brush or hard sponge (*loofa*). Hot and cold alternative showers etc. mentioned in the section about the Water Element activate the circulation.

In the case of a too active Fire Energy, cooling water therapies should be considered. Water is not only the polarity of Fire, but the Chinese believe that such opposites always carry each other inside as the famous *Yin* and *Yang* symbol shows. A person with a fiery temperament is thus well advised to take up swimming, have cooling drinks, eat cooling food and live in an appropriate climate and learn such calming techniques as meditation.

The Air/Metal Element also has its part to play. Blood needs to be properly oxygenated to carry out its task thus breathing correctly is of vital importance. A fiery person would greatly benefit from the calming regeneration *pranayama* offers. Wood/Space Energy (i.e. a well functioning liver) also contributes, providing appropriate fuel; right amounts of nutrients. The Earth Element as the child of Fire has a special distinct influence. To have a good stable relationship, a home, caring about one's origins (family) are all 'grounding' for the Fire Energy.

Emotional stress has long been recognised for its effect on the heart and circulation. Hence businesses have stress councillors and stress release programs, occasionally even meditation groups built into their systems. The answer to caring for the heart often lies, though, simply **in a change of lifestyle.** A way should be found to remove the source of stress put on the heart and the other organ-systems of the Fire Element. The problems in the affected person's life need to be found and addressed. Switching to a different job might help, a different place to live, a different relationship to others or even to oneself. Self-hypnosis, Autogenics, Autosuggestion, Yoga, walking, painting, music, sports or swimming, anything that relaxes helps.

As we know, diet plays a major role in heart disease; i.e. the consumption of cholesterol, fatty foods, meats etc. are high risk factors and are often accompanied by a low intake of dietary fibre. Diets are never out of the news, since in the 60's heart disease had become one of the most common causes of 'untimely death.' As for supplementing the diet, depending on whether the Fire energy needs stimulating or cooling, such herbs as ginseng, lycii, rehmania, lily bulbs, poria root and carthamus flower, corn silk, honeysuckle etc. are recommended. A Nutritionist or herbalist should be consulted for more specific advice. [33]

As with all the elements, balancing food has two sides. A Fire energy that needs cooling should contain much cold food like salads and fresh fruit, whereas Fire energy that needs stimulating needs spicy and cooked, warming food, such as porridge, soups and stews. Now interestingly, Ayurveda approaches the subject in the reverse way. Accordingly cold foods need a long time to digest, thus they end up stimulating the fire of *Agni* or rot in the digestive system. To cool the fire energy we have to eat spicy food, which has quick bursts of fire; like a straw fire, they make you immediately sweat – which cools one down, provides the nutrients but no excess heat.

11: b) Balancing the Mental/Spiritual Level.

Where <u>Fire energy</u> is prominent (high frequency), when activity is high (or especially low/ feeble) in the Temporal and Occipital Lobes, vision and speech are important; Science think they have actually found a God-spot! On the inside of the Temporal lobe where divine vision is generated, feelings of 'a presence' arises. [34]

A 'fiery mind' thrives on external energetic input. If the mind does not get enough input and constant stimulation, such a mind can develop a violent, destructive, even self-destructive tendency. 'If there is nothing to burn, I burn myself;' 'if there is nobody to blame, I blame myself.' Their initial tendency is extremely outgoing – yet they easily turn 'to ashes.'

They often have an especially good (bad) longterm memory.

Their intense need to burn can be tempered by cooling fluid activities, such as swimming, listening to music or by controlled physical activity such as dancing, sports etc. Keeping 'cool' - detachment and dispassion come about by shift of focus.

The brain changes with learning! We just need to train it!

What can we say about the **influence of Fire energies on the mind.** If we watch the activities of such a mind, we will find it like fireworks; constantly throwing off sparks, filled with inspiration. Inspiration is followed by a short burst of trying to put ideas into practise - then the project is deemed complete or abundant. This relatively short cycle leaves Fire forever dissatisfied, looking for the next completion, searching for the next inspiration. Its path is littered with 'goodbyes.' But once something is truly completed, that Fire celebrates.

Most traditions celebrate such completed cycles; each birthday is completing a cycle, as is moving out of childhood; moving from womanhood into the phase of the wise crone. Completion acknowledges the furthest extension, fulfilment of the highest goal; a new process starts. When we are conscious of this completion, joy is celebrated with fireworks, candles and light. As outside, so inside.

> Let the heavens be glad before the Lord
> and let the earth rejoice,
> Let seas and all that is therein,
> cry out and make a noise
> let fields rejoice and everything that
> springs from the earth,
> then every tree shall sing
> with great joy before the Lord. (Psalm 96)

Our lives are made up of cycle after cycle. It means that completion constantly happens, even if we are not aware of it; every completion has a measure of joy with it; wave after wave of such joy makes up our lives – our life could be one long celebration – unfortunately we don't let it. On the contrary, in our hectic and superficial lives, we are haunted by incomplete cycles, incomplete dealings with others and ourselves, leaving unsolved problems. The latter are like these open wounds until we resolve them; until we complete them they will be problems that influence our body, mind and spirit. When life looks bleak and dark we need to call into our awareness where completion is needed. We need to focus on the problem that has to be solved and bring it to completion, so that it can be let go of, released from the body and mind, so that the light can rise again.

Many techniques are available to become aware of those issues that need completion. The ending will have to come, that is just as certain as one pulsation of the heart following another. Everything that has started needs an end; it is a cosmic law. Any action has consequences; any cause has an effect; every effect had a cause. Whatever we have started, however long ago, or unintended, it will seek its completion. When that is done, there will be joy. We need to trust this will happen. That trust, as well as that joy after having completed an experience - is the joy of being alive that lives in the heart. That joy comes from our hearts singing with the energy of love. This song of our heart carries that love to others, so that we can stand anywhere, and suddenly we become aware that some struggle has been completed. Joy and love follow swiftly. We might stand in the bus, or ride in a full train, stand in a filled schoolroom or a secluded garden and suddenly that love pours out and we realise - much to our own astonishment, 'that just now, I love all these strangers, I love the whole world.'

They say this happens out of grace; a veil is suddenly removed from our hearts so we can see our true nature. The more frequently that veil is removed and those waves of love flood us, the closer we are to a stage called bliss or *Ananda*. Bliss does not mean one goes around all day grinning like a clown; it is not even necessarily accompanied by great emotions; it is more an inner awareness of being secure in the totality. There is nothing apart from this All; it is being in harmony with all there is.

For that we need to listen to the quietness of our hearts, there we might sense the love in ourselves. For anybody seeking love - and who is not - it must be the most stunning revelation that love is not given to us from anybody; not from you, not from a husband or child, not from any agent outside ourselves. This love is in us! It is the nature of pure life energy, it is us; it flows through us, for us, to nourish us, to warm us and from us to give to others. We are the source of the love we need and the instrument of the love we give. Indian philosophy has it, that we are characterised by three qualities: Sat (existence) chid (consciousness) ananda (bliss, joy). We exist, we are aware, and we are joy. Not bad! Meditate on that!

To prepare for such deep meditations there are two useful ways I have come across. One is doing the right kind of exercise, like Yoga, Tai Chi or *Makkaho* exercises, to balance and quieten our body energy. Once that is done we become comfortable and stable to sit for Meditation. This is what Patanjali suggests as the third limb of his eight points for Yoga. Once we have achieved a stable posture, *asana*, start withdrawing the outer attention (there are many ways to do that) and focus inside. After some practise, we can contact the love inside us, and we will know that it is the power of love that has taken on 'my form'; it is love that loves through me! It is not the 'I' that loves.

There remains one factor to consider. The mind that is primarily influenced by Fire energy throws out thoughts at vast speed; thoughts appear disjointed: oh look - a car, a bird flies, my mother called, his trousers are too long... A lot of the 'sparks triggered,' are due to visual input, requiring an immediate expression - then they are gone. A frantically restless mind indeed! As everything seen will set the mind off - so closing the eyes is very helpful - but especially at the beginning that might be scary.

There is one particular practice that helps to tame such a mind. *Trātaka*, also called *trotana*: Gaze steadily without blinking at a small object; this might be a statue, a small dot, a circle, a spiral, a flame etc. It helps to preserve energy, to increase the power of concentration, decreases 'rajasic' energy; it activates subtle vision and increases visual power etc. [35] One is to stare at the object until the eyes water. The most common form is probably to practise on a flame. Make sure the room is draft free and place the flame about 1½ meters to 2 meters away from the eyes. It is best to use a flame from 'ghee', clarified butter, as the characteristics of the flame tend to affect the 'mood.' *Ghee* is sattvic, subtle and peaceful. Such flame is referred to as *Shiv*, (root of Shiva) or Parabrahma.

One of the benefits of this kind of practise is that one gains control over the involuntary muscles of the body (eyelids and respiration). The mind does not get completely steady without gaining control over involuntary muscles. Once one gains control over these two, other involuntary actions of the body are automatically controlled. According to Ayurveda, educating these *raja* components reduces *pitta*.

There is also another 'open eye meditation.' It starts with the awareness that 'all is Brahman.' Our eyes see, but the mind that sees does not get pulled into associating other thoughts with it; we simply know that all we see is Shiva. 'Our great masters tell us a very simple way. See the divine presence in the chirping of the birds, in the running of the brooks, in the cracking sound of dry leaves, in the summer forest. If we are able to discover the divine presence in these, and get absorbed in it, we disappear.' Only the experience remains. 'Experience without an experiencer is the reality.' [36] When we are able to experience the pulsating presence of divinity in this world, we practise open eye meditation. Established in this, we live meditation...

Chapter Twelve: Balancing the Air Element

AIR'S particular 'theme' is movement; a constant pulse moves the 'universe' from the furthest extension, gathering, taking all in and moving out again. The classical authority, the Nei Ching, talks frequently about this where outside turns to inside; for example air from outside gets gathered, sucked into the lungs, then taken as oxygen into the tiniest, deepest vessels in our body and after animating us, it journeys back. In fact the Nei Ching calls this vital function the animating spirit, or *PO*, [37] Recall how in the Judaeo-Christian tradition, God breathed life into the clay figure, changing it into the first man, (Adam); one could indeed say, we are the 'Breath of God.'

Another important insight into aspects of the Air/Metal Element comes from contemplating our skin. The skin is the outer periphery of the body. Its condition reveals how we literally 'hold ourselves together', how we deal with the 'onslaught' of the outside world. How do we choose what to take in, what to repel? We reject some things that we shouldn't have taken in and erupt in sores and spots, or even eczema! We tighten and tense the skin in an attempt to keep things in and literally 'crack up.' Do we feel stretched and exhausted from trying to contain what we have; letting no new experiences in, we try to stay the same, to stay forever young? Is our skin tired and wrinkled from all the action and demands that the outside world has made? Or do we look clear and adequate for our age because we react appropriately?

Furthermore our posture and our habits give insights into the state of our Air Element. To recall: the associated meridians are Lung (LU) and Large Intestines (LI). LI starts either side of the nostrils, runs along the crest of the shoulder bone to the hollow in front of the arm. In the hollow in front of the arm socket, LU starts. Then almost parallel, they run along the outer edge of the front of the upper body and along the outside back edge of the legs (a branch along the upper ridge of each arm to the thumb and index finger). If these lines were strings and they are either too tight or too loose, the puppeteer would not be pleased.

In the first instance the puppet would have drawn-up shoulders, arching forward with the head pulled down (similar to the person with characteristic Earth Energy). The arms would look tensed up, close to the body; the posture expressing 'a drawing inward', armoured to protect one's emotions and to keep others out. The legs would be tensed at the outside edge seemingly opening the knees. The feet point outwards, pulling away from the mid-line; an altogether hard, stiff, inflexible looking puppet, walking heavy but upright; with a top-heavy chest and a 'disconnected lower body.'

In the second case, with the meridian too slack, the person appears collapsed, sunken into herself. Such a person might constantly 'twiddle their thumbs' or stroke various parts of their face with the thumb and index finger. They might frequently sit with their elbow supported on the table, their head resting on the thumb that is tucked under the chin, and the index finger either resting or rubbing at the side of the nostrils. They might have the habit of pinching the side of the jawbone half way between chin and ear, pulling the skin. Smokers often rub the index finger and thumb against each other, in a circular motion or a picking or clicking of the nails of the two fingers. Some people twiddle their hair around the thumb and index finger. These 'little habits' look just like nervous distractions, yet they are subconscious work on the Air energy-network. Another example that comes to mind is the thumb sucking baby (and child). Could it be that it is a stimulation mechanism of the lung-meridian, to strengthen their breathing? There are many more of these outer manifestations of 'involuntary' stimulation; scratching and itching are obvious links.

Once we recognise that these habits, gestures and even postures are due to an imbalance in the Air/Metal Element, **what can we do about it**? Obviously many practises of complementary medicine can be drawn upon. But how can we help ourselves to a more balanced state?

12: a) Let's look at Balancing Air in General.

Balanced appropriately, this energy is constantly on the move, taking what the body needs to the centre and <u>leaving behind</u> what it does not need. If this function fails we need to find ways of restoring it. The solution is almost too obvious to mention and yet most of us forget it. I am talking about <u>breathing</u>. Most of us breathe shallowly and use only a small part of our full breathing potential: we deny ourselves the taking in of life energy or *Prana*. Why do we do it? Some would say, we are lazy! Others say, it is because we do not really want to be here on this earth, in this incarnation, in this family! Others still say – our traumatic birth experience makes us fear life; and still others imagine we feel threatened by the subconscious memory of previous death. Be that as it may – the fact remains - we are conscious energy! The way we are born, the where and why, are choices of the consciousness entity we are, and we can change it! We can learn how to breathe properly, leaving the negativity behind and choose not to hinder the Movement of life!

For that, we need to be aware and discriminate between what is **good** for us, and what is not, even if it might be pleasant! The first step is to become aware of the breath, from moment to moment. Be aware of it when you walk to work, when you watch television, when you brush your teeth or sit on the toilet. Follow with your attention, the flow of the air as it touches your nostrils, feel the temperature change in your nose. Become aware how it fills your lungs, how your chest expands, how your diaphragm lifts and relaxes. Now, do it now, while you read. - Watch your breath, feel your body relaxing with it; focus on the out- breath, a long, long conscious out-breath. Let it go! Don't hold on to it, it has done its job, let it go! All of it!

When all the used 'stuff' is gone you are free to take in the 'new', the fresh energy of life! Keep watching your breath!

'The moment you breathe deeply, more energy becomes available in your body. Where there is energy flow, there is motion. You can experience this motion in many different ways: as a sensation like tingling and numbness or vibration, or as emotion such as sadness, joy or anger. So therefore, if you are afraid to feel, one of the most effective ways to keep yourself from feeling is to control your breath. ' [38]

Conscious breathing reveals, there are distinct turning points in breathing, once at the point of fullest inhalation, the second at the point of complete exhalation. Each time the furthest perimeter is reached, you can neither stay at the point of greatest expansion - nor at the point of greatest contraction; furthermore you can decide to turn deliberately or life turns it for you. The teaching here is twofold. From time to time we need to stop, think and decide on what to leave behind! If we neglect this shifting process, life will do it for us, it never stays still, it will turn us. We have the choice of moving with live or being moved by life - or whether we are moved as a pawn in other peoples games even. So 'Letting go' has a very positive aspect, it empowers us to make our own decisions and choices, to take charge of our lives. Leaving the unwanted - we are ready to create our own destiny; we are pure creative life energy.

Both the process of breath and that of elimination (Large Intestines) have repetition as one of their characteristics; imbalances here therefore might suggest focusing attention on the routines in a person's life. Listen to a smoker: "every time I have a drink, I crave for a cigarette!" We have acquired so many habits: from Sunday lunch to walking the dog at 7am, from the drink after work - to the job itself. Our life revolves around such routines that keep us from enjoying the moment. We have even habitual expectations and desires, needing success, craving approval, demanding attention; are these not simply addictions? Do you still eat (talk, tell stories, read) the same things now, as you did twenty years ago? Are you still reacting in ways you learned as a five-year-old? Do you still cling to old grief, surplus attitudes or relationships?

One of the biggest, most difficult issues is to let go of the image we have of ourselves, of our cleverness and superiority, or on the other hand our smallness, unworthiness, timidity and loneliness; our individuality, our sense of isolation and separateness. The older we are, the more roles and identities we have acquired. To let go of all this ballast and to see through it, to who we really are, is like being stripped naked of all social, psychological and philosophical conditioning. Finally we are asked to let go of our body identification (more later on).

Air energy seriously asks - look at the turning point! It might be NOW. Let go, let go of the old and useless and turn to the Now! Maybe it is time to clean out a cupboard, desk, or loft - maybe clothes, books etc. need to be given away. Move on; move into the now, as each breath is happening in the now. You can encourage this by swimming, doing Hatha Yoga, Tai Chi or Qi Quong etc. On the other hand if there is too little Metal Energy, more focus, more routine and self-discipline might be asked for.

In the Chen-Ko Cycle, Fire too has an important relationship with Metal/Air. The Nei Ching says, 'when people are hurt through extreme heat of summer they will get intermittent fever in fall.' [39] We know that Fire 'eats' Metal/Air; contemplating this, we can easily see the connections in the world around us, but also in our physiology. Dry heat will parch the lungs, the body cannot process dry air and the villi (little hair-like fingers) that moisten the air, when dried up, make it easy for bacteria to invade. Dry heat dehydrates the body internally and makes skin shrivel. Heat and dryness damages Metal/Air energy, literally and metaphorically. Emotions such as passionate love, a passion for sport or dangerous games, even a passionate attachment to a job can challenge Metal/Air to self-destruction. On the other end of the scale, a passionate love might entice somebody out of their rut. It is all in the balance!

To strengthen and/or harmonise Metal/Air Energy, we look for food that will strengthen and/or clear the Lungs and the Large Intestines, thus free the flow of *Qi*. Food helps that will moisturise air passages and intestines or conversely depress humidity if there is excess in either of these. In general we should eat food that grows locally, in this case it is also recommended to eat food, that ripens in the autumn and that grows in temperate climates. A range of vegetables such as beans, artichoke, beets, potatoes, spinach, watercress, seaweed and tomatoes are said to moisturise, and so do nuts and sea-foods. Onions, peppers, fennel, cabbage, kale and cauliflower, carrots and mushrooms as well as almonds, sesame seed, brown rice and all fibrous foods help with decongestion. Red meat, dairy products and fried food are said to clog the system. Grapefruit, pears, oranges and especially orange peel, fresh ginger and glehnia- root are recommended to aid digestion. Astralagus, ginseng, radishes of all sorts are stimulating to the Lung-organ-network, as are tangerines (promote expectoration), water chestnut, grapes, apples, pears, (lemons, mangoes, melons), blueberries, and strawberries are all thought to be beneficial for the tendencies of imbalance in the Metal/Air Element.

We understood that we need give up many issues and roles that have become surplus, otherwise they become blocks hindering the life energy to flow through us freely. How do we know what to give up - what not? This brings us straight to our mind; it has an in-built tendency to be attached to what is mine and wants to keep it! The more attracted our senses get to the many objects (and ideas) in life like money, food, beauty, time or even energy, the more our mind holds on – and feeds the ego with it! We need certain foods, certain people, money etc., but are these so important, that they control us? That is the big issue at stake here, so to solve it, we need to cultivate a core 'Air aspect' which is: **discrimination**. This is an important wisdom-tool that we have to learn, if we want to walk into health and wholeness. This brings us right to looking into the more **mental and spiritual level.**

(12: b) Mental and Spiritual Level

How can we train our ability to discriminate? First we need to be aware what our sense actually do, and then leave them at what they can do best: to see, to hear, to touch... *without* getting the mind involved; without getting the mind attached to what they see and how they like or dislike this! I.e. we need to learn to see without pulling the mental file out which says: I like what I see and I want it! To see without the desire to possess; to hear a song without needing to buy the record. To taste the food and enjoy it, or the wine, or the air without wanting to eat or drink it for the rest of your life. That sounds easy; but how about the women whose touch we crave; the man whose smile we want to see 'for the rest of our life'? How about the house we want to own, the garden we want to plant? Our mind gets involved and attached to all sense impressions, like the monkey to his food! We all have such patterns as part of our personality, but to balance ourselves, we need to re-examine these!

Where Air energy is dominant, (or especially slack) it shows in those areas of the brain where touch and communication is processed; noteworthy activity is to be observed in two parts, the unemotional frontal cortex, (abstract thinking) and the posterior part of the Frontal and Parietal Lobe. Air's sharp and penetrating intellect affects the former; it is tremendously valuable in gathering, organising and storing factual knowledge. With it comes a great skill for creativity in problem solving! Such a mind habitually inquires: how something works, why this is like that? Can it be done better in a different way? Such people can be like a library, or the typical intellectual or technical wizard, yet the person rarely lets the knowledge affect her. People like that flourish in today's technical society. There might come a point where such a person sees that the world our senses perceive is in fact 'unreal,' (as modern scientists have discovered). Which then either will 'pull the carpet from under their feet'... or they will delve deep to 'discriminate between the true and the false... (and come to a firm conviction about the underlying reality. This aids the discovery of 'what I am' and 'what I am not' and produces joy when letting go of 'what I am not', the spiritual goal for Air energy.

It is obvious that such a mind could best be disciplined by study; regular study of any ancient scripture is an effective way of keeping such a mind under control. It becomes a powerful tool on the path of knowledge, *JnanaYoga*. On the path of knowledge the mind is given an alternative field for occupation. 'It is in the nature of the mind to entertain thoughts... Therefore it is enjoyed in all the Yogas, that the mind should be soaked some way or other with an idea greater, nobler and more divine than sense objects. Unless we train the mind to revel in a subtler and more divine field, it cannot redeem itself from the ordinary pursuits... therefore a mind basking in the contemplation of the all pervading consciousness awareness... can successfully detach itself from sense objects... the more we gain control over the mind... the more will it become equanimous, peaceful and serene...'[40]

Such calmness of the mind is supreme goal of Yoga. Once we discover its joy, the dogmatic intellectual activity will be a thing of the past, it will be balanced by more accepting softer, emotional aspects; it will acknowledge impermanence and vulnerability, and foster compassion and loving-kindness to others. As it says in the poem:

The impossible mind!

For understanding Him, mind is a useless tool
Bound by its limits it makes us into a fool.
Whatever we think results from what we've sown,
Thoughts move only from known to known;
Trapped within, how to reach the Unknown?
Striving to understand, mind creates its own goal
Thoughts creating God – cannot go beyond my soul.
Conditioning must go, simply treat it as sport,
No body, no mind can understand the Lord;
- Without thinking we've a chance - of sorts.
The silent mind does not seek to understand,
Yet, it might be the womb that serves the end!
The mind must be still, only then is it free
Passive, receptive, innocent let it be!
Once pure, with no movement - it may see!

Chapter Thirteen: Balancing the Space/Wood Element

PICTURE a slice of freshly cut tree trunk; its colour rich golden green, still dripping wet with the moisture of each cut cell; revealing an inner pattern that seems to radiate from the centre outwards. Each ring is clearly distinguishable; on close inspection each cell can be made out, with its simple structured walls whose strength builds the whole tree.

To me this symbolises a balanced Wood energy. Let us contemplate it. Bold rings show the new growth, added spring in a steady natural rhythm. Dormant withdrawn periods alternate with a time of rapid growth, stretching from the centre in ever widening circles. Each cell is structured in a controlled shape, governed by its own inherent biological laws that dictate the growth pattern in harmony with the adjacent cells. Each cell is filled with sap, rich nutritious moisture that rose up from the root travelling to the branches and leaves, expanding to all sides and up through the leaves seemingly reaching to the sky. Each cell is unique. Despite its blueprint each has its own unique character, like each leaf has its unique identity. Even though it grows uniquely, forever creative balanced Wood Energy is aware of its interconnectedness. It is confident in its conviction, yet in tune with the repetitive cycles of organisms.

This image holds true for Space too; Space holds eternal laws according to which all planets move, according to which all life moves; in tune with the pulse of creation it expands and contracts. These laws keep harmony amongst all - Space does not collapse, planets do not collide and lettuces don't grow cherries. Each part of creation has a unique blueprint according to which its *dharma* unfolds. All are held by a supreme intelligence that is forever going forward, withholding nothing.

There is a beautiful story about the Indian God Indra, the greatest of the Hindu pantheon. It tells about Indra and his battle with Vritra, the one that resists and withholds. Vritra takes on the form of a cloud and holds back the life giving rains. It resulted in gloom and doom on the earth, there was only depression, sadness and darkness; there was no growth neither of plants nor human life. Indra decided to help the world. He drank three lakes of nectar, and thus armed, tackled Vritra, striking him with a thunderbolt in his back and in his face with a pointed dagger. When he had killed the demon, water burst from the clouds and from springs on earth and immediately growth started, the plains and fields started to bloom everywhere, trees started to sprout, light and joy was there again accompanying life and growth.

Withholding is - as can be seen, the greatest enemy of growth. As the rain of the cloud, the sap in Wood so is the life energy, the Liver energy in the body. As we can see from the above story, one way to ensure its proper working is to make available plenty of Water Energy. Growth, expansion needs the fluidity of the Water energy. Regular, even expansion (as in the rings of a tree), are rare in human terms. We usually grow more erratic, things happen we react, and frequently not very appropriate. Life's influences come, distort our patters and imbalances appear. Why? Because we get so involved! We aim to go in a certain reaction, something happens and we get confused proceeding this way and that; we need to take control over a certain situation and we over-control; we need to reach out and we over-expand. Because we loose sight of the overall picture, we loose our sense of balance, the rising sap gets blocked and frustration and anger distorts our being.

We can observe these distortion in the posture. Remember that the energy pathways for Wood/Space are those of the liver- and gall bladder meridians. The former rises from the big toe along the inside of the chin-bone, through the middle of the inner thigh. The latter descends from the temples along the side of the neck, trunk and legs literally along the side of the whole body. If we exaggerate and think of these lines as planks, then a picture arises of a man being held between two wooden planks. If these planks are contracted and squeezed together too hard, the body itself will be squeezed between those two planks. He or she will look inflexible, with stiff legs and a 'wooden gait.'

On the other hand if there is no support from the wooden planks on either side of the body, both (GB, LV) meridians are loose and slack without energy, then there is nothing to hold the body up. Sagging and floppy it might oscillate from side to side, without the strength to hold it up. As a consequence some such people might not to be able to walk in a straight line. They always seem to bump into the person walking next to them. This is not so just for the body, they mentally sway from side to side, without direction, without purpose (like a tree in the wind). Some people with these imbalances might hold their heads to one side or craning their necks, straining out of the tight vice. Some might stand with their hands habitually pressed onto or resting on the hips. Some might habitually rub their flank, or rub the 'seams of unseen trousers' in an attempt to ease the strain in GB. A serious imbalances shows in the eyes; people who are cross-eyed, or where the right eye looks to the right, the left eye to the left, have problems in Wood energy.

Our feet usually also give clues about a state of our energy. If a person has a big toe overlapping the second toe, it is not only to be put down to 'small shoes', but it maybe that the liver energy (meridian endpoint) is overpowering the Earth energy (second toe - stomach meridian). The gall bladder meridian runs across the top of the foot to the fourth toe. Not only have people often bunions on this toe (why?) but a look at their shoes might reveal that the outside of the shoe is especially worn just along the outside rim of the foot. Could it be that the person rests with most of their weight on the outer side of the foot, along the gall bladder and bladder meridians; again a typical wood imbalance? If the shoes reveal that the toe area is more worn than other parts it usually means that the liver energy is excessive. [41]

So, once we have observed and found in these postures, habits or gestures, what can we do to redress it?

13: a) Let's look at balancing Space in General:
Well, as with the other Elements, there are various ways of getting help from Acupuncture, Shiatsu, Kinesiology etc. But the very character of Wood/Space is permanent activity, such a person is less likely to want help from others, but more inclined to help him/herself. Having a larger perspective than most, such a person does not only 'see the problem', but also looks for 'a plan' to put things right. Such independents such quality of leadership is inherent in the 'Space person.'

As this energy field is connected to tendons and ligaments which make movement possible, the obvious advice is to do exercises: Yoga, Martial Arts, Qi Quong, Tai Chi, even walking! Any form of Self-Healing provides the feeling of 'doing something' and of 'control.' Do-it-yourself books fill the shelves of bookshops. This ever-increasing, popular industry is not without danger. Most dangers come from our mind leading us astray; pride, anger and desires colouring our analysis - we see what we want to see, we cure what we want to cure! There is nothing wrong with this 'placebo-effect', but the danger lies doing the wrong things, for the wrong reasons, for the sake of our ego.

One method I have come across pretty much excludes this. The Tibetan way of Self-Healing introduced by Lama Gangchen Rinpoche, called *Ngal-So* relaxes body and mind completely; *Ngal* refers to relative truth, while *So* refers to absolute truth; *Ngal* also means darkness, *So* means light (much like the Sanskrit: *Gu-ru*). [42] Here like in all Buddhists thought, good health is a matter of creating good circumstances in the mind. The healing process thus includes creating good thoughts and shifting from ordinary perception, relative truth to absolute truth.

If we experience physical pain, that is relative truth, which is experienced by the ordinary mind. On the absolute level 'I' know it is merely play of energies, and from the point of the all-pervading witness consciousness that expresses through these energies, 'I' put the pain there, so 'I' (the larger impersonal all-pervading I), can remove it. Ngal-So helps to focus on this wider perspective through an ancient praxis that integrates colour therapy, sound therapy, therapy to open blockages using gestures, syllables and symbols, as well as visualisations and breathing.

And there is of course, as we have mentioned in the other sections, the area of food. Food specifically beneficial for balancing the Wood energy should be chosen for its ability to help distribute nutrients and blood, to activate and circulate *Qi* and for its ability to replenish blood and moisture.

So food with a stimulating as well as enriching character, such as sweet, sour, juicy and astringent food, is looked for. Nuts such as pine nuts, almonds, sesame and chestnuts are recommended. Honey is advised as a sweetener; vegetables are suggested such as leeks, carrots, spinach, beets, Chinese cabbage and watercress; fruits such as dates, cherries, blackberries and strawberries are recommended, as well as apples, pears, bananas, olives etc.; and of course all manor of beans, rice, sea foods etc. It is as well to keep in mind that foods should be chosen carefully, in accordance with the season, and within the latitude in which one lives, yet much more detailed advice is needed than can be given here. [43]

Wood/Space energy is creativity par excellence; for this, other elements are roped in - easy, as Space contains them all. Just as we take paint, water and paper and create a picture, we take words, ideas, a pen and paper and create a poem or write a book. We take food, water, thoughts, feelings and impressions and constantly create ourselves. All that is alive partakes in this process, constantly procreating or co-creating. When this urge to create is frustrated, energy gets blocked and imbalances and illnesses result. Just think of the mental pain over infertility of a couple that desires a child; or the flare of anger over a burnt meal; of the mental agony and dissatisfaction over spoilt plans for a certain lifestyle. Think of the resulting irritability because 'I cannot go to a certain concert because I lack the money', or the irritation of not finding the right words to express oneself, or the impatience that one's arthritic joints will not allow one to go 'just anywhere.'

As the concept of homeopathy teaches us - like can be cured with like. The imbalances of Wood/Space energy arising out of frustrated creativity might be healed by freeing creative energy, letting it flow into another branch, another direction. To find new and different ways of being creative might thus help to balance Wood energy. Many projects of art therapy can show the success of this. Even severely handicapped people found great fulfilment and improvement by getting involved in various creative arts, from dance therapy to painting, making pottery, writing poems etc. To channel creative energy into a new direction (if one is blocked off) is thus an intrinsic way to heal Wood energy, even on a very physical level. We all have heard stories where a couple tried in vain to have a child, but as soon as they have adopted a child, the mother gets pregnant; life energy is freed. To become creative is a truly profound way to free Wood energy, but let us go even deeper.

Wood/Space can be creative, because it has the potential already in itself; the unfoldment is merely an expression of what is there. If there are no hurdles put up, without interference - things will evolve according to their intrinsic possibility, according to their own nature, their integrity, their purpose, or as the old sages would say, their *dharma*. To live according to one's *dharma* will then automatically lead to the right unfoldment; what is meant to happen, will happen! The acorn has the potential of the tree, when nothing is put in its way it will become an oak tree. It is not what we add to life that is important, but what we don't add! Contemplating this makes it clear that Wood/Space energy can be balanced simply by living the right *dharma*. It is easy to see the *dharma* of the acorn, 'the tree is treeing', that is its 'suchness', yet what is our purpose? To search for such purpose of one's life is the balancing issue that will affect the Wood/Space energy. Finding the answer to the ultimate question of 'What am I here for?' includes the right *dharma* i.e. 'how do I live it?' Once we are established in this level of awareness and live in it, with total integrity, the highest potential of every living Being unfolds; it is the legacy of space that propels us beyond even space (recall the three upper Chakras).

And yes, like in a helix, we come to this point on various levels. It sounds completely mad to think that by doing some exercises, changing one's diet and thinking about the purpose of life, gallstones, arthritis or a choleric temper can be influenced. Yet masses of disillusioned and depressed people suffer from these states, because they have not addressed this ultimate question; they can see no purpose to their lives and subsequently no joy. The acid of frustration eats at them.

Practising the above will change energy! It will benefit you. From the level where we experience life normally with all its suffering and insecurity, there are steps on the way to answer this ultimate question. One method is to ask ourselves, any time we experience discomfort in body and mind 'what is this saying to me?' and once we understood, then we ask: 'what can I do about it?' Contemplate these, your inner wisdom will reveal the answers. In the stillness of meditation you will find solutions. The stillness also prevents you from being fooled by your own mind, i.e. producing 'wild, useless shoots.' Become a witness of the activities of your own mind and body; observe and take charge of your life. Nothing is an accident; we experience what we need to experience. What is it I need to experience? What have I always wanted to do and why? If something really appeals to me, should I do it, but why? Is this the divine will carrying me into a certain direction? Does the pattern of my life's experience reveal a certain direction, my truth? my path? This practice will lay down the fear of having wasted your life and save you from the ultimate frustration of being helpless in acting out our true purpose.

Once the quest has revealed what we need to know, then it is in the nature of Wood/Space to act upon it. This action will affect others, this energy field gets involved with others, others to create for, work with or on the highest level – to serve! It cannot stay in contemplation of its own truth forever and withhold its energy, it has to share it, come out and apply it to life, to others.

Just as a true painter does not just paint pictures secretly in a back room, but has the pictures shown to others, exhibited, vented under the public eye, and eventually let go, sold. Music has not just to be written down, or heard in one's own ears, but to be played with instruments, performed in concerts etc.

We are all familiar with the painted faces of American Indians; they were originally not primarily to frighten the enemy, or even less to hide behind, quite the opposite. The painted faces used in ceremonies as well as wars were showing the beauty and the achievement, the identity of the individual soul. The design and colour was chosen to express the individual's inner truth, or medicine. The painted face is a way of self-expression. It is an expression of who and what the wearer truly is - not what we on the outside perceive him to be. It allows others to see, and in a way opens up their reactions to the truth of the wearer; the wearer offers his real Self to be relied on, to be used by others.

Wood/Space energy rises from within and spreads outward, on different levels. On the level of the physical body, the liver and gall bladder spread energy throughout the body. On the emotional level the anger and frustrations that rise, can be felt right into our toes. On a soul level, awareness of purpose is carried into interaction with the world; it is why we are here, why the Soul choose a body to incarnate.

13: b) A Look at the More Mental and Spiritual Level

Especially with this Element it is nearly impossible to separate the physical and the spiritual, as we have seen. Where Space energy is especially influencing the brain activity, there might be unusually more (or less) activity in the Parietal Lobes in the areas that deal with spatial awareness, which does actually more than that, it carves out a personal space frame in which we act; they are egocentric! From here personal space is built, growing into space beyond immediate knowledge eventually to infinite space. Furthermore the hippocampus seems to be an important meeting point between personal memories, spatial awareness and even the mechanics of 'paying attention;' all these are central to consciousness. They are involved in 'finding one's way around - even metaphorically.'

As Space is also associated with Sound, there is of course poignant activity in the area of sound; people tend to be active listeners to - (or deny) - their inner 'tune', tend to be either introvert (inner scientists/ mystics etc).

But then the Space energy field is less about the bodily side of things; it is more subtle than that. Fittingly, its creative aspect works especially with the harmonising peaceful nature of energy, which in Yoga philosophy is called *sattva*. It is described as 'the quality of love and life, the higher or spiritual force that allows us to evolve in consciousness. It imparts *dharmic* virtues of faith, honesty, self-control, modesty and truthfulness.' [44] Spiritual traditions of all shades emphasis the need to develop these qualities. *Sattva* itself is the state of balance, that positive field of harmoniously working together, that makes healing happen.

In Yoga, two aspects of this are important: to evolve we need to develop *sattva* - meaning to purify body and mind from all its damaging patterns and habits. But then we need to transcend even *sattva* - leaving manifesting energies behind all together and ascend to the realms of pure existence, of consciousness.

In order to develop **sattvic energy we need to control the senses and control and purify the mind; and these need to be supported by right diet!**

Anyone with spiritual aspirations should eat fruit, especially fresh and sweet fruit; all vegetables - yet not too much onion and garlic; all grains; beans in moderation except mung, aduki and tofu. Nuts and seeds; plant based oils and ghee; dairy products from happy cows (but no hard and mouldy cheeses), raw sugars and honey; sweet spices such as cinnamon, cardamom, fennel, turmeric etc.; herbal teas, water and fruit juices - and most of all, food prepared with love. As you can see **it excludes** all animal fat and meats, fish, eggs – all artificial, processed, canned and pre-packed food, fried food of all types, white flour and white sugar/artificial sweeteners. It excludes all stimulants: alcohol, tobacco drugs and artificial beverages, irradiated and micro-waved foods, genetically engineered foods and food eaten in a disturbed environment and eaten too quickly. 45

Physical purification is practised through *pranayama* (breath control) and through purifying the five *pranas*, (mentioned previously) which include regular cleansing of the bowels possibly with using appropriate herbs (see Yoga and Ayurveda). There are also special yogic techniques for purifying the nose (*neti*) the abdomen (*nauli*).

Of course the most important is mental purification which comes from control of the senses (*pratyahara*), meaning to gain mastery over external influences. We talked previously about being in charge of what we take in through our senses. This goes far beyond the intake of food or chemicals (preservatives and pollutants). It is a question of what we feed to our mind. Most of us suffer from sensory overload, i.e. constant bombardment by TV, radio, computers, newspapers, even books!

We are aware of junk food, but are we aware of junk- impressions? To foster *sattva* energy it helps to give yourself 'time out' each day. Sit quietly... even block the input by using the Yoni mudra - (blocking eyes, ears, nose and mouth!); sit without taking in impressions: look - seeing; to hear without listening etc. Or gaze at the sky, the sea etc... allowing only a uniform input. Anyway you get the gist!

Lastly we come to the control of the mind. When the 'Space- mind' is unbalanced, its plagued by creativity without structure; this is mental chaos! There are herbs which help to calm the mind such as nutmeg, passion flower, kava kava etc.

But mainly such a mind needs to control and structure thoughts, which brings us back to the two main aspects we met throughout: **Meditation and living according to one's *dharma*.** They are mutually supportive. Contrary to common belief, meditation is not cutting off from the world, but it is gathering the energy from centre of our being to be able to act in the world according to the right *dharma*. If we do not know the right action, nor have the energy to act upon it, what is there we can give to the world? If I have nothing, I can give nothing. To give oneself, one has have found oneself. To spread love and wisdom, peace and kindness - the sattvic qualities of the Space Element - we have to have them first ourselves. Otherwise we act inadequately and inappropriately: we shout at our children when they really need help. We give expensive presents instead of a caring word. We hide behind jokes when we want to ask for solace. We even kill, when we really are shouting for help.

A Space mind cannot only be chaotic, but it also can be 'lost in Space.' When such people sit for meditation, they quickly get into a nice comfortable dozy space. They mistake this for a highly alert, awareness; they are inclined to rest there; their mind has neither the energy nor the wisdom that it needs to apply awareness. Such a mind might benefit from taking some herbs to build strength of mind (intelligence and awareness), such as ashwaganda

(Winter cherry, an Indian equivalent of Ginseng), lotus seeds, Shatavari, (again a rejuvenation herb, especially for women), or Haritaki which is sacred to Shiva (Hara), imparting his energy of pure awareness. [46]

As for spiritual practice, it might help such a mind to focus on a revered person or object. Devotion to God, Guru or a murti (statue) might tie down such mind.

Before Meditation, place one of those, or the Divine Mother (Creativity itself) or the Divine Father (Shiva the Lord of Yogis) or... or... in your heart.

A more developed mind that has a capacity for abstraction might explore the nature of truth, the immortal changeless Self, simply the purity of NOW or the divine Lord of All who has no attributes or qualifications – who is simply THAT.

Summer night
The night sky sparkles, the Lord of Space
Reveals his most glamorous face,
More stars and pulsars whiz through his veins,
Then our earth has sand, or grains
Black holes tear at passing galaxies
Digesting planets - as so many fallacies.
Suns burn like beating hearts,
Millions of explosions send forth parts
Nothing exist outside of my Lord,
No snake slithers, no worm comes forward
No eagle flies – no man is born
Without your grace, oh Lord of Space.*
And yet – this Lord is neither
man nor woman - containing either.
He is no concept or idea, fits no rule,
Not of religion nor philosophical school.
This Lord is simply That –
Pure existence is where he's at.
How does That, know 'little me'?
Because He alone can Be
He is within me as Me
As I am within Him as Him
As Him, I am the bug, tiger, whale and rook
I am the daisy, oak, weed and spud
I am the Lord of the Universe,
- am planets, stars and galaxies,
- am suns and million moons
- am vast space; pulsing in his tune:
I am
I am
I am
- and yet I disappear, when I am born.

Chapter Fourteen: Conclusion

WE BEGAN the exploration about the Five Elements, by establishing their source in the indescribable One, Energy that unfolds into three types (inert, kinetics, harmony) and that these combine into five energy fields. We researched into these fields, their qualities, their gifts, their effects on our lives and bodies, their imbalances and how to redress them in order to bring them into harmony within themselves and amongst each other. From that harmony, they return back to the One from which they originated.

In the context of the human experience this means, that the perspective of the plurality in which we normally live, changes into the realisation of the Oneness; this Oneness behind all existence, is the Divine Totality

Western society has laid great emphasis on 'being an Individual', on 'standing out from the masses'! This very 'achievement' cuts us off, isolates us from the awareness of our true nature, which is embedded in the whole of all that exists, whatever we call it: 'being one with God', interdependence, the Web of Wicca or, or, or!

As the world appears to our senses, each item, including ourselves – stands out; we are convinced we are separate, limited by our skin, imprisoned in our character. How often have you heard 'I can't be different - that's the way I am.'

And yet it is the fundamental law of nature that everything changes. Being alive is constantly changing; imagine you were a blood cell in your body; you have a life span; a function, you reproduce yourself, you do a job, you travel through the veins, you live and you die - all as part of this body. In the same way, we as people are part of one divine organism, the body of the universe, the body of God! Within this, as expression of this, we have a life span, a task, etc. The 'blood cell 'could not do the function as a muscle cell, or a liver cell; similarly we are 'individual', special, yet at the same time the totality, just as a drop of water is still water.

We have to shift our mental attitude, our perception to see that we are part of 'IT.' We are the perfect part of the larger whole that is life! Take this one step further... and you will realise that you are not the body but a manifestation of the entire 'Being'; WE are the world! Without us - the world does not exist!

'Every subatomic interaction consists of annihilation of the original particle and the creation of new subatomic particles. The subatomic world is a continual dance of creation and annihilation, of mass changing into energy and energy changing into mass. Transient forms sparkle in and out of existence, creating a never-ending, forever newly created reality.' [47] **What an enormous chance to recreate ourselves! We can - because we are IT!**

As soon as we identify with the body, we return to a insular (skin-tight) identity - and yet, anything we do, or think, anything that happens to us, even illness, drought, disaster and war, are part of a gigantic n-th dimensional network of life energy. We are no more separate from our neighbour, from our family, from you, or the elephant in Africa than the smell of the rose from the flower. Can you separate the warmth of sunlight from the sun? Can you separate the wetness from water?

As the One, we share one unchangeable essence, as the individual body we are permanent change. Both aspects are true.

We might even understand this, but knowledge gathered only in the head is like a big library - it stores books but they do little else but gather dust. Knowledge becomes effective when it sinks into our Being. One of the people who describe this well is Mark Twain in his book 'Life on the Mississippi.' He writes about the early days of steam boat travel and his apprenticeship to Horax Bixby, the riverboat pilot, who teaches him the science of navigating this mighty river; the river takes on meaning beyond that of a mere body of water:

> 'At the end of what seemed a tedious while, I had managed to pack my head full of islands, towns, bars, 'points' and bends... in as much as I could shut my eyes and reel of a good long string of these names... I began to feel that I could take a boat down to New Orleans... (It was not long) before Mr. Bixby would think of something (to put me into place). "My boy, you have got to know the shape of the river perfectly."
>
> "Do you mean to say, that I've got to know all the million trifling variations of shapes in the banks of this interminable river... "
>
> "You got to know them better than any man ever did know the shapes of the halls in his own house... and in a pitch dark night (and in) a starlight night... Then there is your grey mist (and) different kinds of moonlight..."
>
> "Have I got to learn the shape of the river according to all these five hundred thousand different ways? If I tried to carry all that cargo in my head it would make me stoop-shouldered."
>
> "No! You only learn the <u>shape</u> of the river; and you learn it with such absolute certainty that you can always steer by the shape that's in your head, and never mind the one that's before your eyes."
>
> I went to work now to learn the shape of the river... Nothing had ever the same shape when I was coming downstream that it had borne when I went up. I mentioned these little difficulties to Mr. Bixby. He said:
>
> "That is the very main virtue of the thing. If the shapes didn't change every three seconds, they wouldn't be of any use... " [48]

The knowledge that was required to navigate the river, for Mark Twain had to become symbiotic, one with his whole being; he became totally immersed in the river, he knew it like himself. He did not need to see the landmarks any more, and then compute his course; he knew them in his heart, in his Being! Knowing the river so intimately, the river gave his knowledge freely to him. This comes from wisdom, not from academic knowledge. The difference is clear: the river can be just so much water, with bends and landmarks, with cities on its bank or opportunities for business and personal relationships. Or it can be listened to and taken into your heart and then it talks and it becomes a source of wisdom.

To hear the wisdom of the Five Elements, to take their knowledge into the heart, into the core of our being, for that we need to be quiet and listen. This is what meditation and contemplation offers us. It offers us a great jewel, the wisdom of our heart, our nature, the inner Self. From there we change; from there we grow to be at peace with ourselves and others quite naturally; and thus can act appropriately in the presence, in the Now.

Mark Twain writes, 'Throughout the long twelve hundred miles, there was never a page that was void of interest, never one that you could leave unread without loss, never one that you want to skip, thinking you could find higher enjoyment in some other things. There never was so wonderful a book written by man.'

With deep observation of our-self, the knowledge of the head becomes purified and sinks down to fertilise intuition, the wisdom of the heart. The dictionary defines intuition as, 'the immediate knowing of something without the conscious use of the mind.' A sudden knowing rises from within like a small bird that darts across the sky of our mind. It is like the tiniest voice that whispers and disappears. It speaks without words, it is behind the idea, behind the sculptor's image, behind the painter's inspiration or the scientist's insight. To notice this creative spark, we need to slow down and become silent, then we will hear the voice of intuition.

In Western societies we are taught from being a small child onwards, that we have to do things in order to achieve something. Throughout school we are pushed to invest in achieving the next goal; to 'make something out of ourselves.' This constant drive to achieve, <u>to aim for the next</u> thing is a driving force that even dominates our dreams and relationships; it prevents us from ever feeling content and at ease. This 'push' goes so far that our bodies cannot follow and we get sick, that our emotions cannot follow which lead to ever increasing suicidal rates, and our minds get so pressured that anger and aggression are the necessary consequence. We need to let off steam!

To be able to step out of this madness, we have to give up the illusion that we are an isolated being and recognise that we are at all times, part of a larger whole, an 'interminable river... whose shape has five hundred thousand different ways.'

And all these are nothing as an expression of the Divine, in Five Elements and so St.Francis of Assisi composed a hymn to God; Creator **in** the Five Elements: Altissimu omnipotente bon Signore (Most highest, almighty Lord...)

Be praised my Lord, especially Sir brother sun... who takes meaning from you, Most High; ...and sister Moon and the stars in heaven...

Be praised my Lord, through brother wind; through the air and... every kind of weather, by which you give sustenance to your creatures.

Be praised, my Lord, through sister water, who is useful and humble and precious and pure.

Be praised, my Lord through brother fire through whom you illuminate the night, beautiful, joyful, vigorous and strong.

Be praised, my Lord through sister our mother earth, who sustains and rules and produces different fruits with coloured flowers and grass. [49]

The divine itself has taken many forms, which have been grouped into these five gross energy fields, in constant interaction. We observe and we learn from them; we work with them and let their wisdom sink in our hearts; just like the old sage in the Shrimad Bhagavatam (Indian sacred text) who learned the highest wisdom from his environment. He confessed to have 24 Gurus (teachers) and it is said that his face 'shone with the brilliance of wisdom.' Here is a conversation, in which he explains to a king:

"Mother Earth is my first Guru. She told me to hold lovingly in my heart all those who trample on me, scratch me, hurt me, just as she does. She taught me, to give them my best, remembering that their acts are normal and natural from their standpoint. The earth through its trees and mountains taught me that life is for unselfishly, humbly serving all."

"Who is your second Guru?"

"Water. This force contains life and purity. It cleanses whatever it touches and provides life to whoever drinks it. Water flows unceasingly. If it stops it becomes stagnant. 'Keep moving, keep moving' is the lesson I learned from water."

"Your third Guru?"

"Fire. It burns everything, transforming it into flame. By consuming dead logs, it produces warmth and light. Thus I learn to absorb everything life brings and turn it into a flame that enlightens my life. In that light others can walk safely."

"Who is your fourth guru, sir?"

"Air is my fourth guru. The wind moves unceasingly, touching flowers and thorns alike, but it never attaches itself to the objects it touches. Like the wind, I learned not to prefer flowers over thorns, friends over foes. Like the wind my goal is to provide freshness to all without becoming attached."

"And your fifth guru, sir?"

"'All-pervading and all-embracing space is my fifth guru. Space has room for the sun, moon and stars-and yet it remains untouched and unconfined. I too, must have room for all the diversities of existence and still remain unaffected by what I contain. All visible and invisible objects have their rightful place within me, but they have no power to confine my consciousness. The Self is all pervading and like Space, is unchanged by forms appearing and disappearing." [50]

Swami Muktananda of Ganeshpuri writes in his Autobiography: 'I made myself understand that the five Elements, the rivers, oceans, mountains and caves were the body of Nityananda.' [51]

Likewise, I bow to Nityananda, my Guru, who is my 'twenty-four-thousand' teachers, with gratitude and love.

Notes

INTRODUCTION
x) *Jnana Sindhu* in Swami Muktananda *Play of Consciousness* (South Fallsburg: SYDA, 1990) p. 57.
1) Howells, G. *The Soul of India* (London: Kingsgate Press, 1909), p. 282.
2) Hunt, V. *Infinite Mind; Science of Human Vibrations of Consciousness* (Malibu, California: 1996).
3) Lama Gangchen Tulku Rinpoche *Making Peace with the Environment* (New Delhi: Indian Institute of Ecology and Environment, 1996) p. 63.

PART I
1) Lama Angarika Govinda *Foundations of Tibetan Mysticism* (Yorkbead: Weiser 1969) p. 72.
2) R. E. Hume, *Chandogya Upanishad, 6th.Prapathaka, 12th Khanda*, from *Thirteen Principal Upanishads* (Oxford University Press, 1979).
3) S. Rinpoche *The Tibetan Book of Living and Dying* (London: Rider, 1992).
4) *Sri Guru Gita, Sri Skanda Purana* from *The Nectar of Chanting* (Ganeshpuri, India: 1987) v. 36-42.
5) Skolimowski, H. *The Participatory Mind* (London: Arkana 1994).
6*) Sakala Sant Gatha, Kashinath Ananta Joshi, Sant Vanmaya Prakasham.Mandir* translated by Anand Mudra. (Poona: 1975).
7) Amit Goswami Phd. *The Self-Aware Universe* (New York: Penguin - Putman Inc. 1995) p. 71 ff.
8) Dyczkowski, Mark S. G. *The Doctrine of Vibration* (Sate University of New York Press, 1987).
9) Coomaraswamy A.K. *The Dance of Shiva* (The Noonday Press, 1969).
10) Swami Chinmayananda *The Holy Geeta* (Mumbai: Chinmaya Mission Trust, 1996) p. 652. 11) i.b.i.d. 1062.
12) Swami Sivananda *Lord Shiva and his Worship* (Garwahl U.P. India: Yoga Vedanta-Forest-Academy Press, 1992).
13) Swami Venkatesananda *Yoga Vashista* (Albany: SUNY, 1993) p. 51 ff.
14) Sri Aurobindu *The Bhagavad Gita* (Pondicherry: Divine Life Trust, 2000) p. 466.
15) Swami Chinmayananda *Talks on Shankara's Vivekachoodamani* (Mumbai: Chinmaya Mission Trust, 1999) p. 127.
16) i.b.i.d. p 108.
17) Swami Shivananda i.b.i.d. pp. 131/267.
18) i.b.i.d. p. 217.
19) Br. Sudhanshu Chaitanya *Pancadasi I* (Mumbai: Central Chinmaya Mission Trust 1994) pp. 80/87.
20) Sri Nirsargadatta Maharaj (ed. Jean Dunn Chetana) *Consciousness and the Absolute* (Mumbai: 1997) p. 26.
21) Madhava-Vidyaranya *Sankara-Dig-Vijaya* (Madras: Sri Ramakrishna Math, 1996) p. 47.

22) Gerson, Scott *Ayurveda* (Shaftesbury: Element, 1993) pp. 3-4.

23) Thich Nath Than *Old Path White Clouds* (New Delhi: Full Circle, 1997) p. 321.

24) Snelling, J. *The Buddhist Handbook* (London: Rider, 1995) p. 68.

25) Sogyal Rinpoche *Living and Dying* (Rider, 1993) p. 247.

26) *Ambrosia Heart Tantra* trans. Dr. Yeshi Dhonden and Jhampa Kelsang (Dharamsala: Tibetan Archives, 1977) p. 33.

27) Evans- Wentz, W.Y. *The Tibetan Book of the Dead* (Oxford University Press, 1996) p. 13.

28) Crook, J. Fontana, D. *Space in Mind* (Longmead, Dorset: Element Books, 1990) p. 190.

29) Evans-Wetz *The Tibetan Book...* i.b.i.d. pp. 201/202.

30) Lama Gangchen, TYS *Making Peace with the Environment* (Milan: Gangchen Publications, 1996) p. 143 ff. For further info. contact: Gumpen Lama Gangchen, Via Marco Polo 13, Milan.

31) Pandit Rajmani Tigunat *Seven Philosophies Systems of Indian Philosophy* (Pennsylvania: Himalayan Institute of Yoga Honisdale, 1983) p. 29 ff.

32) Tsultrim Allione *Women of Wisdom* (London: Arkana, 1986) pp. 27/28.

33) Lama Gangchen *Seven Astrological Purifications* (Milan: Gangchen Publications, 1997).

34) Lama Gangchen TYS *The Borobudur Stupa Mandala* (Milan: LGPP 1997).

35) Lama Gangchen, TYS *Making Peace with the Aura* (Milan: LGPP 1997) pp. 19/27.

36) Veith, I. *The Yellow Emperors's Classic of Internal Medicine*, pp. 10/11.

37) Watts, A. *Tao, The Watercourse Way* (Harmondsworth: Pelican books, 1979) p. xiv.

38) Smullyan, R. M. *The Tao is Silent* (London: Harper and Row, 1977).

39) Watts. i.b.i.d. pp. 75, 47.

40) Veitz. i.b.i.d. pp. 11-18.

41) Wilhelm, Richard. *I Ching* (London: Routledge and Kegan, 1978) pp. 308, 309.

42) Temelie, B. Trebuth. *Das fuenf Elemente Kochbuch* (Sulzberg: Joy Verlag, 1993) pp. 28-40.

43) Willis, Ben *The Tao of Art* (London: Century Paperbacks, 1987) p. 70.

––––

44) Cowen, J, *Mysteries of the Dream-time Prism-unity* (Dorset: 1992) p. 60.

45) i.b.i.d. p. 91.

46) Watts *The Two Hands of God* (London: Rider, 1978).

47) Cowan, J.G. *Myths of the Dreaming* (Dorset: Prism Press, 1994) pp. 2,4, 5.

48) Reed, A.W. (London: P.T.Y Ltd., 1977) p. 137.

49) Mountford, Charles/Ainslie Roberts *The Dreamtime* (Rigby, Adelaide: 1974).

50) i.b.i.d. p. 38.

51) Stevens, Christine *White Man's Dreaming* (Oxford: Oxford University Press, 1994) pp. 27/8.

52) Cowan *Myths of the Dreaming* (Dorset: Prism Press, 1994) pp. 25-32.

53) Baglin, Douglas/Barbara Mullins *Aboriginal Art of Australia* (Sydney: Reed, 1978) pp. 30/31.

―――

54) Ali. A. Mazrui. *The Africans* (London: BBC Publ., 1986) p. 296.

55) i.b.i.d. p..50.

56) Vusamazulu Credo Mutwa *Indaba, My Children* (Johannesburg: Blue Crane Books, 196?) p. 455.

57) Malidoma Patrice Somé *The Healing Wisdom of Africa* (London: Thorsons, 1999).

58) Vasamazulu Credo Mutwa i.b.i.d. pp. 452 and 3-15.

59) Malidoma Patrice Somé *The Healing Wisdom* i.b.i.d. p. 169 ff.

60) Malidoma Patrice Somé *Of Water and the Spirit* (London/ NewYork: Arkana, 1995) pp. 198-201.

61) i.b.i.d. p. 254.

62) Malidoma Patrice Somé *Healing Wisdom* i.b.i.d. p. 179.

―――

63) Argüelles, José *The Mayan Factor* (Santa Fe: Bear & Co., 1987) p. 34.

64) Gilbert, A. G. and Maurice M. Cotterell *The Mayan Prophecy* (Shaftesbury: Element, 1996) p. 58.

65) Séjourné, Lauretta *Burning Water* (Thames and Hudson, 1978) p. 72.

66) Caso, Alfonso *El Pueblo del Sol* (Mexico: Fondo de Cutura Económica, 1953) p. 40.

67) Séjourné i..b.i.d. pp. 55-57.

68) i.b.i.d. pp. 62/63.

69) i.b.i.d. p. 110.

70) the list has been compiled using R. Montgomery's *Twenty Count* (Santa Fe: Bear and Co.) info. from Arguelles *Mayan Factor* and *Rainbow-Hawk's Glyphs of the Emaha Tribe.*

―――

71) Schenk, Amelia, translated after, *Die Weisheit der Indianerfrauen* (Wien: Scherz, without date)

72) Chokecherry Gall Eagle *Beyond the Lodge of the Sun*, (Shaftesbury: Element, 1997) pp. 29/48

73) Sun-Bear and Wabun *The Medicine Wheel* (New York: A Fireside Book, 1992) pp. 4/5.

74) Sams, Jamie *Sacred Path Cards* (San Francisco, New York: Harper 1990) p. 86.

75) Chokecherry, i.b.i.d. pp. 69/129.

76) Sams i.b.i.d. p. 87.

77) Sun Bear and Wabun, i.b.i.d. p. 198.

78) told after: Sun Bear and Wabun, i.b.i.d. and also Gibbings *The North American Indian* (Llanerch, Lampeter: 1993) p. 14 ff

79) After Joseph Campbell *The Flight of the Wild Gander* (Harper Perennial, 1995) p. 78 ff.

―――

80) Plotinus *The Enneads* (London: Penguin Classic, 1990) pp. lxviii ff / 139
81) i.b.i.d. p. 480 f.
82) Hamilton, Robert *Earthdream, the Marriage of Reason and Intuition* Bideford: Green Books, 1990) p. 44.
83) Fox, Mathew *Illuminations of Hildegard von Bingen*, (Santa Fe New Mexico: Bear & Co., 1985) p. 18.
84) Schipperges, H /Hildegard Von Bingen *Heilkunde* (Salzburg: Otto Mueller Verlag, 1992) p. 13
85) i.b.i.d. pp. 56-59.
86) i.b.i.d. pp. 76 ff.
87) Skolimowski, Henryk *The Participatory Mind* (London: Arkana, 1994) p. 126.
88) Skolimowski, i.b.i.d. p. 130.
89) Jung, CG *Memories, Dreams and Reflections* (London: Fontana Press, 1995) and Bladon, Sue *The Four Functions in Astrology* (unpublished paper 1994) pp. 1/2
90) Capra, F. *The Turning Point* (London: Flamingo, 1988) pp. 71, 76, 89.
91)Eden, Donna with David Feinstein, *Energy Medicine*, Piatkus 1998, pp. 209-211.
92) Linn, Denise, *Sacred Space* (London: Rider, 1995) p. 226 f.

———

93) S. Masunaga *Zen Imagery Exercises* (Tokyo-New York: Japan Publications, 19 87) p. 16.
94) Pandit Rajmani Tigunait *At the Eleventh Hour* (Honsdale, Penns.: Himalayan Institute Press, 2001) p. 349.
95) G. Parrinder *The Bhagavad Gita* (London: Sheldon Press, 1974).
96) R.Gerber i.b.i.d. p. 22 f.
97) Deepak Chopra *Quantum Healing* i.b.i.d. p. 48 f.
98) Barbara Ann Brennan *Hands of Light* (Bantam Books, 1988) pp. 41/53.
99) Linda Johnson *Daughters of the Goddess* (YCS International Publishers).
100) Ohashi *Reading the Body, Ohashi's Book of Oriental Diagnosis* (Aquarian/Thorsons, 1992).
101) Benjamin Hoff *The Tao of Pooh* (Mandarin Paperback, 1991) p. 39.

PART II
All references of anatomy or physiology are based on:
Ross & Wilson *Anatomy and Physiology in Health and Illness*, Kathleen J. W. Wilson OBE. (Edinburgh: Churchill Livingstone, et al. 1990 Seventh Edition).
1) Pandit Rajmani Tigunait *The Eleventh Hour* (Himalayan Institute Press, 2001) p. 363.
2) Beinfield Korngold *Between Heaven and Earth*, (New York: Ballantine Books, 1991) p. 87.

———

EARTH

3) R. Hamilton *Earthdream* (Bideford, 1990) p. 22.

4) J. Cowan *Myth of the Dreaming* (Prism Press, 1994) p. 115.

5) Swami Kripananda *Jnaneshwar's Gita* (SUNY, 1989) and RD. Rande, *Jnaneshwar The Guru's Guru* (SUNY, 1994).

6) Veith.I. *The Yellow Emperor Classic of Internal Medicine* i.b.i.d. p. 112.

7) Masunaga.S/Ohashi/Wataru *Zen Shiatsu* (Japan Publications, 1977) p. 38.

8) Sonia Moriceau. Excerpts from guidelines compiled for Shiatsu practitioners.

9) i.b.i.d.

10) Hildegard von Bingen *Heilkunde* (Otto Mueller Verlag...) pp. 84/ 106.

11) Lama Gangchen, TYS *Ngal-So How to Relax Body, Mind and Speech* (Milan: Institute of Tibetan, Medicine) p. 15.

12) Barbara Brennan *Light Emerging* (Bantam, 1993).

13) Veith I. i.b.i.d. p. 28.

14) i.b.i.d. p. 141.

15) Lama Angarika Govinda *Tibetan Mysticism* (Maine: Samuel Weiser, 1996) p. 134.

16) Veith.I. i.b.i.d. p. 119.

17) i.b.i.d. p. 109.

18) H.Wilhelms *Chinese Horoskopes* (Pan Books, 1980) p. 31 ff.

19) Jamie Sams *Sacred Path Cards* (San Francisco: Harper Collins 1990) p. 279.

20) Dr. Ros, F. *Aurvedic Acupuncture* i.b.i.d. p..51.

21) H. von Bingen *Heilkunde* i.b.i.d. p. 84.

22) Veith, .I. i.b.i.d. p 112.

23) Swami Anubhavananda *Guided Meditation* (Mumbai: SAT Bhavana Trust, 1999).

24) Harish Johari *Chakras* (Rochester: Destiny, 2000) pp. 75-85.

25) Devreux G. *Elements of Yoga* (London: Thorsons, 2002) p. 111ff.

26) Swami Hariharaananda Aranya *Yoga Philosophy of Patanjali* (Albany: SUNY 1981).

27) Harish Johari i..b.id. p. 77.

28) Swami Chinmayananda *The Holy Geeta* (Mumbai: Chinmaya Mission Trust) inspired by p. 1095.

29) i.b.i.d.

30) Goodmann, D. *Be as You Are, The Teachings of Sri Ramana Maharshi* (London: Arkana, 1985).
 Graf.K.von.Durkheim *Hara, The Vital Centre of Man* (London: Mandala Books Unwin 1989).

31) Malidoma Patrice Somé*Of Water and the Spirit* (London: Arkana, 1994).

32) H.Corbin *Cyclical Time and Ismaili Gnosis* (London: Kegan Paul International, 1983).

―――

WATER
33) Hildegard von Bingen *Heilkunde* i.b.i.d. p. 77.
34) R. C. Gregg *Athanasius: The Life of Anthony and the letter to Marceliius* (N.Y.: Pandit Press, 1989).and B. Ward *The Sayings of the Desert Fathers* (Cistercian Publ. 1984) T. .Merton *Wisdom of the Desert* (New Direction Publication Co.)
35) J. and C. Bord *Sacred Waters* (London: Granada, 1985).
36) *Vankatananhara's Corrunentary in: Concept of Saraswati* Dr.RanhunathAiri (New Delhi: Mustiran Monoharlal, 1977) and Rabindranath Tagore *The River must become the Sea Sadhana the Realisation of Life* (New York: McMillan, 1914).
37) N. Weeks *The Medical Discovery of Physician* (Walden: Eduard Bach, 1993). M. Schaeffer, *Bach Flower Therapy* (London: Thorsons, 1986).
38) Omran Mikhael Aivanov *The Mysteries of Fire and Water* (France: Prosveta, 1993).
39) Matthews, John and Caitlin *The Encyclopaedia of Celtic Wisdom* (Shaftesbury: Element, 1994) and C. Punkola Estees *Women who Run with Wolves* (London: Rider 1994).
40) Sonja Moriceau *Life Cycle*, Excerpts from *Guidelines for Shiatsu Practitioners* (Paper 1992).
40) i.b.i.d.
41) J. & C. Matthews *Celtic Wisdom* (Shaftesbury: Element, 1993) p. 26.
42) after I. Veith *Nei Ching* p. 133.
43) A. Tomatis for info: Tomatis Centre, Eccleston Square 26 London SW 1 1NS.
44) W. Johnston *Cloud of Unknowing* (Faunt, 1997) p. 30 ff.
45) Hildegard von Bingen i.b.i.d. p. 75.
46) Nor Hall *The Moon and the Virgin* (New York: Harper Row, 1980) p. 44 and T. Suttrim Allione *Women of Wisdom*, (London Arkana, 1986) pp. 31/32.
47) Hildegard von Bingen i.b.i.d. p. 78.
48) D. Frawley *Yoga and Ayurveda* i.b.i.d. p. 124.
49) Harish Johari Chakra, p. 97 ff.
50) C. Ingram, In the footsteps of Ghandi Parallax, California, 1990) and Eknath Easwarum, Petalume, *Ghandi the Man* (Nilgiri Press, 1978).
51) D. Frawley *Yoga and Ayurveda* i.b.i.d. p. 304.
52) Swami Kripananda, *Jnaneshwar's Gita* SUNY, 1989) Chapter 16.
53) D. Frawley *Yoga and Ayurveda* i.b.i.d. p. 307.

FIRE
54) J.Shinoda Bolen, MD *Goddess in Every Woman* (Colophon: Harper &Row, 1985).
55) Hiranyavarna *Rig Veda VII.77.1* in R. Panokkar, *The Vedic Experience* (1977).
56) Sadguru Sant Keshavadas *Gayatri* (London : Kegan Paul, 1993) p. 125.
57) *Sharan Shiva* Jonathan Star, unpublished manuscript quoted in *Darshan Magazine No. 53* (South Fallsburg: SYDA Publications) p. 66.

58) A. Dante *Divine Comedy*.

59) S. Noffke *The Dialogue* (New York: Paulist Press, 1980) and C. *Keams The Life of Catherine of Sienna* (Wilmington: Michele Glazier Inc., 1980).

60) Ohashi *Reading the body, Ohashi's Book of Oriental Diagnosis* (Aquarian/Thorsons, 1992).

61) J. Sams *Sacred Path Cards* i.b.i.d. p. 29.

62) Hildegard von Bingen *Heilkunde* i.b.i.d. p. 128.

63) i.b.i.d. p. 112.

64) Eknath Easwaran *Dialogue with Death* (Nilgiri Press, 1992) p. 136 f.

65) W. Ohashi *Reading the body* i.b.i.d. p. 90ff.

66) Ross Dr. F. *Ayurvedic Acupuncture* p. 40.

67) O. Karrer *Die grosse Glut,Textgeschichte der Mystic im mittelalter* (Muenchen: 1926).

68) Amit Goswami *Self-Aware Universe* (Penguin Putman, 1995).

─────

AIR/ METAL

69) Ross and Wilson *Anatomy and Physiology* (Edinburgh/London: Churchill Livingston, 1992).

70) M. Aurelius, in *Darshan, No. 92* (South Fallsburg, N.Y.: SYDA) p. 2.

71) *'Holding On', Darshan, No. 60* (South Fallsburg, N.Y.: SYDA).

72) M. Fox *Meister Eckhardt* (Santa Fe: Bear and Co., 1983).

73) Plotinus in Stephen McKenna, *First Ennead* (London: Faber & Faber, 1962).

74) Ross Dr. F. *Ayurvedic Acupuncture* (Wisconsin: Lotus Press, 1994) pp. 16/17

75) Johnston W. *The Cloud of Unknowing* (Fount, 1997).

76) Veith, I *Nei Ching* i.b.i.d. p. 103.

77) Sams, J. *Sacred Path Cards* i.b.i.d. p. 10.

78) Veith, I. *Nei Ching* i.b.i.d. p. 147.

79) Shaykh Fadhlalla Haerri *Sufism* (Shaftesbury: Element, 1990) p. 49.

80) Giovanni Maciocia *The Psyche in Chinese Medicine* (European Journal of Oriental Medicine, 1/1, Spring 1993) pp. 16/17.

81) Alan Isaacs et al. *The Physical World* (Penguin Books, 1976) p. 82.

82) *Hutchinsons Encyclopedia* i.b.i.d. p. 1239.

83) Ilza Veith *Nei Ching* pp. 207/141.

84) Swami Chetanananda *The Breath of God* (Cambridge, Massachusetts: Rudra Press, 1977) pp. 23/24, also: Thich Nath Hahn *The Sutra on the Full Awareness of Breath* (Parallax Press, 1988).

85) Lama, Anagarika Govinda *The Way of The White Clouds* (London: Rider Books, 1992) p. 244.

86) Swami Chetanananda i.b.i.d. p. 23.

87) Beinfield/Korngold *Between Heaven and Earth* i.b.i.d. p. 119.

88) Veith, I. *Nei Ching* i.b.i.d. p. 120.

89) Lama Angarika Govinda *Foundation of Tibetan Mysticism* i.b.i.d. p. 178.

90) Harish Johari *Chakras* i.b.i.d. p. 122.

91) Swami Venkatesananda *Yoga Vashista* (SUNY 1993).

92) Swami Chinmayananda *The Holy Geeta* i.b.i.d. p. 1095 f.

93) Wilhelm, R. *I Ching or Book of Changes* (London: Routledge and Kegan, 1978).
94) Frawley, D. *Yoga and Ayurveda* i.b.i.d. p. 300.
———

SPACE
95) Swami Chinmayananda *The Holy Geeta* i.b.i.d. pp. 652, 922 ff.
96) *Oxford Children's Encyclopedia* (Oxford University Press, 1991).
97) E. Eswaran in *Dialoque with Death* i.b.i.d. writes brilliantly about body identification.
98) R. Dawkins *God's Utility Function* (Phoenix: Orion Books, 1995) p. 1.
99) R. Weber *Dialogue with Scientists and Sages* (London: Arkana, 1986).
100) F. Capra, *The Tao of Physics*, (London: Fontana, 1980).
101) J. Sams, *Sacred Path Cards,* (San Francisco: Harper, 1990).
102) D. Linn, *Sacred Space* (London: Rider 1995).
103) Veith., I. *Nei Ching* i.b.i.d. p. 133.
104) i.b.i.d. p. 133.
105) Sonia Moriceau *Excerpts from Guidelines* i..b.i.d.
106) D. Ross *Ayurveda and Acupuncture...* i.b.i.d. p. 24.
107) Veith, I. *Nei Ching* i..b.i.d.
108) Jamie Sams *Sacred Path Cards* i.b.i.d. pp. 89/90.
109) Lama Gangchen *Ngal-So* i.b.i.d. p. 59.
110) G. Parrinder *The Bhagavad Gita* (London: Sheldon Press, 1974) p. 38.
111) Jnaneshwar Maharaj *The Nectar of Self-Awareness* (Siddha Yoga Publications, 1979).
112) *Corpus Hermeticum* ed. and trans. W.Scott, (New York: Oxford University Press, 1986).
113) Harish Johari *Chakras* i.b.i.d. p. 131.
114) Dr. P. V. Karamelbar *Patanjala Yoga Sutras* (Kaivalyadham, Lonavalla, India) Pada III S. 51.
115) Teilhard de Chardin *Spirit of Fire* (New York: Ursula King Orbis Books 1996) pp. 88/89, 173.
116) Chinmayananda, Swami *The Holy Geeta...* i.b.i.d. p. 1095 f.
117) R. Dawkins i.b.i.d.
118) *Mahabharata* in *Darshan No. 71* (South Fallsburg: SYDA, 1993).
119) R. Quong *Chinese Written Characters, their Wit and Wisdom* (Beacon Press, 1973).
120) Plato, Phoedo, trans: GMA Grube *Five Dialogues* (Indianapolis: Hackett Publ. 1981).
121) S. Moriceau, *Prayer from the Heart Sutra* (private translation - with permission, 1995).

PART III
1) B. Ingles and R. West *The Alternative Health Guide* (London: Michael Joseph Ltd. 1983) p. 7.
2) After: *Dhammapada* Eknath Easwaran, (London: Penguin Arkana, 1986) p. 78.

3) Milarepa *Autobiography of a Tibetan Yogi* i.b.i.d. p. 246.

4) Farid-Ud-din-Ahar *The Conference of Birds* (Penguin Classics, 1984) p. 166.

5) M. Buber *Tales of the Hasidim* (New York: Schocken Books 1947).

Balancing EARTH

6) M.H. Woodcott, A. Schumway *Cook Development of Posture and Gait across the Life Span* (University of South Carolina Press, 1989).

7) C. A. Meier *Healing Dream and Ritual* (Switzerland: Daimon, 1989) p. 1.

8) i.b.i.d. pp. 52/53.

9) Veith, I. *Nei Ching* i.b.i.d. p. 149.

10) Lama Gangchen *Ngal-So* i.b.i.d. p. 153.

11) Veith, I. *Nei Ching* i.b.i.d. p. 55.

12) Beinfield, Krongold *Between Heaven and Earth* i.b.i.d. p. 332.

13) Ohashi, W. *Reading the Body* i.b.i.d. p. 171.

14) Jamie Sams *Sacred Path Cards* i.b.i.d. p. 141.

15) V. W. Odajnyk, *Gathering the Light, a Psychology of Meditation* (London: Shambala, 1993).

16) Veith, I. *Nei Ching* i.b.i.d. p. 148.

17) i.b.i.d.

18) Rumi *Open Secret, Versions of Rumi* (Putney: Threshold Books, 1984).

21) Swami Chinmayananda *Vivekachoodamani* (Mumbai: Chinmaya Mission Trust, 1999) p. 343.

Balancing WATER

20) Ohashi *Reading the Body* i.b.i.d. p. 126.

21) Janet and Colin Bord *Sacred Waters* (Granada, 1985) p. 2.

22) Vivianne Crowley *Phoenix from the Flame* (Aquarian/Thorsons, 1994) p. 61.

23) Susanne Cooper, The Dark is Rising Sequence (Harmandsworth: Penguin, 1984) p. 763.

24) Ingles and West *Guide to Alternative Medicine* London: Michael Joseph, 1983) pp. 24/5.

25) Ohashi *Reading the Body* i.b.i.d. p. 54.

26) i.b.i.d. p. 58.

27) R. Panikkar *The Vedic Experience* (London: Darton, Longman and Todd, 1977) p. 114.

28) i.b.i.d. p. 117.

29) i.b.i.d.

30) Chapter 6 of *The Thirteen Principal Upanishads* (Oxford University Press) p. 248.

Balancing FIRE

31)From: *Tintern Abbey - William Wordsworth's The Prelude* ed. by Carlos Baker, Holt, Reihort and Winston (New York: 1965).

32) To be found in Masunaga/Ohashi *Zen Shiatsu* (NY: Japan Publication, Inc. Tokyo, 1977).

33) For further information see: Beinfield/Krongold *Between Heaven and Earth* i.b.i.d.
34) R. Carter *Mapping the Mind* i.b.i.d. p. 208.
35) *Science of Spirituality Vol 15: Path of Deliberate Rigour* (India: Sanatan Bharatiya Sanskruti Sanstha, 1998).
36) Swami Anubhavananda *Open-eye Meditation* (Mumbai: Sat Bhavana Trust, 2003) p. 23.

Balancing AIR
37) Veith, I. *Nei Ching* i.b.i.d. p. 139 ff.
38) Bruno Hans Geba *Breathe Away your Tension* (New York: Random House, 1973) p. 38.
39) Veith, I. i.b.i.d. p. 117.
40) Swami Chinmayananda *Vivekachoodamani* i.b.i.d. pp. 32/34.

Balancing SPACE
41) For further information, see: Ohashi *Reading the Body* i.b.i.d. p. 143 ff.
42) For further information please contact: Kunpen Lama Gangchen KLG, Institute for the Propagation of the Tibetan Medical Tradition, Via Marco Polo B, 20124 Milan, Italy.
43) For further reference : Beinfield/ Krongold, Between Heaven and Earth, i.b.i.d.
44) Frawley D. *Yoga and Ayurveda* i.b.i.d. p. 27.
45) i.b.i.d. p. 184.
46) Frawley, D. & Lad Vasant *The Yoga of Herbs* (Lotus Press, 1988) p. 174.

CONCLUSION
47) Gary Zukav *The Dancing WU-Li Masters* (New York: Bantam, 1980) p. 197.
48) M. Twain *Life on the Mississipi* (New York: Vintage Books 1991)
49) Brendan Smith *The Silence of Divine Love* (London: Darton Longman Todd, 1998) after pp. 150/151.
50) Pandit Rajmani Tigunat *The Himalaya Masters* (Honesdale: Himalayan Institute Press, 2002) p. 40 f. and Swami Venkatesananda *The Conscise Srimad Bhagavatam* (Albany: SUNY, 1989).
51) Swami Muktananda *Play of Consciousness* i.b.i.d. p. 60.

Selective Bibliography

Argüelles, J. *The Mayan Factor*. Santa Fe: Bear & Co., 1987
Beinfield, H. and E. Korngold. *Between Heaven and Earth*. N.Y.: Ballentines, 1991
Brennan, B. A. *Hands of Light*. Bantam Books, 1988
——. *Light Emerging*. Bantam Books, 1993
Buber, M. *Tales of the Hasidini*. N.Y.: Schocken Books, 1947
Bucke, R.M. *Cosmic Consciousness*. Penguin, Arkana, 1991
Capra, F. *The Turning point, Science, Society and the Rising Culture*. London: Fontana
——. *The Tao of Physics*. London: Fontana, 1980
Carter, R. *Mapping the Mind*. London: Phoenix, 1998
——. *Consciousness*. London: Weidenfeld & Nicholson, 2002
Chokecherry Gall Eagle. *Beyond the Lodge of the Sun*. Shaftesbury, Dorset: Element, 1997
Chopra, D. *Perfect Health*. London: Bantam Books, 1992
——. *Quantum Healing*. Bantam Books, 1989
Connelly, D.M. *Traditonelle Akupunktur, Das Gesetz der fuenf Elemente*. Heidelberg: A.C.Endrich, 1987
Cowan, J.G. *Myths of the Dreaming*. Dorset: Prism Press, 1994
——. *Mysteries of the Dream-time*. 1992
Darshan: In the Company of Saints. Monthly Magazine of the SYDA Foundation, Siddha   Yoga Publishing, South Fallsburg, NY (Issues: 53, 60, 71, 77/78, 79, 92, 99)
Dawkins, R. *God's Utility Function*. Phoenix: Orion Books, 1995
Devreux, G. *Elements of Yoga*. London: Thorsons, 2002
Dyczkowski, M. S. G. *The Doctrine of Vibration*. Albany: SUNY, 1987
Eknath Easwaram, Petalum. *Ghandi the Man*. Nilgri Press, 1978
——. *Dialogue with Death*. Nilgiri Press, 1992
——. *Milarepa, Tibet's Great Yogi*. Oxford University Press, 1996
Fox, M. *Illuminations of Hildegard of Bingen*. Santa Fe: Bear & Co., 1985
——. *Meister Eckhardt*. Santa Fe: Bear and Co., 1993
Frawley, D. *Yoga and Ayurveda*. Lotus Press, 1999
Gerber,R. MD. *Vibrational Medicine*. Santa Fe: Bear & Co., 1988
Gerson, S. MD. *Ayurveda*. Shaftesbury: Element, 1993
Goswami, A. *Self-Aware Universe*. Penguin Putman, 1995
Harish Johari. *Chakras*. Rochester: Destiny, 2000
Herrmann, C-M. *The Movement of Life in the Five Elements*. Madrid: Centeur, 1996
Hoff, B. *The Tao of Pooh*. Mandarin Paperback, 1991
Hume, R. R. *The Thirteen Upanishads*. Oxford University Press, 1979
Hunt, V. V. *Infinite Mind*. Malibu: 1996
Ingles, B. and West, R. *The Alternative Health Guide*. London: Michael Joseph Ltd., 1983
Iyengar, B. K. S. *Light on the Yoga Sutras of Patanjali*. London: Thorsons, 1993
——. *The Tree of Yoga*. Boston: Shambala, 2002

Jnaneshwar Maharaj. *The Nectar of Self-Awareness*. South Fallsburg, N.Y.: Siddha Yoga Publications, 1979

Johnston, W. *Cloud of Unknowing*. Faunt, 1997

Keams, C. *The Life of Catherine of Sienna*. Wilmington: Michele Glazier, Inc., 1980

Lad, Dr. V. *Ayurveda, the Science of Self-Healing*. Twin Lakes: Lotus Press, 1994

Lama Angarika Govinda. *Foundation of Tibetan Mysticism*. Maine: Samuel Weiser, 1969

Lama Gangchen T.Y.S. Rinpoche. *Making Peace with the Environment*. New Delhi: Indian Institute of Ecology and Environment, 1996

——. *Ngal-So, Self-Healing III*. Milan: Lama Gangchen Peace Publications, 1994

Lama Surya Dass. *Awakening the Buddha Within*. Bantam Books, 1997

Malidoma Patrice Some. *Of Water and the Spirit*. London: Arkana, 1994

——. *The Healing Wisdom of Africa*. London: Thorsons, 1999

Masunaga S. *Zen Imagery Exercises*. Tokyo-New York: Japan Publications, 1987

Matsumoto, K. and Birch, S. *Five Elements and Ten Stems*. Brookline: Pradigma Public

Matthews, J. and Caitlin. *The Encyclopaedia of Celtic Wisdom*. Element, Shaftesbury: 1994

Mc.Connelly D. *Traditional Acupuncture, the Law of the Five Elements*. Maryland: 1979

Montgomery, R., *Twenty Count*. Santa Fe: Bear and Co.

Noffke, S. *The Dialogue*. New York: Paulist Press, 1980

Odajiyk, V. W. *Gathering Light, a Psychology of Meditation*. London: Shambala, 1993

Ohashi, W. *Reading the Body*. London: Thorsons, 1992

Omraam Mikhael Aivanhov. *The Mysteries of Fire and Water*. France: Prosveta, 1993

Pandit Rajmani Tigunait, Ph.D. *At the Eleventh Hour*. Honesdale: Himalayan Institute Pr.

——. *The Himalaya Masters*. Honesdale: Himalayan Institute Pr., 2002

——. *Seven Systems of Indian Philosophy*. Honesdale: HIP

Panikkar, R. Mantramanjari. *The Vedic Experience*. London: Darton, Longmann, Todd, 1977

Parahamsa Yogananda. *Autobiography of a Yogi*. London: Rider 1995

Plato, Phoedo, (trans: G. M. A.Grube). *Five Dialogues*. Indianapolis: Hackett Publ., 1981

Plotinus. *The Enneads*. London: Penguin Classics, 1991

Rabindranath Tagore. *The River Must Become the Sea*. New York: McMillan, 1914

——. *Sadhana*. London: Mcmillan and Co., 1932

Rande, R. D. *Jnaneshwar*. The Guru's Guru. SUNY, 1994

——. *Mysticism in India*. SUNY, 1983

Ros, Dr. F. *The Lost Secrets of Ayurvedic Acupuncture.* Twin Lakes: Lotus Press, 1994

Ross & Wilson. *Anatomy and Physiology.* Edinburg/London: Churchill Livingston, 1992

——. *The Eye of Shiva.* London: Condor Books, 1980

Rumie. *Open Secret, Versions of Rumie.* Putney: Threshold Books, 1984

Sadguru Sant Keshavadas. *Gayatri, the Highest Meditation.* London: Kegan Paul, 1993

Sams, J. *Sacred Path Card.* San Francisco: Harper, 1990

Schaeffer, M. *Bach Flower Therapy.* London: Thorsons, 1986

Séjourné, Lauretta. *Burning Water.* Thames and Hudson, 1978

Shaykh Fadhlalla Haerri. *Sufism.* Shaftesbury: Element, 1990

Shear, A. *Buddha, the Intelligent Heart.* London: Thames Hudson, 1992

Shipperges, H. *Hildegard von Bingen, Heilkunde.* Salzburg: Otto Mueller Verlag, 1992

Shinoda-Bolen, J. MD. *Goddesses in Every Woman.* Harper & Row, Colophon: 1985

Skolimowski, H. The Participatory Mind. London: Arkana, 1994

Soengal Rinpoche. The Tibetan Book of Living and Dying. London: Rider, 1992

Sri Aurobindo. The Bhagavad Gita. Pondicherry: Divine life Trust, 2000

Sri Guru Gita, Sri Skanda Purana, from The Nectar of Chanting. Ganeshpuri: 1987

Sri Nirsargadatta. *Consciousness and the Absolute.* Mumbai: Chetana, 1994

St.Theresa of Avila. (trans: Kieran Kavanaugh OCD & O. Rodriguez OCD). *Autobiography.*
New York: Book of the Month Club, 1995

Swami Anantananda. *What's On My Mind.* S.F., N.Y.: Siddha Yoga Publication SYDA, 1996

Swami Anubhavananda. *Guided Meditation.* Mumbai: Sat Bhavana Trust, 1999

——. *Open-eye Meditation.* Mumbai: Sat Bhavana Trust, 2003

Swami Chetananda. *The Breath of God.* Cambridge, Mass.: Rudra Press, 1973

Swami Chidvilasananda. *Enthusiasm.* S. F., N.Y.: SYDA Foundation Publishing, 1997

——. *The Yoga of Discipline.* S. F., N.Y.: Siddha Yoga Publications SYDA, 1996

Swami Chinmayananda. *The Holy Geeta.* Mumbai: Central Chinmaya Mission Trust

——. *Vivekachoodamani (Talks on).* Mumbai: CCM Trust, 1999

Swami Hariharananda Aranya. *Yoga Philosophy of Patanjali.* Albany: SUNY, 1981

Swami Kripananda. *Jnaneshwar's Gita, A Rendering of the Jnaneshwari.* SUNY, 1989

Swami Muktananda. *The Perfect Relationship.* S.F. N.Y.: Siddha Yoga Publications, SYDA, 1980

——. *From the Finite to the Infinite*. S.F., N.Y.: Siddha Yoga, Publications, SYDA, 1994

——. *Play of Consciousness*. S.F., N.Y.: Siddha Yoga Publications, SYDA, 1978

Swami Nityamuktananda. *Seeing Yoga, Path and Goal*, Mumbai: Sat Bhavana Trust. 2004

Swami Nityamuktananda. *Seeing Yoga* A contemplation of Patanjali's Yoga Sutras; Ediciones Ambrosia, 2005

Swami Sivananda. *Lord Shiva and his Worship*. Their Garwahl, Himlayas: Yoga-Vedanta Forest Academy Press, 1992

Swami Venkatesananda. *Yoga Vashista*. SUNY, 1993

——. *The Concise Srimad Bhagavatam*. Albany: SUNY, 1989

Teilhard de Chardin. *Spirit of Fire*, New York: Ursula King, Orbis Books, 1996

Thich Nhat Than. *Transformation and Healing*. London: Rider, 1993

——. *Peace is Every Step*. London: Bantam Books, 1992

Twain. M. *Life on the Mississippi*. New York: Vintage Books, 1991

Veith, I. *The Yellow Emperor's Classic of Internal Medicine*. Berkley/L.A.: University of Cal. Press, 1972

Wandsworth, W. (ed. by Carlos Baker, Holt, Reihort and Winston). *The Prelude, Tintern Abbey*. New York: 1965.

Ward, B. *The Sayings of the Desert Fathers*. Cistercian Pub., 1984

Watts, A. *The Watercourse Way*. London: Penguin, 1975

——. *Two Hands of God*. London: Rider, 1963

Weber, R. *Dialogue with Scientists and Sages*. London: Arkana, 1986

Wilhelm, R. I. *Ching or the Book of Changes*. London: Routledge and Kegan, 1978

Willis, B. *The Tao of Art, Century Paperbacks*. London: 1987

Wilson Ross, N. *Three Ways of Asian Wisdom*. N.Y.: Simon Schuster, 1966

Woodcott, M. H., Schumway Cook. *Development of Posture and Gait across the Life Span*. University of South Carolina Press, 1989

Zaehner, R. C. *Hindu and Muslim Mysticism*. Oxford: Oneworld, 1994

Zukav. *The Dancing WU-Li Masters*. N.Y.: Bantam, 1980

About the Author

Swami Nityamuktananda, (Order of Saraswati) has dedicated her life to the realisation of the divine Truth and the dissemination of it in whatever form, creed or context.

German by birth, and naturalised British, she now lives, after many years of study and world-wide travel, in the far west of Cornwall. Although she originally studied Theology, her studies soon expanded to Education, Psychology, Art and Design (Ceramics) and Philosophy. Different teaching jobs (in colleges and universities) in various countries followed. At the centre of her studies (as well as teaching) was always the subject of 'Self-awareness.' Extensive travel and life in Asia (China, Japan and India) awakened her interest in Eastern Philosophy and led via the Zen arts of Raku and Shiatsu - to deep involvement in Meditation, Sattipahana (mindfulness) and finally Yoga and Vedanta. She also studied/practised several complementary medical practices.

Over the last 15 years, she has worked with several great spiritual Masters: (Zen Master S. Moriceau, T.Y.S. Lama Gangchen, Tulku, Tibetan Buddhism, Swami Chidvilasananda (Siddha Yoga), and ultimately with Swami Anubhavananda, Acharya of Vedanta).

In 1997 she completed her doctorate in Eco-philosophy and has since contributed world-wide in conferences and workshops on 'The Five Elements' and Yoga Philosophy in its widest sense: be it in the context of Complementary Medicine (Italy, Spain, Indonesia, Nepal, etc.), Ethics (House of Lords/London Univ. Complutense, Madrid; 16th Congress International for Research on Aggression, Sri Lanka etc.) or in connection with Yoga and Indian Philosophy (Mumbai, Singapore etc).

At present she teaches primarily in the context of Yoga Teacher Training - Ethics and Philosophy of Yoga.

In 1997 she was awarded a **"World Peace Prize"** for contributions to World Peace (LGWPF), NGO of UN).

Her publications include:
Seeing Yoga; Contemplation of the Yoga Sutras by Patanjali; Ediciones Ambrosia 2005
'GU-RU' Contemplation of a Sanskrit Hymn, Sat Bhavana Trust, Mumbai, Jan. 2001
The Movement of Life in the Five Elements, Centeur, Madrid, 1996; 2nd Ed.: Paul Coughlin, UK, 2000
The Way of Raku Patten Press, Penzance, Cornwall, UK 1988.

Questionnaire to the Elements in You

Physical ~ Emotional ~ Spiritual

(Find the key to the questionnaire after the Element Cycles)

	1	2	3	4	5
Your Build	Solid/strong / stocky	Tall/soft	Medium/energetic	Short/wiry/thin	Tall/noticeable/upright
Bones/Frame	Hips – large/strong	well proportioned	Moderate/flexible	Thin bones	Good muscles/easily tight joints
Weight	Heavy (hard to loose) weight	Heavy/full	Moderate – up and down	Low – hard to hold	Steady
Skin Tone	Cool/damp	White/soft	Ruddy/lustrous	Pale/dry/blemishes	Thin/transparent
Eyes	Large/steady	Clear/white	Piercing/lively	Small/nervous	steady/radiant
Hair	Thick/shiny	Fine/wavy/oily	Thin/shiny/curly	Dry/thin	Strong/plenty
Teeth	Large well formed	Well formed/straight	Small/bleeding gums	Poorly formed	Spaced loosely
Nails	Strong/white	Soft/pink	Pink/brittle	Rough/brittle	Rough/grooved
Joints	Firm/large	Large/light	Loose/flexible	Stiff	Problems
Circulation	Moderate/good	Slow	Good/warm	Poor	Variable
Appetite	Constant/nibbling	Uninterested/ moderate	High/excessive	Nervous	Variable
Thirst	Moderate	Fairly strong	High	Scanty	Low
Sweating	Can be profuse	Low/hardly	Profuse/long	Scanty	Even
Stool	Well formed/irritable	Tendency soft	Too loose	Hard/dry	Well formed to dry
Urination	Clear	Moderate/strong smell	Profuse/yellow	Scanty	Clear to yellowish
Immune system	Good	High	Moderate/ sensitive to heat	Low	Strong
Sensitivity To	Dampness	Coldness	Sunlight/heat	Dry cold	Wind/damp cold
Tendency to diseases	Congestion	Toxicity	Fever/edema	Lung / colon disease	Inflammation/ rheumatism / arthritis
Sleep	High/excess	plenty	Restless	Disturbed	Needs little
Sexual Activity	High	Variable	Passionate	Controlled	Low
Endurance	High	Determined	Moderate/ Jumpy	Easily exhausted	Focused
TOTALS					

	Space/Wood	Air/Metal	Fire	Water	Earth
Organs	Liver, gallbladder	Lung, large intestines	Heart, small intestines	Kidney, bladder	Spleen, stomach
Typical Diseases:	Liver disorder, peripheral nerve co-ordination, cramps, spasms, nausea	Upper respiratory disorder, skin and mucus disorder, breathing disorder, coughs, allergies	Cardiovascular, disturbance of sleep, speech, heart rhythm, metabolism	Problems with fertility, disorder central nervous system, fluids, teeth, ears	Indigestion, veins, muscular, flesh, abdominal stuff, malnutrition, malabsorption
Subject to injury from	Wind	Dry	Heat	Cold	damp
Injuries enter	Head, neck, upper back	Skin, throat, mouth, nose	Nose, mouth, throat, upper back	Lower back, hips/legs	Lower back, abdomen
Desires	Purpose	Order	Fulfillment	Truth	Connectedness
Archetype	Pioneer	Alchemist	Wizard	Philosopher	Peacemaker
Talent	Initiative	Discrimination	Performance	Imagination	Negotiation
Virtue	Fervor	Righteousness	Charisma	Honesty	Loyalty
Preoccupation	Work	Rituals	Stimulation	Secrets	Details
Compelled to	Win	Control	Consume	Criticise	Interfere
Obsessed with	Change & Independence	Order & Perfection	Pleasure Seeking & intimacy	Mysteries & Facing death	Pleasing others and security
Aversion to	Bondage	Spontaneity	Boredom	Exposure	Change
Tends to	Stay busy	Make Judgment	Seek Excitement	Seek Solitude	Seek Comfort
Emotional Addiction	To be aroused	To be right	To be in Love	To be protected	To be needed
Spiritual Fear	To be Helpless	To be Corrupt	To be Cut Off	To be Extinct	To be Lost
Path	Action/ Creativity	Mastery	Compassion	Knowledge	Service
Existential Issue – Goals	What to do?	What I am and am not?	How far can I go?	What is my past and my future?	What's my role and where am I?
Sense and Perception	Vision, Speech, Comprehension (Temporal and Parietal Lobe)	Touch (frontal cortex)	Sight/speech (Temporal/occipital lobe)	Taste (lower frontal lobe)	Smell (upper frontal lobe)
Types of Memory	Spatial memory	Technical memory	Long-term memory	Fears and trauma	Genetic memory/ planning info.
Seeks the perfect. . .	Cause	System	Lover	Teacher	Family
Tends to	Risk; stay busy	Follow higher order	Seek excitement / make contact	Seek solitude / avoid exposure	Seek comfort/ avoid isolation
Major Emotion	Anger	Grief	Joy	Fear	Sympathy
Associated Season	Spring	Autumn	Summer	Winter	Late summer
Direction	East	West	South	North	Centre
Taste	Sour	Pungent	Hot	Salty	Sweet
Helpful foods	Wheat, peaches, chicken	Rice, onions, chestnuts	Millet, ;plums, cabbage, raspberry	Beans, dates, leek	Millet, squash, apricots
Colour	White / green	White / transparent	Red	Blue	Yellow
Aggregate	All pervading	Gaseous	Transforming	Fluid	Solid
Nourished by	Water	Earth	Space	Air	Fire
Controls	Earth	Space	Air	Fire	Water
Is restrained by	Air	Fire	Water	Earth	space

The Chen-Ko Cycle

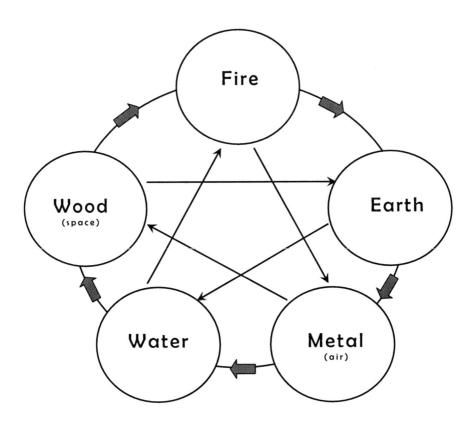

The Chen-Ko Cycle was a further development of Chinese thought. In the previous symbol, the cosmological circle, the Earth is the centre, equal to China's perception of the 'Middle Kingdom'. Later on, Earth became part of the transition between Fire and Metal, (Yang and Yin, between Summer and Autumn).

In the Chen-Ko cycle, the outer circle, the (Shen or Sheng) describes the quality of nourishing, supporting and even generating. The inner sequences of relationship (Ke or Ko) represent the dynamic of restraint, inhibition, control. Together they are like good parents, they support and nurture, but they also limit, control and set boundaries; without such restraint, the child would grow wild, overstep it's boundaries and possibly destroy itself.

For example: - Water nourishes Wood, but restrains Fire by quenching it. Wood provides Fire with combustible material yet inhibits Earth by holding it with it's roots.

Elemental Tree

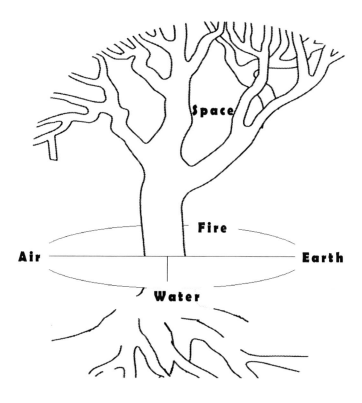

This symbolic representation is found with small variations in the Celtic culture, the American Indian culture and the Australian Aboriginal.

The centre pole, or tree is representative of the Great Mystery; The Divine Power, the upper and lower worlds; - the other dimension respectively.

Life in ordinary dimension follows a circle, in accordance with the four Elements, which are linked to the directions (East, West, North and South). The various traditions only vary in the amount of detail.

The Cosmological Cycle

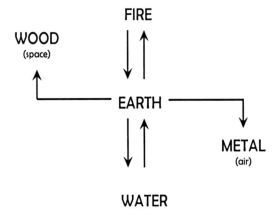

The Cosmological Cycle is strongly connected to Traditional Chinese Medicine. There the energy is called Qi. The focus of the Cosmological Cycle is the Earth, it is based in the centre, and the main axle of activity is between Fire and Water. The interplay between these two elements is controlled and enriched by the Earth. 'Metal' and 'Wood' feed and support this main interplay. This theory is mainly used in respect to the body, it's physical organs and energy meridians. Consequently it is relevant to Acupuncture, Shiatsu and other healing arts.

The Fire energy descends; The Heart – Qi (Energy) transforms Food-Qi into Blood. The Water-energy rises to cool the Fire this function is mainly connected to the kidneys energy.

Metal energy, is connected to the lungs'; lung-energy descends and provides the inner organ with energy.

Wood energy, connected to the liver and gallbladder transports Qi into all directions and floats upwards.

The Wheel Of Creation

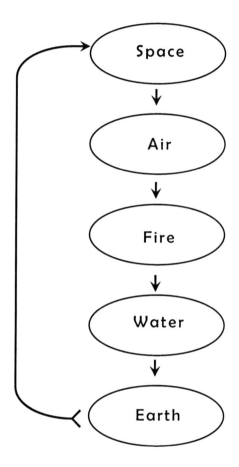

In the Vedic tradition, the Five Elements are thought of as having appeared in a specific order, so as to form the Cosmos. This primordial order appeared in a cycle or wheel, the 'Wheel of Creation'. In the sequence it is thought, that each element helped to create the next in line, from the most subtle to the most physical. Prana, the life-energy, the most subtle contained them all. This Wheel of Creation can be said, to describe the birth process of the universe, macrocosm and microcosm.

Don't Read This Before You've Completed the Questionnaire
~ As your mind is the greatest trickster ~

Key to the Questionnaire

5 = Space
4 = Air
3 = Fire
2 = Water
1 = Earth

The sum total of the first page - relates more to your constitutional element (what you came into the world with).

The sum total of the second page - relates more to experience and emotions since.

The sum total of both pages - gives you a tentative insight into your present dominant element.

Most probably, you will find one element dominant, or occasionally two. Dominance could express itself as too much or too little. The element with the lowest score is obviously what you are lacking. It is easier to replenish what is lacking than to reduce that which is too much. We aim for balance – Balance is Health. Imbalance causes problems even illness.

In Yoga, we aim at overall balance first then encourage to go beyond the gross elements altogether to cultivate more sattvic energy i.e. a dominance of space representing the Spiritual element.

Warning – refrain from putting yourself in a box. Life is constant movement and change. For a more detailed analysis, visit your local practitioner of Traditional Chinese Medicine or Ayurveda.

	1	2	3	4	5
Memory	steady/slow recall	Good/excellent	Sharp/clear erratic	Absent minded	Quick/ sharp
Speech	Slow, singing	Pronounced	Sharp/cutting/ Clipped	Clear/fast	Calm
Cleanliness	Low/ tendency to be lazy	Moderate	Sporadic	High	Important
Temperament	Content	Adaptable	Motivated/inspiring	Nervous	Focused/ unpredictable
Positive Emotions	Love/reliability	Nurturing	Courage	Directness	Adaptability/ acceptance
Negative Emotions	Attachment/ stubbornness	Fear/worry	Anger/ Irresponsibility	Isolation especially oneself	Anxiety/frustration/ anger
Faith	Steady/ unchangeable	Committed	Determined/ Devotion	Erratic	Central to life
Works For	Serving others, organising	Helps others	Oneself/ Self-interest	Fulfillment of Personal interests	Self-less / for the good of all
Stimulants (inc. alcohol & Drugs)	Taken frequently	Occasionally	Often	infrequently	Oscillating between never and always
Depression	Occasionally	Frequently and easily	Deeply changeable	Rarely	Never
Violent Behaviour	Rarely	Occasionally against oneself	Relatively easy	Never	Rarely
Attachment to money/belongings	Important but generous giver	Fairly	Easily gained easily spent	Little	Not/unimportant
Forgiveness	Long grudges	Not easy	With effort	Easy	Totally and simply
Concentration	Fair	Poor/improves with practice	Poor with great difficulty	Good	Easily controlled
Truthful - Honest	Not important /pleasing others	Supportive/high	Performing/ Manipulative	Mostly	Always naturally/ too direct
Creativity	Low	Supportive/high	High/ transforming	Analytical	High
Spiritual	More material interested	Often/ mystical	No interest/ once discovered – Devotional	Ritualistic	Naturally with ease
Attraction to meditation	Rarely	Easily	Very difficult / hard to practice	Occasional	Highly
Page2 Total					
Page1 total					
TOTAL					

Printed in the United Kingdom
by Lightning Source UK Ltd.
127034UK00001B/190-219/A